The Wall

Prophecy, Politics and Middle East "Peace"

RAMON BENNETT

SHEKINAH BOOKS
L T D

"They lead My people astray, saying, 'Peace,' when there is no peace, and when a partition wall is built, they cover it with whitewash, therefore tell those who cover it with whitewash that it is going to fall. Flooding rains will come, great hailstones shall hurtle down and a raging wind will burst forth."

(Ezekiel 13:10-11 Lit. translation)

Dedication

To the small number of Jews who truly wait for God.
May their faith be richly rewarded.

Acknowledgements

My sincere appreciation goes to all my readers who have written or called over the years urging me to continue writing. Without such encouragement, I probably would have sought a different occupation.

I would like to acknowledge my editor, Marilyn Bryant, who, since my first faltering words as an author, has been a constant source of help and encouragement. I owe her much.

A debt is also owed to Martha Farmer, who so willingly gave of her time and professional talents to proof-edit this work and make it more readable.

I also wish to express my gratitude to all the wonderful Norwegian friends who helped me during the years it took to put this work together. Special thanks go to Finn Frestad, Kjell-Guner Lohne and Lars-Toralf Storstrand.

Last, but not least, I want to thank my most precious life partner, Zipporah, who not only loves me, but also allows me the freedom to work undisturbed for as long as I wish. I would feel empty and lost without this very dear and lovely friend.

Contents

Preface

Often, when I lecture on subjects included in this present work, I am invariably told that people are simply not aware of the things I speak about. Therefore, within these pages the reader will find information that CNN, the world's largest purveyor of news, chooses not to tell. There is also information the White House, the U.S. State Department, the CIA, and others, would rather the reader did not know—information that is far too damaging. But even when Christians are in possession of the truth, precious few of them raise their voices in protest.

As a general rule, world leaders possess very little spiritual acumen. The Bible is full of prophecies, and many of them are finding their fulfillment in our day. No biblical prophecy, however, came by the will of man. They are the result of the foreknowledge of Almighty God, Creator and Possessor of heaven and earth and everything within these realms. God communicated His fore-knowledge of future events to holy, God-fearing men who *spoke as they were moved by the Holy Spirit* (2 Peter 1:21), these later committed the prophecies to writing.

For prophecies of future events to find their fulfillment they must, of necessity, have a human agency. More often than not the human element is supplied by political leaders. Many leaders believe they not only create history, but that they also control the destiny of nations. In reality, they only help orchestrate chaos. God alone controls the destiny of nations, and He wrote history aeons before it or the politicians were thought about. The ability to foretell history with such accuracy, however, necessarily implies the ability to control history. We need to remind ourselves often that God is firmly in control of events, even when it appears that He is not.

Political leaders usually belong to one of the following three groups: Those who do not know; those who do not want to know; and those who do not care.

The government of the United States literally gets away with murder around the world today, because most leaders of other nations either belong to one of the above camps or are too spineless to speak out against the ethics of the sole superpower that intends to rule the world.

The concept of *peace, peace!* (Jeremiah 6:14) has addled the brains of godless Israeli leaders, and constant U.S. meddling has only succeeded in muddying the waters further.

For the most part, Israel has turned its back again upon *the Holy One of Israel*. Scorn and disdain are now heaped upon those in Israel who continue to revere His Name. The gathering over Israel of the clouds of fury and righteous judgment of a greatly provoked God will shortly bring a deluge of wrath upon the inhabitants. Instability is endemic to the Middle East, but Israel's pursuit of a false "peace" instead of the knowledge of the Almighty will wreak havoc in the region and beyond.

The Muslim vision of a Middle East is one in which Israel disappears. The Arab world, along with Iran and Pakistan, are working towards the fulfillment of the vision, and Israel's apostasy is working hand-in-hand with them.

The "peace process" is a process that leads only to war. Since the signing of the Oslo Accords in September 1993, the Arab nations have become the world's largest arms purchasers, and America is the foremost dealer. Together with radically Islamic Iran and Pakistan, the Arab nations have stockpiled sufficient chemical, biological, bacteriological and nuclear weapons to extinguish all life on planet earth several times over. The terrible signs of a nuclear, chemical and biological holocaust have appeared on the horizon, and our lives are in danger of being snuffed out in an inferno of cosmic proportions. A conflagration could be ignited at a moment's notice at the whim of any one person who believes he controls the destiny of nations.

Only a living, personal and intimate relationship with Jesus Christ will provide us with hope for tomorrow. Faith in God's Son is the only faith that can dare to hold its own in these perilous times.

Please read this work carefully and prayerfully and know that because He lives, we can face tomorrow.

Ramon Bennett
Jerusalem
Tuesday, March 21, 2000.

I

The Promise

The Bible declares that *the fool has said in his heart, "There is no God"* (Psalms 14:1, 53:1). It is not very flattering to be categorized as a *"fool,"* but that is how man's Creator has labeled all those who deny His existence. Sincere, honest and intelligent persons that study biblical prophecy in depth, together with open history books, soon arrive at the understanding that history was written in detail long before it happened. Thus, the One who predicts history with such accuracy must also control it. And the One who predicts natural events such as earthquakes with frightening accuracy must, also, control nature. Therefore, Bible believing people can take comfort in knowing that the future is a lot less out of control than is generally thought and, consequently, a lot less terrifying.

I firmly believe the Bible to be the inerrant and living word of the active, living God who is very much involved in the affairs of man. I know that many millions of liberal Jewish and Gentile secular humanists do not hold to this view. They long ago tossed aside the Book of books as being a mere collection of winsome fables.

Secular humanism is a naive form of atheism. It assumes the inherent goodness of man despite the 1,000 or so wars that have taken place in the West alone during the last 2,500 years. Secular humanists say there is no God, and they are, therefore, *"fools"* according to God. Given the rise of secular humanism in the West, and considering the fact that there are far more people alive today than at any other time in history, one does not need to be a professor of higher mathematics to realize there must be more *"fools"* around today than at any time previously. Our nations are full of them and generally run by them. The Western world today is really nothing less than a ship of *"fools"* steaming toward an iceberg called Armageddon, on which it will end its days.

The focus of some of today's *"fools"* is fixed upon a tiny sliver of land situated in the very heart of the Muslim Middle East. That sliver of land is called Israel, and the greater portion of this oversized parking lot is said to be "one of the most densely populated countries in the Western world."[1] The population of Israel is largely made up of survivors and de-scendants of survivors of Arab, Nazi and Communist aggression.

Some of the world's more powerful *"fools"* are pushing Israel to placate the Arab and Muslim worlds by giving up land it captured while defending itself against attacks from its Arab neighbors. International law gives Israel the right to retain the captured land, as it was taken during wars of self defense and virtually purchased with the lives of thousands of Israeli soldiers. It is also a fact that whoever endangers his neighbor's independence by an act of military force must first be ready to suffer the loss of territory, if his aggression does not succeed. But Israel is being coerced into giving up politically what it won militarily by defending itself. The concessions Israel is being forced to make greatly affects its ability to defend itself against further attacks from outside its borders.

The combined land area held by Israel's Arab neighbors is a staggering 5.4 million square miles[2] (14 million square kilometers). This is equivalent to 10 percent of our entire planet's land surface—the most land held by any ethnic group in the world. Israel, however, exists on a minuscule 7,847 square miles[3] (20,324 square kilometers).

Even *"fools"* should be able to arrive at the conclusion that it is not a pressing shortage of space that causes the Arabs to demand a return of lost land. Nor does the disputed land contain sufficient oil to give it value. The Arab nations possess two-thirds of the world's known oil reserves.[4] Israel, however, can barely produce sufficient oil to lubricate the nation's sewing machines.

The captured land, though, has great strategic value militarily, and it was from these areas that three wars were launched against Israel. A return of the land means a return to bloody wars. The fact that the world's leading *"fools"* apparently have not arrived at these most obvious conclusions is by intent, not ignorance. And this shutting out of facts is due to their own plans and aims for the Middle East from which they hope to magnificently profit.

To my previously stated premise that the Bible is the inerrant, living word of the living, active God, I add another: I firmly believe that when God made promises, either for blessing or for judgment, He was not acting like a Western politician seeking re-election. With God, a promise is a promise is a promise. If God said it, then it is as certain to come to pass as surely as day follows night:

The grass withers, the flower fades, but the word of our God stands forever (Isaiah 40:8).

If the reader desires to test the validity of God's promises, it will only take time and perseverance. Simply take a Bible, and beginning in the first chapter of Genesis and working through until the end of the book of Malachi, note all the promises of blessing or judgment to specific nations, peoples and individuals. Then take an assortment of good encyclopedias and history books and read up on the histories of those same nations, peoples and individuals. I myself undertook a comprehensive study of specific promises to the nation of Israel. I documented fulfillments of God's promises to the Jewish people up until the present day from history books, encyclopedias, newspapers, magazines, television and radio news programs. Some of the findings are in my book entitled "When Day and Night Cease." It has opened thousands of hearts and minds in over 100 countries to the truth of God's faithfulness to His word and confirmed it to even more. God is not slack concerning His promises and, indeed, it is only a "*fool*" who would deny the involvement of God in the affairs of today's modern nations.

Prophecy in Fulfillment

I believe we are living in perhaps the most exciting period of all of human history. I believe we are in the last days of the End Times and racing toward the end of time, as man understands time. More biblical prophecies have been fulfilled during the past 50 years than in the preceding two millennia—a good number of prophecies are in the process of fulfillment today. Nearly all of the prophecies of the last half century have directly involved the Jewish people and the modern state of Israel. Is it any wonder that the eyes of the world have fixed their gaze upon this little pocket of rocky real estate in the Middle East?

The One who sits enthroned as King of the universe, controlling the stars, history and the destiny of nations, long ago determined Israel's destiny. He not only fixed the boundaries of its land, but also declared its destructions, determined its exiles, organized the nation's rebirth and opened the highways and byways for His people to return.

God says Israel is *the dearly beloved of My soul* (Jeremiah 12:7), and His wife—*I am married to you* (Jeremiah 3:14). And

He personally gave to Israel a special little parcel of land in the Middle East as an inheritance. It is special because it is God's own land, and for this reason Israel's inheritance is never to be permanently disposed of:

> _The land shall not be sold permanently, for **the land is Mine**_ (Leviticus 25:23).

Israel's land is special because God, _the Holy One of Israel,_[5] cares for it and watches over it:

> _[It is] a land for which the LORD your God cares; the eyes of the LORD your God are always on it from the beginning of the year to the very end of the year_ (Deuteronomy 11:12).

And it is special because it includes Zion and Jerusalem—where God chooses to dwell:

> _This is My resting place **forever;** Here I will dwell, for I have desired it_ (Psalms 132:14).

The title deed to Israel's inheritance belongs to Almighty God. Jerusalem, _the city of the great King_ (Psalms 48:2), is His dwelling place by His own choice. It is, therefore, to be fully expected that the forces of hell will try to wrest the land from the hand of Israel, and divide up Jerusalem between themselves. From the time of King David (from whose bloodline Jesus the Jewish Messiah came) Jerusalem has been the most fought over city in the world. Jerusalem, the eternal city, has arisen from the ashes of destruction 37 times.

For a thousand years or more nations and empires came against ancient Israel in attempts to destroy it and take its inheritance for themselves. Some effected modest successes, and a small few enjoyed nearly complete successes. But without exception and within a relatively short period of time, all those nations and empires suffered the same fate they had inflicted or desired to inflict upon Israel, and some never raised their heads again. Only history books and archeological journals can point back to their former existence.

Israel, however, is not only back on its land, but is a nuclear power and rated the third most powerful military force in the world.[6] It also enjoys one of the world's most advanced economies. All this is entirely due to the intervention of Israel's God. It behooves the leaders of all nations currently involved in the "peace process" to stop and ponder the ramifications of their involvement. However, _the **fool** has said in his heart, "There is no God."_

Israel's Faithful God

Israel is a most unique nation. It was set apart by God, and has been set apart by the nations of the modern world. God Almighty chose Israel and set it apart for His purposes, and the nations of the world chose to set Israel apart for their purposes. The nations of the world have two standards: one by which they judge themselves, and one by which they judge Israel. Israel is the only nation in history to be repeatedly attacked by neighboring armies, and after inflicting humiliating defeats upon them, is forced to adopt the posture of a defeated nation by suing for peace and returning captured territory.

Millions of people today believe that Israel has little or no right to any of the land it now possesses, let alone that which was captured in wars of self defense. Anyone mentioning that the Jewish people have a continuous 3,500-year-old presence in the Holy Land and that the land was given to them by divine decree, usually has a Latin proverb quoted to them: *"rebus sic stansibus"*—circumstances have changed. Most politicians—including many Israeli ones—tell us the same thing, as does the world's news media. Even worse, this view is also shared by millions of Christians.

Are you, dear Christian reader, one who holds such a view? Would you believe the heavenly God, or do you rather choose to believe the worldly politicians and journalists—those *"fools"* who say in their hearts *"There is no God"*?

Outside of Jesus, Abraham is the person most frequently mentioned in the Bible. And Abraham is the only person recorded in the Bible who was called the *friend* of God (2 Chronicles 20:7; Isaiah 41:8; James 2:23). Why was Abraham so singularly different? The answer is both strange and simple: **Abraham believed God!** That is what the Bible says—

> *Abraham believed God, and it was accounted to him for righteousness. And **he was called the friend of God***
> (James 2:23).

Abraham was greatly blessed by God and became very wealthy, mega-rich by today's standards. But Abraham was 85 years-old, and his wife, Sarah, was 75 years-old and barren—unable to bear children. Abraham planned to leave his wealth to his trusted servant, Eliezer (Genesis 15:2), but God had other ideas. God told Abraham to count the stars if he was able, and then told him that his descendants would be just as numerous (Genesis 15:5). Abraham's age, together with Sarah's age and condition, made this totally impossible in the natural, and Abraham was painfully aware of those facts.

But, over and against the facts which stared him in the face daily, Abraham chose to believe God's word. And thus it is recorded:

> *he believed the Lord and He accounted it to him for righteousness* (Genesis 15:6).

This, and other similar actions that are also recorded in the Bible, set Abraham apart from all others. They earned him a place dear to God's heart and the unique designation *friend of God*.

Since Abraham's time it is only those of like faith who are called sons of Abraham, and it is only those who imitate Abraham's faith who will inherit the Kingdom of God. A passage from the great apostle Paul's letter to the Galatians makes this abundantly clear:

> **Abraham believed God,** *and it was accounted to him for righteousness.* **Therefore know that only those who are of faith are sons of Abraham** (Galatians 3:6-7).

Perhaps a popular paraphrase gives the sense even better:

> **God declared [Abraham] fit for heaven only because he believed God's promises.** *You can see from this that the real* **children of Abraham are all the men of faith who truly trust in God** (Galatians 3:6-7 TLB).

We cannot possibly fit into the category of being a son of Abraham and fit for heaven and God's kingdom, if we hold or even lean toward the view that God's promises change with the years! We are to **truly trust** and **believe** God, period. We must strive to emulate Abraham's faith in God's promises. Abraham completely ignored the natural aspect—the deadness of his body, the deadness of Sarah's womb—and grasped God's promise with both hands,

> **being fully convinced that what He had promised He was also able to perform** (Romans 4:21).

And that is the stand we are required to take. Politicians speak out lies almost as easily as they breathe in air, but God **cannot** *lie* (Titus 1:2)—it is **impossible** *for God to lie* (Hebrews 6:18). As it

was said earlier, with God a promise is a promise is a promise—
the word of our God stands forever (Isaiah 40:8).

In an age where it is difficult to find faithful people, even
among professing born-again Christians, it is indeed comforting to
know that we have a truly faithful God. Even Jeremiah the prophet,
while mourning Jerusalem's destruction, could say to God, *great
is Your faithfulness* (Lamentations 3:23). When God makes a
promise, whether it is for good or for bad, He is faithful and will
most surely deliver—

> *If we are faithless, He remains faithful; He cannot deny Himself*
> (2 Timothy 2:13).

A reader might say, "but that scripture speaks of Jesus." Correct,
and we find that Jesus Himself said, *I and My Father are one*
(John 10:30). The nature of the Father is also the nature of the
Son. The original Greek of John 10:30 means that the Father and
the Son are one essence—essentially one. The Scriptures witness
to the Father: *I am the LORD, I do not change* (Malachi 3:6). They
also witness to the Son:

> *Jesus Christ is the same yesterday, today, and forever*
> (Hebrews 13:8).

The nature of God is not subject to change; if it was He would not
be God. He is absolute truth and absolute faithfulness—in Him we
can absolutely trust.

Israel was conquered nearly 2,000 years ago by the most formidable
military power of that time, forcing it into a second exile from its
land. But, this did not negate the promise by Almighty God of an
eternal possession. While Israel was in exile experiencing God's
punitive judgment, He reassured the people of His promise by
declaring:

> *I lifted My hand in an oath to give it to your fathers, and this
> land shall fall to you as your inheritance*
> (Ezekiel 47:14).

During Israel's exiles from its land, the land just lay *desolate* (see
Ezekiel 38:8).

Hundreds of years earlier God decreed that the Jews would be
conquered by the Babylonian empire and exiled from their land for
70 years (Jeremiah 29:10). At that time He made the following
promise:

> *I will bring you back from your captivity; I will gather you from all the nations and from all the places where I have driven you, says the LORD, and **I will bring you to the place from which I cause you to be carried away captive***
>
> (Jeremiah 29:14).

Seventy years later that promise was faithfully fulfilled and the Jews returned to their land—the full story is recorded in the books of Daniel, Ezra and Nehemiah.

God had also decreed a second exile, and this was effected by the hand of the Romans. But God had made another promise to His people:

> *It shall come to pass in that day that the LORD shall set His hand **the second time** to recover the remnant of His people*
>
> (Isaiah 11:11).

And it is this second gathering out of the second exile that we are witnessing today. Jews have returned and are returning to Israel from every point of the compass. This is exactly in accordance with what God promised at that time:

> *He will ... assemble **the outcasts of Israel**, and gather together **the dispersed of Judah from the four corners of the earth*** (Isaiah 11:12).

As God had promised so long ago to bring His people back to their land, it is very obvious that the land would need to be waiting for them.

Never, in 5,000 years of recorded history, has a people come back to its land after 2,000 years, as Israel has done. Never, in 5,000 years of recorded history, has a "dead" language been revived into the vernacular, as Hebrew, Israel's common language, has been. Never have so few people been attacked by such great numbers so many times, as Israel has been. Never have so few people inflicted such decisive defeats upon such powerful armies in so few days, as Israel has done. Never has a nation shot an enemy's air force out of the skies without the loss of a single plane, as Israel did. This writer could go on and on, but suffice it to say that not one single "never" could have been accomplished without the intervention of Israel's faithful and trustworthy *Holy One*. Israel has come home after nearly 2,000 years, exactly as God promised. And, in contradiction to what some pundits say, Israel is home to stay.

The Covenant

It is important for all Bible-believing Christians to take a good look at the covenant God made with Abraham concerning the land of Canaan, the Promised Land, and this not just for the reasons of faith and encouragement. The making of the covenant is described in the 15th chapter of Genesis. It is the only biblical record of an actual making or more correctly, a "cutting," of a covenant. The covenant was cut some 4,000 years ago, but it is now highly controversial and literally millions upon millions of Muslims, humanist Jews and liberal Christians reject its validity for today. Even the United States' president Bill Clinton said on April 27, 1998, "As a Christian I do not know how God, if he were to come to earth, would divide the land over which there is such dispute now."[7] Clinton has been a prime mover in coercing Israel to give up its land to its enemies. But, if Clinton, "as a Christian" (a proven history of fornication and lies indicates the depth of his "Christianity," however), understood God's word, he would certainly know that God would not dream of dividing the Promised Land, except perhaps among the tribes of Israel.

God's covenant with Abraham provides the answer for what angers and frustrates the Arab and Muslim worlds, the White House, the European Union, the Kremlin, the Western news media, and not a few others.

When Abraham was still called Abram, living in Chaldea (ancient Syria, but present day Iraq), the land of his birth, God spoke to him:

*Get out of your country, from your family and from your father's house, **to a land** that I will show you*

(Genesis 12:1).

After a period of time, we are told, Abram came to the land of Canaan and there God spoke to him again, and said: ***To your descendants I will give this land*** (Genesis 12:7). God promised to give the land of Canaan to Abram's descendants and symbolically, Abram would possess the land through them.

Abram roamed throughout Canaan, but due to a famine there, went down into Egypt to find some relief. He got himself into trouble with Pharaoh, the Egyptian king, and was subsequently escorted back to the border and deported (Genesis 12:20). Abram was continuing with his nomadic life in Canaan when God spoke to him the third time about the land:

> *Lift your eyes now and look from the place where you are—
> northward, southward, eastward, and westward; for **all the
> land which you see I give to you and your descendants forever**
> … Arise, walk in the land through its length and its width, for
> **I give it to you*** (Genesis 13:14,15,17).

God Almighty had again promised to give the land of Canaan to
Abram and his descendants.

After an interval of time, God spoke to him a fourth time regarding the land:

> *I am the LORD, who **brought you out** of Ur of the Chaldeans,
> **to give you this land** to inherit it* (Genesis 15:7).

Obviously, when God commanded Abram to leave the land of his
birth, it was for one purpose only: to bring him into the land of
Canaan and give it to him. We now have four separate occasions
where God spoke to Abram concerning the land, and three times
where He personally promised to give it to him and his offspring.
But this time Abram asked for confirmation, a sealing of the repeated
promise:

> *LORD GOD, **how shall I know** that I will inherit it?*
>
> (Genesis 15:8).

God's response to Abram provides us with the validity of the
covenant today.

Abram was not staggering in unbelief as some Bible commentators claim. He was simply desiring to follow the custom of the
day and have the promise sealed. God graciously consented to
Abram's request and told him what was required:

> *"Bring Me a three-year-old heifer, a three-year-old female
> goat, a three-year-old ram, a turtledove, and a young pigeon."
> Then he brought all these to Him and cut them in two, down
> the middle, and placed each piece opposite the other; but he
> did not cut the birds in two … And it came to pass, when the
> sun went down and it was dark, that behold, there appeared
> **a smoking oven and a burning torch that passed between
> those pieces**. On the same day **the LORD made a covenant
> with Abram**, saying: "**To your descendants I have given this
> land, from the river of Egypt to the great river, the River
> Euphrates**" (Genesis 15:9,10,17-18).*

In granting Abram's request for a confirmation of the promise, God told him to bring certain animals and birds. Abram was familiar with the custom as no covenant was made in ancient times without sacrifice. After he had brought the birds and animals he slaughtered them, cut the animals in two, and laid the pieces opposite each other.

God Almighty then manifested Himself in the form of fire and smoke, much like He did in the pillars of fire and cloud in the wilderness (Exodus 13:21) and again on Mount Sinai (Exodus 19:18). (It is interesting that there are only three occasions recorded in the Bible where God appeared in these forms. And these three occasions ushered in the events that placed, and continues to place, the Jewish nation apart from all other nations: the bringing of Abram's descendants out of Egypt and the setting of them apart as God's chosen nation—which they still remain; the giving of the law and commandments at Mount Sinai—which they still adhere to; and the giving of the land of Canaan—where Israel thrives today). We now see God passing between the pieces of the animals and sealing the promise He had made to Abram.

In the Bible there are conditional and unconditional covenants. The one God made with Abram concerning Israel's possession of Canaan is an unconditional covenant. In ancient times, it was customary for both parties to a covenant to walk between the pieces of animals and make promises to each other—even marriage covenants were made this way (see Malachi 2:14). But here God alone walked between the pieces. It was He who was binding Himself and affirming His promise to Abram and his descendants— Abram was bound to nothing. The covenant is in no way conditional upon Abram or any of his descendants meeting any conditions in order to keep the covenant in force. Dwelling in the land in an interrupted tenure was conditional however—Israel must cling to its God and to His law:

> *You shall therefore keep all My statutes and all My judgments, and perform them, that the land where I am bringing you to dwell may not vomit you out* (Leviticus 20:22).

Even though God is *a consuming fire* (Exodus 24:17; Deuteronomy 4:24, 9:3; Hebrews 12:29) the birds and animal pieces prepared by Abram were not consumed by the fire of God's presence, because it was a covenant being made, not a sacrifice being offered.

The slaughtering and dividing of animals when making covenants in yesteryear had great importance. The parties to the covenant walking between the birds and pieces of animals signified the following curse:

May it be so done to me if I do not keep my oath and pledge.[8]

God not only promised on oath—_I lifted My hand in an oath_ (Ezekiel 47:14)—to give the land to Abram and his descendants, but the whole ceremony was an enacted curse that He invoked upon Himself. By walking between the pieces He was, in fact, **invoking a curse upon Himself to be slaughtered like the animals if He ever failed to keep His promise!**

At the time when Abram was 90-years-old, God changed his name of Abram (Exalted Father), to Abraham (Father of a Multitude). And when Abraham was 100-years-old he fathered Isaac (Genesis 21:5). God later confirmed to Isaac and his descendants the covenant He had previously made with Abraham:

Dwell in this land, and I will be with you and bless you; for to you and your descendants I give all these lands, and I will perform the oath which I swore to Abraham your father
(Genesis 26:3).

God also confirmed it once more to Isaac's son, Jacob, and his descendants:

I am the Lord God of Abraham your father and the God of Isaac; the land on which you lie I will give to you and your descendants (Genesis 28:13).

Not only did God personally promise the land individually to Abraham, Isaac, Jacob and his descendants, but He had invoked a curse upon Himself, if He failed to fulfill that promise. Therefore, we know with certainty to whom the Promised Land was given, and we also know the boundaries of the covenanted land which God defined:

From the river of Egypt to the great river, the River Euphrates
(Genesis 15:18).

There is, therefore, a confirmed covenant with confirmed boundaries.

Regarding the length of the covenant, the Scriptures are not silent here either: _I give to you and your descendants forever_

(Genesis 13:15). Some would argue that *forever* does not mean forever. The use of *forever* is ambiguous, but it does accurately reflect Almighty God's thinking. This will become clear shortly.

Two almost identical Scripture passages, found in Psalms and in I Chronicles 16:15-18, tell us the term of the covenant. We should realize that when God, by His Holy Spirit, repeats a passage in His written Word, the facts must be important. Here we look at the passage in Psalms:

> *He remembers His **covenant** forever, the word which He commanded, for a **thousand generations**, The covenant which **He made with Abraham**, and **His oath to Isaac**, And **confirmed it to Jacob** for a statute, **to Israel** as an everlasting covenant, saying, "**To you I will give the land of Canaan** as the allotment of your inheritance"* (Psalms 105:8-11).

Here the nation of Israel is also brought into the covenant, and the duration of the covenant is described as *forever, everlasting* and *a thousand generations*. There are no contradictions here. It will become clear that the use of *everlasting* is, like *forever,* describing *a thousand generations.*

The length of a generation is also provided moments before God ratified the covenant with Abram:

> *Know certainly that your descendants will be strangers in a land that is not theirs, and will serve them, and they will afflict them **four hundred years** ... but in the **fourth generation** they shall return here* (Genesis 15:13,16).

On the day the covenant was made, God defined a generation at that time as being a period of 100 years. And in the entry under "generation" in the world's most authoritative dictionary of the English language,[9] we find written *inter alia*:

> In reckoning historically by "generations," the word is taken to mean the interval of time between the birth of the parents and that of their children.

Thus, Scripture declares:

> *Abraham was **one hundred years** old when his son Isaac was born to him* (Genesis 21:5).

And lest we get confused about Ishmael, God only recognizes Abraham's son, Isaac, as being the legitimate son of the promise. He makes this very clear when He tells Abraham:

*Take now your son, **your only son** Isaac...* (Genesis 22:2).

The term of the covenant is, therefore, 1,000 generations multiplied by 100 years which is 100,000 years.

Abraham was born somewhere around the year 2111 B.C. He was 75 years of age when he left the land of his birth (Genesis 12:4) and traveled to the land of Canaan, where God made the covenant with him. Using these dates we can calculate the years of the covenant:

$$2,111 - 75 = 2,036 + 1999 = 4,035$$
$$100,000 - 4,035 = 95,965$$

Since we have only traveled approximately 4,035 years along the path of time since God made the covenant with Abraham, there are almost 96,000 years of the stated duration left. On the basis of this fact, who then has the right of possession today? The descendants of Abraham through the line of Isaac, obviously.

The duration of the covenant has nothing whatever to do with the return of the Lord Jesus Christ. It simply tells us that the seed of Abraham through Isaac, namely Israel, has sole right of possession of the Promised Land for that length of time. The world must pass away (most likely from a thermo-nuclear war) with

a great noise, and will melt with fervent heat (2 Peter 3:10)

giving place to

new heavens and a new earth in which righteousness dwells
(2 Peter 3:13).

This, of course, will happen many tens of thousands of years before the covenant can ever run its course. However, it should now be clear why God saw fit to also use the words *forever* and *everlasting* when describing the term of the covenant.

God Almighty established an unconditional covenant of defined duration for a defined land with defined borders and defined the people who were to possess it. We must remember, however, that the Israelis are the possessors, not the owners of the land. God holds the title deed Himself.

He made this clear to Israel before it undertook the crossing of the Jordan to take possession of its inheritance:

*The land shall not be sold permanently, for **the land is Mine***
(Leviticus 25:23).

God also testifies to the land being His in 2 Chronicles 7:20; Isaiah 14:25; Jeremiah 2:7, 16:18; Ezekiel 36:5; Hosea 9:3; and Joel 1:6, 3:2. God also refers to the nations surrounding His land as *"My wicked **neighbors**"* (Jeremiah 12:14).

Confirmation that ownership of the land is still held by God today, and that Israel is meant to be home on its inheritance, is also found in the Scriptures. Concerning the war between Israel and Gog, which is unmistakably in the future, God says to Gog and his allies:

> *You will come against **My people Israel** like a cloud to cover the land. It will be **in the latter days** that I will bring you against **My land*** (Ezekiel 38:16).

Further proof of modern Israel's right of possession is also found in the passage about the coming war. Scripture says in Ezekiel 38:8 that Gog's troops will gather on *the **mountains of Israel***.

The *mountains of Israel* are the biblical areas of Judea and Samaria—Israel's heartland. Portions of Judea and Samaria have been handed over to Yasser Arafat's PLO (Palestine Liberation Organization), and more is slated to be given in the future. However, we should take note that nowhere in the Bible does it mention "mountains of Palestine," and this should serve to indicate the temporal nature of the Israeli-PLO "peace process."

Israel has been involved in a "peace process" for the past several years. But there can be no lasting peace, either for Israel or for the nations, until Jesus, the *Prince of Peace* (Isaiah 9:6), returns to rule the nations from Jerusalem. Large tracts of Israel's God-given inheritance have been handed over to the sovereignty of a people led by murderers, liars and thieves, and who have no legal or moral right to it.

I must state again that the title deed for this land is held by God. He is the Landlord, and Israel is His tenant. Just imagine the scene that would take place if an ordinary landlord came to collect rent from his tenant and was told by the tenant that he had given the property to the landlord's wicked neighbors! Would not the landlord be extremely angry and demand the return of his property? Would he not tell the tenant in no uncertain terms that he had no right whatsoever to give the property away, because it was not his to give? Only the Owner of the Promised Land has the right to give it away, and He has already made His decision known. Israel cannot give away what does not belong to it, and God will most definitely demand its return. And God will certainly not be opposed to taking it back by force.

Israel has no authority to barter with God's land, selling it for a worthless scrap of paper with the word "peace" scrawled upon it. The world will find out soon enough that the agreements signed between Israel and God's *wicked neighbors* are null and void in the eyes of Him who holds the deeds. And all those forcing Israel's hand will ultimately find themselves in a confrontation with the Owner also.

Christian Incognizance

This writer is stunned by the abysmal ignorance shown by many church leaders regarding God's covenant with Israel. In August 1998 for example, 700 Anglican bishops meeting in Lambeth, England, adopted a resolution calling for Jerusalem to be the capital of both Israel and a future Palestinian state.[10] And in January 1999 it was reported that more than 1,000 American clerics, including Protestant and Catholic bishops, were calling on the Clinton administration to "freeze foreign aid" to Israel and to "pressure Israel to support a Palestinian state."[11] It is expedient for all church leaders and the leaders of all nations to remember this one unshakable fact: God never loses in any confrontation. The greatest threat facing our planet is not AIDS, global warming, stock market collapses, terrorism or fundamental Islam, it is God Almighty. The nations of this world, including Israel, are on a collision course with the Creator of the universe because of the "peace process." But, *the fool has said in his heart, "There is no God."*

2

A Nation Betrayed

Israel is a nation betrayed. It is a nation betrayed by politicians and journalists. Most of these betrayers are Jewish. Many are Israelis, but others still live in the *galut*, the Hebrew word for "exile" from the Land. And some of the latter fall into the self-hating category—Jews who wish they were not.

Jews themselves are often the greatest enemies of the Jewish people. Jews even helped fund and support Adolf Hitler's initial rise to power which resulted in the Nazi Holocaust and the death of six million of their own people. Jews are proud of the fact that Karl Marx was one of their sons. Marx was a satanist and is responsible for more Jewish deaths than Allah, the god of the Muslim Koran.

Latterly, misguided, godless Jews have given birth to the Israel-PLO "peace" process. This "peace" process, born of a desire to be like the Gentile nations, will bring the wrath of God down upon the Jewish nation and cause more Jewish blood to be spilled:

> *What you have in your mind shall never be, when you say, "We will be like the Gentiles, like the families in other countries...". "As I live," says the LORD GOD, "surely* **with a mighty hand, with an outstretched arm, and with fury poured out,** *I will rule over you"* (Ezekiel 20:32-33).

Today, Israel in general dwells in a materialistic fog, more concerned about "peace in our time" than God's promises and calling. And just as Esau despised his birthright and sold it for a bowl of lentil stew (Genesis 25:31-34), so Israeli leaders are despising their inheritance by selling it for White House approval of their actions.

A perpetual over-abundance of godless Jews has been the bane of Israel's existence since time immemorial. The age-old Jewish festival of *Chanukah*, celebrated each year with great joy throughout the Jewish world, would never have seen the light of day were it not for the many godless Jews of yesteryear.

Chanukah, the Jewish Festival of Lights or Feast of Dedication

(John 10:22), is observed for eight consecutive days by Jews everywhere. Family members daily exchange gifts and light candles in a special nine-branched menorah called a *Chanukiyah*. On the first day, one lighted candle is placed in the *Chanukiyah*. Two candles are lighted on the second day, three on the third, four on the fourth, etc., until the eighth day when all eight candles, plus the *shammash*, the "servant" candle, are lit. *Chanukah* recalls the Maccabean revolt and celebrates the victory of the Maccabees over the Seleucid king, Antiochus IV, and his superior Syrian forces on 14th December 164 B.C. *Chanukah* means "dedication," and the festival takes its name from the rededication of the Temple by the Maccabees—exactly three years to the day of its desecration.

The Temple in Jerusalem had been polluted by pagan practices which had even included the sacrificing of pigs to Zeus on the holy altar. After the Maccabees won control of Jerusalem, they immediately proceeded to cleanse the Temple. And in the Temple, they found a single vial of oil for the great menorah, sufficient for one day's light. The Maccabees lit the menorah, even though more of the specially processed oil would take some days to produce. However, instead of burning out, the oil miraculously continued to light the menorah until the eighth day, by which time the fresh oil had become available.

At that time Antiochus IV was using the common culture of Greek Hellenism to unify his Seleucid empire. The high priests of Israel were the nation's powermongers, and Jason offered Antiochus a large payment of money together with a promise to Hellenize the city of Jerusalem, if Antiochus would make him high priest in place of his brother Onias III. Around three years later, Menelaus supplanted Jason by offering Antiochus even more for the high priesthood and an acceleration of the Hellenization of Jerusalem.

Both Jason and Menelaus were repugnant to the orthodox Jews who wished to retain their faith in and observance of Judaism. For these Jews, however, things went from bad to worse. In time, in order to destroy Judaism and force Hellenization upon them, people in Jerusalem were forbidden to observe the Sabbath, forced to eat swine's flesh, and put to death if found with a book of the Law. They were also sentenced to death if they had a child who had been circumcised. Altars were erected and sacrifices made to pagan gods. Swine were sacrificed in the Temple and offered to

Zeus upon his altar, which had been erected over the brazen altar of burnt offering.

The Maccabean revolt began in a little town called Modein, outside of Jerusalem. A priest by the name of Mattathias openly defied a Syrian commissioner and refused to sacrifice to the heathen gods. Mattathias killed the commissioner, a fellow Jew, overturned the altar, and fled with his sons to the hills. Mattathias died around two years later, and the leadership of the revolt was taken over by his son Judas Maccabeus, who was advised by his brother Simon.

Although the Maccabees fought the Syrian forces, the Syrian forces were not the real enemies. The Maccabees were indeed the heroes of *Chanukah*, but the Jews who were more than willing and able to adopt Greek culture were the real enemies. *Chanukah* is celebrated universally by Jews today, but if the Jewish world's secular humanist majority of today—all those who want to be "just like the nations"—were to read and understand the real story of the Maccabean revolt, they would stop celebrating *Chanukah*. And the modern Maccabees, the orthodox Jews of today who look upon the secularization of Israel and denigration of Judaism with re-pugnance, are no longer heroes. They are the "right-wing fanatics," who have been called "scum,"[1] "the putrid fruit of the settlement policy,"[2] etc., by some members of Israeli left-wing government coalitions.

The parallel between the Maccabees and the political and religious unrest in Israel today is all too obvious. The Hellenist Jews—politicians, journalists, and laymen—have sold their souls to the devil. They denigrate both God and Judaism, have legalized prostitution, promoted abortion, opened the nation's businesses on the Sabbath, eat locally produced swine's flesh, and scramble in an impetuous rush to sign away the Promised Land in "peace" agreements with those who hate them and hope to destroy them. They embrace an enemy who uses the language of peace for the purposes of war. They deride the ancient and strategic land of Israel—the dream focus of Jews throughout millennia—as an old fashioned possession made irrelevant by the new era of intellect. These Hellenist Jews have assimilated foreign ideas diametrically opposed to the Jewish faith and, in adopting a tolerance for everything, stand for nothing.

The modern state of Israel was created by Jews who came

from a multitude of countries, rescued from anti-Semitism, annihilation and assimilation. They came to live in their ancient land—an independent Jewish country—and to be responsible for their own fate. Peace for them means being able to get on a bus without being afraid or to buy vegetables and other necessaries of life without fear. But, the number of the "victims of peace" that have died since the Hellenistic Jewish "peace" became a reality in September, 1993, have "far exceeded the casualties of war—the Lebanon war, for example."[3] They swallowed the bogus excuse that Jewish deaths by terror were the price of "peace." They bought the lie that there would be "no more terrorism in our time," just like the British bought Neville Chamberlain's lie of "peace in our time." They thought they would decide their own future, but powerful politicians, mainly those living safely abroad, decide it for them. And stress, like water dripping methodically upon a rock, erodes their psychological makeup. Israel is full of stress today. The specter of terror, the concern for security—for children drafted into the army, the political pressures—all these things and more prevent them from sleeping well at night.

However, Israeli Hellenist Jews like Shimon Peres, Yitzhak Rabin, Yossi Beilin, Chaim Ramon, Yossi Sarid, Shulamit Aloni, Yael Dayan, Naomi Chazan, etc., together with those living in the *galut* like Caspar Weinberger, Henry Kissinger, Mike Wallace, Martin Indyk, Dennis Ross, Madeleine Albright, William Cohen, etc., could not effectively cook their individual and corporate machinations without a Hellenist Jewish press.

The news media is the world's spokesman. And the one who controls the public's information controls the public's judgement. The media is very much aware of its enormous power to manipulate and uses it to full advantage. The world, apparently, has yet to learn that the news media is not a nonprofit organization working for the betterment of the human race. The media competes fiercely for the elite top of the pole positions in the dollar and power games. And without even blushing, it will falsify, fake and fabricate news to achieve its own rancid, secular humanist ends.

Shimon Peres has repeatedly said that "history is nonsense,"[4] and that he will "not allow it to get in his way of a New Middle East."[5] He may scoff at history, but as George Santayana said:

Those who do not learn from history are doomed to repeat it.

Peres, like other Hellenists mentioned, has lost his faith, and history is already repeating itself. Israel at 52 is suffering a severe mid-life crisis.

3

A Tale of
Ten Spies

Most readers will be familiar with the biblical story of the 12
spies that were sent by Moses—on God's instructions—to scout
out the Promised Land in preparation for an Israeli conquest. The
spies returned after 40 days of reconnoitering the length and breadth
of the land. They brought reports of the terrain, the fortification of
cities, the strength of the peoples, and they brought with them an
example of the land's produce—figs, pomegranates and a single
cluster of grapes that required two men to carry it.

Much of the report given in Numbers, chapter 13, was a true
assessment of the actual situation: The land was indeed a land of
milk and honey as God had thrice said it would be (Exodus 3:8,
3:17, 33:3), and the fruits were tangible proof of the abundance
and goodness of the land. *The people who dwell in the land*, they
said,

> *are big and strong, and the cities are large and well fortified*
> (Numbers 13:28).

And they listed the peoples that dwelt in the mountains, on the
coast, and along the banks of the River Jordan. This was a factual
report of the land based upon 40 days of spying out the land.

Caleb (one of the spies) was impatient to begin the conquest
and said:

> *Let us go up at once and take possession, for we are well
> able to overcome it* (Numbers 13:30).

But 10 of the spies cried him down and said:

> *We are not able to go up against the people, for they are
> stronger than we ... The land through which we have gone as
> spies is a land that devours its inhabitants, and all the people
> whom we saw in it are men of great stature ... we saw the
> giants ... we were like grasshoppers in our own sight...*
> (Numbers 13:31, 32, 33).

Here sin and Satan found an entrance wide open into the heart of
the Israelite nation.

Looking Back...

While the Israelites were suffering under Egyptian bondage God had come down to them and promised to deliver them from the hand of Egypt, and to take them into the land of Canaan,

> *to a good and large land, to a land flowing with milk and honey* (Exodus 3:8).

The whole of Israel had subsequently witnessed the hand of Almighty God moving on their behalf. Greater miracles followed each preceding one, until Israel walked out of Egypt a free nation. God's presence went before them to *search out a place* (Deuteronomy 1:33) for them to pitch their tents in the desert—leading them in a pillar of cloud by day and a pillar of fire by night.

After Pharaoh had sufficient time to regret the loss of Egypt's cheap labor force, he gathered the Egyptian army together, chased after the Israelites, and came upon them by the Red Sea. God rolled back the waters of the Red Sea, opening up a highway that allowed Israel to pass through on dry land. God waited until the whole Egyptian army was on the Red Sea road in hot pursuit and then brought the waters back over it, drowning all the Egyptians. When the Israelites saw the bodies of the Egyptians washed up on the shores of the Red Sea, they knew for certain that they were free, because their oppressors were no more.

Now God had brought them to the border of the Promised Land, as he had sworn to do. He had fulfilled His word, and the ancient world had never before witnessed such manifestations of divine power:

> *For ask now concerning the days that are past, which were before you, since the day that God created man on the earth, and ask from one end of heaven to the other, whether any great thing like this has happened, or anything like it has been heard.... did God ever try to go and take for Himself a nation from the midst of another nation, by trials, by signs, by wonders, by war, by a mighty hand and an outstretched arm, and by great terrors, according to all that the LORD your God did for you in Egypt before your eyes? To you it was shown, that you might know that the LORD Himself is God; there is none other besides Him. ... And because He loved your fathers, therefore He chose their descendants after them;*

and He brought you out of Egypt with His Presence, with His mighty power (Deuteronomy 4:32, 34, 36-37).

Yet, after having witnessed such a display of God's mighty power and deliverance, 10 of the spies did not believe He could deliver the Promised Land into Israel's hands. All 12 spies had observed the same facts, and all were in high positions of leadership in their tribes (Numbers 13:2, 3). This conclusively proves that being placed in a position of leadership by man is no guarantee at all that the person possesses the attributes of leadership required by God. Ten of the scouts were dismal failures—only Caleb and Joshua possessed the necessary qualities to lead God's people.

Ten faithless, fearful men can easily out-shout two faithful, fearless men. Fear is the antithesis of faith. Courage goes hand in hand with faith. Fear stems from a lack of faith in God. Both faith and fear have expectations: Faith expects positively, fear expects negatively. **Faithless**ness breeds **fearful**ness. Strength and courage comes from **fearless**ness:

> *Be strong and of good courage, do not fear nor be afraid of them; for the LORD your God, He is the One who goes with you. He will not leave you nor forsake you*
>
> (Deuteronomy 31:6).

The 10 spies began with fear and unbelief, proceeded into exaggeration and fabrication, and eventually dug themselves into a hole from which they could not extricate themselves. That hole in the wilderness finally became big enough to accommodate an entire generation, barring only Moses, Aaron, Caleb and Joshua.

How easy it is for a fearful minority to intimidate the greater mass. A truthful report of an abundant land with large, strong cities became tainted with fear (*they are stronger than we*); and unbelief (*We are not able to go against the people*); and exaggeration (*all the people...are men of great stature...we were like grasshoppers*); and fabrication (*The land...is a land that devours its inhabitants*). We do not possess the full account of what the 10 fearful spies actually said, but it was obviously more than that recorded in the book of Numbers. For example, further wild exaggeration from the spies appears in Deuteronomy 1:28: *the cities are great and fortified up to heaven.* However, to the Israelites, the Promised Land, the *land of milk and honey,* now appeared to be a hostile land—one that *devours its inhabitants.* By speaking evil of the land the faithless spies were, in fact, speaking evil of God. And the huge cluster of grapes that required two men to carry it was no longer evidence of abundance. This was now intimidating and unnerving—a symbol of paralyzing terror. It bore out what the 10 unbelieving, fearful spies had said; it was grim evidence of the size and terribleness of the inhabitants of this formidable land.

The entire congregation was affected:

And all the children of Israel grumbled against Moses and Aaron, and the whole congregation said to them, "If only we had died in the land of Egypt! Or if we had died in this wilderness! Why has the Lord brought us to this land to fall by the sword, that our wives and children should become victims?" (Numbers 14:2,3).

After witnessing firsthand the awesomeness of the Almighty in dealing with the Egyptians, both in Egypt and at the Red Sea, in their minds God was too impotent to complete the task before Him. This was nothing short of blasphemy, and God was far from pleased with them:

...they are a perverse generation, children in whom is no faith (Deuteronomy 32:20).

The hole that the 10 spies had dug with fear and unbelief, with exaggeration, fabrication, distortion and outright lies, became a grave for an unbelieving generation. For 40 years—one year for each day spent spying out the land—Israel wandered in a harsh, dry, hostile environment, until that unbelieving generation was buried beneath the desert sands. Not until the faithless generation was swept away, could Israel again attempt to enter its divine inheritance.

Yesteryear and Yesterday

There are striking similarities between the events of the first days of Israel's ancient history as a nation and those of today's modern State of Israel. From reading the Bible we know of God's intervention in Egypt—the systematic catastrophes which wrought destruction upon the country and, finally, the liquidation of Pharaoh's army in the Red Sea. We know of Israel's failure to enter the Promised Land through unbelief and the resulting 40 years of wandering in the wilderness. We also know of its successful conquest of Canaan under Joshua, and its rise to glory and prosperity under David and Solomon. We have a written record of all of these things, and many archeological finds spanning millennia substantiate them.

The historical record of events during the relatively few years of modern Israel's existence is not only well documented in written works, but much of it is recorded audibly and visually on both tape and film. Like the early days of ancient Israel, the birth and development of the modern State of Israel was also accompanied by many miracles.

On May 15, 1948, for example, the day following the declaration of Israel's statehood, seven[1] Arab armies launched coordinated attacks against the infant nation in a bid to extinguish its life. The Arab armies were made up of fully equipped regular troops who were trained, well organized, and properly supplied. They held the initiative,[2] and they had also been trained and equipped by the British. Lieutenant General Sir John Glubb commanded the Jordanian army and British officers also commanded the Syrians.[3]

Israeli troops, on the other hand, were mostly untrained, and many of their rifles were homemade. Against the seven fully equipped, well organized, coordinated armies, Israel pitted

> about 18,000 fighting men with 10,000 rifles, 3,600 submachine guns, four elderly mountain guns smuggled in from Mexico, some bazookas, and two tanks which had been 'liberated' from a British depot.[4]

Vastly outnumbered and short of weapons—not every fighter could have a gun—the newborn Jewish state emerged victorious from the war. Israel was not only the victor, but its size had almost tripled due to the amount of enemy territory it had captured.

In June 1967, five powerful Arab armies encircled Israel. Their stated intent was, according to the Egyptian leader, to "totally exterminate the State of Israel for all time."[5] When asked at a press conference what would happen to the Israelis if the Arab attack succeeded, the PLO's Ahmed Shukeiry replied: "I estimate that none of them will survive."[6] Israel's reply to the Arabs was a lightening thunderbolt delivered with a clenched, mailed fist. Israel hurled its force of 400 attack-planes deep inside hostile Arab territory and annihilated the enemy's planes and air bases. In just

170 minutes Egypt's air force, the largest in the Middle East, was in complete ruins—its hundreds of combat planes were now flaming wrecks, and the bases were bombed into uselessness.[7] On the same day the air forces of Syria, Jordan, Iraq and Lebanon suffered the same fate.

Israel obliterated the five Arab armies in just six days. Billions of petrodollars had been spent on the military hardware for the bid to exterminate Israel forever. This equipment was now scattered over battlegrounds like twisted, broken and burning wisps of straw. And, Israel had captured such vast areas of enemy territory that its size was tripled once again.

In October 1973, on Yom Kippur (The Day of Atonement), the holiest day in the Jewish calendar, a marriage between the now immense Egyptian and Syrian armies was consummated in a surprise attack upon Israel. The combined number of troops from these two armies alone made up a force of a nearly one million men. Joining this multitude later, together with their planes, tanks and guns, were hundreds of thousands of troops from Jordan, Saudi-Arabia, Kuwait, Yemen, Iraq, Libya, Morocco, Algeria and Tunis.[8]

This surprise attack on a most solemn day when the nation was fasting and attending synagogue services caused the lightly manned Israeli lines to crumple under the tidal wave of invading men and tanks. The nation was largely unaware that a war was being waged for its survival until several hours after the attacks began. And it was days before it realized just how close defeat had come in those early hours.

Facing the Egyptian avalanche of 600,000 men, 2,000 tanks, 2,300 artillery pieces, hundreds of fighter-planes and SAM (Surface to Air) missiles in the south were **precisely 436 Israelis and 177 tanks**.[9] These few men and their handful of tanks were spread out along the 110 mi. (177 km.) length of the Suez Canal. Opposing the Syrian earthquake of nearly 400,000 men and 1,400 tanks in the north were around 2,000 Israelis and some 25 to 50 tanks.

This courageous few, scattered along two front lines, fought and fell. But they sufficiently slowed the momentum of the enemy long enough to enable reinforcements to arrive. It took three days for Israel to fully mobilize its troops, but once mobilized, the IDF (Israel Defense Force) moved swiftly and powerfully.

By day four of fighting, Israel had driven the Arab forces

back across the lines that had existed on day one. By day 12 Israeli troops had fought their way to within 14 mi. (22 km.) of Damascus, and the suburbs of the city were within easy reach of their artillery. Israel's leaders, however, felt the city possessed little military value and held back on any further advance. Leaving a strong force in place to repulse Arab counterattacks, all available men and equipment were then transferred to other fronts.

On the southern front, Israel crossed over to the west bank of the Suez Canal and was decimating the Egyptians as the troops punched their way toward Cairo. On day 17, Anwar Sadat, the Egyptian president and instigator of the war, issued

> panic-stricken appeals to his countrymen to rise up in arms, to fight "to the death" to save Cairo.[10]

Only forceful intervention by America, due to a "threat of unilateral Soviet action"[11] in the final hours of the war, prevented Israel from arriving uninvited in Cairo. Between them, the U.S. and the U.S.S.R. "negotiated" a cease-fire and forced Israel to comply. Twenty-six years later the world still remains unaware of how close it actually came to the reality of nuclear war.

Only a few hundred tanks from the thousands involved in the assault upon Israel managed to return home to their bases. Many thousands of personnel carriers, tanks, antitank and antiaircraft guns, supply vehicles and hundreds of combat aircraft lay in smoldering ruins. Israel's victory over numerically superior forces had been brutal and decisive. In practical terms all that was left of the attacking armies were corpses and mountains of torn and lacerated steel. These covered the battlefields, filled towns and villages, and lined the routes of Israel's advances upon the Syrian and Egyptian capitals.

The Soviet Union, being the chief supplier of arms and military equipment to the Arab nations, was humiliated by Israel's decimation of its equipment. It not only threatened, but was also ready to use, a nuclear option to prevent further humiliation. The Soviet reputation was at stake. A confrontation between the U.S.S.R. and America, resulting from a nuclear strike against Israel, was only averted by the U.S. forcibly forcing Israel to accept the cease fire.

Divine Strategy

God intervened in modern wars on Israel's behalf just as He had done in Israel's ancient battles, and this intervention is often documented through dramatic miracles that occurred during the fighting. (There is insufficient space for inclusion of these miracles here, but a number of them are recorded in my book, "When Day and Night Cease"). A divine strategy is also apparent in the wars modern Israel has been forced to fight to prevent its own annihilation.

Looking at ancient Israel's conquest of the Promised Land, we can see that it was a successful campaign under the command of Joshua, an excellent general. By and large the conquest took around five years and was accompanied by some notable miracles. But brilliant leadership, military expertise and miracles notwithstanding, not all of the enemy was destroyed; some remained in the land. The Bible explains why God allowed that situation:

> ...*to teach warfare to the descendants of the Israelites who had not had previous battle experience* (Judges 3:2 NIV).

In other words, God purposely let some of Israel's enemies hang around in the land so that following generations could learn the art of war by fighting them. This turned out to be a blessing in disguise. By fighting those irritating enemies year after year, Israel learned how to defend itself against attack, and became, until its final rejection of God, the great military power of the region.

During WWI, Britain fought against the Turks in Palestine, and against Germany and other axis powers in different parts of the world. While fighting on several fronts, Britain ran out of acetone, a vital component of gunpowder. Chaim Weizmann, a Jewish chemist, was asked by Winston Churchill to immediately manufacture 28,000 tons of acetone or Britain would be defeated. After Weizmann produced an artificial acetone that made a more powerful high-explosive than the original, he was asked what he required as payment. His reply was:

> If Britain wins the battle for Palestine, I ask for a national home for my people in their ancient land.

To this Britain agreed, and shortly afterward the British Foreign Minister Arthur James Balfour issued a statement to that effect which had been approved by the Cabinet. That statement is known as the Balfour Declaration. Britain defeated the Turks, and 11 days following the capture of Palestine, the war ended.

After the war Britain was given a mandate to establish the Jewish National Home in all of Palestine. Britain, however, soon embarked on a policy of Arab appeasement (which it still pursues today). It gave control of the Golan Heights to the French, who were then occupying Syria. Then, with one swift stroke of a pen, Britain cut off a further 77 percent of Palestine and gave it to Abdullah Ibn Hussein, whose family had been ousted from Arabia by the Sa'ud family. Abdullah formed Transjordan (now Jordan) and became its king. The British also established Abdullah's brother, Feisal, as king over a semi-independent Iraq.

In November 1947, the Jews finally ate the crumbs that dropped from the British table. What remained of Palestine at that time was divided by the League of Nations between Arabs and Jews, with the Jews receiving the smaller allotment. The Jewish National Home which was to have incorporated all of Palestine, now actually constituted less than 11 percent of that land. The State of Israel was formally declared on May 14, 1948, and the first Arab-Israeli war began in earnest the following day.

Now, it would have been a very simple thing for God Almighty to have pulled a few strings and allowed the Jews to take over the whole of Palestine. However, He chose to engineer circumstances that not only gave the Jews a tiny sliver of land, but also gave them war. The moment the Jews dared to call the bit that fell to them their own, they were required to fight fiercely against great odds to keep it. But, remember the Scripture cited previously,

> *He did this only to teach warfare to the descendants of the Israelites who had not had previous battle experience*
>
> (Judges 3:2 NIV)!

Israel was immediately forced to begin learning the art of war in earnest. And at the conclusion of its War of Independence, Israel found itself possessing three times as much land as it had gotten from the League of Nations. How aptly fits the psalm:

> *For they did not gain possession of the land by their own sword, nor did their own arm save them; but it was Your right hand, Your arm, and the light of Your countenance, because You favored them* (Psalms 44:3).

Another passage of Holy Writ that we should not be content to leave buried in antiquity's dust is this:

Little by little I will drive them out from before you, until you have increased, and you inherit the land (Exodus 23:30).

Many scripture passages have two fulfillments, a literal one and a secondary one. Now, consider the conquest of Canaan under Joshua, it was basically over in around five years. This was hardly time for the Israelite population to have increased much, especially in light of the fact that all men of military age were engaged in the conquest. And all the fighting men of the tribes of Reuben, Gad and Manasseh left their "_little ones_" and "_wives_" on the eastern side of the Jordan and did not return to them until they crossed back to their inheritance after the conquest (Joshua 22:9). Modern Israel, on the other hand, began with some 650,000 Jews in 1948, but that number had increased to over three million by the time of the 1973 Yom Kippur War.

Each successive war launched against Israel by its Arab neighbors brought further territorial gains to the Jewish state. At the same time, Israel's army, navy and air force increased in size and power. After 25 years of statehood and four wars with its neighbors, Israeli forces had, according to one of Britain's foremost authorities on military affairs,

progressed from nothing to being one of the most efficient and battle-hardened forces in the world.[12]

Further, drawing from a Jewish population that only topped 4.783 million in December 1998, Israel is, according to the _Jane's Intelligence Review_ of July 1997, rated the **third most powerful fighting force in the world**[13] (only behind America and Russia).

From less than modest beginnings and without initiating a single conflict, Israel, with no small amount of help from God, took possession of most of the land promised to Abraham nearly 4,000 years ago. It had captured the biblical _Negev_ (desert wilderness) in the south; the Old City of Jerusalem containing the Western Wall of the Temple Mount—the last remains of the first and second temples; Hebron—the biblical city where King David began his 40-year reign; Judea and Samaria—the biblical _mountains of Israel_; and biblical _Bashan_—the Golan Heights. Only tracts of land held by Syria and Iraq were missing from Abraham's map of the divine inheritance.

Both Syria and Iraq have been rattling their sabers at Israel for years. Iraq even launched 39 SCUD missiles at Israeli population centers during the 1991 Gulf War, a war in which Israel was not even involved. And, only the refusal by America to give Israel the International Friend or Foe (IFF) codes used by allied aircraft over Iraq[14] prevented savage Israeli retaliation against Iraq.

Israel 1992 - 1996

Aided by the overt interference of America's Bush Administration, Yitzhak Rabin and his socialist Labor party stole the right to govern Israel from the incumbent Likud party in the June 1992 elections and ended 15 years of Likud rule. Labor's previous term in power ended after it had been caught napping at the start of the Yom Kippur War, and many Israeli lives were lost as a result. But when Likud rose to govern, it successfully negotiated Anwar Sadat's Egypt into a signed peace agreement without the loss of any of Israel's divine inheritance. And the Likud government had also begun the Madrid peace conference in 1991, with the aim of achieving a negotiated settlement of the Palestinian and Syrian issues. Likud's stated objective was to again effect a settlement without loss to any part of Israel's ancient inheritance. But, in the guise of being "honest brokers" in the negotiations between Israel and the Arabs, President George Bush and his Secretary of State James Baker promised the Arabs that a Palestinian state would be established on much of Judea and Samaria (Israel's biblical heartland).[15] They also promised Syria that America would return to it the Golan Heights (biblical *Bashan*).[16]

To effect his own agenda, it was necessary for Bush to bring down the Likud government and replace it with a more "pliable" one that would carry out America's bidding. Thus the Bush administration conspired with Yitzhak Rabin, described both as "a weak man in Washington's pocket"[17] and "the symbol of the defeatism which characterizes leftist radicalism,"[18] to effect the Likud's downfall. By secret negotiations with the PLO—Israel's sworn and bitter enemy when negotiations were still classified as an act of treason; by promising the Arabs the moon wrapped in dollar bills—costing Israeli taxpayers hundreds of millions of dollars annually; and stopping "at no dirty deal to assume power,"[19] Rabin's Labor party unseated the Likud government. Rabin subsequently formed perhaps the most godless and corrupt government that has ever ruled over the nation of Israel. Within months of taking office, several members of his coalition were either in prison or on trial for fraud, forgery, corruption and theft of public monies.

Ten unbelieving, fearful spies brought a bad report of the land to Israel, when it was at the doorstep of Canaan. They shouted down those who believed and trusted in God, infecting the whole house of Israel with a virus of fear and unbelief. Rabin and his cabinet colleagues did no less themselves during their short term in office. Rabin had witnessed the founding and establishment of the State of Israel against impossible odds. He and his colleagues had seen 1947's tiny piece of Palestine expand, until Israel was almost in possession of its full biblical inheritance. They had seen Israel become an economic miracle—leading the industrial world in economic growth. They had witnessed a small, largely untrained, ill-equipped band of men become the third most powerful fighting force in the world. Israel had learned the art of war so well that only a fool would now mess with it. But fearing an Arab victory over Israel, the fearful and unbelieving Rabin and Peres governments threw the wheels of fortune in reverse and caused Israel to take the posture of a defeated nation. Nowhere else in history has a victorious nation ever sued its enemies for peace.

On the threshold of possessing the whole of the Promised Land these "_fools_" said in their hearts, "_There is no God._" Instead of having Yasser Arafat executed for murdering more Jews than any man since Adolf Hitler, they "fawned over him and glorified him."[20] Rabin shook Arafat's bloodstained hand, and Peres hugged and kissed Arafat and stood holding his hand while posing for pictures.[21] Both Rabin and Peres gladly took joint acceptance, with Arafat, of the Nobel Peace Prize—

> jointly receiving the world's most prestigious award for peace with a man who was the arch-terrorist of the 20th century.[22]

And then, convinced in their hearts that _there is no God_, they began handing Arafat large areas of Israel's divine inheritance.

Arafat continues his calls for war against Israel. He gives shelter to terrorists operating against Israeli civilians from the territory now under his control and has established a regime "that tortures people to death"[23] in the very heartland of biblical Israel. This travesty of justice came about because Rabin and Peres, and all their advisors, collectively said in their hearts, _There is no God_.

For Rabin and Peres, Israel's God-given inheritance was and is just "real estate,"[24] "holes in the ground"[25] and the Bible is merely an "outdated land-registry book."[26] Peres mocked: "The more land we give up the more Ph.D.s per kilometer we have."[27] How perfectly do the words of the psalmist fit Rabin and Peres:

> *they despised the pleasant land; they did not believe His word*
> (Psalms 106:24).

These unworthy Jewish leaders followed in the footsteps of Esau and despised Israel's birthright by selling it for a bowl of Arafat's lies. They too,

> *are a perverse generation, children in whom is no faith*
> (Deuteronomy 32:20).

Rabin and Peres gathered their fearful, conniving and unbelieving band around themselves:

Yossi Beilin, who earned the nickname of "Soap"[28] in the Israeli army and that of "Peres's poodle"[29] from Rabin himself.

Chaim Ramon, who on television addressed those holding opposing views with an absurd: "This is a **democracy**, and if you don't come around to our way of thinking and join us, **we will crush you**."[30]

Yossi Sarid, who spat hatred and venom at religious Jews—the *Haredim*—and portrayed them as "black masses who must be stopped."[31]

Naomi Chazan who, in a public meeting where religious protestors were told to "shove the Bible up your ass," addressed the audience with: "You cannot have democracy in Israel without fighting the *Haredim* and what they stand for."[32]

Shulamit Aloni, who expressed the collective fear of all the "*fools*" to the press when she said, "Let us not forget that the god of the Moslems has many, many more troops than the God of the Jews."[33]

Yael Dayan, an alleged lesbian, hosted a reception for homosexuals and lesbians in the Israeli Knesset,[34] and also read from the Bible in a Knesset session to "prove" King David was a homosexual.[35]

Amnon Rubenstein, who as Minister of Education, requested on television that students in the Israeli school system "spy on their teachers"[36] if, among other things, the teacher did not agree that the Government's "peace process" was "the only way to go."[37]

Teddy Kollek, who became a legend as mayor of Jerusalem—until the 1993 mayoralty elections that is. (Rabin backed Kollek and argued that the results of the Jerusalem election "would constitute a mandate on his approach to peace."[38] Ehud Olmert, a Likud candidate, stood against both Kollek and Rabin's peace. He ended Kollek's 28-year reign by taking 59.5 percent of the vote[39] compared to Kollek's 34.8 percent). When Kollek was greeted by the Pope at the Vatican, the Pope remarked that Kollek had just come from Jerusalem, "the spiritual center of the world."[40] And after being mayor of Jerusalem for 28 years, but a secular humanist for much longer, Kollek naively replied, "I thought that Rome was."[41]

The men and women listed above were but some of those on board Rabin's ship of _"fools."_ And just as the 10 fearful, unbelieving spies had shouted down those who believed God on the border of Canaan, so those who made up the Rabin and Peres governments shouted down all who expressed opposition to their myopic "peace" policies—

> treating half the population like second-class citizens with contempt, arrogance, scorn and delegitimation.[42]

The 10 fearful spies were clearly guilty of sedition for they _rebelled against the command of the Lord_ (Deuteronomy 1:26) and

> _discouraged the heart of the children of Israel, so that they did not go into the land which the Lord had given them_
>
> (Numbers 32:9).

Therefore, Rabin and Peres and all those who machinated with them are equally as guilty of sedition before God. Like the spies before them, they too are or were

> _a perverse generation, children in whom is no faith; they rebelled against the command of the Lord_ and _discouraged the heart of the children of Israel_
>
> (Deuteronomy 32:20, 1:26; Numbers 32:9).

Most of those who had demonstrated against the policies of Rabin and Peres were religious Israelis. Many of them felt betrayed by Rabin and Peres much like Moses, Aaron, Caleb and Joshua felt betrayed by the 10 spies—leaders of the tribes of Israel. Rabin's Environment Minister, Yossi Sarid, a man proud of being a *"fool,"* urged the police to stop treating the religious demonstrators with "...kid gloves. Give it to them" he urged.[43] The religious have faith in both God and the Bible, and implicitly believe that it was God Himself who had brought the Jews back to their ancient land, as the Bible foretold. Rabbi Gary Cooperberg wrote:

> The God of Israel has given us the ability to return to all the Land of Israel and to rebuild a truly Jewish state here. It is only our fear and blindness which prevents us from bringing instant redemption.[44]

Ten fearful, faithless, blind spies prevented an entire nation from entering its inheritance under Moses around 1,450 B.C. Another fearful, faithless, blind group of leaders prevented the restored people of Israel from possessing their full inheritance as the seventh and last millennium began to shine its light into history.

4

The Indictment
of Israel

Ancient Israel's history paints a beautiful picture of God's love, goodness and patience toward a people whom He chose to embrace as His own. But Israel's canvas of time is also liberally splashed with the vivid and heartbreaking colors of blood, tears, pain and exile from the Land. The Almighty, Eternal, Creator God took Israel to Himself and established it as a nation solely because of the merits of His mortal friend Abraham. The nation of Israel was to be

> *a people for Himself, a special treasure above all the peoples on the face of the earth* (Deuteronomy 7:6).

God would have tapped all the power of the universe on Israel's behalf, but within a relatively short period of time following the settling of the nation in the Promised Land, the people rejected God as their King—

> *they have rejected Me, that I should not reign over them*
>
> (1 Samuel 8:7).

Israel demanded an earthly king, so it could be like all other nations:

> *Now make us a king to judge us like all the nations*
>
> (1 Samuel 8:5).

God allowed Israel's demand for an earthly king and chose Saul to lead His people (1 Samuel 9:17). Saul soon rejected God's commands, and his rebellion brought about his own rejection by God:

> *For rebellion is as the sin of witchcraft, and stubbornness is as iniquity and idolatry. Because you have rejected the word of the Lord, He also has rejected you from being king*
>
> (1 Samuel 15:23).

God replaced Saul with David, *a man after His own heart* (1 Samuel 13:14), and King David subsequently took Israel to the pinnacle of its power. The Bible tells us that

> *David did what was right in the eyes of the Lord, and had not*

turned aside from anything that He commanded him all the days of his life, except in the matter of Uriah the Hittite
(I Kings 15:5).

According to the divine record David's sole sin during his 40-year reign over Judah and Israel was when he lusted for his neighbor's wife, Bathsheba. David committed adultery with her, and after having gotten her pregnant, had her husband Uriah killed in an effort to cover his sin.

After Uriah was dead and Bathsheba had completed her mourning period, David sent for her and she became one of his wives. Bathsheba later gave birth to the child that had been conceived in sin, but God would not allow the baby to live. He became mortally sick and died. Bathsheba became pregnant by David again and this time bore him a famous son, Solomon, who is history's monument to David's sin. Solomon inherited David's throne and

surpassed all the kings of the earth in riches and wisdom
(1 Kings 10:23).

And men of all nations, from all the kings of the earth who had heard of his wisdom, came to hear the wisdom of Solomon
(1 Kings 4:34).

The weight of gold that came to Solomon yearly was six hundred and sixty-six talents of gold, besides that from the traveling merchants, from the income of traders, from all the kings of Arabia, and from the governors of the country.

And King Solomon made two hundred large shields of hammered gold; six hundred shekels of gold went into each shield. He also made three hundred shields of hammered gold; three minas of gold went into each shield. The king put them in the House of the Forest of Lebanon.

Moreover the king made a great throne of ivory, and overlaid it with pure gold. The throne had six steps, and the top of the throne was round at the back; there were armrests on either side of the place of the seat, and two lions stood beside the armrests. Twelve lions stood there, one on each side of the six steps; nothing like this had been made for any other kingdom. All King Solomon's drinking vessels were gold, and all the vessels of the House of the Forest of Lebanon were pure gold. Not one was silver, for this was accounted as nothing in the days of Solomon (1 Kings 10:14-21).

Solomon, however, was not just a monument to David's lust, he was also a recipient of it genetically, and his lust far surpassed that of his father. David had seven wives (1 Chronicles 3:1-3, 5, 9) and at least 10 concubines or sex partners (2 Samuel 20:3), but

> *King Solomon loved* **many** *foreign women, as well as the daughter of Pharaoh: women of the Moabites, Ammonites, Edomites, Sidonians, and Hittites—from the nations of whom the* LORD *had said to the children of Israel, "You shall not intermarry with them, nor they with you. Surely they will turn away your hearts after their gods." Solomon clung to these in love. And he had* **seven hundred wives, princesses, and three hundred concubines;** *and his wives turned away his heart. Solomon* **did evil** *in the sight of the* LORD... . *So the* LORD *became angry with Solomon, because his heart had turned from the* LORD *God of Israel, who had appeared to him twice*
> (1 Kings 11:1-3, 6, 9).

From the latter part of Solomon's life onward—after he had spurned God—everything began to slide downhill for Israel.

Cause and Effect

Israelis, together with most Jews living in the *galut*, would dearly love to see Israel return to the golden days of David and Solomon. Under David Israel rose to the peak of its military power. Under Solomon Israel rode the crest of splendor's wave and no other nation or king could approach being its equal.

With the passing of the years following Solomon's death, however, Israel's military might disappeared. Its majestic glory was trampled in the dust under the feet of a seemingly unending line of conquering armies. Solomon's magnificent gold-overlaid temple in Jerusalem was sacked and burnt, and the inhabitants throughout the length and breadth of the Land died from the sword, famine and disease, or were taken away by their conquerors into captivity. Israel became a reproach and a byword to all the nations round about. And this happened not just once, but twice.

Seventy years following the first devastation and exile of Israel, God ,as His word had foretold, brought His people back to the Land. Israeli life began anew and, in time, an even greater temple than Solomon's was built. But with the passing of time, the same pattern of events took place, and Jerusalem with its second temple was completely destroyed. Millions of Israelis died from the sword, famine and disease, or were taken away by their conquerors.

This writer is an Israeli citizen living in Jerusalem for 20 years. For that length of time I have had to suffer listening to many Jews berating Gentiles for every calamity that has ever befallen the Jewish people. The sufferings of the Jewish nation throughout its history is, according to many Jews, almost entirely attributable to the Gentiles. Rabbis, however, do teach that the second destruction of Jerusalem was due to the Jews not treating their brethren in accordance with the law of Moses. Apart from this confession of Jewish shortcomings toward each other, which is far from the real reason for Jerusalem's destruction, the Jews apparently feel their conduct through the ages has been rather blameless.

A rabbi from New York once had the _hutzpah_ (nerve) to seriously tell this writer a story about the two types of animals in the Bible, the clean and the unclean (Leviticus 11:1-8). He began by paraphrasing the biblical passages and said animals that chew the cud and have cloven hooves are clean animals. He said those chewing the cud but not having cloven hooves or those having a cloven hoof but not chewing the cud are unclean animals. He then said:

> We Jews are the clean animals, we are righteous inside and out, but Gentiles are related to the pig that wallows in its own filth.

No doubt a good number of Israelis, along with other Jews in the _galut_, would readily concur with the rabbi. However, their layers of arrogance and pride are peeled away by the biblical records, and they are shown to be blatant hypocrites.

Israel was an adulterous nation long before they rejected God from ruling over them as King. Listen to the Divine's indictment of Israel:

> _...the children of Israel **did evil** in the sight of the LORD, and ...the anger of the LORD was hot against Israel. So He delivered them into the hands of plunderers who despoiled them; and He sold them into the hands of their enemies all around, so that they could no longer stand before their enemies_
>
> (Judges 2:11, 14).
>
> _...the children of Israel **did evil** in the sight of the LORD. ...Therefore the anger of the LORD was hot against Israel, and_

He sold them into the hand of Cushan-Rishathaim king of Mesopotamia (Judges 3:7, 8).

*...the children of Israel again **did evil** in the sight of the LORD. So the LORD strengthened Eglon king of Moab against Israel, because they had **done evil** in the sight of the LORD. Then he gathered to himself the people of Ammon and Amalek and went and defeated Israel* (Judges 3:12, 13).

*...the children of Israel again **did evil** in the sight of the LORD. So the LORD sold them into the hand of Jabin king of Canaan* (Judges 4:1, 2).

...the children of Israel did evil in the sight of the LORD. So the LORD delivered them into the hand of Midian ...and the hand of Midian prevailed against Israel (Judges 6:1, 2).

*...the children of Israel again **did evil** in the sight of the LORD, and ...they forsook the LORD and did not serve Him. So the anger of the LORD was hot against Israel; and He sold them into the hands of the Philistines and into the hands of the people of Ammon* (Judges 10:6, 7).

*Again the children of Israel **did evil** in the sight of the LORD, and the LORD delivered them into the hand of the Philistines* (Judges 13:1).

At this point we arrive at where Israel rejects God and demands an earthly king. Saul is chosen, crowned, and later rejected by God for rebellion against His commands. Thus David enters into history and provides God with one of the very rare periods where He is obeyed, loved, worshipped and appreciated for who He is. Of a consequence David is exalted, Israel is delivered from all its enemies, all its territory is restored, and Israel becomes the great power of the region.

Solomon, David's son by Bathsheba, succeeded his father and began his reign by following in David's footsteps and walking with God. But Solomon's lust for women became stronger than his love for God. In time, Solomon completely cast God aside:

*Solomon **did evil** in the sight of the LORD, and ...built a high place for Chemosh the abomination of Moab, on the hill that is east of Jerusalem, and for Molech the abomination of the* *people of Ammon. And he did likewise for all his foreign wives* (1 Kings 11:6, 7, 8).

Solomon's sins greatly angered God, and He determined to tear the kingdom from Solomon, but purposed to leave him Judah because of the promise He had made to David:

> *"And it shall be, when your days are fulfilled, when you must go to be with your fathers, that I will set up your seed after you, who will be of your sons.... He shall build Me a house ... and I will not take My mercy away from him, as I took it from him who was before you"* (1 Chronicles 17:11, 12, 13).

Solomon's lust for women turned his heart away from the One who had exalted him, and his sowing of rot and apostasy into Israel's soul was to bring forth a bumper crop. Solomon

> *rested with his fathers, and was buried in the City of David*
> (1 Kings 11:43),

but the nation, however, was to pay a most terrible price for his sins.

Upon Solomon's death, his son Rehoboam became king over all Israel, but God's resolve to rip 10 of the tribes away and give them to Jeroboam, Solomon's former servant (1 Kings 11:26), was inflexible. He sent Ahijah the prophet to Jeroboam:

> *Behold, I will tear the kingdom out of the hand of Solomon and will give ten tribes to you (but he shall have one tribe for the sake of My servant David, and for the sake of Jerusalem, the city which I have chosen out of all the tribes of Israel), because they have forsaken Me, and worshiped Ashtoreth the goddess of the Sidonians, Chemosh the god of the Moabites, and Milcom the god of the people of Ammon, and have not walked in My ways to do what is right in My eyes and keep My statutes and My judgments* (1 Kings 11:31, 32, 33).

Rehoboam was subsequently left only with Judah to rule. Even so, he still chose to walk the same evil path as his father Solomon had done. Disaster was about to begin stalking the Land:

> *Rehoboam the son of Solomon reigned in Judah. ...Now Judah did evil in the sight of the LORD, and they provoked Him to jealousy with their sins which they committed, more than all that their fathers had done. For they also built for themselves high places, sacred pillars, and wooden images on every high*

hill and under every green tree. And there were also perverted persons in the land. They did according to all the abominations of the nations which the LORD had cast out before the children of Israel. It happened in the fifth year of King Rehoboam that Shishak king of Egypt came up against Jerusalem. And he took away the treasures of the house of the LORD and the treasures of the king's house; he took away everything
(1 Kings 14:21, 22-26).

Jeroboam reigned over 10 tribes of Israel, but his sins were greater than all those who had preceded him. He provoked God to such extreme anger that the LORD sent Ahijah the prophet to him saying:

*Thus says the LORD God of Israel: I exalted you from among the people, and made you ruler over My people Israel, and tore the kingdom away from the house of David, and gave it to you ... but you have **done more evil than all who were before you**, for you have gone and made for yourself other gods and molded images to provoke Me to anger, and have cast Me behind your back—therefore behold! I will bring disaster on the house of Jeroboam, and will cut off from Jeroboam every male in Israel, bond and free; I will take away the remnant of the house of Jeroboam, as one takes away refuse until it is all gone. The dogs shall eat whoever belongs to Jeroboam and dies in the city, and the birds of the air shall eat whoever dies in the field; for the LORD has spoken!*
(1 Kings 14:7, 8, 9-11).

Only five kings—Asa (2 Chronicles 14:2), Jehoshaphat (2 Chronicles 17:1, 6), Jotham (2 Chronicles 27:1-2), Hezekiah (2 Chronicles 29:1-2) and Josiah (2 Chronicles 34:1-2), all from Judah—followed the *Holy One of Israel* during their reigns. Every other king followed the evil inclinations of their own hearts and prepared the way for the sky to fall in on Israel. Consider the records:

*Nadab ...became king over Israel ...and he **did evil** in the sight of the LORD* (1 Kings 15:25, 26).

*Baasha ...became king over all Israel ...he **did evil** in the sight of the LORD* (1 Kings 15:33,34).

*Ahab ...became king over Israel; and ...**did evil** in the sight*

of the L*ORD,* **more than all who were before him**
(1 Kings 16:29, 30).

Ahaziah ...became king over Israel and ...he **did evil** *in the sight of the* L*ORD* (1 Kings 22:51,52).

Jehoram the son of Ahab became king over Israel at Samaria ...and he **did evil** *in the sight of the* L*ORD* (2 Kings 3:1, 2).

Jehoram the son of Jehoshaphat began to reign as king of Judah. And he walked in the way of the kings of Israel ...and he **did evil** *in the sight of the* L*ORD* (2 Kings 8:16, 18).

Ahaziah ...became king, and ... **did evil** *in the sight of the* L*ORD* (2 Kings 8:26, 27).

Jehu ...anointed king ...over Israel. But Jehu **took no heed to walk in the law of the** L*ORD* **God** *of Israel*
(2 Kings 9:2, 3, 10:31).

Jehoahaz ...became king over Israel ...and he **did evil** *in the sight of the* L*ORD* (2 Kings 13:1, 2).

Jehoash ...became king over Israel ...and he **did evil** *in the sight of the* L*ORD* (2 Kings 13:10, 11).

Jeroboam ...became king ...and he **did evil** *in the sight of the* L*ORD* (2 Kings 14:23, 24).

Zechariah ...reigned over Israel ...and he **did evil** *in the sight of the* L*ORD* (2 Kings 15:8, 9).

Menahem ...became king over Israel, and ...he **did evil** *in the sight of the* L*ORD* (2 Kings 15: 17, 18).

Pekahiah ...became king over Israel ...and he **did evil** *in the sight of the* L*ORD* (2 Kings 15:23, 24).

Pekah ...became king over Israel ...and he **did evil** *in the sight of the* L*ORD* (2 Kings 15:27, 28).

Hoshea ...became king of Israel ...and he **did evil** *in the sight of the* L*ORD* (2 Kings 17:1, 2).

Manasseh ...became king, and ...he **did evil** *in the sight of the* L*ORD, according to the abominations of the nations*
(2 Kings 21:1, 2).

Amon ...became king, and ...he **did evil** *in the sight of the* L*ORD* (2 Kings 21:19,20).

*Jehoahaz ...became king, and ...he **did evil** in the sight of the LORD* (2 Kings 23:31,32).

*Jehoiakim ...became king, and he ...**did evil** in the sight of the LORD* (2 Kings 23:36, 37).

*Jehoiachin ...became king, and he ...**did evil** in the sight of the LORD* (2 Kings 24:8, 9).

*Zedekiah ...became king, and he ...also **did evil** in the sight of the LORD* (2 Kings 24:18, 19).

What a terrible indictment of the kings of Israel and Judah! The people were to learn the truth of the proverb:

Righteousness exalts a nation, but sin is a reproach to any people (Proverbs 14:34).

When Israel walked before God in righteousness, it was exalted as a nation. When it stiffened its neck and stubbornly insisted on walking in the ways of other nations, it suffered the consequences. For Israel and Judah the fruit of sin became increasingly costly and bitter to the taste.

Valley of Tears

Israelis, together with other Jews living outside the Land, bemoan the sufferings of the Jewish people. Yet, few there are who would have the honesty to say: "We brought it upon ourselves by the many sins we committed against our God—provoking Him to great anger." Israel's recorded history is one of being selected as Almighty God's chosen people—His own *special treasure*. Their fear of Him was brief, their backsliding was rapid, and their apostasy was complete. God sent His prophets to them time and again to warn them:

And the LORD God of their fathers sent warnings to them by His messengers, rising up early and sending them, because He had compassion on His people and on His dwelling place. But they mocked the messengers of God, despised His words, and scoffed at His prophets, until the wrath of the LORD arose against His people, till there was no remedy

(2 Chronicles 36:15-16).

And the LORD has sent to you all His servants the prophets, rising early and sending them, but you have not listened nor _inclined your ear to hear. They said, "Repent now everyone of his evil way and his evil doings, and dwell in the land that the LORD has given to you and your fathers forever and ever. Do not go after other gods to serve them and worship them, and do not provoke Me to anger with the works of your hands; and I will not harm you. Yet you have not listened to Me, says the LORD, that you might provoke Me to anger with the works of your hands to your own hurt"_ (Jeremiah 25:4-7).

The messages of repentance, however, held not the slightest interest for them, and

they did not obey nor incline their ear, but made their neck stiff, that they might not hear nor receive instruction
(Jeremiah 27:23).

Ultimately, the sky fell in on Israel and Judah:

Therefore He brought against them the king of the Chaldeans, who killed their young men with the sword in the house of their sanctuary, and had no compassion on young man or virgin, on the aged or the weak; He gave them all into his hand (2 Chronicles 36:17).

...the anger of the LORD was aroused against Israel, and He delivered them into the hand of Hazael king of Syria, and into the hand of Ben-Hadad the son of Hazael (2 Kings 13:3).

Thus says the LORD God of Israel: "I have anointed [Jehu] king over the people of the LORD, over Israel." But Jehu took no heed to walk in the law of the LORD God of Israel... In those days the LORD began to cut off parts of Israel
(2 Kings 9:2, 3, 10:31, 32).

...the king of Assyria ...carried Israel away ...the children of Israel had sinned against the LORD their God ...and had walked in the statutes of the nations (2 Kings 17:6, 7, 8).

For because of the anger of the LORD this happened in Jerusalem and Judah, till He finally cast them out from His presence (Jeremiah 52:3).

...they would not hear, but stiffened their necks, like the necks of their fathers, who did not believe in the LORD their God. And they rejected His statutes and His covenant ...and went after the nations ...and sold themselves to do evil in the sight *of the LORD, to provoke Him to anger. Therefore the LORD was very angry with Israel, and removed them from His sight; there was none left but the tribe of Judah alone. Also Judah did not keep the commandments of the LORD their God, but walked in the statutes of Israel... And the LORD rejected all the descendants of Israel, afflicted them, and delivered them into the hand of plunderers, until He had cast them from His sight. For ...the children of Israel walked in all the sins ...until the LORD removed Israel out of His sight, as He had said by all His servants the prophets. So Israel was carried away from their own land...*

(2 Kings 17:14,15,16,17,18,19,20,21,22,23).

If God's chosen people would but read His indictment of them, perhaps some might cease to lay the blame for the Jewish nation's woes at the feet of the Gentiles. Many, however, would still concur with the rabbi who said: "We Jews are the clean animals, we are righteous inside and out, but Gentiles are related to the pig that wallows in its own filth." Jesus was handed over to the Romans for crucifixion by such as he—perhaps partly due to His scathing indictment of them:

Woe to you scribes and Pharisees, hypocrites! For you are like whitewashed tombs which indeed appear beautiful outwardly, but inside are full of dead men's bones and all uncleanness (Matthew 23:27).

It was successive centuries of committing sin and doing evil that brought God's punitive judgment upon the whole nation of Israel. A long line of evil, unrepentant kings sank the people deeper and deeper into sin's mire. It is a sad but true fact that a nation will become what its leaders already are. Sheep grow fat from feeding on pasture that shepherds lead them into and leave them to graze upon.

Some Christians can perhaps feel the pain of God's heart more acutely than others, but from the following scripture everyone should get some idea of just how provoked God was by Israel and Judah:

And the LORD spoke by His servants the prophets, saying, "Because Manasseh king of Judah has done these abominations (he has acted more wickedly than all the Amorites *who were before him, and has also made Judah sin with his idols), therefore thus says the L*ORD *God of Israel: Behold, I am bringing such calamity upon Jerusalem and Judah, that whoever hears of it, both his ears will tingle. And I will stretch over Jerusalem the measuring line of Samaria and the plummet of the house of Ahab; I will wipe Jerusalem as one wipes a dish, wiping it and turning it upside down. So I will forsake the remnant of My inheritance and deliver them into the hand of their enemies; and they shall become victims of plunder to all their enemies, because they have done evil in My sight, and have provoked Me to anger since the day their fathers came out of Egypt, even to this day"* (2 Kings 21:10-15).

It was mentioned earlier that there were only five kings who followed the ways of God with a whole heart. One of those kings, Josiah, endeavored with all of his might to bring the people of Judah back to a vibrant relationship with their *Maker*. Despite Josiah's wholehearted love and obedience, however, the *Holy One of Israel* would not relent of the punitive destruction He had purposed to bring because of the sins of former kings:

*Now before him there was no king like [Josiah], who turned to the L*ORD *with all his heart, with all his soul, and with all his might, according to all the Law of Moses; nor after him did any arise like him. Nevertheless the L*ORD *did not turn from the fierceness of His great wrath, with which His anger was aroused against Judah, because of all the provocations with which Manasseh had provoked Him. And the L*ORD *said, "I will also remove Judah from My sight, as I have removed Israel, and will cast off this city Jerusalem which I have chosen, and the house of which I said, 'My name shall be there'"*

(2 Kings 23:25-27).

And God fulfilled His promise of doom down to the last letter. His warnings of impending judgment were clearly and unmistakably delivered by His prophets, but all those warnings were ignored. The joyful, unrepentant years of sin finally reaped a bountiful harvest of destruction, death, pain and misery:

You have fed them with the bread of tears, and given them tears to drink in great measure (Psalms 80:5).

Four centuries later the same drama was to be acted out again, with the same tragic and terrible consequences. The unrepentant people of the Land only had themselves to blame for what befell them:

> *Righteousness exalts a nation, but sin is a reproach to any people* (Proverbs 14:34).

Where Have All The Flowers Gone?

Israel's Jewish population after 50 years of statehood stood at 4.738 million. And current statistics for all of world Jewry is only 13.8 million.[1] Israel's history goes back thousands of years, as does that of China and India. China's population is more than 1.15 billion[2] and India's more than 889.7 million.[3] Had the nation of Israel walked in the ways of God, it could easily be as populous today as China or India.

The Apostle Paul, in Romans 9:29, quoting the Prophet Isaiah, extols the graciousness of God in leaving to Israel even a remnant of its people:

> *Unless the LORD of hosts had left to us a very small remnant, we would have become like Sodom, we would have been made like Gomorrah* (Isaiah 1:9).

Israel in antiquity was so wicked, so corrupt, that only the few pious left to it prevented the name and nation from being swept into extinction like Sodom and Gomorrah. The vast shortfall between Israel's current population and that of India's or China's is entirely due to Jewish stiffnecked rebellion against walking in the ways of the *Holy One of Israel*. It should also be borne in mind that it is no new thing for God to abandon the greatest part of the Jewish nation, when corrupt, and to confine his blessing and favor to the righteous, believing few.

The King of the Jews is today not only rejected, but even the knowledge of Him is banned in Israel. The nation has gone a whoring after a golden calf of materialism, and much prefer to have godless secular humanists rule over them. God is good, God is love, but He does not suffer being trifled with indefinitely.

The Unchanging One

In chapter 2, we spoke about God being faithful to fulfill His promises. It matters not whether His promises are for good or for bad, He is faithful to fulfill them. We know from the divine record that He fulfilled His promises to destroy Israel and the holy city of Jerusalem, and this is also borne out by world history. God told Israel what blessings would fall to them if they followed after Him and obeyed His voice, and He spelled out what would befall them if they chose not to obey His voice. It was a conditional covenant. The blessings were conditional upon Israel obeying God, and the curse was conditional upon them disobeying Him. This very important section of scripture is included here in its entirety—it should be carefully and thoughtfully read through:

1   *Now it shall come to pass, if you diligently obey the voice of the Lord your God, to observe carefully all His commandments which I command you today, that the Lord your God will set you high above all nations of the earth.*

2   *And all these blessings shall come upon you and overtake you, because you obey the voice of the Lord your God:*

3   *Blessed shall you be in the city, and blessed shall you be in the country.*

4   *Blessed shall be the fruit of your body, the produce of your ground and the increase of your herds, the increase of your cattle and the offspring of your flocks.*

5   *Blessed shall be your basket and your kneading bowl.*

6   *Blessed shall you be when you come in, and blessed shall you be when you go out.*

7   *The Lord will cause your enemies who rise against you to be defeated before your face; they shall come out against you one way and flee before you seven ways.*

8   *The Lord will command the blessing on you in your storehouses and in all to which you set your hand, and He will bless you in the land which the Lord your God is giving you.*

9   *The Lord will establish you as a holy people to Himself, just as He has sworn to you, if you keep the commandments of the Lord your God and walk in His ways.*

10   *Then all peoples of the earth shall see that you are called by the name of the Lord, and they shall be afraid of you.*

11   *And the Lord will grant you plenty of goods, in the fruit of your body, in the increase of your livestock, and in the produce of your ground, in the land of which the Lord swore to your fathers to give you.*

12   *The Lord will open to you His good treasure, the heavens, to give the rain to your land in its season, and to bless all the work of your hand. You shall lend to many nations, but you shall not borrow.*

13   *And the Lord will make you the head and not the tail; you shall be above only, and not be beneath, if you heed the commandments of the Lord your God, which I command you today, and are careful to observe them.*

14   *So you shall not turn aside from any of the words which I command you this day, to the right hand or to the left, to go after other gods to serve them.*

15   *But it shall come to pass, if you do not obey the voice of the Lord your God, to observe carefully all His commandments and His statutes which I command you today, that all these curses will come upon you and overtake you:*

16   *Cursed shall you be in the city, and cursed shall you be in the country.*

17   *Cursed shall be your basket and your kneading bowl.*

18   *Cursed shall be the fruit of your body and the produce of your land, the increase of your cattle and the offspring of your flocks.*

19   *Cursed shall you be when you come in, and cursed shall you be when you go out.*

20   *The Lord will send on you cursing, confusion, and rebuke in all that you set your hand to do, until you are destroyed and until you perish quickly, because of the wickedness of your doings in which you have forsaken Me.*

21   *The Lord will make the plague cling to you until He has consumed you from the land which you are going to possess.*

22   *The Lord will strike you with consumption, with fever, with inflammation, with severe burning fever, with the sword, with scorching, and with mildew; they shall pursue you until you perish.*

23   *And your heavens which are over your head shall be bronze, and the earth which is under you shall be iron.*

24   *The Lord will change the rain of your land to powder and dust; from the heaven it shall come down on you until you are destroyed.*

25   *The Lord will cause you to be defeated before your*

enemies; you shall go out one way against them and flee seven ways before them; and you shall become troublesome to all the kingdoms of the earth.

26   Your carcasses shall be food for all the birds of the air and the beasts of the earth, and no one shall frighten them away.

27   The LORD will strike you with the boils of Egypt, with tumors, with the scab, and with the itch, from which you cannot be healed.

28   The LORD will strike you with madness and blindness and confusion of heart.

29   And you shall grope at noonday, as a blind man gropes in darkness; you shall not prosper in your ways; you shall be only oppressed and plundered continually, and no one shall save you.

30   You shall betroth a wife, but another man shall lie with her; you shall build a house, but you shall not dwell in it; you shall plant a vineyard, but shall not gather its grapes.

31   Your ox shall be slaughtered before your eyes, but you shall not eat of it; your donkey shall be violently taken away from before you, and shall not be restored to you; your sheep shall be given to your enemies, and you shall have no one to rescue them.

32   Your sons and your daughters shall be given to another people, and your eyes shall look and fail with longing for them all day long; and there shall be no strength in your hand.

33   A nation whom you have not known shall eat the fruit of your land and the produce of your labor, and you shall be only oppressed and crushed continually.

34   So you shall be driven mad because of the sight which your eyes see.

35   The LORD will strike you in the knees and on the legs with severe boils which cannot be healed, and from the sole of your foot to the top of your head.

36   The LORD will bring you and the king whom you set over you to a nation which neither you nor your fathers have known, and there you shall serve other gods-- wood and stone.

37   And you shall become an astonishment, a proverb, and

a byword among all nations where the Lord *will drive you.*

38   *You shall carry much seed out to the field and gather but little in, for the locust shall consume it.*

39   *You shall plant vineyards and tend them, but you shall neither drink of the wine nor gather the grapes; for the worms shall eat them.*

40   *You shall have olive trees throughout all your territory, but you shall not anoint yourself with the oil; for your olives shall drop off.*

41   *You shall beget sons and daughters, but they shall not be yours; for they shall go into captivity.*

42   *Locusts shall consume all your trees and the produce of your land.*

43   *The alien who is among you shall rise higher and higher above you, and you shall come down lower and lower.*

44   *He shall lend to you, but you shall not lend to him; he shall be the head, and you shall be the tail.*

45   *Moreover all these curses shall come upon you and pursue and overtake you, until you are destroyed, because you did not obey the voice of the* Lord *your God, to keep His commandments and His statutes which He commanded you.*

46   *And they shall be upon you for a sign and a wonder, and on your descendants forever.*

47   *Because you did not serve the* Lord *your God with joy and gladness of heart, for the abundance of everything,*

48   *therefore you shall serve your enemies, whom the* Lord *will send against you, in hunger, in thirst, in nakedness, and in need of everything; and He will put a yoke of iron on your neck until He has destroyed you.*

49   *The* Lord *will bring a nation against you from afar, from the end of the earth, as swift as the eagle flies, a nation whose language you will not understand,*

50   *a nation of fierce countenance, which does not respect the elderly nor show favor to the young.*

51   *And they shall eat the increase of your livestock and the produce of your land, until you are destroyed; they shall not leave you grain or new wine or oil, or the increase of your cattle or the offspring of your flocks, until they have destroyed you.*

52   *They shall besiege you at all your gates until your high and fortified walls, in which you trust, come down throughout all your land; and they shall besiege you at all your gates throughout all your land which the LORD your God has given you.*

53   *You shall eat the fruit of your own body, the flesh of your sons and your daughters whom the LORD your God has given you, in the siege and desperate straits in which your enemy shall distress you.*

54   *The sensitive and very refined man among you will be hostile toward his brother, toward the wife of his bosom, and toward the rest of his children whom he leaves behind,*

55   *so that he will not give any of them the flesh of his children whom he will eat, because he has nothing left in the siege and desperate straits in which your enemy shall distress you at all your gates.*

56   *The tender and delicate woman among you, who would not venture to set the sole of her foot on the ground because of her delicateness and sensitivity, will refuse to the husband of her bosom, and to her son and her daughter,*

57   *her placenta which comes out from between her feet and her children whom she bears; for she will eat them secretly for lack of everything in the siege and desperate straits in which your enemy shall distress you at all your gates.*

58   *If you do not carefully observe all the words of this law that are written in this book, that you may fear this glorious and awesome name, THE LORD YOUR GOD,*

59   *then the LORD will bring upon you and your descendants extraordinary plagues—great and prolonged plagues—and serious and prolonged sicknesses.*

60   *Moreover He will bring back on you all the diseases of Egypt, of which you were afraid, and they shall cling to you.*

61   *Also every sickness and every plague, which is not written in the book of this law, will the LORD bring upon you until you are destroyed.*

62   *You shall be left few in number, whereas you were as the stars of heaven in multitude, because you would not obey the voice of the LORD your God.*

63   *And it shall be, that just as the LORD rejoiced over you to*

do you good and multiply you, so the LORD will rejoice over you to destroy you and bring you to nothing; and you shall be plucked from off the land which you go to possess.

64   *Then the LORD will scatter you among all peoples, from one end of the earth to the other, and there you shall serve other gods, which neither you nor your fathers have known-- wood and stone.*

65   *And among those nations you shall find no rest, nor shall the sole of your foot have a resting place; but there the LORD will give you a trembling heart, failing eyes, and anguish of soul.*

66   *Your life shall hang in doubt before you; you shall fear day and night, and have no assurance of life.*

67   *In the morning you shall say, "Oh, that it were evening!" And at evening you shall say, "Oh, that it were morning!" because of the fear which terrifies your heart, and because of the sight which your eyes see.*

68   *And the LORD will take you back to Egypt in ships, by the way of which I said to you, "You shall never see it again." And there you shall be offered for sale to your enemies as male and female slaves, but no one will buy you*

(Deuteronomy 28:1-68).

After making the *blessing and curse* known to Israel, God also said:

*I call heaven and earth as witnesses today against you, that **I have set before you life and death, blessing and cursing; therefore choose life**, that both you and your descendants may live; that you may love the LORD your God, that you may obey His voice, and that you may cling to Him, for He is your life and the length of your days; and that you may dwell in the land which the LORD swore to your fathers, to Abraham, Isaac, and Jacob, to give them (Deuteronomy 30:19-20).*

Despite God promising Israel that His blessings will *come upon you and overtake you*, they chose not to obey Him, and thereby chose death. God's patience ran out:

I earnestly exhorted your fathers in the day I brought them up out of the land of Egypt, until this day, rising early and exhorting, saying, "Obey My voice." Yet they did not obey or _incline their ear, but everyone followed the dictates of his evil heart; therefore I will bring upon them all the words of this covenant, which I commanded them to do, but which they have not done_ (Jeremiah 11:7-8).

Israel was conquered and destroyed. The survivors were taken into captivity among the nations. Remember, George Santayana said: "Those who do not learn from history are doomed to repeat it." Israel did not learn and, therefore, repeated it. A repeat performance of refusing God's ways brought another complete destruction in the first century A.D., and Israel went back into exile for almost 1900 years. Now God has brought Israel into His land once more and established them for the third time. But how long will it be before His patience wears thin with them again?

Half a century after the establishment of the modern state of Israel, they are turning their back on Him yet again. A large percentage of Israelis today have no belief in Him at all, and they are openly antagonistic to anything that smacks of religion. Many could not care less for His land either; they just want to be left alone to do their own thing—to walk in _the counsels and the dictates of their evil hearts_ (Jeremiah 7:24).

There is, of course, a remnant of Israel today who follow the _Holy One of Israel_ with a whole heart, just as there was a remnant who wholeheartedly followed Him in days gone by. But that godly remnant could not and did not prevent the destructions and horrors that came upon the nation in yesteryear. Neither will today's godly remnant prevent another horrific catastrophe, once God's patience has been sufficiently tried.

Israel and the nations seriously and urgently need to consider the fact that God has not changed with the passing of the years: _I am the Lord, I do not change_ (Malachi 3:6). The behavioral patterns that provoked Him to anger yesterday will also provoke Him to anger today. The terrible consequences that came because of yesterday's events will come again because of similar events taking place today. What is written here should be taken very seriously!

Readers from nations other than Israel should fear to sit in judgment of Israel—they should tremble at the sins of their own nations. God is _the Judge of all the earth_ (Genesis 18:25), not just of His chosen people. Israel has thousands of years of history, while some nations have very little. America, for example, has relatively no history to speak of. Yet, in its brief few years, it has already gone from "One Nation under God" to a nation almost completely under sin. The impeachment process of President Bill Clinton was a time of shame for that nation. The professing "Christian" president twice vetoed the Senate's rejection of late-term abortion bills, resulting in the murder of thousands of near-born babies. He committed adultery with a number of women outside of his marriage, and lied after swearing before the Grand Jury to tell the truth. His acquittal by the House without even a censure of his actions—when all the members knew him to be guilty—will undoubtedly contribute to the wrath of God falling upon the nation in the not too distant future.

Sheep not only follow the shepherd, they also follow the shepherd's example. Someone should certainly tell Bill Clinton that the Bible he is so often seen waving says,

> *the cowardly, unbelieving, abominable, **murderers**, **sexually immoral**, sorcerers, idolaters, and **all liars** shall have their part in the lake which burns with fire and brimstone, which is the second death* (Revelation 21:8).

However, it is not just the president of the United States—he is but indicative of the whole nation. America must repent,

> *dress in sackcloth and roll about in ashes! Make mourning as for an only son, most bitter lamentation; for the plunderer will suddenly come* (Jeremiah 6:26).

Watchman, What of the Night? (Isaiah 21:11)

Yitzhak Rabin's rise to power in Israel was nothing short of a tragedy for the nation. A godless *fool* himself, he chose to be surrounded by other godless *fools*. And in a large gathering of world leaders in 1994—televised worldwide—Rabin said Israel wants "to be like all other nations."[4] What did he care that Israel's desiring to be like the nations around it severely angered God more than two millenniums ago? Rabin also embraced Israel's vilest enemy and delivered large tracts of God's own personal land over to him, because to Rabin Israel's divine inheritance was only "holes in the ground."[5] Rabin pushed ahead with his "peace" process and another *"fool"* revealed how Rabin accomplished so much:

> We succeeded because for the first time the government took God out of the equation.[6]

During Rabin's godless term of governing Israel *the plunderer* came, and death and carnage from the hands of the "Philistines" against Israelis rose by 900 percent.[7] And then Rabin was removed from office by bullets fired from an assassin's gun.

Saul was the first human king of Israel and was, obviously, the first king to rebel against God's word.

> *So Saul died for his unfaithfulness which he had committed against the Lord, because he did not keep the word of the Lord ...therefore He killed him, and turned the kingdom over to David the son of Jesse* (1 Chronicles 10:13,14).

Jeroboam's reign led Israel into deep sin *and the Lord struck him, and he died* (2 Chronicles 13:20). Likewise Manasseh caused Judah to sin greatly and

> *the Lord brought upon them the captains of the army of the king of Assyria, who took Manasseh with hooks, bound him with bronze fetters, and carried him off to Babylon*
> (2 Chronicles 33:11).

God has repeatedly been provoked into disciplining Israel—feeding them with

> *the bread of tears, and [giving] them tears to drink in great measure* (Psalms 80:5).

And God will not be swayed from administering further punitive punishment when necessary. He does not share the modern world's view that children's flesh ought not to feel the stinging discomfort of *the rod of correction* (Proverbs 22:15). He will certainly punish severely, but He will never forsake:

> *For the Lord will not forsake His people, for His great name's sake, because it has pleased the Lord to make [Israel] His people* (1 Samuel 12:22).

> *For You have made Your people Israel Your very own people forever; and You, Lord, have become their God*
> (1 Chronicles 17:22).

The path modern Israel and most Western nations have chosen to take today is a highway leading to catastrophe, pain and tears. Israel today is again being stripped of its divine inheritance. Listen to the voice of *the Holy One of Israel*:

> *Son of man, they who inhabit those ruins in the land of Israel*

> *are saying, "Abraham was only one, and he inherited the*
> *land. But we are many; the land has been given to us as a*
> *possession." Therefore say to them, "Thus says the LORD God:*
> *You eat meat with blood, you lift up your eyes toward your*
> *idols, and shed blood. Should you then possess the land? You*
> *rely on your sword, you commit abominations, and you defile*
> *one another's wives. Should you then possess the land?"*
>
> (Ezekiel 33:24-26).

According to the divine record, when repentance was not forth-coming, the deliverance of Israel's land into the hands of its enemies was ever a prelude to further catastrophe. The last Scripture given above is a fair assessment of Israeli life today. Given the current situation it is simply a matter of time before the axe falls upon the nation's neck once more. But judgment shall not be confined to a truncated Israel alone. Western nations will also be sucked into the vortex of God's fierce anger, along with Arab states.

Watchmen on the walls are duty bound to warn the inhabitants of the city:

> *But if the watchman sees the sword coming and does not blow*
> *the trumpet, and the people are not warned, and the sword*
> *comes and takes any person from among them, he is taken*
> *away in his iniquity; but his blood I will require at the*
> *watchman's hand* (Ezekiel 33:6).

This watchman sees the sword coming and is blowing the trumpet. Will anyone heed the sound?

5

Who Killed Cock Robin?

The "era of peace" negotiated by Rabin and Peres brought a staggering **900 percent increase** in the murder of Israelis compared to the years in the era of open warfare by terrorist organizations against Israel.[1] After the signing away of much of Israel's inheritance to Arafat, the majority of Israelis were against the government's policies due to the fruit they had produced. Like their religious brethren, the secular voices were not only ignored, but they also became objects of taunts, insults and sneers from Rabin and Peres. Hearing accented Hebrew from a demonstrator, who had immigrated with her family many years previously, Polish born Peres told her insultingly: "You don't belong here! Go back where you came from!"[2] Rabin called protesters "cry-babies"[3] and said they were "not real Israelis."[4] He told the residents of the Golan Heights, whom he had utterly duped with bald-faced lies in an election speech, that they could "spin around in their demonstrations like propellers."[5]

Rabin not only taunted and insulted those that did not share either his values or policies, but his language was often "vicious"[6] and "foul-mouthed."[7] Several weeks before Rabin's assassination on November 4, 1995, one of his aides told Thomas Friedman of the *New York Times*:

> We estimate that Rabin had **personally insulted at least two million Israelis** in the past year.[8]

Friedman wrote of this a week after the assassination,[9] and it was as if the aide was proud of what he had shared with the journalist.

Murder!

On page 74 of my book, *Philistine: The Great Deception*, published five months before Rabin was murdered, I wrote: "Barring … **assassination by an irate Israeli**, Yitzhak Rabin will, even at his present age of 75 years, live to rue that fateful day he took Arafat's hand." Numerous readers of the book have written or called to say how prophetic that statement was. This writer does not consider it to have been a "prophetic" statement. He has, he is told, an analytical mind. He simply added two and two together and came up with four as the answer. Now, more than four years after Rabin's assassination, he is still totally mystified as to how so many millions of people never thought this could possibly happen.

Rabin's assassination literally stunned the nation. With Rabin having been a Freemason of high degree[10] many other Masons of high degree among the world's leaders gathered in Jerusalem to pay their last respects. It was here that President Bill Clinton used the Hebrew phrase *shalom haver*[11] (Good-bye friend), which was soon printed in bumper-sticker form and used throughout Israel.

The government now led by Peres blamed the Likud party— even Bibi Netanyahu himself—for having created the atmosphere that incited murder in the hearts of those with right-wing leanings. Horrible things were said by many of the members of the left-wing-humanist government. Rabin's widow, Leah, accepted Arafat's condolences, but refused to hear Netanyahu's.[12] She gladly shook Arafat's bloodstained hand at the funeral, but refused Netanyahu's outstretched hand.[13] She received Arafat into her home three days after the funeral, but denied access to Netanyahu.[14] And she continues "spewing forth her venom"[15] against Netanyahu, the Likud party, and all who did not embrace her husband's policies. All who were not fully supportive of her husband's policies were, she said, "related to the murderer." And then snatches of truth began to trickle out.

Yigal Amir, age 25, was arrested immediately after he fired two shots at absolute point-blank range into the back of Yitzhak Rabin. Amir was so close to Rabin that according to a police source, "Rabin felt the gun before he felt the bullet."[16] Questions were raised: How could the assassin have gotten so close without arousing the suspicions of security men? Where were Rabin's own bodyguards when the premier was shot? Why did they not immediately shoot the assassin? Why was Rabin not wearing a bulletproof vest in view of the threats received against his life? Answers came, but they raised more questions than they resolved. Concerning the vest they said "his bodyguards had not suggested it."[17] As to the bodyguards not responding with gunfire, we are told the assassin's gun "was a toy pistol. It wasn't real."[18] The bullets were "blanks."[19] And of absent security men, they offered:

We were told to gather around Shimon Peres. We had no orders to gather around the Prime Minister.[20]

One of the prime suspects arrested by the police on suspicion of conspiring to murder Prime Minister Yitzhak Rabin was 28-year-old Avishai Raviv. Under heavy guard,

> he had to be dragged into the courtroom. Handcuffed and looking scared, he entered shouting, "This is a political investigation and a false arrest."[21]

Avishai Raviv was the founding member of an extreme right-wing organization called Eyal, and he organized "anti-government demonstrations nationwide."[22]

Former MK and Kiryat Arba settlers' spokeswoman Geula Cohen said of Raviv:

> He was everywhere ... participating in every demonstration, always starting provocations ... He would talk about killing Arabs and killing those Jews who he believed were not 'really' Jews ... Raviv had gone to a local summer camp and preached violence against Jewish soldiers and policemen.[23]

One of Raviv's former followers testified:

> "He would always lead us somewhere, and the army would always be waiting ... He always tried to provoke a confrontation. When he came to Jericho, he would walk around and begin cursing Arabs."[24]

Now under investigation, Raviv had good cause for concern. Several witnesses testified that he had "goaded Yigal Amir to slay Rabin."[25]

> He kept saying to Yigal: "You keep talking about killing Rabin. Why don't you do it? Are you frightened? You say you want to do it. Show us that you're a man! Show us what you are made of!"[26]

Raviv told Amir and others that

> Rabin should die, and whoever killed him was a righteous person.[27]

On Friday afternoons Raviv would take some of his Eyal group to demonstrate in front of Rabin's home. He would chant:

> Rabin and his wife will be hung like Mussolini and his mistress.[28]

And it was not just Rabin who Raviv said was to die.

> He was a real macho. He kept saying: "Kill all the Arabs. Kill Rabin. Kill all the ministers. Kill the *rodfim* [persecutors] like Yossi Sarid and Shulamit Aloni."[29]

Without doubt Avishai Raviv was "the leading agitator on the extreme right."[30]

While Raviv was being investigated, the investigating officer learned from the newspapers[31] that Raviv was a "mole,"[32] a "plant,"[33] an "informer"[34] for the GSS (General Security Services—the *Shin Bet*). The GSS did not tell the police that Raviv was an informer even after he had been arrested and questioned following the murder.[35] More often than not, when an agent's cover is blown, the organization that pays him denies knowledge of him. Obviously, this was the reason for Raviv looking "scared" when he was "dragged" into the courtroom. But slowly, snippet after snippet, bits of truth trickled out and became public. And what is not known today might never be known—ever.

Raviv and the GSS

Avishai Raviv was "not merely some simple informer."[36] He was the "star agent"[37] of the GSS. He was "a full-blooded agent provocateur"[38] who "operated under the code name 'Champagne,'"[39] and had "handlers and case officers—at least ten."[40] This technique of using agent-provocateurs was made into "a chilling, brutal science by the Bolsheviks and Stalin."[41]

A full month before the premier's murder, a notorious photomontage of Rabin in the uniform of a SS commander first appeared in a demonstration and on television.[42] Rabin's government used this incident to

> smear the entire opposition, from Likud Chairman Netanyahu to the extremist right-wing youth groups.[43]

After Avishai Raviv's arrest (and release), it was revealed that he had

> brainwashed two young Gilo boys into making photomontages depicting Rabin as an SS commander. He then gave them to an Israeli TV reporter, pressuring him to air them.[44]

Israel Television's Nitzan Hen, who had covered the demonstration where the photomontage had first appeared, subsequently verified that it was Raviv who gave him the poster and later contacted him to make sure the picture had been telecast.[45]

Security sources also acknowledge that Raviv's handlers, **under pressure from their superiors,**

> gave their star greater and greater freedom to organize and incite right-wing violence.[46]

All of Raviv's activities were part of a government "conspiracy to make the right-wing look bad."[47] Raviv's mission was to incite people to commit acts which would prove there was a right-wing conspiracy to topple the government, when in fact none existed. The assassination sting was only one of the activities, and it was set up so a right-wing activist could be caught in the very act of assassinating the Prime Minister of Israel.

The fruit of Rabin's policies caused his public opinion ratings to sink. Right-wing groups were clearly manipulated—

> to salvage Rabin's future, and enable him to brand the settlers and the Likud (especially its leader Binyamin Netanyahu) enemies of peace, on a par with Hamas and Islamic Jihad [terror groups responsible for attacks against Israeli civilians].[48]

The very nature of Raviv's work meant he could only have operated

> with the approval of former Prime Minister Yitzhak Rabin, the Attorney-General, the State Comptroller and K, the head of the GSS.[49]

Information that leaked out from the State Commission of Inquiry into Rabin's murder and from security sources

> pointed an accusing finger back at the Prime Minister's Office.[50]

The GSS answers directly to the Prime Minister.

> Yitzhak Rabin either ordered the campaign or let it continue when he found out about it.[51]

The GSS could not have run a campaign to discredit the opposition without Rabin's full knowledge. A justice ministry source confirmed that Rabin himself ordered a vigorous operation against the right-wing in 1993.[52] Attorney General Michael Ben-Yair

> approved Raviv's central role in the anti-government campaign,[53]

and Rabin personally

> called State Attorney Dorit Beinish to inform her of the new policy.[54]

The justice ministry source said the operation

> included initiatives by informers to start activity, something that had been used by the GSS against Palestinian opponents.[55]

Thus, on the surface, Rabin's assassination appeared to be a sting that backfired, and

> the police and GSS are frantically trying to cover up the truth.[56]

Avishai Raviv was with a group of people at the peace rally where the assassination took place, when rumors began to circulate that shots had been fired toward Rabin's car. Raviv immediately

> pulled out his cellular phone and spoke to someone who the eyewitnesses could not identify.[57]

Raviv said, "It was Yigal. Don't you know Yigal?"[58] Raviv identified Yigal Amir as Rabin's attacker

> some 40 minutes before a description of the gunman was broadcast.[59]

And, it was Yigal Amir who was subsequently sentenced to life imprisonment for the murder of Yitzhak Rabin, plus a further six years for wounding Yoram Rubin, Rabin's bodyguard. Amir's older brother, Hagai, was convicted of manufacturing the dumdum bullets fired into Rabin's back.

The fact that Raviv's GSS purpose was to goad Amir into an attempt to kill Rabin is indisputable. But, did Amir shoot Rabin as a result of Raviv's goading? Apparently not. Amir had realized Raviv was a GSS plant long before the shooting took place, as did others in Amir's circle.[60] Amir's friend, 20-year-old Margalit Har-Shefi, was also suspicious, but her suspicions were not confirmed until she was questioned by the GSS after the assassination. After hours of questioning, she was left alone in a room with Raviv who was in leg irons, and she then realized that Raviv "was now trying to set her up."[61]

Amir knew Raviv was a GSS plant, and apparently exchanged blank bullets provided by Raviv with the extremely accurate, hard hitting bullets made by his brother, Hagai. When Amir did made his move, the GSS was expecting blanks to be fired. But unbeknown to them, Amir had switched the blank bullets for real ones. Even so, did Amir actually kill Rabin?

Conspiracy?

Yigal Amir admitted firing two bullets into Rabin's back at point-blank range. However, Barry Chamash, an investigative journalist, says that he uncovered irrefutable evidence that Rabin died from a bullet **fired from the front into his chest**. And this bullet was removed from Rabin's chest at the hospital on the night he died. Chamash spent two years investigating Rabin's assassination and says that neither the police or the government would act upon the evidence he collected. Chamash said

> reporters have been warned by their superiors that their jobs will be lost, if they covered my evidence of a murder conspiracy.[62]

Also, the top-rated political talk show *Popolitika* canceled Chamash's slot shortly before the scheduled show, "undoubtedly due to political pressure and threats" says Chamash.[63] Chamash finally dropped his pursuit of the truth about the assassination in November 1997, after receiving numbers of threats against his life. He told this writer personally that he thinks he knows who the killer is, but the welfare of his wife and young children must come first. He is totally convinced that he is a "dead man," if he reveals whom he believes committed the murder.

Chamash is not alone in his belief that a bullet from a gun other than Amir's killed Rabin. Rumors began to circulate shortly after the assassination that a bullet of a type differing from Amir's gun was taken from Rabin's body at the hospital. And in his summation at the trial, Amir's defense lawyer, Gabi Shahar, proposed that "a second party was involved in the shooting."[64] Shahar reiterated that

> there were no eyewitnesses at the murder scene, and that it was not beyond the bounds of possibility that shots were fired by someone else.[65]

It is also a fact that some "mystery" person "left glasses and a watch at the scene."[66]

At his trial Amir showed no remorse for having shot Israel's prime minister. On the contrary, he expressed satisfaction that Rabin was dead. But Amir insisted that he only "intended to paralyze

Rabin and not kill him."[67] His brother, Hagai, admitted making the bullets, but said:

> These bullets are not fatal. I added a ball of iron on the end of the bullet, which forms a hollow, and this hollow enables the bullet to be more accurate, and that's it, it doesn't break up or do anything else. I did it because I wanted to have more accurate bullets, and I gave my brother some of these bullets.[68]

Numbers of questions have not been satisfactorily answered. For example: Amir fired a total of three shots, two into Rabin and one into his bodyguard's shoulder—no shots were fired by security men. So why did Yishai Shuschter, who was close enough to see Rabin fall, say, "there were **four** shots"?[69] When Leah Rabin heard the "pop of the bullets that hit her husband"[70] and asked what happened, she was told by a bodyguard that "it was a toy pistol."[71]

Two or three days later, this writer read a very small news item printed in the *Jerusalem Post* to the effect that

> the body of a man was found in the Jerusalem forest with a bullet wound in the head.

No other details were given, and it was certainly not something this writer would clip and file among his records. Some time later, however, a story began circulating that

> a security guard had committed suicide or been killed and secretly buried.[72]

The story became widespread, and it was not accompanied by denials. The body in the forest was rumored to be that of Yoav Kuriel, the bodyguard who had told Leah Rabin that Amir's gun was "a toy pistol." Interestingly enough, that small news item about a body being found in the Jerusalem forest does not appear on the electronic data base of the *Jerusalem Post* today—it was erased. Dennis Eisenberg, who coauthored with Uri Dan *The Mossad: Secrets of the Israel Secret Service* and other books on the Middle East, also noticed the above news item and later was not able to trace it in the archives of the "Post" either. Eisenberg was writing a book entitled *The Ultimate Conspiracy*, and while researching material, he attended all the public hearings of the Shamgar Commission of Inquiry into the assassination. Eisenberg told this writer that he repeatedly ran straight into thick concrete walls whenever he tried to uncover information about the bodyguard,

Yoav Kuriel, and the body in the forest. The Commission's hearings which involved the activities of the GSS were held behind strictly closed doors.

Someone Knows the Answers

Yoram Rubin, Rabin's wounded bodyguard, testified that

> right after hearing the first shot he heard someone shouting "blanks, blanks."[73]

A GSS man shouts "blanks, blanks," another tells Leah Rabin that the shots are from "a toy pistol," and one (or more) of the men is apparently eliminated. Who were these men, and where are they today?

Why did Rabin's limousine driver not wait for an ambulance to arrive, but chose instead to take the still breathing Rabin to the hospital himself, by "a route almost three times longer"?[74] Why was he stopped at a police roadblock on the way.[75] Why was Leah Rabin prevented from going to the hospital in the car with her wounded husband, but made to travel instead in a separate car taking a different route?[76] For what reason did a GSS agent ask police for Amir's gun after the shooting?[77]

Did Rabin's self-initiated sting backfire and actually cause his own demise? Did someone in the GSS want Rabin dead? Someone inside the GSS certainly allowed Raviv to incite, and Amir to act—but who? Which GSS official ordered bodyguards to gather around Shimon Peres and left the Prime Minister, whose life had been threatened, unprotected? Was Yigal Amir helped by someone inside Rabin's inner circle of guards? Did a GSS man fire a fatal bullet into Rabin's chest? If so, where—in the carpark at the precise time Amir fired his shots or in Rabin's own limousine during the protracted journey to the hospital? Why was there no ambulance on hand at a massive "Peace Rally" where many thousands of people were gathered, and where a terror attack was a distinct possibility? The hospital was unprepared for Rabin, but why was it not notified that the critically injured premier was being brought in? So many questions, but a single satisfactory answer has yet to come forth. Someone, however, knows the answers, but he is not telling.

Adding a rather *picante* flavor to the assassination pottage is the knowledge that Yigal Amir once worked for a government organization that reported directly to the Prime Minister's Office. Officials in the PM's office admitted that Amir

> had been sent to Latvia for a few months by the Liaison Bureau, also known as *Nativ...What* he did there and what *Nativ* does there we cannot answer.[78]

Fourteen days following Rabin's assassination the British *Observer* newspaper quoted "security" sources as saying that,

> on the day of the murder, Amir was carrying an identity card he had received from the GSS during his period in Latvia.[79]

The card,

> signed by the then GSS head Ya'acov Perry, would have enabled him to enter the sterile area, where he waited to assassinate Rabin.[80]

Carmi Gillon, the current head of the GSS, personally handled Avishai Raviv.[81] The night before Rabin's assassination, however, Gillon flew (the coop?) to Paris and thereby escaped personal involvement.[82]

And Avishai Raviv? What of him? One of the few times he has been seen was when he was

> being driven off in a GSS vehicle with Clinton's parting words to Rabin, "*shalom haver,*" on its rear window.[83]

A senior security source says,

> "...the Shamgar commission established to investigate the assassination, will probably not explore Raviv's role. Nobody has any reason for the truth to come out," the source says. "Shamgar does not have the mandate.
>
> "The GSS simply wants this episode to end. Shimon Peres is now in power and doesn't want to rock the boat."[84]

There had been a deal of effort expended by left and right-wing parties interested in forcing the State Attorney's office to put Avishai Raviv on trial. However, the State Prosecutor apparently feared what Raviv might "leak" if he was indicted, and the deliberations continued for about three years. It was a given that if Raviv eventually stood trial, we could be 101 percent sure that he would not be indicted for incitement to murder, but for some minor crime like perjury for having denied being a GSS agent at Yigal Amir's trial. Raviv simply knows too much, and a number of people would not sleep well at night if he were to stand trial for his role in Rabin's assassination. People in Raviv's position—like security guard Yoav Kuriel—often meet with unfortunate "accidents" which guarantees their silence.

Persistent pressure for the investigation and indictment of Raviv finally prevailed in April 1999. But as was fully expected he was indicted on minor charges only—failing to stop the assassination, and with membership of a terrorist organization. Amir's friend, Margalit Har-Shefi, was convicted on the same charge of failing to stop the assassination and was given a prison sentence of two years. So, even if Raviv is found guilty of those charges he might still take his secrets to the grave, which, as was alluded to earlier, might be a lot sooner than he cares to think about.

The assassination of Yitzhak Rabin has all the hallmarks of a JFK conspiracy. Conspiracies, however, are like murders—perfect ones remain undiscovered.

The person who gained the most from Rabin's assassination was Shimon Peres, Rabin's longtime rival. Peres immediately assumed leadership of the nation, affording him the opportunity to push the "peace process" along at a faster rate than Rabin had done. And, there has been and still is, a pointing of fingers at Peres, insinuating that he was somehow involved with the assassination. Peres has called these insinuations a "blood libel,"[85] Nevertheless, it is now past four full years since the accusations first surfaced, and Peres has not called for an investigation into the activities of Avishai Raviv and the GSS. And further, the Oslo-backers within the left-wing establishment are still not done with their attempts to trash the Oslo opponents and discredit them in the eyes of the world. In the opening hours of 1998, another ugly scene began to unfold.

Early in the last week of December 1997, Israeli police announced the arrest of "two right-wing extremists."[86] The men were taken into custody, before they could carry out a plan to take a pig's head onto the Muslim controlled Temple Mount, and throw it into the Al-Aqsa mosque compound during the Muslim's holy fast-month of Ramadan. The arrest received "worldwide media coverage,"[87] and according to police, "had diverted certain bloodshed."[88] However, the odds for success in getting a pig's head through the tight Israeli security and onto the Mount during Ramadan are about the same as for a tadpole becoming a surrogate mother to a brontosaurus.

This minute detail obviously escaped the notice of the "very leftist,"[89] hawk-eyed former police chief, Assaf Hafetz. And when Barry Chamash, the investigative journalist, said that one of the arrested men, Avigdor Eskin, is "a known _Shabak_ (GSS—_Shin Bet_) 'provocateur,'"[90] the ensuing stench reminds us of the 1995 Raviv–Amir assassination setup. Chamash claims the "pig plot was stage managed,"[91] and another Middle East commentator also believes

> the arrests and announcement of the pig plan was part of a campaign to smear the Israeli right.[92]

In March 1998, the attorney for the other arrested man presented evidence to the court that a certain Harel Hershtik had opined various ideas to his client. Among the suggestions was one of

> using a catapult to propel pig heads with Korans stuffed in their mouths onto the Temple Mount during Muslim prayers.[93]

The attorney produced GSS memos showing Hershtik to be "acting under orders of the security service itself," and that he was "a _Shin Bet_ plant."[94] Apparently, Rabin's assassination only brought about a leadership reshuffle among _"fools,"_ it did not change their tactics.

Further information concerning the assassination of Yitzhak Rabin and the trial of Avishai Raviv was sent to the author by Barry Chamish just before this book went to print. This information has been included in the Addenda, 1–3.

6

Israeli Politics

Life in the Middle East seems to float from crisis to crisis amid scattered islands of calm. No one anywhere can tell what is going to happen tomorrow, and this is especially true of the political arena. Nothing is permanent in the Middle East except instability and mayhem. Arab dictator regimes eliminate opponents by disposing of them and their bodies. And every leader's secret mission is to survive and never forget his ancestors' inheritance—this makes for perpetual tension, conspiracy and war.

Israel—the only democracy in the Middle East—sits in the midst of this precarious turmoil. Israeli democracy, however, differs from Western democracy. The evolutionary democratic process has not taken it many rungs higher on the ladder than either its Arab neighbors or the former Soviet Bloc.

Hundreds of thousands of Jews from Arab countries were some of the first immigrants into Israel. They fled ever-increasing Arab hatred as Palestine writhed in labor with Israel. Today, these refugees and their children comprise well over 50 percent of Israel's Jewish[1] population. Consequently, the mentality of this majority group is strikingly Arab. For the most part, they think and act much as Arabs do.

Also among the earliest Jewish immigrants into Israel were those who came on the first great Aliyah from the Soviet Union. Joining these and their children are the almost one million who have emigrated from the former Soviet Union during the past two decades. Therefore, all those who have come from the former Soviet Union, together with their descendants, now form more than 25 percent of Israel's Jewish population. Add this figure to the previously mentioned 50 percent plus from the Arab world, and we can understand why the Arab and Socialist ways of thinking are so deeply ingrained into the soul of Israel's particular brand of democracy.

Israeli democracy is very aptly portrayed in the statement quoted on page 47 made by Chaim Ramon, a leading member of both Yitzhak Rabin's and Shimon Peres's governments:

This is a democracy, and if you don't come around to our way of thinking and join us, we will crush you.

Ramon saw no discrepancy between "democracy" and the words "we will crush you" in the same sentence. This is the political vernacular of both the Arab and Soviet psyches. In the Middle East, ego and power have insatiable appetites and few morals. Only a rare few of Israeli politicians are actually motivated by real concern for their country.

Israeli Knesset sessions often descend below gutter level. Members have used their fists against opponents, frequently use foul language, and often tell outright lies. Deceit of every possible shape and hue is practiced, and for some politicians, is as natural as brushing one's teeth. The most important thing in political life for many Israeli politicians is getting publicity for their overstuffed egos to feed upon. If a politician is part of the government opposition, pulling down the government by any and all available means in order to get his own party into power is the second most important thing. And next in line is climbing the party's political ladder of success—even if it means destroying a few of your comrades.

Labor politicians were angry in December 1997, when Meir Palevsky, a private investigator specializing in personal surveillance, was hired by Labor heads. The angry politicians said that Palevsky's real job would be to "spy on them."[2] Party leader Ehud Barak denied hiring Palevsky, but Barak's office said that Palevsky "was hired with his full approval."[3] Labor's politicians know full well that Palevsky has been used previously within Labor's ranks. At the height of Rabin's feud with Peres, a number of letters were written against Rabin. Palevsky was hired and subsequently uncovered Labor's Yossi Beilin as the perpetrator of the letters.

Almost all Anglo-Saxons, following a so-called "lively" political "debate" in the Knesset, hang their heads in acute embarrassment. Imagine a British MP shouting out in the House that his "honourable colleague" was a "toilet,"[4] as did the Moledet party's leader, Rehavam Ze'evi. Then imagine the "honourable gentleman" screaming back, "And you're the s--t in the toilet!",[5] which was the response of Hadash's Tawfik Zayyad. With only a few exceptions, it is the power hungry and insanely ambitious that want to jump into the filthy shark infested waters of Israeli politics.

The Israeli Media

The Israeli media—both printed and electronic—is firmly in the hand of the left-wing Labor Socialists whose tentacles also control the Army, the Police and the Courts. The media in Israel, therefore, is strongly pro-Hellenist, pro-"peace," anti-religious and anti-right-wing. It was fully supportive of the Rabin and Peres's "peace" policies and worked hard to bring an election victory to Labor in 1996. The media used its own brand of psychological warfare upon the Israeli populace, and there was "a certain discernible and statistically proven double standard"[6] with which it treated the members of the incumbent Hellenist government, as opposed to members of their opposition.

Israel Television's *Channel One* was

> particularly offensive in its servility to the government's cause. Statistically, it was shown to feature government officials four times more often that it did opposition leaders. This channel badgered and interrogated opposition representatives in a manner that can only be called unprofessional.[7]

Likud politicians were

> interviewed with hostility and cut off before completing a sentence.[8]

Interviews with Likud party leader, Bibi Netanyahu, on radio and television were only allowed "at a time when the ratings were lowest,"[9] and "nearly each of his replies was cut off by carping comments."[10] On election day, *Israel Radio* stooped really low and broadcast a fabricated report that "Jewish right-wing extremists were seeking to assassinate Peres."[11] The bulletin was repeated **every half hour**, and throughout the day they kept exhorting Arab voters "to come out and vote for Peres and prevent a Likud victory."[12]

An actual program or printed article might be forgotten by the next day, but the subconscious effects of a biased media are felt long afterward. At the time of this writing, the former Director-General of the prime minister's office, Pinhas Fishler, who served during June and July, 1996, is suing most of the Israeli media for NIS 23 million (US$6.5 million) in damages.[13] Fishler claims that the negative portrayal of him—including vicious, unmitigated lies and fabrications—forced him to leave his post. Among the defendants in the case are *Yediot Aharanot, Ha'aretz, Ma'ariv,*

Globes, Yediot Tikshoret, Kol Yisrael and Israel Television's *Channel One*. Fishler told the court that since leaving the prime minister's office, he had been out of work because the media reports

> achieved their intended goal and severely damaged his reputation.[14]

To say that the Israeli media has difficulty accepting election results that are not to its liking would be a gross understatement. Three years after Netanyahu's win at the polls, the media had still not accepted the result. From the minute Netanyahu confounded Labor and won the elections,

> he faced the most vicious character assassination drive that any prime minister ever did.[15]

Never before in Israel has there been such a concerted, concentrated, hateful attack against a prime minister. In December 1997, Netanyahu said:

> Over the past year and a half, my wife and I, and even our children, have been subjected to humiliations and insults that are unprecedented in the history of the state.[16]

Referring to a nine-page article about his wife Sara in *Yediot Aharanot*, Netanyahu continued,

> this latest article represented a new degree in "loathsomeness and evil" that "violated all boundaries."[17]

Things got worse. In May 1998, four journalists of *Channel One* television "doctored" the soundtrack of Israel Television's main evening news to present Netanyahu waving to a crowd chanting "Death to the Arabs."[18] The terrible attacks were unrelenting and in August 1998, Netanyahu said:

> If I ever thought that there was a limit to how low my opponents were willing to go in order to besmirch me, I now know that I was mistaken. For the past two years, I have been the butt of lies, slander, malicious besmirching, and the like, every day— I, my wife, my children, my colleagues, have all been the subject of lies and slander that were totally not true.[19]

Even an Israeli journalist asked in an article:

> And just how far will Israeli journalists stoop for the inside dirt—and we do mean dirt—on Prime Minister Binyamin Netanyahu and his family?[20]

The article said

> Israeli journalists have offered huge amounts of money, sometimes several thousand dollars, for information[21]

about the Prime Minister and his family. Labor's Chaim Ramon, a member of the committee charged with bringing the Netanyahu government down, said:

> Netanyahu must be given no rest. We must not ease up the pressure on him.[22]

In perhaps the only fair and objective piece of journalistic writing concerning Netanyahu to appear in the Hebrew press since the 1996 elections (quotes will appear later in the chapter), Ari Shavit, a journalist for the prestigious secular, left-wing *Ha'aretz* daily, wrote a series of incisive articles under the title, "1997: The Year of Hating Bibi."[23] Shavit's reward for writing positively about Netanyahu was to be shunned by his colleagues.

The media (along with the members of the secular left-wing opposition) waited like a cat ready to pounce upon anything that exits or enters a mouse hole. If Netanyahu as much as coughed, he was "dividing the people." If he sneezed, he was "leading Israel into war." Chaim Ramon said:

> It is our duty to hammer in the message that Netanyahu is a menace to public safety.[24]

Expecting opposition members to say something positive concerning Netanyahu or the left-wing Israeli media to write anything positive about him was like asking chickens to vote for Colonel Sanders if he was still alive. And at the start of every workday, Netanyahu—referring to the Israel press—asked his spokesman, "What is in the garbage this morning?"[25]

While in office as Israel's premier, Binyamin Netanyahu appeared to have aged ten or more years. Besides wading hip deep through media and political muck every day, he had to also deal with the machinations of opponents, a spiteful opposition, and disloyal members in his own government.

Labor opposition member, Yossi Beilin, took it upon himself to scurry around the Middle East to "conduct private foreign policy" on matters concerning the "peace" process. On his own initiative, Israel's president, Ezer Weizman, a left-wing Labor party member, traveled to Cairo to hold his own talks on the "peace" process with

Egypt's President Mubarak. Israel's presidency is a ceremonial office, but Weizman is well known for "shooting from the lip" and has repeatedly broken his undertaking to keep his political views out of the public realm. He suggested to Secretary of State Madeleine Albright that she "knock together the heads of Netanyahu and Arafat."[26] Two times in 1998 he publicly made disparaging remarks about Prime Minister Netanyahu and called for new elections. In response, Netanyahu accused Weizman of

> siding with the Palestinians against Israel, and urged him to be "statesmanlike."[27]

Labor party leader, Ehud Barak, also held talks with Mubarak concerning the "peace" process. Labor's Shimon Peres, in addition to influencing Arafat against the legitimate government of Israel, had been almost everywhere, speaking to nearly everyone on practically every issue. But he had no authority to speak about anything to anyone.

All these people and more besides undermined the democratically elected government of Israel. They represented no one and could not commit the state of Israel to anything, but they appeared oblivious of the fact that the rules of the democratic game are that there is only one government at a time.

Leah Rabin

Yitzhak Rabin was the most unpopular prime minister in Israel's history.[28] And his widow, Leah, must surely be the nation's most unpopular widow. Yitzhak Rabin died as a result of policies that did not sit well with 60 percent of the Israeli population. Even with a massive national outpouring of grief over the slaying of the premier and sympathy for the government itself, the government could not muster the votes to remain in power and continue Rabin's policies. Over 55 percent of Jews preferred instead to vote for Bibi Netanyahu, and in U.S. politics this would be considered a landslide victory. Netanyahu's win was "the most stunning political upset in Israel's history."[29] If Rabin had not been assassinated, the inevitable, absolutely humiliating punishment of defeat by Netanyahu would just have surely ended his political life.

Leah Rabin, like the Israeli media, cannot accept Netanyahu's win. After his victory was confirmed, she declared to the media networks worldwide:

All I can do is look at where I keep my suitcases and feel like packing them and disappearing from here very quickly. It's that bad.[30]

Numerous Israelis offered to take her to the airport.

Leah Rabin was involved in an illegal foreign currency account scandal in the 1970s, during her husband's first term as prime minister. The scandal not only forced Yitzhak Rabin to resign, it also caused the Labor party to lose the next elections. Such is the established character of Rabin's widow. Following a terrorist bombing at the Mahane Yehuda Market in September 1997, Leah Rabin arrived at the scene with around 100 security men. She was greeted with yells, hissing and booing by the locals.

Israelis could understand the terrible, justified pain emanating from such a raw wound as the murder of her husband, but most cannot accept her vicious, hate-filled attacks against anything and anyone not fully supportive of her husband's bankrupt policies. A Hellenist worthy only of the era of the Maccabees, Leah Rabin showed her pathological hatred of religious Jews when she said,

I would prefer that my children be Arabs rather than Orthodox Jews.[31]

Instead of mourning her loss quietly, Leah Rabin's scheming mind grabbed at a once-in-a-lifetime opportunity to become rich and famous. She requested and received from Labor's finance minister, an office, a car and a driver at a cost of around $150,000 to the Israeli taxpayers. She vowed to bear the torch for her late husband's "peace" policies, even though the Israeli voters had decisively rejected them as a disaster. However, they are forced to continuing paying for them through the travels of his unelected widow, as she meets with heads of state and government dignitaries.

Rabin not only cynically exploits her husband's death for personal gain, but literally spews unadulterated venom at the right-wing element of Israel and Netanyahu in particular. In Oslo, Norway, in November 1999, months after Netanyahu had vacated the premier's chair, Rabin addressed a conference attended by U.S. president Bill Clinton, Norwegian Prime Minister Kjell Magne Bondevik, PLO Chairman Yasser Arafat and others. This was televised worldwide. In an obvious reference to insidious accusations that Netanyahu was somehow responsible for her husband's death, she said: "We do not forgive and we do not forget."[32]

Aggressively elbowing her way in front of TV cameras, before radio reporters, and in the printed media, she has continuously undermined and damaged the policies of all who did not (and do not) bow down to Yitzhak Rabin's policies.

Yitzhak Rabin is remembered by many Israelis as someone who failed at almost every turn. His widow, Leah, will be remembered as

> one of the most self-serving, opportunistic, bitter, hateful, despicable, embarrassing, manipulative, victim posturing, female tyrants in Jewish history.[33]

Shimon Peres

Another prominent figure who could not accept Netanyahu's election as prime minister of Israel is Shimon Peres, who ran against him in 1996. But then, Peres has difficulty in accepting any defeat, period. In fact, Peres is the uncrowned king of electoral defeats. He stood for prime minister more times than anyone else in Israeli history and lost each time.

There is a definite consensus of negative opinion about Shimon Peres held by his colleagues and peers, be they same party members, opposition members, or journalists. Space allows for but a sample of sentiments by those who know him today or knew him well in the past:

Prime Minister David Ben-Gurion said of Peres: "Never believe him and don't get close to him."[34]

Prime Minister Moshe Sharett said:

> I totally and utterly reject Peres and consider his rise to prominence a malignant, immoral disgrace.[35]

Prime Minister Levi Eshkol said:

> Peres engages in poisoning wells, slander and rumor-mongering.[36]

Prime Minister Yitzhak Rabin called Peres a "consummate plotter,"[37] referred to him time and again as a "liar," and said: "I never believed one word of his."[38]

President Ezer Weizman called Peres a "son of a bitch."[39]
Ari Stav, editor of _Nativ Journal_, wrote of Peres as

> an uncontrolled power seeker, which will stop at nothing in achieving his goals.[40]

Moshe Kohn, columnist for the *Jerusalem Post*, called Peres "an unashamed liar,"[41] and likens him to Amalek (Exodus 17:8-16; Deuteronomy 25:17-19)

who came from the rear and attacked the laggards and the weak.[42]

Ruth Matar, cofounder of *Women for Israel's Tomorrow* wrote that Peres "has no qualms about using treachery to obtain his goals."[43]

Seemingly, it is a rare associate indeed who either trusts or believes Peres, and the Israeli public also shows scant confidence in him. Peres remains unfulfilled after having lost five out of five general elections[44]—the public consistently votes his opponents into power. His two terms as prime minister of Israel were both attained by default—the second time around he was handed the premiership by Yigal Amir.

Some people believe Shimon Peres has "near mythical powers as a political sorcerer,"[45] that he is a "never ceasing saboteur and artist of political intrigues"[46] and

a radical opportunist who guesses well where the wind is blowing and changes his position accordingly.[47]

No one, however, thinks as highly of Peres as he does himself. Says Peres,

Many statesmen have also said about me: "If only we all had the IQ like Shimon."[48]

Perhaps Peres's pride is best epitomized in his declaration that he may not know what the people want, but he does know what is good for them.[49] His assumption that he is in a league of his own is not shared by his own party, and his blindness to reality is occasioned by his own vanity. And instead of stepping down graciously, Peres "clings to power like a baby to his mother's nipples."[50]

Rebus Sic Stansibus

In days past, Shimon Peres was the most fervent opponent of any Israeli territorial concession.[51] He said that if Israel returns to the 1949 borders, it will "face annihilation in war."[52] And Peres well understood that Israel's 1967 preemptive strike against the mobilized armies of five Arab nations was necessitated by Israel's lack of defendable borders. He is obviously very much aware of the fact that natural borders, strategic depth and land mass eliminate the necessity of such desperate actions as preemptive wars. When interviewed as Israel's Minister of Defense, Peres stressed the strategic importance of territory in the age of modern warfare. He asserted:

> Perhaps in 1948 one could believe that it was feasible to defend the 'narrow waist' of Israel's most populated area, when the most formidable weapon possessed by both sides was the cannon of limited mobility and range. However, today anti-aircraft and anti-tank missiles will constitute a threat to every plane and helicopter flying in Israeli skies, and to every vehicle traveling on the main roadways of the coastal plain.[53]

Peres also knows full well that the "Palestinians" have no plans for peaceful coexistence with Israel, but plan instead to destroy it. In his book *Tomorrow is Now* he wrote:

> The Arabs are cultivating separate Palestinian nationalism and the myth of 'restoring the rights of the Palestinian people' – in the area of the State of Israel and in her place. They do so not in order to solve the refugee problem, but to destroy Israeli national identity and in order to recreate a Jewish problem of far greater extensiveness. The national Palestinian objective is aimed at eliminating the existence of the State of Israel and not to coexist with her in peace.[54]

The Political process called the "peace process" is the diametrical antithesis of reality, and this is even substantiated by Peres in his own writings and statements. And yet he rushes to sign agreements both with terrorists and dictators, and this after having said,

> the number of agreements signed in the Middle East are as the number of the agreements annulled.[55]

So what rationale brought Peres to a full 180 degree switch to disown everything he has believed, preached and written? *Rebus sic stansibus* he says (circumstances have changed). That is the refuge of an opportunist, but it was noted earlier that Peres is indeed "a radical opportunist."

Only one significant change of measurable proportions has taken place in the Middle East since the founding of Israel's statehood in 1948. That one change happens to be the size of individual standing armies, and the enormous weapons stockpiles available to them. After more than 50 years of recurring warfare the annihilation of Israel still remains the number one objective of the Arab world.

No, it is not *rebus sic stansibus* that is motivating Peres. It is a combination of fear and the greed for power and payoffs. However, Peres in his spiritual and political bankruptcies has misjudged again. The "peace process," if allowed to run its course, would bring Israel to the size and status of a castrated dwarf—waiting for its Arab neighbors to deliver the irresistible, fatal death blow. And if king Peres survived, he would be left holding power over nothing. Professor Howard Adelson so aptly writes:

> ...the entire public relations campaign designed to depict Shimon Peres as a highly intelligent, well educated thinker with a disciplined, logical, analytical mind, was a massive fraud. He was, in fact, a remarkably uneducated individual, a poseur, who tried in vain to present himself as an intellectual, but who was, in truth, incapable of analytical effort that was meaningful.[56]

In order to camouflage his fear of an Arab military victory over Israel and succeed with his "peace process" machinations, Peres wove

> a web of falsity and deceit unprecedented in the history of Israel.[57]

Many of the world's politicians are pathological liars, and apparently Shimon Peres belongs at the head of the group.

In March 1988, Peres addressed the committee of presidents of Jewish organizations in Jerusalem:

> I absolutely object to negotiations with the PLO. All the talk about my being ready for negotiation with the PLO is nothing but nonsense.[58]

But Peres had already initiated contacts with the PLO in 1987, in blatant violation of the law.[59] And, according to Jordanian author Mamdukh Nufal in his book *The Oslo Recipe*, Peres

> requested that the PLO sabotage the ninth round of peace talks held in Washington in 1992, in order to force Yitzhak Rabin to recognize the PLO and the Oslo approach.[60]

The PLO leader, Abu Mazen, made the same accusations in

his published memoirs. Abu Mazen claims that the PLO were not just asked to sabotage the ninth round of talks, but to sabotage the fifth and sixth sessions as well,

> in order to show that the Likud was incapable of making peace.[61]

And in his bid to push forward the Oslo "peace process," Peres held forth his thesis that Arab economies are collapsing under the heavy burden of war, and that Arab nations would therefore prefer a path of peace to one of war. To illustrate the Arabs' "burden of war," he gave the cost of Scud missiles as $2 million per unit. Therefore, 1,000 Scuds would cost the Arab economies $2 billion.[62] Now Peres as a former minister of defense knew very well that there was not a shred of truth in what he presented, and obviously lied deliberately when he gave those figures. He knew that a Scud costs between $150,000 and $250,000, making a maximum possible of $250 million spent for 1,000 Scuds.[63] And $250 million is a negligible sum for Arab economies, about equal to one day's oil production in Saudi Arabia.[64]

In early 1994, Yasser Arafat revealed that Peres had sent a letter the previous year to the Norwegian foreign minister Johan Holst promising Israel would not hamper—would even encourage— "Palestinian" institutions in eastern Jerusalem. For weeks, both Peres and Rabin categorically denied the existence of any such letter. On May 2, 1994, Peres

> gave his passionate word to the Knesset that there had been absolutely no undertaking whatsoever given to the PLO not to tamper with its institutions in Jerusalem.[65]

On May 7, MK (Member of the Knesset) Benny Begin actually produced the letter in the Knesset![66] The letter was personally signed by Peres, but the apparently unflustered Peres "maintained that he had not be caught lying."[67] Later, Peres said that his only regret about the affair was "that it became public."[68]

1992 and all that

General elections in June 1992, saw the fall of Yitzhak Shamir's Likud government and the installation of a Labor government headed by Yitzhak Rabin. Successive Likud governments had led Israel for 15 years. And, Likud policies had raised Israel to where it led the industrial world in economic growth, despite a worldwide economic boycott against it for more than 40 years. The collapse of the Soviet Union in 1991 opened wide the floodgates of Jewish emigration. Hundreds of thousands of Jews from the former Soviet Union poured into Israel. This massive infusion of people stretched every resource and applied unbelievable pressure to the economy. If the Soviet Jews were to be successfully absorbed into Israel, an equally massive infusion of money was also necessary.

Israel looked to its "ally" the United States of America for help. Yitzhak Shamir's government needed help, not a handout. It requested the U.S. government to "guarantee" $10 billion in loans to help Israel absorb the immigrating Jews. By "guaranteeing" the loans, Israel would be spared the payment of millions of dollars in higher interest rates. Israel had always paid its international debts on time, and thus the "guarantee" should have been mere formality. But it was not. The Bush and Baker duo detested Shamir because he insisted upon Israel's right to determine its own policy. Realizing that refusing the loan guarantees could topple Shamir, President Bush refused to grant them. Time and again Israel requested the "guarantees," and as many were the requests were the number of refusals. Secretary of State

James Baker kept postponing his decision on the issue, repeatedly changing the terms of the agreement.[69]

When election time came around, the modalities of the loan guarantees became the deciding issue for the Israeli voter, and Shamir's government fell, because it had been unable to procure them. Like Avishai Raviv's GSS involvement in the Rabin assassination that was to come three years later, the truth also began to leak out through the cloak of secrecy that wrapped the loan guarantees. Shimon Peres had himself

pressed the Bush administration to refrain from approving the guarantees so as to facilitate a Labor victory in the May 1992 elections.[70]

And if Abu Mazen's memoirs are correct (and there is no reason for them not to be), Peres had also opened "secret channels with the PLO to rig the elections."[71]

Yitzhak Rabin has almost been elevated to the station of a saint within Israel—a military man who rose to take the office of prime minister and was cut down by an assassin. As a military man, however, Rabin quite often fell apart at the seams when under pressure and suffered more than one "nervous breakdown," when faced with stressful situations. As IDF Chief of General Staff at the time of the June 1967 war, for example, he suffered a nervous breakdown and "begged" to be relieved of his duties.[72] He was also guilty of making grave errors of judgment in his military decisions, with resulting high losses of life.

The October 1973 Yom Kippur war was the greatest trauma that ever hit Israel; thousands of Israeli soldiers lost their lives, and thousands more remain crippled in body and in mind. Due entirely to the IDF's unpreparedness, Israel was taken by surprise and only narrowly staved off total defeat in the opening days. When Egypt and Syria were both amassing huge armies along Israel's borders, Yitzhak Rabin actually advised against mobilizing Israel's forces.[73] History's annals record this and the consequences.

Unfortunately, Rabin's political record fares little better than the military one. While the world credited him with being the powerful force behind the "peace process," he was, in fact, only the front man who activated the machinations of others—

the straw-man of Shimon Peres, Yossi Beilin and Yossi Sarid.[74]

"It is unthinkable," wrote Ari Stav, Editor of the Israeli journal *Nativ*, that Rabin

> could have implemented the three moves which his policy called for: the ethnic cleansing of Judea and Samaria; the Gaza District and the Golan heights; withdrawal of the Israeli Army from the Golan; partitioning of Jerusalem. A person like Shimon Peres, the great manipulator, is needed for this purpose.[75]

Peres had lost four general elections. The Labor party knew it was inconceivable that the Israeli public would vote Peres into office, if he stood again in 1992. So, Yitzhak Rabin, the old "warrior," was taken down from the shelf, dusted off and brought out to be the front for Shimon Peres. Ethnic Israelis, like their Arab cousins, idolize the military, and retired generals are quickly absorbed into the political scene's top echelon. Take Ehud Barak for example, the current prime minister and leader of the Labor party. Barak is the most decorated soldier in Israel's history. He knows how to expertly kill with explosive, gun, knife and bare hands. Enamored with killing, he even stated on a television program that, if he were an Arab, he would "join a terror group."[76]

Apart from killing he knows very little. He retired from the army, was taken in tow by Rabin prior to his assassination, toppled Peres as Labor party leader, ran for the office of prime minister in the May 1999, elections and was elected. All this, and the camouflage behind his ears having barely wilted. He knows little or nothing about finances, education, health, housing, immigration, etc., but is now running the country and handing the Arabs all they desire at an even faster rate than his mentor Rabin.

But, while Peres received and enjoyed the credit for the "peace process," it actually belongs to Yossi Beilin, Peres's prodigy. Beilin is the real architect of the Oslo agreements and stuck so close to his master's heels that Rabin dubbed him "Peres's poodle."[77] Beilin is a secular-humanist thinker, whose vision is one of "a new world in which Israel would sacrifice for others."[78] Beilin's effect was totally dependent upon a close relationship with Peres, and when he presented his ideas, they became Peres's actions. Professor Adelson concurs:

> It was common statement on the street, repeated frequently by virtually all observers of Israeli political life, that whatever Beilin said publicly would be acted upon in the very near future by Peres as his own policy.[79]

Beilin got Peres, who in turn got Rabin, to promise President Clinton that Israel would cede the entire Golan and also 20% of the Kinneret [Sea of Galilee] to Syria,[80] and allow a Palestinian state in 90% of Judea and Samaria.[81] Israel would also partition the eastern and western sectors of Jerusalem between Israel and the PLO and give the PLO full control over the Temple Mount. Israel would also relinquish its sovereignty over the Old City of Jerusalem.[82]

If Peres had continued at the helm of the ship of "*fools*," Israel would have been shrunk down to the 1948 borders and beyond, retaining only a truncated 3,000 sq. mi. (7,770 sq. km.) of lowland with indefensible borders, whetting the aggressive appetites of its partners in "peace" and inviting military attacks.

Government in Exile

Shimon Peres lost his fifth general election to Binyamin (Bibi) Netanyahu in May 1996. But this did not put a halt to Peres's political chicanery. Netanyahu became the democratically elected prime minister of Israel's 14th Knesset, but Peres, on the other hand, thought he was "leading a government in exile."[83]

Four months after Peres took his fifth punishment at the polls, another furor broke out in Israel. Information was leaked that Major-General Oren Shahor, the top Israeli negotiator for civilian affairs with the Palestinians, had been meeting "secretly and furtively"[84] with Shimon Peres and Yossi Beilin. While Shahor, Peres and Beilin all denied that "classified information" had been passed on, Shahor was immediately suspended and later replaced as a negotiator. Yehoshua Matza, chairman of the Likud party's secretariat, said,

> the meetings were aimed at sabotaging the diplomatic negotiations and efforts to reach a better agreement than the Oslo Accords.
>
> These meetings are the continuation of Peres's other meetings with the heads of Arab states and Palestinians aimed at thwarting the success of the negotiations. Hypocrisy and undermining have characterized Peres's political career.[85]

The Shahor/Peres/Beilin secret meetings were but the storm in a teacup compared to the hurricane that blew in a little later. Israel's largest daily newspaper, *Yediot Aharonot*, broke a story that Peres had advised Yasser Arafat not to sign the Government's agreement on Hebron. The Knesset was in a turmoil. The government of Israel was trying to negotiate the best deal in what it considered to be a suicidal "peace process"— a process which it inherited from the former left-wing–Arab coalition government— and Peres told Arafat of the PLO not to sign, "because Netanyahu is not to be trusted."[86] Peres had earlier admitted that

> through his contacts with Arafat, he tried to give the Palestinian leader "small details and those keys" that will enable Arafat to negotiate directly with Netanyahu.[87]

Peres became prime minister by default after Rabin was assassinated. However, even with all the massive outpouring of grief over Rabin and untold sympathy for the existing government, Peres could not hold onto power. At the time of the assassination the issue of Hebron, Israel's oldest Jewish city, was under negotiation. Hebron was an explosive issue for many Israeli Jews. How could Jews abandon their holy and most ancient city to the Muslims once again?

An agreement on Hebron had been partially formulated while Rabin was alive, and this agreement was ready under Peres. Says Mohammed Mall Alla of the Hashemite Center in Amman, Jordan:

> Shimon Peres refrained from implementing the agreement in Hebron. Legally, he could have done it. But politically, the mandate was given to another prime minister. What Peres did in the last few months as prime minister was killing the peace process.[88]

The reason Peres did not implement the Hebron agreement was because he wanted to see the inevitable Jewish anger and outrage poured into Netanyahu's lap, while he smirked from a safe distance.

Netanyahu renegotiated the Hebron agreement left to him by the former government. And while that final agreement was being debated in the Knesset, this writer was lecturing at an Israel conference in Germany along with other participants from Israel. Being very interested in the proceedings, three of us would closet ourselves in a room to catch the Israeli news on shortwave radio. Each of us—an Israeli leader of a messianic congregation, a Gentile journalist who has lived in Israel for many years, and myself—had quite different perceptions of what the final outcome would be. The journalist's opinion was this:

> Netanyahu will sign the agreement, but it won't be ratified by the government.

The congregation leader said, "Nah, the agreement won't be signed." This writer was convinced otherwise and said: "The agreement will be signed, and the Knesset will ratify it." As it transpired my prediction was proven to be correct. After the signing, I think everyone in Israel, including myself, expected a fierce battle in the Knesset in order to have the agreement ratified. But it was a quick process which surprised us all.

Many people felt that this writer's prediction of the Hebron outcome was prophetic. Again, he will go on record saying that he does not consider it to be prophetic. Like the Rabin assassination, the Hebron outcome was simply a logical deduction: If the Hebron agreement had not been signed there would have been a complete breakdown of the "peace process," and war would have quickly followed. And, if the agreement had been signed but not ratified by the Israeli Knesset, the "peace process" would still have collapsed, bringing us into immediate military confrontation with the

Arab world. There is no modern-day "confrontation" over Hebron mentioned in the Bible. According to the Scriptures, the great confrontation takes place over Jerusalem. Therefore, of necessity the Hebron agreement had to be both signed and ratified in order to reach the confrontation over Jerusalem. We will discuss the Jerusalem confrontation at length in a later chapter—so, please stay tuned.

Peres is still not yet out of the picture. President Clinton openly backed Peres in the 1996 elections, but Peres lost to Bibi Netanyahu. In 1997 Clinton turned his attention to Ehud Barak making it clear to Israel and the world that Barak was now his man. Clinton snubbed Prime Minister Netanyahu by refusing to meet with him and interfered with the 1999 Israeli elections by providing and funding his own campaign manager to oust Netanyahu. But Peres was not deterred by having lost Clinton's backing, and when interviewed at that time by the French weekly *L'express*, Peres said he was

> waiting for the right conditions before reappearing on the Israeli political scene as an alternative to Netanyahu.[89]

The future is sure to reveal a further cabal from the defeatist king of Israeli political deviousness. Apparently, Peres now waits in the wings for the right conditions before reappearing as an alternative to Ehud Barak.

Surely, it was men like Peres of whom the Prophet wrote:

> *We have made a covenant with death, and with Sheol we are in agreement. When the overflowing scourge passes through, it will not come to us, for we have made lies our refuge, and under falsehood we have hidden ourselves* (Isaiah 28:15).

Infantile Behavior

Inside Netanyahu's own government, some members (including a few from his own Likud party) continually stabbed him in the back through petty rivalries or attempts to gain publicity and increase personal voter support in future elections. Hana Evenor, a judge brought in from the outside to arbitrate and render decisions based on the party constitution, became exasperated with the mindless, asinine behavior indulged in by some government Likud members. Besides nauseating the public, the inane behavior threatened to engulf the whole government and bring it down. Judge Evenor admonished them:

I allow myself to warn you that you are cutting down the limb on which you all sit. The public is stunned and bewildered at this senseless self-destruction.[90]

No one, however, gave Netanyahu more trouble than David Levy, a Moroccan-born Jew whose ego is matched only by his vanity. Levy threw a string of childish tantrums over not being chosen to lead the Likud party in 1992. Likud supporters got so fed up with both Levy and the Likud party due to the internal wrangling that tens of thousands of supporters threw away their votes at the 1992 polls, paving Rabin's way to power. Without Levy, the suicidal Israel–PLO "peace" process could not have gotten off the ground and flown.

In due time, after another of his "If I can't be leader, I'm not playing!" tantrums, Levy left Likud to form the Gesher party where he could be leader. Levy garnered sufficient votes from the large contingent of North African Jews in 1996 to win six seats in the Knesset. Netanyahu, unfortunately, needed the six seats of Gesher to form his coalition government, and from day one Levy began throwing his infamous fits: "If I can't be the Foreign Minister, I'm not playing!"; "If my friend Ariel Sharon doesn't get a place in the new government, I'm not playing!"; "If I'm not included in making important decisions, I'm not playing!"

During his months in office as foreign minister, Levy repeatedly embarrassed Israel both at home and abroad. Declaring that he was being "left out of the decision making," he boycotted both cabinet meetings and meetings with foreign dignitaries—including one with the U.S. Secretary of State. Levy also refused to attend a number of meetings overseas. He resigned as Israel's foreign minister in December 1997 and departed the Netanyahu government, joining the opposition, because in his opinion, there was not sufficient monies allocated to the underprivileged. Having previously given notice that he was going to run for prime minister in the next elections, this was no more than an attempt to win votes as a champion of the poor. With Levy's long history of pouting and threatening to resign without ever doing so, the media had heydays and continually mocked him.

Labor party leaders in their bid to topple Netanyahu promised Levy the position of foreign minister in any government formed by them, if he would resign and join Labor. Levy resigned in order to save face and ultimately gained the third slot on Labor's Knesset list which assured him of a senior cabinet position. He pulled his six-seat faction out of the government, leaving it with a very small majority. Levy timed his exit to coincide with a crucial vote on the state budget in his own hope of bringing down the government and forcing Israel into new elections.

During the vote on the state budget, the Knesset gallery was packed with local and foreign media personnel. Global television news networks devoted unproportionate time and energy to the story, and cited numerous commentators' predictions of Netanyahu's imminent fall. Netanyahu, however, said that his government would survive

> despite all predictions to the contrary. If I had to operate according to media predictions, I would have never been elected. I plan to go on defying such predictions, surprising the media anew, disappointing it and shattering its expectations.[91]

Netanyahu outmaneuvered Levy, and the government survived again. Two months later a member of Netanyahu's close circle said:

> With 100 percent of the necessary qualifications and five percent of his time devoted to foreign matters, Netanyahu is getting more done than Levy did as full-time foreign minister.[92]

It took more than Levy's childlike tantrums and combined machinations of Peres, Beilin and Barak to topple Netanyahu and his government. Netanyahu appeared to be an indefatigable survivor.

Ari Shavit wrote of Netanyahu:

> Neither ambition nor marketing skills are sufficient to explain how Netanyahu continues to survive. ... Kick him out of the door and he will return through the window, kick him out of the window and he will return through the chimney, kick him out of the chimney and he will find a crack in the wall. He will wipe the gob of spit off his face, rearrange his tie, and keep on going. He will give the millionth interview, and might even give the false impression that he is giving in a little here and there, that he has lost his way. But all along he is actually doggedly maneuvering himself toward some predefined point. That is how it is with him, ever since he was a kid. He is going to either capture the flag or die trying.[93]

American Interference

In chapter 3 we saw that U.S. President Bush, Secretary of State James Baker, and Shimon Peres conspired to bring down the Shamir government in 1992 and install Yitzhak Rabin. But U.S. interference in the Israeli elections that year was nothing in comparison to 1996. The U.S. State Department staked all on Peres's election—their plans made no provision for a Netanyahu victory. At

> ...no time in the almost 50 years of Israel's existence—during which 10 presidents have served in Washington—has an American president put the power and prestige of the Oval Office behind one Israeli candidate as Bill Clinton has done in supporting Shimon Peres.[94]

Departing from all diplomatic norms, Clinton implied that those who do not vote for Peres are opposed to peace when he said:

> I want the people of Israel to know they have to make a decision whether they want to pursue the peace process or not.[95]

Charles Krauthammer of *The Washington Post* wrote:

> Not since the CIA went around Iran and Guatemala renting mobs and overthrowing governments in the early 1950s, has the U.S. given more attention to making sure the right folk win the contest for power in a foreign country. The Clinton administration wants to re-elect Prime Minister Peres almost as badly as it wants to re-elect Bill Clinton.[96]

The 1996 elections turned out to be a war, and in a war there are winners and losers. The winner was Bibi Netanyahu; the losers were Peres, Clinton, the U.S. State Department, and the media. Peres was ahead in the polls, but Netanyahu was ahead in reality. And all the while the losers perceived Peres to be winning, democracy was seen to be working. But, when it was proven that Netanyahu had won, democracy had failed.

The American media continued its own demonization of Netanyahu. *The New York Times*, for example, ran a photo of Netanyahu beside a massive blowup of himself as though a demagogue had seized power over a subjected people. *The Boston Globe* said that Netanyahu's victory was "a blow to peace." *CNN*'s Dan Rather said Netanyahu's victory over Peres raised "questions about the future of the Middle East." *CNN*'s *Crossfire* host Robert Novak said, "people all around the world are going to be terribly depressed." Novak went on to say,

I'll tell you who did the nose thumbing. It was the majority of Jews in Israel who said, "The hell with you, United States. We'll pick our own prime minister."[97]

Apparently, the American media's brand of democracy requires blind obedience to American dictate by all nations of the world. Anything less is viewed as treachery.

Same Old Story

While Israel was still some months away from the early elections set for May 17, 1999, President Bill Clinton cast his vote ahead of time by sending his fast-talking advisor James Carville to Israel, "to share campaign tips" with Labor leader Ehud Barak.[98] Carville, who stymied polls by helping Clinton achieve victory in 1992, worked together with Stanley Greenberg and Robert Shrum. This trio helped bring success to the campaigns of British Prime Minister Tony Blair and German Chancellor Gerhard Schroeder.[99]

Britain's Prime Minister Tony Blair also cast an early vote for Ehud Barak. Blair asked Peter Mandelson to advise Barak's campaign staff. Mandelson virtually single-handedly recreated Blair's "New Labour" party and made it electable after almost two decades on the opposition benches.[100] Nothing much had changed since Labor's 1996 election debacle. The U.S. and British governments desperately wanted Netanyahu out of power. And they equally as desperately wanted to have the Israeli leader of their choice elected—one who can be manipulated into doing all their will, like Rabin and Peres did.

News reports—especially those of the *Reuter* news agency—habitually refer to Netanyahu as the "hardline" prime minister, or the "hardline" Likud leader, as though the attached epithet was part of his name. This is simply another form of media brainwashing. If Netanyahu is "hardline," then it stands to reason that Shimon Peres must be "limpline." And while the "limpline" Peres blamed a "weak Arab vote" for Labor's 1996 election defeat, 19,000 Arabs[101] actually voted against him by voting for the "hardline" Netanyahu.

Labor's Nightmare

Labor members squabbled like children, pointed their fingers at one another, and blamed each other for the 1996 election defeat. The fiasco had no father. But it did have one thousand and one supposed explanations, and cheating and fraud at the polling were among them. The Labor party appealed to the Jerusalem District court against the results—it wanted a nationwide re-examination of all ballot boxes. The limpline Labor party faction chairman Ra'anan Cohen charged the Likud with election fraud, and because of the importance of the issue, the Interior Ministry's national supervisor of elections investigated all of his charges personally.

After the investigation the court not only refused to overturn the election results, but also "sharply criticized" Labor.[102] In an affidavit to the court, director-general of the Central Elections Committee Tamar Edri said:

> This election appeal constitutes an abuse of the judicial system. The appellant knew that the facts did not uphold his claims, but the appellant—a public figure, an MK, chairman of the Labor faction and vice-chairman of the Central Elections Committee—chose to present a false picture in an affidavit to this court.[103]

Besides electoral fraud and cheating at the polling stations, other putative explanations included: not enough mobilization of voters, poor slogan, voter apathy, etc. Everything was used except the real reason—that the majority of Israelis had rejected the Left's bankrupt policies. Israeli voters are among the best educated in the world, and since they were not consulted in the first place over the Oslo accords, the 1996 election represented the first referendum on its merits.

Bibi Netanyahu did not win the election—the Oslo accords lost it. The majority of Israelis did not so much vote for Bibi Netanyahu as vote against Shimon Peres. Peres held all the aces: the backing of Bill Clinton, the State Department, the U.S. media, the Israeli media; the sympathy overflow of Rabin's assassination; and a campaign personally managed by France's mythological media whiz, Jacques Seguela, whose awesome campaigns were credited with bringing François Mitterand to power (twice). But Israelis had thoughtfully and somewhat sadly concluded that the Oslo agreements had worsened Israel's situation and, therefore, required revision.

Bibi Netanyahu

Binyamin Netanyahu is not the first member of the Netanyahu family to become famous in Israel. His brother Yonatan (Yoni) commanded the famous Israeli commando raid on Uganda's Entebbe airport in July 1976. Yoni led some of Israel's finest fighting men in a split-second-timed operation that successfully released Jewish hostages taken by Arab terrorists from a hijacked jet. Yoni was shot in the back and died during the near perfect operation—the only Israeli to fall.

Binyamin (Bibi) Netanyahu was a former IDF captain and served for five years with the *sayeret matkal*, an elite special forces unit—the same unit in which Yoni served. The Netanyahu brothers climbed to the top rungs on the ladder of bravery and fighting ability. At age 22, Bibi participated with other commandos in the successful storming of a hijacked Sabena Airlines' jet at Ben-Gurion airport in 1972. Bibi served as Israel's Ambassador to the United Nations from 1984 to 1988. He was elected to the Knesset in 1988, and became Israel's deputy foreign minister the same year. An articulate and photogenic person, he became a familiar face to millions of viewers of television news during the Gulf War, especially after he appeared wearing a gas mask. He was elected the leader of the Likud party in 1993, and was strongly opposed to the policies of Yitzhak Rabin and Shimon Peres.

The name, Binyamin (Benjamin) Netanyahu, was perhaps a significant one for an Israeli premier in the dark days of Israel's struggle for survival. Binyamin means "the son of the right hand of God," and Netanyahu means "given by God." Also, Netanyahu's ancestry is prestigious. On his father's side he is a descendant of "The Gaon Mevilna" (Rabbi Eliahu of Vilna), and on his mother's side from "Rashi," one of Jewry's greatest scholars. It is believed that the 12th century Rashi was descended from the line of King David.

A great many Israelis believe that Netanyahu was raised up by God to lead Israel. Even Netanyahu himself holds a

> deep conviction that if it were not for him, the State of Israel would not survive.[104]

Outwardly, Bibi Netanyahu is not an orthodox Jew or a secular Jew, neither has he shown any sign that he is a Jew who believes in Yeshua (Jesus) as the true messiah. Netanyahu is a Jew who believes Israel must continue as an independent Jewish country responsible for its own fate.

Netanyahu raised an absolute storm in October 1997, after he was secretly recorded confiding to a rabbi at a government meeting. After some left-wing politicians had sounded off about how the "peace" process was in danger of collapse, Netanyahu whispered to the rabbi that "the Left has forgotten what it is to be Jews."[105] His remarks were taken quite out of context and had nothing at all to do with anyone being an orthodox Jew, a secular Jew, or any other brand of Jew. He made the point that Israel was created by Jews rescued from anti-Semitism, annihilation and assimilation. He pointed out that the Labor–left-wing politicians had forgotten why Israel was born, and for what purpose. As would be expected, nobody at all raised a fuss about the nasty, sneaky recording of the Prime Minister's private remarks.

Continuing his recorded whisperings in the rabbi's ear about the left-wing political faction, Netanyahu said:

> They think we will put our security in the hands of the Arabs— that Arabs will take care of us. We'll give them part of Israel and they'll take care of us. Who ever heard of such a thing! It's as if the spies came and said, 'Not only are they mighty and we're afraid of them, but they're mighty and we'll let them protect us.' Incredible![106]

Netanyahu, as a former member of a special force elite commando unit, was mocking the left-wing's fear of Israel's destruction by Arab armies. An author of books on how to combat terrorism, Netanyahu has tremendous confidence, even great pride, in Israel's ability to take care of itself:

> Our war on terrorism is tough and continual, and unfortunately, bloody. The minute terrorists think they can get away with it, they will. We won't let them get away with it.[107]

And it was a fact that during Netanyahu's term in office, terrorist attacks against Israelis were reduced by 80 percent.[108]

Netanyahu's whisperings to the rabbi compared the Labor–left-wing Bloc unfavorably with the infamous spies of the Bible, as this book has also done. But, it is impossible to comprehend what drives Netanyahu, without understanding the importance he attaches to the biblical story of the Israelite spies. Joshua ben-Nun and Caleb ben-Yefuna sought to do the right thing and got stoned for their efforts by the children of Israel. The more he was stoned, the more Netanyahu became convinced that he was the right person doing the right thing at the right time.

Bibi, the Gentleman

In June 1996, an article appeared in the Tel Aviv weekly *Ha'ir* inferring, but providing no evidence, that Bibi Netanyahu had created several false identities in the U.S. According to *Ha'ir*, its information had been pulled from the Transunion Credit Bureau's files—one of three major federally regulated credit bureaus operating in the U.S. *Ha'ir* also claimed that the same information was in Netanyahu's U.S. Social Security file (Netanyahu had studied and also worked in America). *Ha'ir* claimed that the names Benjamin Netanyahu, Benjamin Neitay, John Jay Sullivan, and John Jay Sullivan Jr., all appeared in Netanyahu's file and all held the same Social Security number.

For several weeks following the article's publication, both the media and the opposition had a party lashing out at Netanyahu. The wave of publicity was insinuating that Netanyahu had created false identities, because he secretly wanted to live in the U.S. permanently; that he used one or more names "as an alias for unknown activities;"[109] and that he might have deliberately used a Social Security number belonging to one John Jay Sullivan in order to use his credit rating or "as a cover to receive payments as an informant for the CIA."[110] The accusations voiced by the both the opposition and media were endless.

John Jay Sullivan was located in California by New York investigator, Steve Rambam. Sullivan turned out to be a U.S. federal agent who had possessed his Social Security card since age 15, and had no idea how his name and number could have gotten connected to Netanyahu.

Transunion officials said that

> someone got access to the system and apparently entered incorrect information about Netanyahu to make the names appear together.[111]

But when Transunion officials conducted a later search of the same Social Security number, only Sullivan's name appeared. All reference to Netanyahu had been removed.[112] Transunion believed that

> someone, perhaps the same person, gained access a second time to remove records. The company says it is investigating. No one has yet been able to determine the source of the high-level computer break-in, but the federally regulated company

is convinced that only federal U.S. agencies are capable of accomplishing such a break in.[113]

And when Netanyahu's Social Security file was found to include no reference to individuals other than family members, it was apparent that it, too, had been tampered with. An official stated that

> any attempt to enter such a file without proper authorization is considered a federal offense.[114]

The following question still remains unanswered today: Who executed the computer break-ins, inserted the false information and removed it again later—and why? Netanyahu's lone comment on the whole issue was that he

> cannot remember his Social Security number, has no record of it, and has never heard of Sullivan.[115]

Another deluge of abuse and accusations that poured down upon the head of Netanyahu came after the opening of the 2,200-year-old Hasmonean tunnel exit in September 1996. The tunnel had been opened onto the Via Dolorosa ("The Way of Sorrows") four years previously, but the PLO kicked up a fuss, and the accommodating limpline left-wing government obligingly closed it again for them.

Very early in 1996 when Peres was still in power, Arafat requested permission for Muslims to use a site on the Temple Mount known as Solomon's Stables for prayers during Ramadan. Peres acceded to the request with two provisos: It was to be a strictly one-time usage and provided that Israel could quietly open the Hasmonean tunnel exit onto the Via Dolorosa. Arafat agreed. But when Netanyahu opened the tunnel later in the year, Arafat called for violence against Israel and his "policemen" turned their guns against Israeli soldiers killing 16 of them. A mini-war broke out and in addition to the 16 Israeli soldiers that died in the opening minutes, 55 Arabs also died and nearly 1,600 people were injured. At an ensuing press conference Israel's top security officials explained that they had

> warned against opening the exit, and the severe ramifications which would result.[116]

Netanyahu took full responsibility for the opening of the tunnel. Despite the violence and in face of the international pressure, he refused to close it, and the tunnel remains open to this day.

The Labor-led opposition and the media took its usual shortcut through the sewer to besmirch Netanyahu as a menace to Israeli society and one who was leading into war with the Arab and Muslim worlds. Netanyahu grimaced and bore it.

During a television interview in the following December, Emmanuel Rosen of _Channel Two_ pointed out that Netanyahu had not heeded the advice of security experts in the Hasmonean tunnel incident and hoped he "would learn his lesson."[117] Netanyahu responded that

> despite reports to the contrary, he was told by security officials that opening the Hasmonean tunnel exit would not bring about any radical reaction by the Palestinians. He added that security officials had encouraged the opening.[118]

To say that an uproar ensued would be the understatement of the year. The _Ma'ariv_ newspaper headlines the following day read:

> Shock in the General Security Service over Netanyahu's remarks.

GSS officials said "Netanyahu's statements are 'not true,'"[119] and that his statements "are divorced from reality."[120] Labor supporters held a rally at the Knesset where they held placards aloft reading: "Bibi is harming the security,"[121] and "Bibi is a pathological liar."[122] Labor party faction chairman Ra'anan Cohen said: "I believe the head of the GSS. The Prime Minister is lying."[123] Then the truth came out. The headline in the next day's _Ha'aretz_ read:

> The head of the GSS confirms that he encouraged Netanyahu to open the Hasmonean tunnel—regardless of timing.[124]

Ma'ariv's headline featured a quote from the then head of the GSS, Ami Ayalon, in which he said:

> In a number of meetings, I encouraged the Prime Minister to open the tunnel, and I emphasized that the timing was not a major issue.[125]

For over two months, Netanyahu knew he was being slandered, yet chose to remain silent in the face of merciless criticism. GSS officials lied to the media and to the nation in order to save their own faces. Netanyahu went against the wishes of advisors and confidants, who urged him to publicize the transcripts of meetings dealing with the opening of the tunnel. These transcripts would have cleared Netanyahu at the beginning, but he opted to sacrifice his reputation for what he perceived to be in the national interest.

Netanyahu is one of the rare few in Israeli politics who really cares more about his country than himself. He is a man who is very much on his own. When there are no strangers around and no one to challenge him,

> the expression on his face is almost sorrowful. It is the expression of someone who feels that it was not supposed to be like this.[126]

Equally as disturbing as the lying by GSS officials over the opening of the tunnel is the statement made by a senior PLO official after the mini war:

> The truth is we thought we gave Labor an excellent chance to get rid of Netanyahu and it didn't seize the opportunity. Some of us are saying that we spilled our blood to help Labor and it never helped us in return.[127]

Labor members did, however, help the PLO in their attempts to topple Netanyahu.

> Their activities include supporting Yasser Arafat, advising him and guiding him on how to outfox the legally-elected Prime Minister and destroy his administration. They are feeding Arafat with inside information about the problems afflicting Netanyahu. They outline strategies they believe will bring him to his knees.[128]

In January 1996, Labor's Housing Minister, Binyamin Ben-Eliezer boasted in an interview with *Ma'ariv* that Labor had a plan to guarantee its win in the next elections.

> We will reach an arrangement with Yasser Arafat. He will not allow a single Palestinian into Israeli territory for the next 10 months. The economic compensation for this, to the tune of a quarter of a billion dollars, will be transferred to him from us by American money. The result is that until the elections there will be no terrorist attacks, we will win big, and thereby Arafat, from his point of view, will get a considerable advantage toward the permanent settlement which will also answer our interests.[129]

Labor planned to spend hundreds of millions of dollars on buying a false temporary peace in order to remain in power. Rabin committed Israel to pay billions of dollars to the Arabs to effect Labor's win in 1992, and Peres's government followed the party line. In 1998, with Ehud Barak sitting in Labor's helm seat, it was reported in the media that Labor had reached another understanding with Yasser Arafat. In order to reduce Netanyahu's chances in the 1999 elections, Arafat would hold off declaring a Palestinian state on May 4, 1999, as he had repeatedly promised to do.[130] Yossi Beilin spearheaded the drive to convince Arafat to postpone his declaration of independence for eight months, in order that the declaration would not play into Netanyahu's hands.[131]

A Palestinian state is forbidden under the terms of the Oslo agreements which Arafat has signed with Israel. A unilateral declaration of a Palestinian state by Arafat would have brought a swift response by Netanyahu. He would have enjoyed the support of around 60 percent of all Jewish Israelis for his actions—almost certainly ensuring a Netanyahu victory on May 17, 1999. But his Israeli humanist opponents were ready and willing to make deals with Israel's enemy in their efforts to deny him that victory.

With these constant machinations from Labor, it was almost unreasonable to expect Netanyahu to prepare for the diplomatic front. He was busy all day with Labor's internal political intrigues.

Why they Hated Bibi

Jews and Gentiles should recall that in 1819, an anti-Semitic movement called "Hep, Hep" arose in Germany. This name became a battle-cry against Jews, and was derived from an acronym of the three Latin words, _Hierosolyma est perdida_, meaning "Jerusalem is lost." Had the Hellenist governments of either Rabin or Peres prolonged their reigns, Jerusalem would almost certainly have been lost again, along with a significantly large portion of the land of Israel. But Bibi Netanyahu arose to rule in Israel by a 55 percent plus majority vote of Israeli Jews. An election promise of Netanyahu's was: Jerusalem will never be lost again.

Bibi Netanyahu took control over an entire country at a most critical time in its history. He managed to do this against all odds—against the entire world. He is not a "yes sir, no sir, three-bags-full-sir," politician. He tells it like it is and has incurred the wrath of the whole world for doing so.

President Bill Clinton really wanted Shimon Peres in Israel's driving seat in 1996. This was not just because Peres is putty in

Clinton's hands, but also because Netanyahu's reputation in Washington was already known. In 1990 Netanyahu was barred from the State Department by then-Secretary of State James Baker. Netanyahu charged that U.S. policy was "built upon a foundation of distortion and lies."[132] Absolutely true, but saying it loud and clear did not exactly endear Netanyahu to the State Department's heart. And Baker's top aide at that time was Dennis Ross, and he still remains the head of U.S. "peace" efforts in the Middle East today.

Since that time things went from bad to worse. Netanyahu dared to say "No!" to Bill Clinton, Dennis Ross and Secretary of State Madeleine Albright (who even "wagged"[133] her finger at him in a meeting). Referring to Netanyahu's refusal to bow to every U.S. dictate, Clinton's Commerce Secretary William Daley said, in December 1998,

> new elections may be needed in Israel before its government behaved....[134]

Netanyahu reacted strongly, telling *Israel Radio*:

> Israel is nobody's protectorate, Israel is the Jewish people's sovereign state, and only the people of Israel will decide on who their leaders are to be. ...I expect an apology and an unequivocal retraction.[135]

Daley apologized.

Colonel David Hackworth, author of "Hazardous Duty" and other books, said during a 1998 U.S. radio interview that he had been hearing from his friends at the CIA headquarters in Langely that

> "Netanyahu has to be gotten rid of, because he won't go along to get along."[136]

Colonel Hackworth said that he heard the CIA had an

> active program to get rid of Netanyahu, and it comes from the White House.[137]

Getting rid of Netanyahu could have meant increased political pressure or an even uglier scenario. Only now do we know the answer, and this we will address shortly.

American Jews also became increasingly frustrated with Netanyahu. He did not bow to their wishes any more than he did to those of the White House. Hellenism is the dominating force among the 6,000,000 plus Jews in America. Reform and Conservative faiths constitute the major beliefs of American Judaism. Most Reform Jews are only marginally removed from atheism, many are total atheists, and many Conservative Jews follow close behind. All share one thing in common—all choose to live in the _galut_ rather than in the Jewish homeland. Eighty-five percent of American Jewry is in favor of the "peace" process, and the same percentage was in favor of the U.S. pressuring Netanyahu to make concessions to the Palestinians.[138]

In an April 1997, meeting with American Jewish leaders in Washington, Netanyahu showed his feelings in a rather pointed way. When the Jewish leaders placed their hands on their hearts and pledged allegiance to the American flag, Netanyahu strikingly turned the other way. _U.S. News & World Report_ carried a photo of his act on page 52 in its November 17 issue.

Although Netanyahu lived, studied and worked in the U.S. and has an obvious love for the nation and its people, he believes a Jew's allegiance should be to the Jewish state. He is a little contemptuous of Jews who remain in the _galut_, but from their place of opulence and safety, tell Israel how it should conduct its affairs.

Europe

European leaders stopped only a little short of gnashing their teeth at Netanyahu. After pouring hundreds of millions of dollars into building an embryonic Palestinian state, their ambitions were temporally stymied by Netanyahu as Israel's prime minister. While it pretends to be "impartial" in the Arab-Israeli conflict, the European Union is in reality a very strong supporter of the Arab world.

In November 1997, a letter was delivered to Jerusalem by the French Foreign Minister Hubert Vedrine, attacking Netanyahu for stopping the Oslo process. The letter was sent by French President Jacques Chirac, German Chancellor Helmut Kohl, and British Prime Minister Tony Blair.[139] The letter contained a "very forceful demand" for Israel to implement another troop withdrawal in the West Bank.[140] Jacques Chirac is openly hostile toward Israel and adapts his political position to cater

> to what he deems to be the prevailing sentiment in the Arab world.[141]

Chirac was responsible for Iraq's French-built nuclear reactor that Israel bombed and destroyed in June 1981. The official name of the reactor was "Osiraq," but Israelis referred to it as "O-Chiraq." France was building a nuclear facility for Saddam Hussein and supplying him with sophisticated weaponry. The French were aware that Saddam was breathing out threats of destruction of the Jewish state, but they strictly enforced their 30-year blockade of arms to Israel.

In August 1998, the "impartial" European Union called on its member nations to boycott all Israeli goods produced in Judea, Samaria, east Jerusalem and the Golan Heights. According to the EU Commission these areas constitute "disputed territory." Goods from these areas are to be excluded from the free trade agreement between Europe and Israel.[142] Encouraged by the EU's stand, Israel's nearly one million Arab citizens announced a boycott of 120 goods made in Jewish "settlements."[143] Israeli businessmen responded with a threat to dismiss the 13,000 Arabs employed in the manufacture of those goods, but this did not prevent the boycott from going into effect.

Netanyahu visited England for a three-day visit in January 1998. There Tony Blair gave him a "frosty reception"[144] and addressed him in "stern tones."[145] Netanyahu was not moved. He was elected by the Israeli public to apply the brakes to the runaway "peace" concessions to the Arabs that were initiated by Yitzhak Rabin and cultivated further by Shimon Peres. British Foreign Secretary Robin Cook said in February 1998:

> It was unacceptable that the Israeli government should give in to domestic demands which contradicted the expectations of the international community.[146]

There you have it. The wishes of the Israeli people are of no importance, of no concern. They should accept what the members of greedmongers international decide.

Betrayal

Historical documents prove that the English deliberately initiated the bloodshed between Jews and Arabs during the British Mandate period in Palestine.[147] It was done in a bid to foil the establishment of the Jewish state. The subsequent collapse of the once vast British Empire can be pinpointed to its own treacherous acts against the

Jews during the mandate. And more than 50 years down the line the British have still not forgiven Israel for being established—it ruined their plans for an unbroken overland empire stretching from the Middle East right through to India.

British ministers, who condescend to visit the Jewish state, act as if Israelis are still under Britain's colonial rule. David Mellor, as British Secretary of State for Foreign Affairs in 1988, proved his pro-Arab credentials when in insufferable arrogance he publicly berated an Israeli colonel for Israel's "cruel treatment" of the Palestinians. Mellor knew full well that the colonel was forbidden by regulations to reply to the humiliating, verbal whiplashing, and the incident was broadcast around the world. Mellor, who enjoyed an adulterous affair with a porn star,[148] was later forced to resign his government seat, when it became known that he was receiving large financial gifts from the daughter of the PLO's finance minister.[149] The daughter, Mona Bauwens, also funded Mellor's holidays in Spain.[150]

Britain's Foreign Secretary, Robin Cook, received a cool reception when he made a stop in Israel in March 1998. (A few weeks previously he had left his wife of 28 years after admitting involvement in a years-long adulterous relationship. Cook then dismissed his secretary and installed his mistress in her stead.) He caused a furor in Israel by words and actions that beggared belief, and further strained Israeli–British relations by acting like a bull in a china shop. A visit to Jerusalem's Yad Vashem Holocaust memorial is standard procedure for all ministers visiting for the first time. But Cook became the first foreign official to refuse to visit the memorial. Instead, he met with PLO officials at the controversial Jewish neighborhood of Har Homa, after expressly being asked not to do so by the Israeli government and giving his word that he would not. And when he was greeted with "Welcome to Jerusalem, the capital of Israel," by a representative of the Israeli Foreign Ministry, Cook replied: "We recognize only Tel Aviv as the capital of Israel."[151] Cook's manner was pompous and rude throughout his entire visit—he even forced the Prime Minister and Minister of Defense to wait for him.

Cook made no attempt at all to conceal his overt left-wing views or his pro-Arab feelings. Meeting Yasser Arafat in Gaza, he

> hugged his startled host before the PLO chief could even purse his lips to kiss the cheeks of his English gentleman guest.[152]

This was in stark contrast to the arrogant, ill-mannered way he spoke to and treated his Israeli hosts. Due to Cook's insulting behavior, Prime Minister Netanyahu cut short his private meeting with him and canceled the dinner at which Cook was to be the guest of honor.

The British government needs reminding that its Mandate in "Palestine" expired five decades ago. There are now hopeful signs that an end to the 800-year-old "British problem" in Northern Ireland may be in sight. But, like Israel, the Irish might have to suffer British hypocrisy and "humbug" a good while longer.

In the early 1980s, I befriended an Iranian Jew living alone in Jerusalem. He was a very closed man with a sad countenance. After several months of seeing him most every day, he felt sufficiently comfortable to confide in me. He had been a translator working in the U.S. Embassy in Teheran, both during and after the time of the Shah, and by chance had uncovered a spy in his department working with the fanatical Ayatollah Khomeini. After gathering sufficient evidence, he reported to his superior, who said that he would look into the matter. He realized by his superior's questions and attitude that he, too, was a spy. Convinced that his life was in danger, he feigned a heart attack and was admitted to a hospital in Teheran. From there friends helped him to reach Germany, ostensibly to obtain medical help unavailable in Iran. From Germany he made his way to Israel.

His wife and daughter were held in Iran to prevent him from going public with what he had uncovered—namely, the British had borrowed millions from the Shah to develop the North Sea oilfields. To avoid the necessity of repaying the Shah's huge loan, they financed Khomeini in France to overthrow him.

Some of the missing pieces to a puzzle fall into place. It answers the question of why Britain remained so warm to Khomeini during the Iranian revolution, when many countries were severing their relations. It also provides the logic for the British warning Khomeini of an attempted assassination of his son, etc. Apparently, the Jews are not the only people the British have betrayed.

Israel

When Rabin was in power, he set out his vision of a final settlement with the PLO in the Oslo 2 accords. Speaking to the Knesset in

October 1995, he said:

> We are setting out on a new road which is likely to lead us to an age of peace, to an end of wars.[153]

The facts speak for themselves. In the first two years following the September 1993 signing of "peace" agreements, after Rabin had begun to usher in Israel's golden "age of peace," Arab terrorism against Israeli civilians and the subsequent deaths of innocent men, women, children and babies rose 900 percent—worse than any period since the founding of the state.

Rabin's "age of peace" speech lasted 45 minutes. Afterwards, Bibi Netanyahu rose to his feet and determinedly opposed Rabin:

> Don't tell us stories that what guided you in your policy were Jewish values,[154]

he said.

> This government is the one most removed from Jewish values that there has ever been.[155]

Netanyahu continued with

> apart from the security and strategic threats arising from the agreement, the greatest threat is its damage to the vision of and faith in a Jewish homeland by acting as if Israel were a foreign invader.
>
> What will you say to Yasser Arafat and Hamas's Sheikh Ahmed Yassin when they demand the Triangle and Galilee? What will you say when they demand the right to return to Jaffa, Acre, and Sheikh Munis, on whose ruins Tel Aviv University stands?[156]

He repeatedly described Rabin's "vision" as a "tiny, threatened country, dependent on Arafat for its security."[157] He ridiculed Rabin's description of a wide Jerusalem corridor. He said,

> Why should there be a corridor, a cul de sac, a one way alley to Jerusalem? ... So don't tell us about Jerusalem. You are strangling Jerusalem. I saw the maps, and they are a shocking sight.[158]

Netanyahu could not stop the Oslo accords being ratified. The Oslo suicide pact vote was passed through the Knesset by a majority of one. But that one vote was all Rabin needed in order to hand Arafat large chunks of Israel's inheritance and supply his "policemen" with automatic weapons which were used later to kill Israelis—soldiers and civilians. Seven Israeli-Arab members of the Knesset voted in favor of the Oslo accords. Had it not been for them, the Oslo agreements would have been rejected by the Jews.

Before the vote, when members of the Netanyahu-led opposition protested that only Jews can decide the future of the Jewish state, they were labeled "racists." So, PLO-supporting Arabs actually decided the Jewish state's most crucial vote ever!

Among these Israeli-Arab politicians are Yasser Arafat's advisor Ahmed Tibi, who showed his hatred of Jews when he called them "scum."[159] And in February 1998, Tibi relished the idea of Iraqi missiles with chemical or biological warheads hitting Israel in retaliation for a U.S. airstrike against Saddam Hussein. At the height of the Iraq-U.S. crisis over UN freedom to inspect sites thought to contain Iraqi weapons of mass destruction—when things looked like they could end in the U.S. waging war upon Iraq—Tibi spoke at a forum on "Co-Existence and Neighborliness between Jews and Arabs." He said, gleefully:

> You Israelis are preparing your shelters, while we are cleaning our roofs[160]

—referring to the Palestinians dancing on the roofs with glee during the Gulf war when scores of Iraqi Scud missiles hit Tel Aviv.

Also, a member of the infamous seven is Abdul Wahab Derawshe, who "approved" of the five-year-long *intifada* that took such a high toll of Israeli lives. In August 1997, four years after the *intifada*, Derawshe visited Syria and wished them well in their next war with Israel. He also told thousands of Arabs: "I swear to Allah that you will return to Palestine."[161] Another Arab MK, who frequently makes the news with his blind hatred of Israel, is Hashem Mahameed. He was filmed by a news crew inciting Palestinian Arabs to violence against Israel. He had no qualms about clarifying to the Israelis later that "any weapons are justified"[162] in the Arabs' "armed struggle against the nation."[163] And so it goes on.

First under Rabin and then under Peres, the Arab MKs—who hope and pray for Israel's destruction and work toward that end—effectively controlled the direction of the nation. Did Israel go through four devastating, Arab-initiated wars for this? Only a *"fool"* would encourage a vanquished Arab aggressor to turn itself into a political fifth column and enable it to determine Israel's fate.

Through the Knesset, helped by the spiritual and moral bankruptcy of Hellenist Jews, the Arabs are accomplishing politically what they failed to do militarily.

It is now widely accepted that Rabin and Peres intended to pull Israel back to the 1948 lines—borders that not only invite war—but borders in which Israel would cease to exist. Their denials carried no weight, as neither of them were given to telling the truth even in the best of times. Rabin was cut down by an assassin's bullets. Peres was cut down by votes from thinking Jews. Votes can be almost as powerful as bullets.

Netanyahu inherited a catastrophic mess, politically and economically. But he knew exactly where he was going. And that was as far as possible from the Oslo trap into which Israel had been led by the previous Israeli administration. Indeed, Netanyahu performed a veritable juggling act while walking a political tightrope. He neither violated the Oslo accords nor upheld them. He derailed the "peace" process, but carefully avoided a direct conflict with the Arabs. He bought the nation a "time-out" from Oslo's "peace," and that "time-out" was used to make Israel stronger.

Ari Shavit says that Bibi Netanyahu would not have chosen this description, but

> essentially he relates to himself as a one-man drug rehabilitation institution. His task, he believes, is to wean the Arab addicts from the overdose of one-sided Israeli concessions to which they have grown accustomed, to wean the Israeli Left from the overdose of exaggerated expectations of what peace will bring, and to wean the Israeli Right from the false drug of believing in the status quo. It is no wonder then that all three groups are so opposed to him. For this is how addicts behave during rehabilitation; they transfer all their rage to the rehabilitator.[164]

Shavit also stated that, as of December 25, 1997,

> Netanyahu has not made a single move that might be interpreted as improper use of force.[165]

> Netanyahu has not taken a single action that might be considered a war crime.[166]

> Netanyahu bears responsibility for less bloodshed and less

harm to human rights than the two patrons of peace who occupied the prime minister's chair before him. So why do we hate him so much?[167]

Shavit answers his own question, both as a journalist and as an Israeli:

When all is said and done, the truth is that we hate Netanyahu so much because the hatred makes life easier for us. Because this hatred responds to our deepest emotional needs. Because hatred of Netanyahu saves us from having to deal with our own internal contradictions and errors. And because hatred of Netanyahu enables us to conveniently forget that before the bubble burst, we had acted like fools. We fooled ourselves with illusions. We were bedazzled into committing a collective act of messianic drunkenness.

Hatred of Netanyahu also gives us a chance to forget that it was not the rise of Netanyahu that brought on the paralysis of Oslo, but the paralysis of Oslo brought on the rise of Netanyahu. The hatred permits us to keep harboring the notion that everything is really much more simple, that if we only pull back, if we only recognize Palestinian statehood.... The hatred lets us divert our attention from the renewed strength of the Egyptian army, from the pinpoint accuracy of the Syrian missiles, from the Iraqi anthrax and from the Iranian nuclear program. Thanks to our hatred of Netanyahu, we can convince ourselves that if we only beat up our prime minister a little harder, if we could only manage to break his political bones, if we could only vanquish him and get him out of our lives, then everything would revert to the simple sweet life that once was.[168]

Due to no fault of his own, Netanyahu was locked into the "peace" process. The entire inherited situation from the former Hellenist government is practically irreversible—the Oslo accords, the economic problems, the ballistic missile threat. But, Netanyahu reduced the expectations of all parties—Arab, Israeli, U.S., Russian and European alike. The building of the controversial Jewish neighborhood at Har Homa was not a mistake, it was deliberate. By this one act alone, he let the other side know that there was a new government in town, that policy had changed, and that things would not be the same anymore. Concerning the backlash some of his policies had upon the international community, Netanyahu would say, "the world will now have to readjust."[169]

Squaring Up for May '99

Having failed to garner sufficient government support in December 1998 for his handling of the Wye River Agreement, Netanyahu took the initiative and set early elections in motion. Had he not moved for early elections, they would have been forced upon him, and they would have taken place in only six weeks instead of 20 weeks plus—on May 17th. Thus, he once again outfoxed his opponents and remained in office for a further six months, which was just one year less than his full term.

On the surface of things, it looked impossible for Netanyahu to win the May 1999 election. His opponents were being advised by possibly the most awesome political campaign managers in the world, and many of the top Likud personalities either bolted the party in bids to topple Netanyahu or remained in the party to work on toppling him from within. They all hoped to either fill Netanyahu's seat themselves or to receive a choice post at the side of a popular prime ministerial candidate, who might bring him down. Party loyalty counts for very little in the power games of Israeli politics. But, as it was pointed out earlier, Bibi Netanyahu is an indefatigable survivor and, therefore, a Netanyahu victory in 1999 simply could not be ruled out despite the seemingly impossible situation.

Netanyahu is a courageous, lonely man and is supported by a large portion of the Israeli public. Its support is partly because

> Israelis regard him as the nation's ultimate braking mechanism, its last line of defense, the last real goalkeeper in the Jewish national soccer team, alone between the goal posts. Nearly all the other team members have become too tired and left the field, scattering in every direction, after having failed to understand the rules of the game.[170]

With all the international help Barak was receiving and with less than three months to go before the election, Netanyahu was still leading in the polls at 33 percent, just edging out Barak at 32 percent. However, the road from late February to May 17th was not only long, but also very dirty. And it was not just the Israeli politicians who played dirty. The nastiest tricks came out of the

White House. Bill Clinton was not satisfied to just send his own advisor to open an office in Jerusalem in order to facilitate an on-the-spot not-so-subtle war against Netanyahu (Carville, dubbed "Bill Clinton's political rottweiler"[171] reported progress back to his boss each day), but Clinton also brought the big guns of the U.S. State Department to bear against Netanyahu.

Just as president Bush had withheld the loan guarantees from Shamir in 1992 to effect his downfall, so Washington announced in early March that it would now suspend the transfer of $1.2 billion of special aid pledged to Israel at the signing of the Wye Agreement. The State Department said it would continue with its plans to transfer the promised $400 million a year to the PLO.[172] This and other actions were meant to influence Israeli voters to throw Netanyahu out in the May elections.

The pressure and insults heaped upon Netanyahu and the Likud knew no bounds. It is perhaps difficult for those living outside of Israel to even begin to understand the weight of the scorn and hatred showered upon a man who gave his all for his country. Besides the overt interference of the Clinton administration, Netanyahu was required to keep swallowing a continual onslaught of insults from left-wing secular humanists like Ben-Gurion University professor and Meretz member Chaim Gordon, who remarked on television that:

> Prime Minister Binyamin Netanyahu was "filthy scum" and "excrement" and that he would be happy should Foreign Minister Ariel Sharon drop dead from a heart attack.[173]

Enter the Military

Sabra (native-born) Israelis are very much like Arabs when it comes to worshipping the military. Thus, when Israel's Chief of Staff Amnon Lipkin-Shahak made it known in January 1999 that he would retire from the army, form a new "centrist" party and run for prime minister, many Israelis were overjoyed. Opinion polls quickly showed Lipkin-Shahak to be the most popular candidate for prime minister even before he had finished with his military career or had one single day in politics.

Lipkin-Shahak's appointment as Chief of Staff in 1994 was a political one. Remember, the left-wing Labor Socialists control the Media, Army, Police and the Courts. Lipkin-Shahak's appointment as Chief of Staff was made possible by Yitzhak Rabin positioning him for the appointment through "a sweeping rotation in the high echelons of the army."[174] Lipkin Shahak was "Israel's former chief negotiator"[175] with the Palestinians in the Oslo "peace" process. His involvement was criticized as excessive involvement by a senior officer of the IDF in the "peace" process,[176] but Lipkin-Shahak

> was selected by Rabin, because he had been chief negotiator of the Cairo accord with the Palestinians.[177]

Lipkin-Shahak may have formed the new "centrist" party, but his political leanings are definitely left-wing. The "centrist" label was an overt effort to pull votes from each side of center of the political spectrum. Lipkin-Shahak's first ever political statement was given in Tel Aviv in early January and broadcast nationwide:

> I am here today because I want to be elected as prime minister of Israel.[178]

A complete political novice, his ratings quickly fell to 17 percent in the opinion polls, but despite this he was still slated to become Israel's next prime minister at the time. However, he withdrew early from the race for the prime minister's chair in light of his poor ratings, and the wooing of Yitzhak Mordechai into the newly created centrist party.

In late January 1999, Bibi Netanyahu suddenly sacked Israel's Defense Minister Major-Gen. (res.) Yitzhak Mordechai. Mordechai had been negotiating surreptitiously with Lipkin-Shahak about joining his new party. When Netanyahu became aware of Mordechai's deviousness, he sacked him for disloyalty to the Likud party.

Mordechai, an Iraqi-born Kurd and former OC Northern Command, retired from the army after Amnon Lipkin-Shahak was appointed Chief of General Staff in October 1994, and refused to appoint Mordechai his deputy.[179] Mordechai, long regarded as the most dovish member of Netanyahu's cabinet, turned his allegiance from Labor to Likud after Shimon Peres refused his requests for appointment to one of several positions. This included a cabinet post and head of the _Shin Bet_ security service.[180] Mordechai reportedly joined the ranks of the Likud in late 1995, after he was promised the post of defense minister if the Likud won the coming elections.[181]

After Likud won the May 1996 elections and Mordechai was rumored to be the next defense minister, Lipkin-Shahak was then reported to be threatening to resign as Chief of Staff, if the appointment took place.[182] However, Mordechai became defense minister, Lipkin-Shahak remained in his post, and Mordechai became Lipkin-Shahak's boss. The two remained on "bad terms,"[183] until Lipkin-Shahak formed his new centrist party and took Mordechai in, which then cost Mordechai his defense post. Politics breed strange bedfellows.

Mordechai ran for prime minister in the May elections, but withdrew his candidacy one day before Israel went to the polls, and endorsed Ehud Barak instead. Amid much fanfare he told the Israeli voters that he was withdrawing "solely for the good of the country."[184] However, his ego would not allow him to say that he was devastated by his humiliating three percent showing in the polls. He also neglected to say he had received a firm commitment from Barak of a ministerial portfolio in Barak's government if he endorsed him publicly.

Mordechai subsequently became Minister of Transport in Barak's government, but in early March 2000 Mordechai took leave of absence from his office due to an unnamed 23-year-old female filing sexual assault charges against him.[185] The young woman, who worked under him, had hesitated for some time before going to the police, and only filed charges after passing a lie-detector test.[186] Her courage has since inspired several other young women have come forward with complaints of sexual harassment by Mordechai.[187] The police investigation of the transport minister was continuing as this book went to print.

Other PM Hopefuls

Uzi Landau was the first non-defecting Likud member to openly oppose Netanyahu in the run up to the May elections. Landau chaired the prestigious Foreign Affairs and Defense Committee, and after making disparaging comments about Netanyahu, announced that he would challenge him for party leadership in the January primaries. Landau said that if his bid to head the Likud was successful, he would be the party's candidate for prime minister. But, when Moshe Arens, a former Likud minister, announced he would challenge both Netanyahu and Landau for party leadership,

Landau bowed out from the leadership race. Landau said Arens had a better chance of defeating Netanyahu, and he was withdrawing "to avoid splitting the anti-Netanyahu vote."[188]

Moshe Arens—former defense minister and former foreign minister —is widely regarded to be Netanyahu's political mentor and credited with bringing him into politics. Arens had become critical of Netanyahu's handling of the Oslo "peace" process and decided to stand against him for Likud party leadership. He would then run for Israel's number one political slot himself.

Arens is a well-liked politician at home and abroad, and given his popularity, diplomacy and wide experience, many Israelis felt he would defeat Netanyahu, especially in the face of such strong anti-Netanyahu sentiments expressed by senior Likud members. However, when the Likud primaries were held on January 25, 1999, Netanyahu received an incredible 80 percent of the total vote, easily defeating his mentor Arens.

After the result of the vote was certain, Netanyahu appointed Arens to the post of defense minister. The position had become vacant a few days earlier following Netanyahu's sacking of Yitzhak Mordechai. The defeat in the primaries told Arens in no uncertain terms who Likud wanted at the party's helm. Arens gracefully accepted Netanyahu as his leader, and backed him fully in the national election campaign.

Ze'ev (Benny) Begin, son of former Premier Menachem Begin, left the Likud party in order to resurrect his father's *Herut* (National Union) party and run for the office of prime minister. Begin was Science Minister in Netanyahu's government, but resigned his post in protest against most of Hebron being turned over to "those hoodlums,"[189] as he termed Yasser Arafat and company. Begin was a scrupulously honest, intensely patriotic politician, but he lacked the charismatic qualities needed to become an effective leader. His lack of charisma quickly showed in the opinion polls, where his eight percent ratings had him wallowing in one of the lowest positions.

Begin's run for the highest position in the land drew ultra right-wing Likud voters away from Netanyahu, and those lost votes were to be crucial ones indeed for the incumbent prime minister. Like Mordechai, Begin's poor showings in the polls caused him to withdraw from the prime ministerial race the day before the elections, but he was so miffed that he refused to endorse Netanyahu as Mordechai had done for Barak.

Begin's *Herut* party gained four seats in the Knesset, but this was too disappointing for Begin and he quit political life completely. He told *Israel Radio*:

> My job was to serve the public and to be effective, but apparently I don't have a public. Therefore I have decided to end my public activities.[190]

Ehud Barak, head of the Labor party and another former Chief of Staff, ran for prime minister on the Labor party ticket. As Israel's most decorated soldier, he was looking for any and every conceivable way to politically kill Netanyahu in his quest to add a prime ministerial ribbon to his impressive list of decorations.

Advised and stage managed by campaign managers from President Clinton of the U.S., Prime Minister Blair of Britain, President Chirac of France and Chancellor Gerhard Schroeder of Germany, Barak did manage to oust Netanyahu. But Barak only headed him off in the Jewish vote by a mere 1.6 percent. Barak's larger majority was garnered from pro-PLO Arab votes. Yitzhak Rabin and Shimon Peres, acutely aware that Arab votes were crucial to Labor if it was to hold power, accelerated the granting of Israeli passports to Arabs knowing most would vote Labor. It is indeed a sad day for any country when that nation's enemies decide its political course.

However, despite the grossest possible political smear campaign run by the world's highest paid election campaign managers, the results clearly showed that Netanyahu was still preferred by 48.4 percent of all Jewish voters. The media claimed a "stunning" landslide victory when, in fact, no such thing existed.

Netanyahu resigned his Knesset seat after the elections and also the leadership of the Likud party. Many Israelis, however, wish to see him back in politics, and ultimately, back in power. Ariel Sharon became Likud party leader on a temporary basis, until elections for the position take place in 2000. In September 1999, it appeared that Sharon was preparing the ground for a Netanyahu return, and some Israelis got their hopes raised.

The raising of hopes in Netanyahu supporters was accompanied by corresponding panic among his opponents. The following month the police "raided" Netanyahu's home and also his office.

There is no precedent for the raiding of a former Israeli prime minister's home, but remember, the police are controlled by the left-wing Labor party. Not only were Netanyahu's home and office raided by the police, but the police "leaked" news of the raid to the media, so that it had men and cameras ready and waiting to cover it. That evening Israeli television viewers were treated to scenes of police removing several large cardboard boxes of household goods from the Netanyahu premises.

Both Netanyahu and his wife Sarah were questioned for days (sometimes enduring eight continuous hours of questioning) on allegations of "corruption."[191] To be sure, the left-wing media revelled in it and made the most of it.

The allegations of "corruption" stemmed from the fact that the Netanyahu's had not handed back all official gifts received while Netanyahu was in office. Netanyahu later summoned the television networks and took them into a room where numbers of cardboard cartons were stored. He pointed out that since moving out of the prime minister's official residence their household belongings had not been unpacked. It was also pointed out that the Netanyahu's did not pack the boxes in the first place. Those that had dreamed up the "corruption" charges and organized the raids were well aware of the fact that there were official gifts packed in the boxes, and these would have been handed over in due time.

When mud is slung, however, some of it sticks. The object of the exercise was to smear the Netanyahus as corrupt thieves, thus diminishing further the chances of him regaining power.

One hundred thousand party members voted in the Labor primaries on February 15, 1999, and top placings on the Knesset list—after the first two slots which are reserved for Barak and Shimon Peres—went to Shlomo Ben-Ami and Yossi Beilin. (In order to draw David Levy into the Labor fold, Barak later gave him the number three slot ahead of Ben-Ami, forcing him and Beilin down one rung on the ladder). Ben-Ami holds ultra-left-wing humanist views as does Beilin, and political commentators in Israel agreed that Labor was now as far-left as it was possible to go.

In interviews given the day following the primaries, Ben-Ami said: "Left is beautiful, we are a peace party."[192] Beilin said: "Left is right and Right is wrong."[193] When asked what was the difference now between Labor and the ultra-left-wing humanist Meretz party led by Yossi Sarid, Beilin replied:

> Let's not talk about differences, let's just say there is no more reason for Meretz to exist.[194]

After Labor's win in the May 1999 elections, these Hellenist *"fools"* became Barak's right hand men. Yitzhak Rabin's anti-Zionist policies brought widespread protests that often involved hundreds of thousands of demonstrators. These protests just as often turned violent, and Rabin finally paid for his policies with his own life. Barak's government could well bring about another bloody revolt by today's Maccabees.

Premier Barak

The frantic pace of Ehud Barak's sprint to make "peace" with Arab neighbors by opening the floodgates of Israeli concessions, is that of a man who knows his chances of holding power after 2003 is next to nil. Rabin was not only Barak's mentor, he set a pace of concessions that cost him his life. Apparently, Barak aims to exceed Rabin in concessions, and Barak is hurrying much, much faster than common sense allows.

Holding power by a corruptly gained majority of only 1.6 percent of Jewish votes allows Barak no mandate to deviate from Netanyahu's policy. Matters affecting the Jewish homeland should be decided and voted upon by the Jewish people, not Arabs who pray to Allah for Israel's annihilation.

While Barak was busy in the U.S. "negotiating peace" with Syrian officials by offering them a full Israeli withdrawal from the Golan Heights in return for another piece of paper with the words "Peace Agreement" scrawled on it, the Likud was equally as busy bringing a vote of "No Confidence" against him in the Knesset.

The no confidence vote was not over Barak's bid to outdo Rabin's record of concessions, but over the fact that there was an investigation underway by the State Comptroller alleging Barak received hundreds of millions of dollars in illegal funds for his election campaign.[195] The Likud also charged that the police were not investigating the allegations.

After an initial investigation of Barak's campaign funding, the State Comptroller fined Barak's One Israel party 13.8 million shekels (US$3.4 million) for "trampling on election laws," and ordered a full-scale police investigation. One of those thus far named as an illegal contributor of funds to Barak's campaign is Lord Levy, British Prime Minister Tony Blair's personal envoy to the Middle East.[196] (Ezer Weizman, president of Israel and an outspoken opponent of Netanyahu, is also under police investigation for receiving hundreds of thousands of dollars in cash gifts from a French businessman over a period of five years while he was an MK).[197] The police investigations of Barak and Weizman were continuing as this book went to print.

Rabin broke practically every election promise he made concerning Arafat, the PLO and Israel's security. Barak is also breaking his promises. Among his promises was one that no Palestinian prisoner with blood on his hands would be released. However, numbers of Arabs convicted of murder of both Jews and Arabs have been released by the Barak government.[198]

The promise most Israelis were relieved to hear was that Jerusalem would never be divided and would remain under Jewish sovereignty. However, *Ha'aretz* reported in late December 1999 that unnamed Israeli officials have revealed that a number of Jerusalem neighborhoods will be given over to PLO jurisdiction, and that an acceptable arrangement for the Old City would need to be found. All those named in the *Ha'aretz* article, both the Israelis and their Arab counterparts—Oded Eran, Yasser Abbed Rabbo, Chaim Ramon and Feisal al-Husseini—denied the substance of the report.[199] Initial Israeli relief turned into despair two weeks later, however, when Chaim Ramon officially announced that all Arab neighborhoods surrounding Jerusalem will be given over to full PLO control.[200]

Some of the neighborhoods promised to the PLO are directly linked to the Old City, and thus many Israelis are convinced that Barak will eventually turn it over to the PLO also. If, before the final status talks begin, Barak has promised all the surrounding Arab neighborhoods will go to the PLO, what chips does he have left to play with? Only the Old City and the Israeli populated western half of Jerusalem. And Feisal al-Husseini, the PLO's head man in Jerusalem—Arafat's cousin and grand-nephew of Haj Amin al-Husseini, Adolf Hitler's ally and confidant—said, in the London-based *Al-Hayat* newspaper, that

> Palestinians will insist on discussing the western half of Jerusalem as well as the eastern half, claiming 70 percent of western Jerusalem is owned by Arabs.[201]

An old English *adage* says: Fools rush in where angels fear to tread. And Barak's mad rush into the "peace" process has left Yitzhak Rabin looking like a rank amateur.

Barak has publicly said on several occasions that there would be no return of refugees to Israel. However, Barak's Minister of Immigration, Yuli Tamir, was reported to have been advising PLO officials on how to absorb refugees into PLO-ruled areas.[202] This caused a storm of criticism to beat against Barak as it was interpreted to be his tacit support for a return of refugees. A bill was brought before the Knesset by the government opposition which would require an 80 percent Knesset majority vote before 1948 refugees would be allowed to return to Israel. When the bill was put to the vote the government defeated the bill. Super*fool*, Yossi Beilin said afterwards on Israel Radio:

> We are negotiating a "peace" agreement with the Palestinians— the government must not have its hands tied.[203]

Apparently, Barak's government is about to open the floodgates that will allow several more millions of Arabs to pour into Israel proper.

It was mentioned earlier about Arafat's request of Peres to use Solomon's Stables as a temporary mosque.[204] Arafat ensured that mosque became a permanent fixture on the Temple Mount, but in late 1999, the PLO began using excavators and tractors to dig under the Temple Mount to enlarge the mosque. Terrible damage was done to ancient Jewish archaeological sites dating back as far as the first temple period. Jerusalem's mayor, Ehud Olmert, a Likud MK, took legal steps to stop the work and close the site, but Barak personally intervened. He told Olmert to stop his legal action, and allowed the work to continue.

A large protest rally was held after archaeology students displayed for the media a "treasure trove" of Temple-era antiquities taken from heaps of dirt dumped by the Muslims in the Kidron valley.[205] The students claimed the Muslims had sifted through the dirt before dumping it outside of the Temple Mount, and had removed many large and valuable Jewish antiquities.[206] But what does Barak care? He is a Hellenist Jew, a *"fool"* by God's definition.

Barak "negotiated" a "Safe-Passage" route with the PLO, allowing Palestinians to travel between Gaza and Hebron. This caused a great deal of unease among Israelis. They felt the Israeli cities and towns which the route bypasses would be open to terrorist attacks and to a new spate of thievery. To make matters worse the PLO insisted that

> Israel may not arrest any Palestinian using the route, even it they are wanted for terrorism in Israel.[207]

Barak agreed, but assured the Israeli public that its fears were unfounded. Israeli security forces, he said, would be in control, and they would determine which Palestinians would be able to use the route. At the end of the inaugural week of the route's usage in October 1999 it was reported that

> as many as 17 Palestinians traveling on the new southern "safe-passage" route last week simply disappeared at rest stops along the way to Gaza, having evaded Israeli security troops.[208]

Those Arabs "disappeared" into Israeli cities and towns in order to commit more than mischief.

On February 24, 2000 *Israel Radio* broadcast a staggering report that since the opening of the "safe passage" route some 40,000 Syrians, Egyptians and other Arabs from the PLO areas had exploited the route in order to enter Israel.[209]

In the opening hours of March 2000, Israeli security forces laid siege to a Hamas hideout in Taiba, an Israeli Arab town not far from Netanya. In the two-story apartment building were six terrorists and three bombs that were destined to be exploded simultaneously in three high-rise buildings in Netanya that day. During the siege three of the terrorists were killed—one by Israeli gunfire and two from one of their bombs exploding—one was arrested and two managed to escape.

The father of one of the dead terrorists said his son had entered Israel by using the "safe passage" route with a permit issued by the Israeli security forces.[210] The possibility that the whole terror group had used the "safe passage" route to enter Israel was being investigated.[211] "Safe-passage" indeed! Safe for whom?

Ehud Barak was Israel's most decorated soldier and Israel's 14th Chief of General Staff. Active military commanders are concerned about their nation's defense and security and also the morale of the fighting men. However, it is a sad fact of life that the majority of those men, when placed in high profile political positions, quickly lose concern for the defense and security of their country and bow before their obsession with their personal political image. In 1992, Yitzhak Rabin stated categorically:

> ...it is inconceivable that even in peacetime we should come down from the Golan. Whoever even thinks of leaving the Golan wantonly abandons, wantonly abandons, the security of Israel.[212]

Yet in 1993, he was ready to withdraw fully from the Golan at the behest of U.S. President Clinton.

Ehud Barak was Israel's Chief of Staff in 1993, and he argued with Yitzhak Rabin against withdrawing from the Golan Heights. Rabin rebuked Barak for saying publicly:

> From a military standpoint, the IDF must retain control of the Golan Heights, even in peace time.[213]

After donning the prime minister's hat, however, Barak became willing—nay, eager—to hand the entire Golan to Syria, and to dismantle the cities and towns that Israelis have spent 25 years of their lives building. He became ready to evacuate, forcefully if necessary, over 18,000 Israelis from their homes—all at the behest of U.S. President Bill Clinton.

Clinton is desperate to be written up in history books for "brokering" a Middle East "peace," not for turning the White House into a regular house of ill fame. That such a highly intelligent and courageous soldier like Barak would do the bidding of a sexual deviant and draft dodger boggles the imagination. This writer is convinced there has to be an extremely lucrative payoff to Barak somewhere along the line. But that payoff will pale into nothingness when compared to the payoff God will hand out on Judgment Day.

The Wye River Agreement negotiated by Netanyahu in November 1998 was the best agreement negotiated by Israel since the PLO–Israel "peace" process kicked off five years earlier. Yet Netanyahu's government fell because of it, and a radical secular humanist Hellenistic party came into power.

Many thousands of ardent Christians, in Israel and around the world, prayed that God would put the man He wanted into power. So, either prayer is of no value or God put Barak into power. Knowing the answer to the first hypothesis gives us the answer to the second—Barak sits in Israel's helmseat because God wants him in it. Therefore, it is this writer's firm conviction that

God has fully determined to strip off the militarily strategic sections of Israel's inheritance and give it over to its enemies.

7

The "Piece" Process

Our daily lives are affected by decisions reached in Washington, Moscow, Bonn, Paris or London—decisions in which we have no voice. We are simply pawns in a great ideological chess game played by the world's power brokers. Pawns are often sacrificed in order to obtain strategic positions on the game board. Thus, it is in politics and, thus, it is in bids for world domination.

The word "politic" has a number of definitions: "shrewd"; "artfully contrived"; and "expedient, as a plan;" are but some of them.[1] Definitions of "shrewd" include, "evil;" "bad;" "sly;" and "wicked."[2] Among definitions of "artful" are, "artificial;" "cunning;" and "crafty."[3] The word "expedient" is defined in part as, "convenient under the circumstances;" "advantageous;" "contributing or tending to contribute to present advantage or self interest;" and "any means which may be employed to accomplish an end."[4] Here, then, is politics defined:

> An evil, crafty, artificial, self-interest game using any means to gain advantage and progress toward accomplishing a contrived plan.

Knowing the true nature of politics gives an understanding for why it spawns a particular brand of person who is, more often than not, a pathological liar with a conveniently short memory.

When it comes to the Arab-Israeli conflict in the Middle East, world leaders' memories become extremely short. They "forget" that it was a Jewish chemist that saved Britain from losing WWI, and in return the British Government promised to establish a Jewish National Home in all of Palestine, if it defeated the Turks and Germans in the Holy Land.[5] They "forget" that Britain treacherously lopped off 77 percent of the promised Jewish National Home and gave it to Abdullah Ibn Hussein.[6] In their rush to establish a PLO-controlled state of "Palestine" today, world leaders "forget" there is already a homeland for "Palestinians" in existence—a country named Jordan. They "forget" that Abdullah Ibn Hussein originally wanted his country to be called "The Hashemite Kingdom of

Palestine," but gave in to British pressure and accepted Transjordan (now "The Hashemite Kingdom of Jordan").[7] They "forget" that 70 percent of the population of Jordan today is "Palestinian." They "forget" that Jordan has 28 percent less of a population than Israel,[8] but its land area is 336 percent bigger than Israel.[9] These same leaders "forget" that in 1981 the late King Hussein of Jordan said, in Paris: "The truth is that Jordan is Palestine and Palestine is Jordan."[10] They "forget" that three years later he repeated the same conviction in Kuwait: "Jordan is Palestine... Jordan in itself is Palestine."[11]

They "forget" that Prince Hussein, while he was still the Crown Prince and heir to the throne of Jordan, said, "Palestine is Jordan and Jordan is Palestine. There is one people and one land, with one history and one destiny."[12] They "forget" that PLO head Yasser Arafat has also stated: "What you call Jordan is actually Palestine."[13] They "forget" that Arafat's deputy, Abu Iyad, said, too, with regard to the Jordanians and those under PLO rule today, "We are one and the same people."[14] But, today the politicians want to create yet another Palestinian country, at Israel's expense again.

World leaders "forget" that Palestine was a virtual uninhabited wasteland for centuries, and that it was the Jewish cultivation and development of the late 19th and early 20th centuries that enticed Arabs to immigrate to Palestine from other countries.[15] They "forget" it was the Arab nations that initiated every Arab-Israeli war. They "forget" that the land the Arabs are now demanding is what Israel won in its wars of self defense. And they "forget" that the Supreme Soviet—referring specifically to the Soviet Union's occupation of Eastern Europe during and after World War II when it defeated Nazi invading forces—formulated the following:

> A people which has been attacked, has defended itself and wins wars, is bound by sacred duty to establish for itself in perpetuity a political situation which will ensure the liquidation of the sources of aggression. It is entitled to maintain this state of affairs as long as the danger of aggression does not cease.
>
> A nation which has attained security at the cost of numerous victims, will never agree to the restoration of the previous borders. No territories are to be returned as long as the danger of aggression still prevails.[16]

This applied to enemy lands captured by the Soviets, and it was fully acceptable to the international community. What was good for the Soviet Union, however, is not allowable for Israel. The international community, including Russia, calls for Israel to return captured land and withdraw to its boundaries of yesteryear.

Lessons from History

Georg Wilhelm Friedrich Hegel left these immortal words: "History teaches us that man learns nothing from history." The reason men learn nothing from history is found in the words of one defined by God as a "*fool,*"[17]—former Israeli prime minister Shimon Peres: "History is nonsense."[18] And, as George Santayana has said, "Those who do not learn from history are doomed to repeat it."[19] Thus we have a continuous cycle of men repeating the mistakes of history because they are too obtuse to learn anything from it.

The conquest of Czechoslovakia was central to Adolf Hitler's plans for overrunning Europe. Czechoslovakia was a small country strategically placed in the heart of Europe and possessed one of Europe's strongest armies. It could field over 800,000 men, and its arms industry was renowned and highly efficient.

Complicating matters further for Hitler was the physical barrier of the Sudeten mountain range that bordered Germany. The mountains guarded access to Czechoslovakia's heart as well as Prague, its capital. Over the years the mountain passes had been extremely well fortified by the Czechs, making any assault on them very costly in terms of men and equipment. Hitler's generals were unanimous in their opposition to any attempt to try and force a passage through. They felt the cost would be too great, the chance of success almost impossible.

With the military option ruled out by his generals, Hitler opted for a "diplomatic" solution. He planned to politically force the Czechs to give up the mountain passes, and by doing so, render Czechoslovakia defenseless.

Hitler embarked on a campaign to convince the Western powers, especially England and France, that 3,000,000 Germans lived in Sudeten and, therefore, Sudeten rightfully belonged to Germany. The Sudeten Germans enjoyed economic prosperity and full civil rights, but Hitler's propaganda minister Paul Josef Goebbels produced an awesome campaign that presented them as "oppressed" and living under "occupation."

Hitler created and funded a Sudeten political organization subservient to his needs—one that demanded so much that it was impossible to satisfy. The German minority in Czechoslovakia was only a subterfuge, but it provided plausible rationale to Hitler's plan to have the Sudetenland annexed to Germany. The leaders of England and France were unable to see the wood for the trees. Hitler convinced them that all he wanted was justice for his German brothers. Hitler said his Sudeten brethren must have the right of "self-determination," and must also be brought out from under "Czech occupation."

Hitler organized well planned, violent uprisings which the Czechs had to put down by force. Then he presented the Czechs as being the obstacle to world peace. Hitler continually stiffened his demands until he wanted the Sudetenland occupied by the German army and the Czechoslovaks evacuated from the area by September 28, 1938. If his demands were not met, said Hitler, the whole region would be thrown into war. Hitler continued to make inflammatory speeches demanding that Germans in Czechoslovakia be reunited with their homeland, and war seemed imminent.

France had a military alliance with Czechoslovakia, and Britain was committed to standing by France. These powers were not prepared to defend Czechoslovakia, however, and both were anxious to avoid a military confrontation with Germany at almost any cost. French Premier Édouard Daladier and Britain's Prime Minister Neville Chamberlain embarked on a journey of appeasement of Hitler at Czechoslovakia's expense. Hitler kept making demands, and the Czechs were forced by Britain and France to comply.

In September, in a last-minute effort to avoid war, Chamberlain, Daladier, and the Italian dictator Benito Mussolini met in Munich. Mussolini produced what became known as the "Munich Agreement." Years later the so-called Italian plan was found to have been prepared in the German Foreign Office. The Agreement was signed. The German army was to complete the occupation of the Sudetenland, and an international commission would decide the future of other disputed areas.

Both Daladier and Chamberlain returned home to jubilant, crowds relieved that the threat of war had passed. Chamberlain told the British public that he had achieved "peace with honor. I believe it is peace in our time." Czechoslovakia was subsequently informed by Britain and France that it could either resist Germany alone or submit to the prescribed annexations. The Czechoslovak government had no choice but to submit.

Chamberlain and Daladier were discredited the following year. Hitler annexed the remainder of Czechoslovakia in March and then precipitated World War II by invading Poland in September.

Land for Peace

The so-called "peace process" that the American, European, and Russian State Departments are foisting upon Israel does not resemble a real peace. Their actions are purely in their own respective political self-interests—they all wish to appease the Arab world and curry favor with it. America is heavily reliant upon Arab oil and all are eying the vast Arab market for arms and consumer goods.

The "peace process," they say, can only be built upon Israel's recognition of the principle of "land for peace." Perhaps they should have begun by asking the American Indians how successful the principle of "land for peace" was for them!

According to the nations' State Department experts, and the news media, the reason for the continuous state of war between Israel and the Arabs is because Israel is occupying Arab land. By endless repetition, this line of political propaganda has been engraved upon people's minds. The Arabs, however, were making war against Israel when the Arabs held the land—that is how they came to lose it! Israel's very existence is the problem—within any boundary. When the Arab world demands a "just peace," it is saying in effect that "peace" can only come when Israel no longer exists and there are "just" Arab nations in the Middle East.

History Repeated

From the day following David Ben-Gurion's declaration of the state of Israel on May 14, 1948, Arab armies have repeatedly attacked Israel in bids to destroy it. Each war saw multiples of larger and better equipped armies attack Israel. When the Arabs lost the fourth war in 1973 they ruled out the military option—temporarily. Outnumbering the IDF four-to-one in men and machines and having the advantage of a surprise attack, the Arab armies were again decimated within days by Israel. Realizing that "diplomacy" was the only way to defeat Israel, the Arab leaders opted for a "political" solution.

Many Westerners think Arabs generally are inclined to be a bit half-witted. This is very untrue and most unfair. Cultural differences can create great chasms between the ways people act and express themselves. And the Arab culture is such that most Westerners do not even begin to comprehend it at all. Arabs are better at many things than their Western counterparts. Arabs are often shrewd while Westerners can be somewhat naive, and Arab leaders will take full advantage of this.

Jews are credited with having the highest overall intelligence of any race, but as we have seen in our quotes, selfish ambition negates even the highest intelligence. Shimon Peres boasts of having a high IQ but says that "history is nonsense," thereby bearing out the truths of both Hegel and Santayana.[20] Palestine Liberation Organization (PLO) leader Yasser Arafat, on the other hand, thinks exactly the opposite of Peres. Arafat quotes the Arab proverb that one can "remedy the present only with the remedies of the past."[21] Arabs prove there are exceptions to Hegel's rule. They understand that by learning from the lessons in history they can effect the present. In the Middle East "peace process" they are proving to be avid students of history. Western leaders, however, have apparently not gotten any smarter than Chamberlain and Daladier—they are unable to see the forest for the trees, too.

Shades of Munich

Like most Muslim Arabs, Yasser Arafat is a keen admirer of Adolf Hitler and keeps a copy of Hitler's *Mein Kampf* on his desk. Under Arafat's leadership the PLO adopted the two most important symbols of the Nazis, namely the portrayal of the eagle and the infamous raised-arm salute.

Arafat's uncle, Haj Amin al-Husseini, was the virulently anti-Semitic Grand Mufti of Jerusalem. The Mufti was a close confidant of Hitler and helped him plan "the final solution"—the mass extermination of Jews in Europe.

Yasser Arafat is not Arafat's real name. Arafat is a first name, not his family name. He took the name Yasser in memory of Yasser al-Birah, a leader of the Grand Mufti's reign of terror against the Jews in the 1930s.[22] Arafat's family name is al-Husseini.[23] He does not use his family name as he wants to hide the blood relationship to his uncle. Yitzhak Rabin's government overtly helped Arafat by having a very large and famous photograph of Hitler sitting with the Mufti removed from display in *Yad Vashem*—Israel's Holocaust museum in Jerusalem. The museum claims it does not know where the picture is today.

People like Haj Amin al-Husseini made the Holocaust possible. It needed a Hitler, a Himler, an Eichman and a Nazi leadership, but without the willing collaboration of the likes of Arafat's uncle, the scope of the Holocaust would have been greatly reduced.

The fourth Arab military attack in 1973 against an unprepared Israel ended in a humiliating defeat for the attackers. Therefore, since 1974, the PLO strategy for the destruction of Israel has been firmly modeled upon Hitler's "political" dealings with Czechoslovakia. The Arab world has organized a propaganda machine that would have won Goebbels's approval. It is funded with billions of Arab petrodollars and practically every news, educational, informational and travel medium has been impregnated by it.

The Arab propaganda campaign is aimed at delegitimatizing the Jews in their historic land. The Arabs have propagated hundreds of bald-faced lies which many millions of generally naive and gullible people with anti-Semitic tendencies have eagerly swallowed. Lies such as "Jews have no historical or religious ties to Palestine," or "Jerusalem has been an Arab city for 5,000 years," are ludicrous to the extreme, but are believed nonetheless. Indisputable biblical records and museum exhibits aside, one can easily visit the ancient tombs of Israel's kings and prophets dating back 3,000 years or more and realize the extent of Arab propaganda lies. But, as Hitler's propaganda chief Goebbels rightly argued, "a lie spreads in proportion to its size."[24]

Mix into this fearful anti-Israel propaganda stew a liberal use of brutal terror attacks against Israeli civilians, then season the pot well with organized, violent uprisings like the *intifada* and the mini war that greeted Israel's opening of the 2,200 year old Hasmonean Tunnel, and the message is clear: Israel is an "obstacle to world peace." It is obviously an expansionist, racist entity that has stolen ancient Arab lands, oppresses the true owners, and forces them to live a deprived life under brutal military occupation. "Peace" can only be assured when the "Palestinians" are out from under "Israeli occupation," have the "right of self determination," and the Jewish aggressors return all land "rightfully belonging to the Arabs."

Inflammatory speeches against Israel are made daily, and all of Hitler's cliches concerning Czechoslovakia have been taken from mothballs and used. And if the "just" demands of the PLO are not met, "the whole region will be thrown into war."

A "Palestinian Police Force" (the PLO army in disguise) must occupy the "liberated" land and all Jews must be "evacuated." In South Africa's parliamentary chamber in August 1998, Arafat called for "effective economic sanctions against the Israeli Government"[25] in order to force it to accede to PLO demands. Arafat went on to say,

> What is needed is real and effective pressure on the Israeli Government by the American Administration, European Union and international communities.[26]

Arafat was received with a "standing ovation."[27]

The land demanded by the PLO is biblical *Judea* and *Samaria* —*the **mountains** of Israel* (Ezekiel 6:23; 19:9; 33:28; 34:13, 14; 35:12; 36:1, 4, 8; 37:22; 38:8; 39:2, 4, 17), and it wants to see Syria in control of the Golan Heights—biblical *Bashan*, the inheritance of the tribe of Manasseh (Deuteronomy 4:43; Joshua 20:8, 21:27). Israel has its early warning systems installed upon the high mountain areas of *Judea*, *Samaria* and the *Golan*. Technological developments have not eliminated the strategic value of observation points on mountain tops. The loss of the high ground, the early warning systems, and the room to manoeuvre its military equipment renders Israel virtually defenseless.

Nearly 80 percent of Israel's water comes from aqueducts under *Judea* and *Samaria* and from springs on the *Golan*. Deprived of life-giving water, Israel could be overrun by its enemies within days, certainly within weeks.

America says it understands Israel's problems, but pressures Israel to give up the territory nevertheless. The current U.S. administration has even offered to guarantee Israel's security. In the past, however, America has broken practically every pledge it ever made to Israel in the military sphere. There is little reason for Israel to believe America would act differently in the future. It is a strategic fallacy to attach great importance to signed agreements and to believe that political entities are bound by them. Nations abide by agreements only as long as it is in their interest to do so. Another "Munich Agreement" could be produced in the PLO's

Foreign Office and get presented to Israel as an "American initiative."

National Suicide

Secret negotiations took place between some of Yitzhak Rabin's "*fools*" and PLO officials in Oslo, Norway, in 1993. The fruit of these clandestine meetings—strictly forbidden by Israel's Order for Prevention of Terrorism—is officially called the "Oslo Accords." The PLO has found the fruit sweet to its taste. For Israel, however, the fruit has proven to be bitter and rancid. The begetting of the Oslo Accords was tainted, their birth was illegitimate, and they have effected the most unmitigated manifestations of Palestinian hatred and resentment for Israel. The Oslo Accords are not only a mixture of self-delusion and self-destruction, they are also a mockery. Oslo was the beginning of the process of Israel's self-destruction. Indeed, Oslo is a four-letter word for "suicide."

On November 17, 1973, Jonatan (Yoni) Netanyahu, re-membered among the greatest of Israel, wrote:

> … I see with sorrow and great anger how a part of the people still clings to hopes of reaching a peaceful settlement with the Arabs. Common sense tells them, too, that the Arabs haven't abandoned their basic aim of destroying the State; but the self-delusions and self-deception that have always plagued the Jews are at work again. It's our great misfortune. They want to believe, so they believe. They want not to see, so they shut their eyes. They want not to learn from thousands of years of history, so they distort it. They want to bring about a sacrifice, and they do indeed. It would be comic if it wasn't so tragic.[28]

Oslo

Many Norwegians are proud of their country's secret "peace-making" efforts between Rabin's cadres and the PLO. Some of these proud Norwegians are born-again Christians. There are, however, thousands of born-again Christians in Norway who are convinced their country has sold Israel out to its enemies. They desire, hope and pray to see the Oslo Accords abrogated. Those making up this latter group obviously know both their Bibles and their God. They have not been fooled by Yasser Arafat like Chamberlain and Daladier were by Hitler.

Millions believe the Oslo Accords to be nothing less than a

courageous leap of faith by two traditional enemies in order to end a long and bloody conflict. They also believe the Norwegians who hosted the secret meetings between the parties are to be highly commended.

Yitzhak Rabin was known to be a man who crumpled under pressure. He took office in the beginning of July 1992, and almost immediately Syria test-fired two Scud C missiles capable of hitting any part of Israel. Syria's president Assad wanted to send Rabin a message, and he got it. Rabin quickly forgot all his election promises and scuttled to recognize the PLO terrorist organization, throwing the "peace process" into overdrive.

Under Yasser Arafat's leadership, the PLO terror groups carried out hundreds of attacks around the world—"bombings, shootings, hijackings, rocket attacks and kidnappings in 26 countries."[29] Arafat is responsible for the shedding of more Jewish blood than anyone since Hitler. Even so, most of his victims and more than 90 percent of the thousands of hostages were not Israelis.[30] Terror won Arafat fame and fortune as the godfather of international terrorism, but terror could not destroy the state of Israel. He switched tracks to those which Hitler used for the conquest of Czechoslovakia. Hitler fooled England's Chamberlain and France's Daladier and was nominated for the Nobel Peace Prize. Arafat has outdone Hitler. He has duped most of the world and took receipt of the Nobel Peace Prize in December 1994.

Far from being a courageous leap of faith, it was Rabin's faithlessness and fear that drove him to shake the bloodstained hand of Israel's worst enemy. And it was Islam and its hatred of Jews that brought Arafat to the "bargaining table." So, we might ask, what made the Norwegians host secret meetings? What was their motivation?

Responsibility for the initiation and mediation of the secret meetings between Rabin's godless government and the PLO belongs to Terje Roed Larsen and his wife, Mona Juul. Roed Larsen was Norwegian planning minister in Prime Minister Thorbjoern Jagland's government. He was also director of the Institute of Applied Social Science (FAFO) in Norway. His involvement with FAFO ended abruptly in 1996, when he was deeply implicated in a financial scandal involving FAFO funds to the tune of millions of Norwegian kroner.[31] Roed Larsen was formerly involved in the "upper echelons of the druid organization."[32] He is a former member of the Marxist-Leninist faction of Norway's Workers Communist Party (AKP-ml), and also of the country's Labor Party Youth Organization (AUF).[33]

Roed Larsen holds strong anti-Israel and pro-Arab views. He was on the editorial committee of the Norwegian publication *Palestine News* (Issue No. 1) when it stated:

> Fight the Zionist State of Israel, U.S. imperialism, and the enemies of the Palestinian people in the Arab world. "No" to a two-state solution—support the battle for the liberation of all of Palestine.[34]

In May 1994, the UN's Arab secretary general Boutros Boutros-Ghali created a brand-new post for Terje Roed Larsen, and he became UN deputy secretary general for the Middle East.[35] It was fairly stated that same year that, "Nowhere is raw anti-Semitism more blatant than in the UN itself."[36]

Roed Larsen lived and worked in Gaza where his office was located. He was responsible for formulating the plan which led to the introduction of the Norwegian Observer Force in Hebron. Concerning the Force, it was reported in an Israeli news broadcast: "The Norwegian Observer Force in Hebron is 'Anti-Israel.' They take almost no notice of Arab stone-throwing, etc. It was the PLO who asked them to come."[37] Similarly, the Norwegian UNIFIL unit in Lebanon has also been anti-Israel. When Israeli soldiers captured a PLO bunker in Lebanon during the 1982 Peace for Galilee operation, they found "a written agreement between the commander of the Norwegian UNIFIL unit and the PLO that promised non-interference by the Norwegians in any terrorist activity that took place in their zone."[38]

Roed Larsen's wife, Mona Juul, was head of the Norwegian Prime Minister's Bureau, and as such was involved in organizing some of the clandestine arrangements.[39] Juul is currently the No. 2 diplomat in the Norwegian Embassy in Tel Aviv.[40]

Prime Minister Gro Harlem Brundtland formed her first government in 1981 as Norway's youngest and first female prime minister.[41] Brundtland was a "long time fan"[42] of Yasser Arafat and continued to speak "glowingly"[43] of him following their meeting in 1983. Twelve years later she took the arch-terrorist by the hand and led him along the red carpet to receive the Nobel Peace Prize.[44]

Brundtland stepped down in October 1996 and took over the reins of the World Health Organization.

Thorbjoern Jagland, a "leftist radical,"[45] succeeded Brundtland as Norway's premier. During his inauguration as Brundtland's successor Jagland

> revealed his long-term love affair with the PLO when he proudly recalled his meeting 'in the darkness of the night' with Arafat in Beirut in 1978.[46]

This was during the time

> when the PLO was raping and pillaging Lebanon, and hijacking and killing civilians on buses in Israel.[47]

On assuming office Jagland immediately appointed Terje Roen Larsen to his cabinet even though he apparently knew of the FAFO funds scandal.[48] Two weeks later, however, the scandal broke, and one month later Roen Larsen was forced to resign his new post.[49] Jagland's first foreign guest was Yasser Arafat.[50] Jagland said he was "happy his first official duty as prime minister was to greet Arafat,"[51] and Arafat acknowledged "I am here to get help from our Norwegian friends."[52]

Tom Berntzen is chief of the News department of NRK, Norway's pro-PLO television station. Berntzen is Jagland's brother-in-law.

Johann Joergen Holst was Foreign Minister in Brundtland's government and was a "long-term friend of Arafat."[53] Holst was involved in the secret meetings and oversaw the signing of the Oslo Agreement. He died suddenly of an "apparent stroke"[54] just four months after the signing. He was married to Marianne Heiberg.

Marianne Heiberg was involved in the secret meetings between the PLO and Rabin's government. Heiberg conducted research at the FAFO when Roed Larsen was the director-general.[55] She was a researcher of Palestinian economic conditions in Gaza[56] and is currently director of the United Nations Relief and Works Agency (UNRWA) in Jerusalem which deals with Arab "refugee" relief.[57]

Bjoern Tore Godal became foreign minister after the death of Holst and had been involved with the secret Oslo meetings. Godal is a close friend of Terje Roed Larsen,[58] and is a former chairman of the AUF. In his capacity as chairman of the AUF Godal approved the following statement:

> The AUF will support the forces which struggle for the national and social liberation of the Palestinian people. The qualification for lasting peace must be that Israel ceases to exist as a Jewish state, and that a progressive Palestinian state is established where all ethnic groups can live side by side in complete equality.[59]

The Norwegian daily *Dagen* described the AUF resolution as "the turning point in Norway's previously warm relations with Israel."[60] Godal remains "a strong advocate of a Palestinian state."[61]

Godal was elated when his friend Roed Larsen was asked by former UN Secretary-General Boutros Boutros-Ghali to be his deputy in Gaza. Godal said:

> We had wanted a stronger role for the UN in the Middle East and this will contribute to that.[62]

With his friend Roed Larsen sitting in Gaza forming plans to install the first foreign presence in Israel, Godal saw his dream move toward fulfillment. And on May 14, 1996 Godal arrived in Hebron to see the redeployment of the Observer Force[63] comprising 120 Norwegians, Italians and Danes.

Knut Frydenlund, a former Norwegian foreign minister, was also involved in the clandestine Oslo meetings. He had visited Arafat in Tunis shortly after Israel expelled the PLO from Lebanon. Frydenlund personally found Arafat to be a sincere person and held this view until his death.

Thorvald Stoltenberg was another Norwegian midwife who helped deliver the Oslo monstrosity. Stoltenberg was a former foreign minister and had also visited Arafat in Tunis after his expulsion from Beirut. Stoltenberg was enamored with Arafat.

Jan Egeland was departmental secretary for the Norwegian Foreign Affairs Office and was involved in the secret meetings in Oslo. Egeland was a former head of Amnesty International in Norway.[64] Amnesty International has been biased against Israel almost since its inception. Most every year Israel must protest Amnesty's report on Israel. In 1989, even

> the Israeli Justice Ministry lambasted Amnesty's latest report on Israel as "biased, unbalanced and lacking in objectivity."[65]

No, the Norwegians are not to be commended. The apparent desire of the Norwegian leaders involved in the Oslo process is to see the

State of Israel replaced by a second Arab Palestinian state. This has always been the prime objective of both the Arab and Muslim worlds and now their reasons for participation in the "peace process."

In 1994 United Nations' Secretary-General Boutros Boutros-Ghali said:

> The Jews must give up their status as a nation and Israel as a state, and assimilate as a community in the Arab world.[66]

The alternative, he predicted, would be "repeated wars."[67] In 1996 Egypt's Foreign Minister Amr Moussa said the same thing in different words. He said that

> within the framework of the overall peace arrangements, Israel will return to its natural stature, in other words, with no ability to threaten Arabs, and in the end will be absorbed into the Arab expanse.[68]

Boutros-Ghali and Moussa are both speaking for the Arab and Muslim worlds and their message is clear: There is no room in the Muslim Middle East for a Jewish state. Israel must cease to exist as a state, and the Jews are to be accorded *dhimmi* status—second class citizens with little or no rights—and absorbed into the Arab milieu.

Israeli super*fool* Shimon Peres was one of the main paladins of the "peace initiative" involving the PLO, and was in attendance at the final secret meeting in Oslo. Spelling out his vision for a "New Middle East" in November 1994, Peres said he envisions an "integration of Israel into the Muslim Middle East."[69] Even as Peres hugs and kisses his new-found Muslim Arab leader friends, they continue working toward their vision for the region—the *dis*integration of Israel in the Muslim Middle East.

Since Norway birthed Oslo it has experienced its "worst economic crisis in a decade."[70] As the world's second largest exporter of oil and natural gas, Norway badly felt the 35 percent fall in world oil prices. The resulting speculation against the Norwegian Krone forced repeated rises in interest rates which in turn doubled mortgage rates, cutting home sales in half.[71] The nation's woes are matched by those of the pro-Oslo politicians—dead, disgraced and depressed. *Time* magazine called it Norway's "Dark Night of the Soul."[72]

Kjell Magne Bondevik became Prime Minister in 1997 after

his Christian Democrat Party defeated Labor's Thorbjoern Jagland at the polls in September. Bondevik, an ordained Lutheran minister, made several election promises regarding Israel, but failed to keep any of them. As a Christian minister Bondevik should know that Israel's God clearly says:

> *I will bless those who bless you, and I will curse him who despises you* (Genesis 12:3 literal translation).

Instead, Bondevik sided with the pro-Oslo crowd and the PLO against Israel. He became sick and depressed, and was forced to seek prayer from his father.[73] Bondevik's government was short-lived. It lost a parliamentary vote of confidence in March 2000, and left-wing Jens Stoltenberg of the pro-Oslo Labor party was then asked by Norway's King Harald to form a new government. Jens Stoltenberg is the son of Thorvald Stoltenberg who visited Arafat in Tunis after Israel drove him and his PLO terrorist forces from Beirut.

Charades

Israel's main "partner" in the peace charade is the PLO. The very definition of peace includes the absence of violence and war, but the PLO has never even tried to hide its true intentions. For Yasser Arafat, "diplomacy" has never been more than a war conducted by other means. He continues to wear a quasi military uniform with a gun on his hip, and sports a beard stubble representing the growth that a frontline soldier would grow in the trenches. His *keffiyeh* (head covering) is always meticulously arranged into the form of the state of Israel to depict what he is fighting for. Arafat is sending visual messages to the Arab and Muslim worlds—and anyone else who cares enough to look—that he is fully occupied in fighting a war for the destruction of the state of Israel.

Inflammatory and inciteful speeches are Arafat's hallmark and in September 1966, he made several such speeches in a period of a few days. In Gaza on September 24, he addressed his "security forces"—the 45,000 man[74] "police force" that Rabin and Peres equipped with machine guns—

> We will fight for the cause of Allah and kill and be killed, and this is a solemn oath... Our blood is cheap compared with the cause which has brought us together ... Palestine is our land and Jerusalem is our capital.[75]

Two days later his PLO "policemen," on joint patrols with IDF soldiers, suddenly turned their guns on the unprepared Israelis killing 16 of them.

A member of the PLO "negotiating" team and its head man in Jerusalem, Feisal al-Husseini—Arafat's cousin and grand-nephew of Hitler's confidant and ally, the Grand Mufti Haj Amin al-Husseini —said publicly in November 1994, 14 months after the Oslo Accords were signed:

> Peace for us means the destruction of Israel. We are preparing for an all-out war... we have become the most dangerous enemy that Israel has. We shall not rest... until we destroy Israel.[76]

On August 4, 1999 Arafat celebrated his 70th birthday. To mark the occasion he told his many well-wishers:

> Allah willing, we will continue with our struggle, our Jihad... and once again enter the city of Jerusalem as the Muslims did for the first time.[77]

When the Muslims entered Jerusalem for the first time in 638 A.D. the Byzantine Christians surrendered without a struggle. The subsequent treaty drawn up between the Muslims and the Byzantine rulers included a condition that prohibited Jews from settling in the city. It was to this that Arafat referred.

Those responsible for the Oslo agreements, and those laying the foundations for a new state of "Palestine," turn blind eyes and deaf ears to PLO violence and rhetoric.

International donors are pouring billions of dollars into the Palestinian autonomous areas with the expectation of reaping huge profits once Arafat formally declares a state of "Palestine." According to an internal audit conducted in mid-1997, however, 40 percent of the Palestinian Authority's budget could not be accounted for.[78] Even the proven fact that $323 million of their cash was siphoned off into private bank accounts held by Arafat and his top aides in one year did not deter the champions of greed— "They told Arafat privately to **clean up his act.**"[79]

Biting the hand that feeds them, Nabil Sha'ath, a high ranking PLO official, said in an interview with Radio Monte Carlo concerning the corruption:

> To my sorrow, the corruption is in the contributing states, not in the Palestinian Authority. They don't give money directly

to the PA, but channel it through the World Bank and the UN Development Project (UNDP) to contractors and suppliers. The PA gets nothing. Europe's problem is the corruption in the European Community, which affects the PA.[80]

The most ludicrous reaction to the wholesale corruption in Arafat's administration came from the womb that bore the Oslo fiasco. A Norwegian government official explained to the nation's taxpayers on television that the stolen millions were moneys that came from other donor countries—donated Norwegian money was not involved. Norwegians have a reputation for being "blue eyed." Those that swallowed their government's "explanation" certainly deserve that reputation.

Arafat was "publicly claiming 'bankruptcy'"[81] when the PLO began to receive billions of dollars in aid from Western donor countries, including $500 million a year from the U.S.[82] All recipients of U.S. aid must open their books to Congress, but the General Accounting Office (a branch of the U.S. Congress) met "a solid stone wall"[83] when it asked to see the PLO's books.

Congress "slapped a hold on U.S. funds to the PA"[84] until it obtained the information it wanted. A report was filed detailing the secret assets of Arafat and the PLO, and an informed source, familiar with the contents of the report, could only confirm that Arafat and the PLO held over $10 billion in assets.[85] These assets are controlled only by Arafat,[86] and at a time when thousands of Gazans were without jobs, food or medical supplies, he was sitting upon a literal mountain of gold. And between 1995 and 1997, the Government of Israel had also paid over one billion dollars into Arafat's private bank account in Tel Aviv.[87] Today, the Barak government continues to pay NIS 35 million ($8.3 million) each month into Arafat's account.[88]

Fulfilled Obligations

Much of the wording of the Oslo Agreement was the brain child of Shimon Peres. In May 1993, Peres repeated what he had said on several occasions previously, namely: "Only Israel can give, while the Palestinians can only take."[89] Such statements should win Israel a place in the Guinness Book of Records! History surely cannot have any precedent where a country enters into negotiations by telling its enemies it expects nothing from them. It is too ludicrous for words.

As stipulated under the terms of the Oslo Agreement, Israel has handed thousands of square kilometers of land to the PLO as well as billions of dollars in cash.[90] Israel has released thousands of Arabs who were imprisoned for their involvement in terror attacks against Israel, and allows over 100,000 Palestinians to find employment inside Israel every day.[91] Despite what the pundits have to say, Israel has fulfilled all of its obligations under Oslo, and more besides. The PLO falls very far short of this.

PLO Violations: PNC Covenant

The Oslo Agreement was signed on September 13, 1995. Yasser Arafat signed on behalf of the PLO and agreed first and foremost to cancel the clauses of the PLO Covenant that call for the destruction of Israel. He undertook to fight terrorism in every area under PLO control, to extradite to Israel Palestinians involved in terror attacks against Israel after the signing of the Oslo Agreement, and to refrain from inciting hatred against Israel in particular and Jews in general.

As mentioned above, Shimon Peres said that only Israel can give and should expect nothing from the PLO. Perhaps a ninth beatitude should be created just for Peres: "Blessed is he who expects nothing: for he shall not be disappointed." At the time of writing, more than six years have passed since Oslo was signed. The PLO Covenant remains an unchanged inspiration to Palestinians. Terrorism grew to mammoth proportions, and repeated requests by Israel for the extradition of Palestinian terrorists have all been completely ignored. Anti-Israel, anti-Jew and hate-filled rhetoric is the norm for members of the Palestinian Authority (PA), in its newspapers and television and radio programs. And neither has the PLO fulfilled any of its other Oslo obligations.

Thirty of the Palestine Liberation Organization's Covenant's 33 clauses call for Israel's destruction.[92] (Since no Palestinian state has ever existed, the Covenant defines "Palestine" by the borders of the British Mandate, a territory granted Britain by the League of Nations for the explicit purpose of establishing a Jewish national home.) The last three clauses deal with procedural matters and are devoid of references to the annihilation of Israel. The final clause 33 states that a two-thirds majority of all PLO National Council members may amend the covenant.

From day one Israel received promises from Arafat that the

Covenant would be amended. By the end of 1995 Israel had handed to Arafat full control of seven major cities of *Judea* and *Samaria*, plus complete civilian control and partial security control of some 400 villages.[93] Even Yitzhak Rabin got tired of unfulfilled promises and issued Arafat with an ultimatum:

> fulfill your undertaking regarding the Covenant, or we halt the negotiations.[94]

Arafat promised, but no amendment of the Covenant took place.

Following Rabin's assassination in November 1995, Peres reaffirmed the ultimatum for appearance's sake:

> If the clauses weren't gone by March 1996 the "train" of the peace process would "stop."[95]

Arafat promised. March came and went, but no removal took place.

Amid great fanfare the Palestine National Council (PNC) finally met on April 24, 1996, to discuss changes in the Covenant. A two-thirds majority of its official 669 membership[96] was required to amend it. After a short debate it was announced that the PNC had voted by a 504 vote majority[97] to amend clauses in the Covenant that called for Israel's destruction. A flurry of headlines and articles from the pens of animated Israeli and foreign journalists greeted their equally wishful-thinking readers: PNC VOTES TO AMEND PALESTINIAN COVENANT;[98] PLO FINALLY CONCEDES ISRAEL IS HERE TO STAY;[99] COVENANT HEADED FOR OVERHAUL[100] etc. Shimon Peres was beside himself and described the vote as "the most important development in our region in a hundred years."[101] More important, obviously, than the founding of the Jewish state 48 years earlier.

A non-euphoric headline was: NETANYAHU CAUTIOUS OVER COVENANT CHANGES.[102] Bibi Netanyahu cautioned against cheering changes in the PLO Covenant, "because," he said, "these amendments are not at all clear-cut at the moment."[103] Netanyahu advised waiting until the dust had settled before hailing the event as "historic" as Peres had rushed to do.
Netanyahu's caution subsequently proved itself to be good advice indeed, but it fell mainly on deaf ears.

The Institute for Peace Education had sent an Arab TV crew to cover the convening of the Palestine National Council. Their video recording shows that after a debate by members of the PNC Arafat had called for a vote. At this crucial point "Arafat's lieutenants ordered all foreign press to leave."[104] Being Arab, the Institute's crew remained.[105] Arafat then announced that

> the vote would be on the subject of referring the whole matter to a newly formed "PNC legal committee" with a recommendation for changes in a session of the PNC that would take place at an unspecified date.[106]

Arafat's lieutenants then summoned the foreign press corps back and "informed them that the PNC had changed its covenant."[107] The following morning the Palestinian news media was filled with reports that "the matter was deferred to a future meeting."[108]

Arafat sent a letter to Shimon Peres in which he informed him that "the Covenant is hereby amended."[109] Peres distributed this in the Israeli government. Arafat sent another letter to the American Consulate General in Jerusalem. The original Arabic states that "a decision was made 'to amend' (*ta'dil*) the Covenant,"[110] and this was sent to Washington. The translation distributed by Peres translates the Arabic inaccurately, but the translation sent to Washington translates it correctly.[111] The fact that Arafat sent Peres an incorrect translation should clearly indicate to everyone that the PNC show was a staged sham.

One of the most valid criticisms the Netanyahu-led Likud had of the Oslo process was that the Rabin and Peres's governments essentially allowed Arafat to sell them the same merchandise three times over. Under the 1993 Oslo Accords, Israel granted the PLO diplomatic recognition in exchange for a promise that the PLO would amend its covenant. The 1994 Cairo Agreement gave the PLO control of Gaza and Jericho in exchange for the same promise. The 1995 Interim Agreement gave the PLO seven major cities in *Judea* and *Samaria*, plus civilian control of most of the smaller towns and villages there, in exchange for yet another promise that the PLO covenant would be amended.

After buying the same goods three times over Rabin issued Arafat with an ultimatum, but was assassinated. Peres reissued the ultimatum and set a firm deadline. The deadline passed quietly by without a whimper of protest. Arafat staged a 600-man show under the bright lights of the world's media, but put the foreign media out at the crucial moment. He declared the Covenant amended and sent Peres a letter to that effect. Peres was fooled completely and declared Arafat's hoax an "historic breakthrough."[112] The U.S.

State Department received from Arafat a letter with wording differing to what Arafat sent to Peres. Arafat stated only that a "decision was made to amend the Covenant," and not "the Covenant is hereby amended."

U.S. Secretary of State Warren Christopher, however, issued a statement that "confirmed" the PNC had "canceled its Covenant calling for the destruction of Israel."[113] Christopher was fully aware that the Covenant had not been canceled. He knew the PNC had only made a decision to cancel it sometime in the future (presumably this would be after the demise of Israel when the Covenant would be obsolete). Thus the U.S. State Department became an accomplice in Arafat's conspiracy by publishing a demonstrable lie. Christopher compounded the offence by also saying that the PLO had lived up to

> the U.S. requirements for the Palestinian Authority to receive $100 million in annual aid.[114]

Arafat was duly rewarded with the ultimate American gesture of recognition and respect—President Clinton received Arafat at the Oval Office. Afterwards, Arafat was a guest at the National Press Club in Washington. According to *Associated Press*, when Arafat was asked, "Have the Palestinians changed their dream of taking control of all of Palestine", Arafat became "suddenly angry,"[115] saying, "I, I not answer this—this is unfair question."[116]

Netanyahu was correct with his warning to exercise caution before celebrating the Covenant's demise. The day following Arafat's declaration of the Covenant being "hereby amended" the Palestinian media reported that the matter had been "deferred to a future meeting." A few days later, an internal document of the Fatah faction of the PLO which Arafat heads, published this:

> The text of the Palestine National Covenant remains as it was, and no changes whatsoever were made to it.[117]

Libyan leader Muammar Gaddafi bore this out at a press conference when he said he had met with Arafat and was told "nothing has changed"[118] in the PLO Covenant. Gaddafi quoted Arafat as having told him that "the Palestinian Covenant hasn't been amended,"[119] and continued by saying:

> I am now reassured that the Palestinian Charter has not been abandoned.[120]

Nine months after his Gaza vaudeville act, Arafat made it quite clear that the Covenant calling for Israel's destruction has not been amended or abrogated. And in January 1997 interviews in Paris Arafat said he would "not amend the charter until Israel adopts a constitution."[121] Arafat also repeated this line to the Arabs living under PLO control.[122] In February 1998 the *Syrian News Agency* published a report on the PLO's latest Executive meeting. The report stated: "Samir 'Osha, a member of the Executive who participated in the meeting said that the Executive had refused to approve changes in the Charter...".[123]

After taking office as Israel's Prime Minister in mid-June 1996, Bibi Netanyahu requested a letter from Arafat listing the specific articles of the PLO Charter which had been annulled. He received a letter from Arafat on July 24, identical to the one sent to Shimon Peres in May.[124] Netanyahu was confident the April show was simply another Arafat ploy and insisted the Covenant be abrogated before Israel considers making further concessions to the PLO.

In December 1998, President Clinton made a visit to Israel and Gaza. Facing impeachment proceedings, Clinton needed something of a foreign policy success in order to enhance his image at home. He showed his disdain of Netanyahu by snubbing Israel in declining to address the Knesset as traditional protocol for visiting heads of state require,[125] and addressed "Palestine's provisional parliament" instead.

The purpose of Clinton's visit was ostensibly to move the "peace process" forward and, in particular, be present at a meeting in Gaza on December 14, 1998 where the Palestine National Council would "confirm" its decision to amend articles in the PLO Covenant calling for Israel's destruction.

When Arafat, in Clinton's presence, called for a show of hands, many went up and the "historic vote," as it was called, made the world jubilant once more. However, in an article published the previous day in the *Jerusalem Post*, an Israeli official had said U.S. negotiators had already worked out the voting procedure.[126] So, the vote was not at all spontaneous, but prearranged by Clinton officials.

Following Arafat's speech Clinton, in his address to the assembly, rewarded Arafat by telling the Palestinians "they were free to determine their own destiny on their own land".[127] This was in effect a U.S. defacto recognition of Arafat's longed for "Palestinian state." And Hilary Rodham Clinton is on record as having said, "it's time for a Palestinian state."[128] But any future Palestinian state would be another breach of the Oslo Accords and also another sellout of Israel by the U.S.

Most of the delegates who raised their hands to make the "historic vote," however, were not part of the PNC, but members of other Palestinian groups. And the media even pointed out at the time that many PNC members who did attend remained seated and did not raise their hands. So, besides the vote having been rigged earlier by the U.S., the PNC "vote" was also fraudulent by the simple fact that people without authority "voted" in the PNC's stead. If that were not enough, we also have a bogus "vote" by reason of the fact that there were a total of 727[129] delegates in attendance—including all the non-PNC members—and only 456[130] of these raised their hands in the "vote." The Covenant itself states that only a two-third majority vote of PNC members can alter it, and there was no such two-third majority "vote" even when all the "PNC stand-ins" raised their hands.

All 456 of those that raised their hands—whoever they were—they were still supposed to be confirming the nullifying of some 30 clauses in the PLO Covenant that call for Israel's destruction. We must, therefore, ask the following question: When exactly did this momentous decision to amend the Covenant take place? And we are told that this took place on April 24, 1996, when the 504 PNC members voted for the nullifying of the Covenant. But we already know, and have ample proof of the fact, that nothing of the sort took place. We know that all foreign journalists were put out while the PNC actually voted to postpone amending the Covenant, but went ahead and told the media and Israel that the Covenant had been amended.

Arafat is both crafty and a liar, but a liar requires a good memory which Arafat does not possess. In his speech immediately prior to the taking of the "historic vote" on December 1998 in Gaza, Arafat mentioned a letter he had sent to President Clinton in January 1998 detailing the clauses nullified in the Covenant. But, the reader should remember, the *Syrian News Agency* published a report in February 1998 stating that "the PLO Executive had refused to approve changes in the Charter"! The Covenant has been amended? Who is kidding whom?

Yasser Arafat went to a deal of trouble to come up with the "believable" PNC voting show for Clinton, but that was not the only show that Arafat produced and directed for his American benefactor. A week prior to Clinton's visit to Gaza a leaflet was distributed calling on residents to regard December 14, the date of Clinton's visit, "a special day of exacerbation in the clashes with Israel."[131] The leaflet was published by the Fatah faction of the PLO that Arafat personally heads, and the violent demonstrations against Israel were intensified for the duration of Clinton's visit. The violent Palestinian clashes with Israel were intensified expressly for Clinton's consumption, and the objective was to coerce him into increasing U.S. pressure on Israel.

Information obtained by the Israeli defence establishment showed the violent clashes "were personally ordered by Yasser Arafat and carried out with the encouragement and active involvement of PA officials."[132] For being such an accommodating man of peace, the Norwegians bestowed upon Arafat the prestigious Nobel Prize.

Same Goods Sold Over

The White House, the U.S. State Department, and the CIA are all aware of each of the reports mentioned in this chapter concerning the blatant deceit about the Covenant's nullification and are, therefore, parties to Arafat's deceit. The Rabin and Peres's governments bought the same rug three times from Arafat. After Netanyahu took hold of the reins the State Department pressured him hard to buy the rug for yet a fourth time. In exchange for handing Arafat territory, equivalent to some 13 times the size of Tel Aviv, U.S. Peace Envoy Dennis Ross would secure PLO "guarantees" that it would fulfill its commitments under the Oslo Accords.

At that time Netanyahu showed no interest in the bargain offered him, but Arafat, with the overt help of Clinton and the U.S. State Department, apparently managed to sell Netanyahu the rug also. After the December 1998 "historic vote" that never was, Netanyahu commented that

> five years after the signing of the Oslo Accords, the Palestinians had finally dumped their "covenant of death."[133]

But they have not "dumped their 'covenant of death,'" and have no intention of dumping it. Without the Covenant the PLO has no reason for existence.

Some want to play down the importance of the Covenant. The Israeli super*fool* Yossi Beilin said, "The Palestinian Covenant is a pathetic, outdated document."[134] To belittle the importance of the PLO Covenant is foolish in the extreme. What Beilin called "a pathetic, outdated document" is what a leading PLO member calls his "Bible."[135] The issue of the Covenant is obviously not trivial in the eyes of the PLO leadership, and Israel should take the matter of amending the Covenant very seriously.

On September 13, 1993, the same day that Yasser Arafat and Yitzhak Rabin signed the "peace agreement" on the White House lawn, Arafat made a speech in Arabic on *Jordan Television*:

> Since we cannot defeat Israel in war we do this in stages. We take any and every territory that we can of Palestine, and establish a sovereignty there, and we use it as a springboard to take more. When the time comes, we can get the Arab nations to join us for the final blow against Israel.[136]

A transcript of Arafat's speech was made available to the U.S. State Department. And the evidence presented above proving the Covenant has not been canceled, is also in the hands of the State Department in its original form. Despite this, the notoriously one-sided State Department and the U.S. news media still continue to pressure Israel into making further concessions to the PLO. This shows both the media's bias against Israel, and also that the U.S. State Department is not and cannot be an honest broker in the Middle East conflict.

PLO Violations: No crackdown on terror

Prior to the May 1999 elections, in the last days of Netanyahu's government, Netanyahu was unbending in his demand that the PLO fulfill its signed commitments before Israel made further concessions. For his insistence on reciprocity he was quickly branded worldwide as a "hardliner" and an "obstacle to peace."

The Oslo process got firmly bogged down in the mud of Arafat's aeons-long non-compliance. Netanyahu insisted the PLO crack down on the many terror groups operating freely from territory under its control. The PLO had long been providing safe refuge for terrorists. The head of the PLO Authority Preventative Security Service, Colonel Jibril Rajoub, said in a May 27, 1998 television broadcast that

> the Palestinian Authority openly approves of terrorist attacks against Israel as long as they do not implicate the Authority.[137]

Rajoub told his interviewer on _Al-Jazira_ television that the PA views the Hamas terror group "as part of the national and Islamic liberation movement," and outside of the areas under PLO control

> they can do as they wish... They can go to Jordan to carry out armed operations and they can also carry out such operations from Syria... At the top of my list of priorities is the Israeli occupation and not Hamas... We are not interested in arrests.[138]

Netanyahu demanded that Arafat take action to "rip out the heart" of Palestinian terrorism before the "peace" process could move ahead. And Arafat gave his response:

> We reject Israeli demands that we act against our brothers, and do not intend to accept dictates on this from anyone.[139]

U.S. "peace" envoy Dennis Ross told Netanyahu not to "force the issue."[140]

At least 21 terrorists wanted by Israel are currently serving in PA security forces under Jibril Rajoub.[141] Another fact is that in the five years that followed the signing of Oslo, more Israelis were killed by Palestinian terrorists than in the preceding 15 years.[142] Many attacks against Israelis are perpetrated by PLO "Policemen." The PLO "Police Force" is a stratagem used by Arafat to rebuild the PLO army that Israel destroyed in Lebanon.

Under the terms of the Wye River Agreement the PLO was permitted to raise its "police force" to a maximum number of 30,000 men. However, almost two years before the Wye agreement came into existence the number of PLO police was already more than 50,000[143]—exceeding the Wye limit by more than 66 percent. One policeman for every 45 residents makes the PLO autonomous areas the most heavily policed state in the world. However, Palestinian human rights activist Bassam Eid said in a January 1997 meeting in London that

> there were at least 80,000 "policemen," including preventative security officers, plainclothes agents and intelligence agents.[144]

This figure was corroborated by Israeli defense sources in September 1996, when they said they

> must contend with at least 80,000 Palestinian fighters with automatic weapons.[145]

When Arafat's police chief Ghazi Jabali was asked how he was going to reduce the current size of his police force to the permitted Wye level of 30,000, he airily replied that he would simply take thousands away "and give them another listing".[146]

In addition to Arafat's "regular" troops the PLO has also been training young Palestinians in preparation for street fighting. In September 1998, *United Press International (UPI)* reported that

> Arafat's Fatah faction of the PLO has just completed its third two-month training course in automatic weapons use and street fighting for young Palestinians.
>
> About 100 participants aged 11-20 were instructed in the use of automatic weapons, pistols and handguns.[147]

A course coordinator, Abdel Raouf Barbakh, said the participants were

> "very brave" as they trained in the use of Kalashnikovs (AK47 assault rifles), pistols and knives.[148]

UPI reported that

> blindfolded children demonstrated an ability to dismantle and reassemble M16 machine guns in seconds. Visiting journalists were also shown demonstrations of "street fighting skills and disarming techniques."[149]

Barbakh said: "This is a message to the Israeli government."[150]

Bibi Netanyahu got the message and was fully justified in demanding Arafat clamp down on terrorism and reduce the size of the PLO "Police Force" before any further concessions are made by Israel. He should have also forcefully brought to the notice of the U.S. administration and the international community that the UN Convention on the Rights of the Child prohibits the use of children in armed conflict.

PLO Violations: Refusal to disarm terror groups

Besides the huge force of armed men in the PLO army that hides under the guise of a "police force," there are thousands of Palestinians that belong to terror and militia groups. These men openly parade through the streets of Gaza and other PLO autonomous areas brandishing and often firing their machine guns. Arafat pledged himself to disarm all these groups and confiscate all their weapons, but six years after the signing of Oslo not one of these groups has been disarmed or disbanded.

Netanyahu had insisted the PLO carry out its commitment to confiscate the thousands of illegal weapons. PLO police chief Ghazi Jabali's solution to the unacceptable level of "policemen" is to take thousands away from the unacceptable figure and simply list them as something other than "policemen." When asked by the Palestinian media how he was going to solve the illegal weapons issue, PLO police chief Jabali said: "No problem—we will give their owners licenses".[151] An alternative solution was proposed by the PLO's representative to the Arab League Muhammed Sabih. Referring specifically to the thousands of illegal weapons held by the Hamas terror organization, Sabih said on Saudi Arabia's _Orbit Television_ that

> if Hamas succeeds in hiding them in areas where the Israel Army is present, they are free to do so.[152]

So, terrorist owners of illegal weapons in the PLO autonomous areas will either be issued with licenses, or they can hide them in Israeli controlled areas ready for use against Israelis. And the U.S. just turns a blind eye and calls this chicanery "compliance" by Arafat.

PLO Violations: Refusal to extradite terrorists

Under the terms of the Oslo Accords (Annex IV, Article II, 7) Arafat is obligated to turn over to Israel for trial anyone for whom Israel provides an arrest warrant and proof of involvement in terrorism. The governments of Rabin, Peres and Netanyahu had together made extradition requests for 45 terrorists.[153] Not only has every request been completely ignored, but Ami Ayalon, head of the GSS, told the Israeli cabinet that many of those wanted by Israel are serving in the PLO "security services."[154] And Palestinian security chief Jibril Rajoub has said:

> no Palestinian will ever be transferred to Israel, Oslo notwithstanding.[155]

In 1998 the PLO began executing Palestinians convicted of murdering Arabs. In March 1999, Raed Attar, a member of the

PLO "security forces," was sentenced to die by firing squad for shooting dead a PLO policeman who was trying to arrest him and two other "policemen."[156] All three of the Palestinians were wanted by Israel for the murder of Guy Ovadia, an Israeli army lieutenant, but the PLO had refused to extradite them.[157] Obviously, the murder of an Arab is a crime worthy of death, but the murder of Israelis merits promotion to the PLO "security services"—a euphemism for the PLO army.

PLO Violations: Continued release of convicted terrorists

As mentioned above, the terms of Oslo obligate Arafat to hand over any terrorist for whom Israel provides an arrest warrant and proof of involvement in terrorism. All 45 requests made for extradition have not only been ignored, but a number of the wanted terrorists have been taken into the PLO "security services."

The terrorists wanted by Israel are quickly traced and arrested by the PLO "police," soon after the murderous attacks against Israelis take place. Within days the terrorists are "tried" in a PLO court, found guilty, and sentenced from two to 10 years in prison. The same procedure is applied to the masterminds and other activists of the terror organizations from which the convicted murderers came. This rapid execution of PLO "justice" is meant for international consumption and, also, to keep the terrorists out of Israeli hands.

Within a short space of time, however, the imprisoned killers are quietly released in what has become known as the "revolving door" policy. Release can come within days of imprisonment, a few weeks or a few months, and in rare cases after a year or two for those having committed the more heinous attacks. Some of the released killers have soon gotten involved in further attacks against Israeli civilians.

After the signing of the Wye agreement in October 1998, the CIA was to monitor PLO prisons and ensure that convicted terrorists served their full terms. And U.S. Secretary of State Madeline Albright gave the Israeli government a written undertaking that

> the U.S. administration will protest any release of terrorists involved in attacks against Israel.[158]

However, convicted terrorists have still been released to roam the streets again without a whimper of protest from the CIA or any

White House or State Department official. With all the U.S. fanfare about fighting terrorism and its organizing of international anti-terrorism conferences, it gives not a hoot about terrorism or its victims, if this interferes with its political ambitions.

America's oft stated resolve to combat terrorism with all its might when it touches American lives is only a big balloon filled with political hot air. Why has it not demanded Yasser Arafat hand over Palestinian terrorists that were identified as taking part in the murders of Americans and who are now living in Arafat's territory under his protection? Why has the U.S. not asked Arafat to hand over Abu Abbas who ordered the murder of wheelchair-bound American Leon Klinghoffer after the PLO seized the Italian luxury liner Achille Lauro in 1985, and who now lives as a free man in Gaza? Why has the U.S. not demanded Arafat hand over Amin al-Hindi who masterminded the murder of Israel's Olympic athletes—including an American weight lifter—at the 1972 Munich Olympics, and today heads Arafat's General Intelligence Service? U.S. political ambitions in the Middle East far outweigh the lives of a mere handful of American citizens.

In January 1999, the Israeli government released a memorandum which listed the names of five terrorists who had been set free as part of a prisoner release to mark the Muslim feast of _Eid al-Fitr_. PLO security chief, Jibril Rajoub, called Israeli Prime Minister Netanyahu "'a liar' despite the fact that he had not seen the list of names."[159] Rajoub said "We did not release one person who killed. ... This is a matter of principle for us."[160] And the U.S. response? An American official said:

> Even if the information proved correct, Israel should have notified the U.S. before releasing a public memorandum.[161]

An Israeli official countered with:

> the Americans don't need us to tell them what is going on. Some of these releases happened two weeks ago and the CIA should know about them.[162]

American indifference to the release of the terrorists named in Israel's public memorandum shows the real heart of American involvement in the Middle East "peace" process. Each of those terrorists had been involved in terror attacks in which Americans were among the victims. The names of the released terrorists are: Hassam Alimani and Talal Baz—complicit in a Jerusalem bombing in July 1997 in which an American was one of 15 killed;[163] Jihad Suwiti and Arafat Kawasmeh—complicit in a February 1996 bus bombing in which three Americans were among the 60 killed;[164] Bashir Daher—complicit in both the July 1997 bombing and another Jerusalem attack in the same year.[165] The lack of protest by anyone from the Clinton administration proves that it cares not a wit about American lives or PLO compliance with the agreements signed with Israel—only about its own political interests.

In June 1999, Israel formally asked Arafat to hand over Muhammed Deif, a terrorist who masterminded the killings of at least 47 people, including five Americans. One American that Deif murdered was Nachshon Wachsman. And in 1966, in Jerusalem, "a moist-eyed President Clinton"[166] vowed at the graveside of the kidnapped and murdered Israeli-American that he would not pressure Israel to push the "peace" process forward with the Palestinians "until the man responsible for the murder was brought to justice."[167]

Nachshon Wachsman's mother was there at the graveside with Clinton. She told *CNS* News: "He said it with tears in his eyes, and his hands on the stones."[168] But four years later, Muhammed Deif still walks around in Gaza a free man, unmolested by the PLO, the teary-eyed Clinton, the CIA or the U.S. State Department. Wachsman was apparently just another sacrifice made on the altar of peace, an altar made wet from crocodile tears.

Under the Wye agreement Israel was to release 750 Palestinians held in Israeli jails. When the first of three releases of 250 prisoners took place, widespread Palestinian violence and riots broke out. The PLO was apparently angry because only 60 of those set free were "political" prisoners while the rest were common criminals. The PLO claimed that Israel should be freeing 750 "political" prisoners—convicted murderers and Hamas terrorists—but Israel said there was no such undertaking given during the Wye negotiations, and said it would not release prisoners with blood on their hands.

In February 1999, in a gesture designed to promote peace and reconciliation, Israel's ceremonial President Ezer Weizman reduced the sentences of seven Israelis convicted of killing or plotting to kill Arabs, together with five Arabs convicted of causing casualties by placing bombs on buses and murdering Israeli soldiers.[169] Weizman was also reviewing the files of around 20 Israeli Arab "political" prisoners.[170]

During the years of the "peace" negotiations, thousands of Palestinian prisoners had been released for political reasons, and Weizman had even pardoned a number of Palestinian women who had murdered Jews and set them free.[171] But, because Weizman reduced prison sentences of Israelis (one sentence was reduced down to 40 years), the PLO objected! PLO officials said that reducing the prison sentences of Israelis "would encourage other extremists to attack Arabs."[172] PLO hypocrisy is the norm, not the exception.

PLO Violations: Unilateral declaration of Palestinian state

Oslo makes provision for heavy Arab population areas under Israeli control to be given over to PLO autonomy, turning them into self-rule areas linked together by free-access roads. The Oslo agreements provide for autonomy only and deny PLO sovereignty over the areas. A sovereign Palestinian state is, therefore, forbidden under the terms of the agreements.

When Oslo was first drawn up—with large measures of Western duplicity laced with left-wing Israeli stupidity—the farce of "peace" negotiations were judged to be complete around May 4, 1999, and this symbolic date was entered into the agreements. Arafat, however, seized upon this date and announced time and again that he intended to unilaterally declare a sovereign Palestinian state on May 4, 1999. And such sovereign Palestinian state would not simply encompass the areas turned over to the PLO by Israel, but would also include all territory outside of the borders of pre-1967 Israel.

Bibi Netanyahu immediately warned Arafat that if he carried out his threat to unilaterally declare a Palestinian state in May 1999, Israel would take whatever action it deemed necessary, including a military option. Netanyahu said the consequences for Arafat would not only be very serious, but the "peace" process would be irrevocably terminated. Netanyahu's government position was that further troop withdrawals from areas specified in the Wye agreement would be suspended until Arafat

> unambiguously and publicly retracts his intention to unilaterally declare an independent state next May.[173]

The Israeli Government repeated the same warnings each time

Arafat repeated his intention of declaring a Palestinian state. But Arafat knew that he would get away with his threat because he has gotten away with everything else—multiple bank robberies, multiple hijackings of passenger planes and passenger ships, the murder of literally hundreds of thousands of people (Jews and non-Jews alike), and the violation of every single important clause in the Oslo Accords. Arafat's response to Israel's warning was:

> We will declare our independent state on May 4, 1999, with noble Jerusalem as its capital, whether they like it or not.... Our rifles are ready, and we are ready to raise them if they try to stop us.[174]

Being an "honest broker," and of late, the compliance referee between Israel and the PLO, the U.S. again raised no objection to Arafat's blatant provocation of Israel, but instead criticized Israel for not turning over more land to the PLO. To make matters worse, in a televised broadcast to Israeli and Arab teenagers, Hillary Rodham Clinton (whom many believe to be the real U.S. President) said that there should be

> a state of Palestine... "a functioning modern state that is on the same footing as other states."[175]

And as mentioned on page 115, Israel's left-wing Labor party made a deal with Arafat whereby he would postpone declaring a Palestinian state until after the Israeli elections in May 1999. The declaration of a sovereign state prior to the elections would work to Netanyahu's advantage, and neither Labor nor Arafat wanted that to happen.

Yasser Arafat, a longtime Muslim terrorist and leader of an international band of murderers, has been the honored guest at the White House on several occasions. On February 4, 1999, he returned to Washington to meet privately with President Clinton. This scheduled meeting followed his invited speech at the Congressional Prayer Breakfast.

PLO Violations: Continued incitement to violence

Under Oslo the PLO agreed to refrain from inciting hatred against Israel in particular and Jews in general, but a steady stream has flowed unabated from Arafat, his lieutenants, and the PA's official media mouthpieces.

Numerous articles vilifying Jews and denying the Holocaust

have been published or broadcast widely on radio and television. For example, the official PA newspaper *Al Hayat Al-Jadida* carried the following article on July 2, 1998 which said *inter alia*:

Jews managed to take control of America's media, as well as media in Europe and elsewhere. Thus they managed to some extent, to change the image of Jews as ugly and vile in the eyes of the world. They proved particularly successful in America and Europe.

When Nazi persecution of the Jews began, the winds began blowing in their favor. What Hitler did to the Jews actually exposed the Jewish plot. World public opinion, manipulated by the Jews, took advantage of these persecutions, disseminating stories about a collective massacre. They concocted horrible stories of gas chambers which Hitler, they claimed, used to burn them alive. The press overflowed with pictures of Jews being gunned down by Hitler's machine guns or being pushed into gas chambers. The press focused on suffering women, children and elderly people in order to rouse empathy and claim reparations, donations and grants from around the world.

The truth is that such persecution was a malicious fabrication by the Jews. It is a myth which they named "The Holocaust" in order to rouse empathy. Credible historians challenge this Jewish myth.[176]

The Wye River Agreement reiterated the Oslo provision that the PLO stop incitement against Israel, but as the following quotation from the official PLO mouthpiece *Al Hayat Al-Jadida* shows, Arafat has no intention of doing so. This article appeared on November 7, 1998—after the Wye Agreement was signed:

Corruption is part of the nature of Jews. So much so that only rarely one finds corruption in which Jews are not implicated. Their intense love of money... is well known and they do not care by what method they achieve it... If one studies their history, it becomes clear that Jews were subjected to losses and expulsion as a result of their wickedness and despicable acts. All this occurred after their true nature and their responsibility for destroying the world were revealed... It is interesting how those harmed by them remain under their influence among them Bill Clinton.[177]

Incitement and violence are "legitimized and encouraged by the Palestinian Authority, the central Palestinian governing body."[178] PA "police" stood idly by while some 15,000 Palestinians gathered in Nablus and engaged themselves in calls for further terrorist attacks on Israel.[179] The same thing happened the following day when a similar rally was held in Bir-Zeit University near Ramallah and featured a "simulated blowing up of an Israeli bus."[180]

PLO foreign minister Farouk Kadoumi defined the goals of Palestinian terrorism to an Egyptian newspaper:

> The martyrdom operations [suicide bombings] are one means of pressuring Israel. They are necessary actions.[181]

Hate indoctrination is a normal part of a Palestinian child's education and also standard fare on official PLO children's television. Hatred of Jews and Israel is taught to children throughout the Arab world as part of the school curriculum.[182] A former Syrian Minister of Education wrote:

> The hatred which we indoctrinate into the minds of our children from their birth is sacred.[183]

The terms of the Oslo Accords notwithstanding, there has been no abatement of hate indoctrination of Palestinian children. As Maha Nashashibi, principal of the Ramallah College for Girls put it:

> We are not allowed to teach things against the Jews, but you have to tell children the truth.[184]

And U.S. Senators are among those who have viewed video footage of

> Palestinian youngsters, some as young as five or six, chanting slogans glorifying violence against Jews on a children's programme.[185]

Since 1994, the Palestinian Broadcasting Corporation has received about $500,000 from the U.S. government.

Former Prime Minister Netanyahu was standing on firm ground when he insisted that the PA puts a stop to the incitement of violence and hatred toward Israel in particular and Jews in general.

The gross violations of the Oslo Accords by the PLO presented in this chapter are but the tip of the iceberg insofar as PLO non-compliance goes.

Yasser Arafat is the leader of the Fatah faction of the PLO.

The word "Fatah" is derived from the reversed letters of the Arabic word "_hataf_" meaning "sudden death." The PLO was formed specifically to destroy the state of Israel, and the reader gets no points for correctly guessing who or what the "sudden death" is meant for. The Oslo Accords were signed in September 1993, and the world lauded its entrance into a new era of peace. However, in mid-1998 Arafat's Fatah placed its constitution on its Internet website. Netanyahu's senior advisor David Bar-Illan said that

> the Fatah Constitution is in some ways worse than the Palestinian Covenant that Israel is trying to get Arafat to amend.[186]

Among the Constitution's many articles is Fatah's goal:

> The complete liberation of Palestine and eradication of Zionist economic, political, military and cultural existence.[187]

After repeated refusals to amend the PLO Covenant since 1993, Arafat posts an equally, if not more, lethal document on the Internet in 1998. Yet Arafat, wearing his "sincere" look, continues to go from one capital to the next around the world declaring that

> Palestinians had fulfilled their obligations, but that Israel had turned its back on peace deals struck in Oslo and Madrid.[188]

And this is the one whom the media has dubbed the "man of peace," who said in November 1998: "Our rifles are ready, and we are ready to raise them."[189] Arafat is always threatening violence, for he knows no path except the one of violence, terror and murder.

Unwanted Neighbors

Under the PLO-accommodating rule of Yitzhak Rabin and Shimon Peres a new era was ushered in. Instead of the promised "era of peace," though, there came one of terror. Arab terrorism against Israelis grew to mammoth proportions. Israelis were blown to pieces by suicide bombers—on buses, at bus stations, in shopping malls, vegetable markets and in cafes. Israelis were stabbed going to work, at work, coming home, at home and at play. The Arab terrorists did not discriminate between soldiers or civilians, males or females, adults, teenagers or little children. And if Israelis drove past Arab villages their cars were usually stoned or firebombed. Israelis were even beaten to death in their cars by Arab mobs, and the cars torched. Anything Israeli was a legitimate target for hate-filled Muslim Arabs.

Some Israelis had rented property in Arab neighborhoods, but local Arabs threatened to kill any Jew that moved into their area. A few Israelis had purchased homes in Arab neighborhoods and were determined to occupy their legally purchased property despite the threats of bodily harm, but 24-hour police guards were required to protect them. One time, when Israelis moved into property they had purchased on Jerusalem's Mount of Olives, even the White House, the U.S. State Department and the EU called it a "provocation," and the Israelis had to move out again. The new "era of peace" and political correctness apparently justifies discrimination against Jews.

The upsurge of Arab violence and terror attacks were the result of the bankrupt policies of Rabin and Peres, and Israelis were fearing for their lives. Many Israelis would not ride a bus, many more refused to leave the safety of their homes at night, and most every Arab began to be viewed with suspicion. Some Israeli landlords now refuse Arab tenants, and while it was perfectly acceptable for Jews to be banned from Arab neighborhoods on pain of death, it was totally unacceptable the other way around. Said Yousef Jabareen of the Association of Civil Rights in Israel:

> The refusal of Jews to rent to Arabs is a blow to the dignity of the Arab population and is indicative of a racist attitude towards them.[190]

After taking control of the autonomous areas the PLO "police" began murdering real estate brokers it suspected of selling property to Jews. Arafat's advisor and member of the Israeli Knesset, Ahmed Tibi, spoke on *Israel Radio* in May 1997 and said, "someone who sells land to Jews has sold his soul to the devil."[191] The day following Tibi's radio appearance another Arab land-dealer was murdered.[192] Salah Salim, another Arab member of Israel's Knesset said, in front of reporters:

> Arab land-dealers who sell property to Jews "should be killed off and made into meatballs." Go ahead and record it well![193]

And these "gentlemen" are full-fledged members of the Israeli Knesset.

Two weeks after Tibi spoke on *Israel Radio* the director general of the JNF (Jewish National Fund) Yitzhak Elyashiv made public the information that:

Arabs are purchasing hundreds of dunams of land throughout Israel.[194]

He said that at present the Israel Lands Administration "has no powers of enforcement to prevent sales."[195] That Israel could possibly consider an alteration to its land laws to prevent continued Palestinian Arab purchases of large blocks of state-owned land was too much for such a fair-minded Arab MK as Ahmed Tibi. He told journalists that "Israeli laws controlling the sale of land are racist."[196]

In 1998 the PA passed a law making it "a capital offence for Arabs to sell any property to an Israeli."[197] The law also

prohibits any Israeli ownership of real estate 'in Palestine'—on pain of death.[198]

The law provides no borders for "Palestine" which is defined as any place "that the Palestinians determine is Palestine."[199] According to the conventional Palestinian view, "Palestine" incorporates all land occupied by Israel proper, and all that taken up by Israeli "settlements" as well as the PLO autonomous areas.

Any Israeli owning property within the PLO's definition of "Palestine" will be sentenced to death. And the law also states: "The property itself will be seized by the PA."[200] Arafat has through this law nailed his true colors to the mast. Just as Hitler's Nazi Europe was to be *Judenrein*—free of any contamination by Jews—so, too, is Arafat's "Palestine" to be *Judenrein*. Hitler's answer to ridding Europe of its Jews was the Holocaust, and his ally who collaborated in this was Haj Amin al-Husseini—Arafat's uncle. Arafat's way of ridding "Palestine" of its Jews is to be exactly the same as Hitler's—kill them and confiscate their property.

Arafat calls for sanctions against Israel and appeals to the international community, particularly the U.S., to increase pressure on Israel to implement the Oslo Accords. His plaintive whine before the international court of public opinion of,

I am not asking for the moon. I only want what has been agreed upon[201]

jerks the heartstrings of an inherently anti-Semitic world. It is absolutely disgraceful that the world's leaders and statesmen—who long ago accepted the principle that agreements signed with Jews bind only the Jews—lay red carpets out for this arch-terrorist turned con-man (at this time of writing Norway alone had laid its red carpet five times for this prince of murderers). Arafat is even being addressed by Christians with singularly fawning, obsequious titles like

> ...his Highness (*sic*) Excellency (*sic*) President (*sic*) Yasser Arafat...[202]

Twice-born Christians everywhere should earnestly beseech God to raise up men to lead our nations instead of *"fools,"* wimps, eunuchs and greed merchants.

Another Berlin Wall?

Following an Arab terror attack in January 1995, in which 21 Israelis died and more than 60 were injured, Yitzhak Rabin exhorted Israelis "not to be demoralized"[203] by the terror attacks. In that rare address to the nation Rabin said the "peace" talks were

> ultimately aimed at bringing about a separation between Israelis and Palestinians.[204]

And Rabin had

> thoughts of actually establishing a fence that would separate Jews from Palestinians.[205]

Indeed, the main argument put forward by the leaders of the left-wing bloc in favor of Oslo and the ceding of territory to the PLO is the need to separate Israeli Jews from Palestinian Arabs. These *"fools"* apparently all suffer from myopia.

Four political tenets held by the left-wing bloc are:

- Security and demography demand Israeli Jews be separated from Palestinian Arabs by a border which leaves the Arab population of *Judea*, *Samaria* and the Gaza strip under PLO rule.
- Israeli Jews must never be separated from Israeli Arabs.
- Israeli Arabs have the same right to determine the political future of Israel.
- Israel must shoulder the responsibility for the economic welfare of Arabs under PLO rule and allow them to work in Israel in large numbers.

The above tenets are absurd and utterly inconsistent with reality. They are based upon totally false assumptions, not the least being that Israeli Arabs are not Palestinian Arabs, but Israeli citizens loyal to their country.

In August 1997, a delegation comprising 44 "Israeli Arab" intellectuals and politicians visited Syria and met with President Hafez Assad in Damascus. Members of the delegation left no doubt as to where their loyalties lay. Some members "wished Syria success in its next war"[206] with Israel, and MK Taleb a-Sanaa went so far as to say that he "hoped for a Syrian victory."[207] MK Abdul Malik Dahamshe declared:

> Palestine and Syria are one homeland. The Arab people will win by the sword; the victory will be won by the Jihad of the Arab world.[208]

Addressing more than 20,000 refugees from one of the camps around Damascus, MK Abdul Wahab Darawashe said:

> There is no difference between one Palestinian and another. We are all Palestinians and we are all Syrian Arabs. ... I swear on Allah that you will return to Palestine.[209]

The delegation stood silently while the crowd shouted:

> Haifa and Jaffa are calling us! With blood and fire we shall redeem Palestine.[210]

Members of the delegation met with Nawaf Hawatmeh and Ahmed Jibril, the heads of two major Palestinian terror groups operating out of Damascus.[211] Neither group recognizes Israel's right to exist.[212] And when the delegation visited the Martyrs Cemetery outside of Damascus, Palestinian poet Samih Kassim told reporters:

> This nation that offered this big number of honored martyrs will be able to defeat all its enemies.[213]

The delegation expressed the general sentiments of the great majority of "Israeli Arabs" whose numbers had reached 901,000 by the end of 1998.[214] Each of the Arab MKs—from the Labor, Meretz, Hadash and Democratic Arab parties—are typical of all of Israel's Arab MKs, and some anti-Jew, anti-Israel sentiments expressed by other Arab MKs have already been seen: Ahmed Tibi, pages 123, 175; Salah Salim, page 175; Tawfik Zayyad, page 88; Hashem Mahameed, page 123. All these "Israeli Arab" MKs are members of Israel's government. Yitzhak Rabin forced the whole Oslo process through the Knesset by a 1 vote majority with the help of 7 Arab votes. Rabin angrily denounced as "racist" the view that only Jews could control the destiny of an independent Jewish state.[215]

After Oslo only a small proportion of Israeli Arabs actually remained loyal to Israel. The silent majority pretends to be loyal, but its real loyalty is to the PLO and many of them have now been convicted of involvement in terrorism against Israel. Murders of Jewish Israelis,[216] suicide bombings[217] and car bombings[218] by Israeli Arabs are now commonplace. The Israeli Arab population today makes up more than 20 percent of Israel's total population figure, and Israel is harboring a potential fifth column in any war in which it becomes involved.

We have seen the real heart of Israeli Arab MKs, and extending to Israeli Arabs the same right to determine the political future of Israel as Jews is suicidal. Given the rate of expansion of the Israeli Arab population against that of the Jewish population, within 20 to 30 years there will be an Arab majority. It would then be but a step and a jump before Israeli Arab MKs constitute a majority in the government, and anti-Jewish laws would quickly be pushed through the Knesset. The Jewish state would soon cease to exist.

In March 1999, another Israeli Arab MK, Azmi Bishara, announced his candidacy for prime minister of Israel in the May elections. After announcing his candidacy Bishara was quoted as saying: "The Jewish nation was a 'fiction with no right to exist.'"[219] Therefore Bishara is playing in the same league as all the Arab MKs quoted earlier.

The tenet that Israel must shoulder the responsibility for the economic welfare of Arabs under PLO rule and allow them to work in Israel in large numbers has taken a terrible toll on Israeli life, and on the Israeli economy. Besides the hundreds of Israelis who have been murdered or maimed by Palestinians who gained access to Israel by holding work permits, they also steal everything in Israel that is not nailed down. And, if they can prise it loose, it is obviously not nailed down.

The effects of allowing Palestinian Arabs to enter Israel to work in large numbers can be seen, for example, in car thefts. In 1997 alone, 45,273[220] new or near new Israeli cars were stolen— one car every 12 minutes. They were stolen "nearly entirely by Palestinian thieves,"[221] and their value was upwards of NIS 1.7

billion (US$423.2 million).[222] Almost all of these cars were either sold to Palestinians in the PLO autonomous areas for practically nothing, or they found their way into sophisticated Palestinian workshops known as "chop shops" where they are broken down for spare parts, literally within minutes.[223] The spare parts eventually find their way back across the borders and are then sold back to the Israelis.[224] The tenet of allowing Palestinians to work in Israel in large numbers not only sucks the blood from the nation, but also shows the foolishness of the tenet that Israeli Jews must be separated from Palestinian Arabs by a border which leaves the Arab population of *Judea*, *Samaria* and the Gaza strip under PLO rule. Palestinians who work in Israel need only travel the few kilometers—as the stolen car drives—to the safety of the PLO areas with the day's plunder, or in order to rinse the victim's blood from his hands. Israel cannot pursue fleeing Palestinians into PLO controlled areas.

Israeli Jews must never be separated from Israeli Arabs, says the left-wing bloc. As was made very clear by members of the Israeli Arab delegation to Syria, the Israeli Arabs consider themselves to be Palestinians. And most Israeli Arabs are either openly antagonistic toward Israel, or remain quietly loyal to the PLO while pretending their loyalty is to Israel. Palestinians have also made it clear that they consider it totally unacceptable for Jews to live in Arab areas, and most Jews do not want Arabs too close to them. They have learned from bitter experience that Palestinians rape, murder and pillage.

There appears to be only two possible solutions to the dreadful situation that exists today. The real (and eventual) solution is for all Jews and Arabs to accept God's salvation accomplished through the atoning work of the Lord Jesus Christ on the cross at Calvary. The alternative human solution would be to transfer all Arabs out of Israel leaving only the small, genuinely loyal minority, and these should be well rewarded for their loyalty.

The leaders of the left-wing bloc will never agree to either solution because, first of all, they do not believe in God, Jesus or the Bible and, second of all, they need a large Arab vote if they are to hold power in Israel. Therefore, under the leadership of left-wing *"fools"* Arab murder and mayhem will return to previous levels. And the situation will continue to escalate for as long as it takes Israel to learn its lessons the hard way, until it is brought to its knees and God finally intervenes on its behalf.

Apart from a sovereign act of grace from the *Holy One of Israel*, a Netanyahu-led government would also reject out-of-hand the first solution put forward. It might, however, conceivably opt for the second solution. Once the Arabs had been transferred and transformed into full-fledged Palestinians, the Israelis would then have had to build a Berlin Wall between themselves and the Palestinians—a wall that even a bug could not cross.

External Players

Statesmen, politicians and journalists have lied deliberately throughout history. The lies of democratic statesmen are often as monumental as the lies of the most tyrannical dictators. In both cases, the motives are love of power and greed. Most of the players in the Middle East "peace process" are conducting their politics according to the definition at the beginning of this chapter.

Cheating most people most of the time has been the norm in politics since the world was created. However, the age of rapid air transportation, television and computers has created a world in which cheating all the people all the time is easier than at any time since Adam. Global hypocrisy has now arrived upon the world's scene.

Superpowers have always been able to lie and cheat more effectively than other states. The collapse of the Soviet Union brought the United States forth as the only superpower, so truth has now become what Washington wants it to be. When Washington's "truth" does not correspond to facts, the facts are buried beneath a barrage of propaganda from a kowtowing media. Ignoring truth is one of the recognized methods of propagating lies, and U.S. policy makers and power brokers protect themselves by a smokescreen of lies disseminated by the media. In the long run, the lying propaganda in the Western media might destroy the West itself.

The Media

The media is the world's spokesman. And the one who controls your information also controls your judgment. The media is not unaware of the enormous power it wields over the masses and the governments of nations. The media is fully cognizant that it has the ability to effectively change the entire world's perception of an event or issue by its "News" coverage. Therefore, the printed media has few qualms about publishing false photographs and false stories,[225] if it considers the import of an issue warrants this. In the same way the electronic media will also hire "actors" and create news clips for its cameras.[226] Neither is it adverse to cutting film footages and splicing the pieces together to give a false visual view of events, and false audio stories will be aired to match the visual.[227]

Peter Jennings, of *ABC-TV*, said: "There's no such thing as truth, only news."[228] Senior *CNN* correspondent Frank Sesno said: "We decide what the public wants to know—what they need to know."[229] And in February 1998, anchor man for *CBS*, Dan Rather, in full pancake makeup, was seen together with Pentagon correspondent David Martin going through the motions of covering a U.S. bombing raid on Iraq. Rather was seen on television for 20 minutes, and at one point stated that "it was not known how many casualties were caused by the bombings."[230] There were, of course, no U.S. bombings of Iraq anywhere near that time—*CBS* was simply getting its "live coverage" ready ahead of time. However, someone mistakenly beamed it to television affiliates via satellite, totally embarrassing *CBS NEWS*. The media has the ability and power to fool most of the people most of the time. How long before it finds ways to fool all of the people all of the time? And how long will it be before the public wakes up to the fact that the media is not a non-profit organization dedicated to the betterment of mankind?

Israel long ago lost the sympathy of the media by stubbornly refusing to be defeated by Arab armies. Today the media wants to help establish a Palestinian state on Israel's land. So, when push comes to shove, most of today's "news" concerning Israel is simply media propaganda and disinformation, and some journalists are "at war with Israel."[231]

CNN is by far the most influential of the television networks and, sadly, world leaders are even known to make far-reaching decisions based on *CNN News*.[232] However, CAMERA[233] lashes out at *CNN's* reporting on Israel and charges it with fostering "a pattern of reporting that flouts the basics of decent journalism."[234] *CNN's* Jerusalem Bureau Chief Walter Rodgers kowtows to Arab sensibilities while disregarding Israel's. In the same breath Rodgers would speak of "President Clinton," "President Arafat" and "Mr.

Netanyahu." Arafat is president of absolutely nothing, but Rodgers paints a picture of a Palestinian state with a "President Arafat" at its head. Rodgers detested Netanyahu and liked to deny him the courtesy of being addressed as "Prime Minister." Reporting on a speech by Netanyahu at Washington's National Press Club, Rodgers said Netanyahu's remarks were

> a very slick effort by the arch practitioner of propaganda to reingratiate himself with the American public.[235]

Over and over again, we hear *CNN* reporters and anchors referring to Arafat as "President" as though it was fact, and we also see it printed in the daily newspapers. We can also read other subtle lies like: "the motorcade passed the Palestinian embassy en route to...".[236] At the time of writing Arafat is not a president, and there is no Palestinian embassy in existence anywhere in the world, except in the mind of the media. Arafat is the head of the PLO—Palestinian Liberation Organization—the richest and most brutal terror organization this world has ever known.

The United Nations

The PLO is the only terror group to have been granted UN recognition, and such recognition cloaked a vile organization with respectability. In 1974, the UN granted the PLO observer status. In 1988 the General Assembly upgraded the PLO mission's designation to "Palestine," thus giving international recognition to a nonexistent sovereign Palestinian state. In 1998, the UN passed a resolution stating that Israeli sovereignty and law in Jerusalem was illegal. One hundred and forty-nine countries voted in favor of the resolution—the U.S. and another six countries abstained. Only Israel voted against the resolution. Practically all the nations of the world are against Jerusalem as the capital of Israel—they would have it be the capital of a second Palestinian state with the godfather of international terrorism as its premier.

King David made Jerusalem the capital of Israel more than 3,000 years ago, and throughout the last three millenniums Jerusalem has never been the capital of any nation other than Israel. The modern recreated state of Israel officially established Jerusalem as its capital again over 50 years ago, and many Jews today—perhaps even the great majority—would rather die than lose their holy city's capital status to that of a PLO state.

The Bible tells us clearly in several passages that there will be a great conflict over Jerusalem in the End Times. And in that day God—the

> _Holy One of Israel—will make Jerusalem a very heavy stone for all peoples; all who would heave it away will surely be cut in pieces, though all nations of the earth are gathered against it_ (Zechariah 12:3).

The nations of the earth have already lined themselves up against Israel over the issue of Jerusalem, but they are, in fact, about to confront Israel's God. We should remember that Almighty God never loses in any confrontation:

> _It shall be in that day that I will seek to destroy all the nations that come against Jerusalem ... And it shall come to pass that everyone who is left of all the nations which came against Jerusalem shall go up from year to year to worship the King, the Lord of hosts_ (Zechariah 12:9, 14:16).

All the nations of the earth that are to come against Israel will, in all probability, assemble for battle under the banner of the UN. The UN is one of the most anti-Semitic organizations in the world, and it constitutes integral parts of the New World Order, the New Age Movement and the One World Government.[237] The UN is linked to the occult, and therefore its designs for Jerusalem are satanic. The UN's longtime strategy has been to isolate Israel from the other nations and to delegitimize the existence of the Jewish state. The UN has devoted 30 percent of its meetings and a full one-third of all its resolutions to Israel.[238]

The forerunner of the UN was the League of Nations, and this august body voted Israel into existence. The credible League of Nations encouraged and helped birth the modern state of Israel, but its pro-Arab successor spends almost one third of its days trying to destroy it! When the 50th anniversary of the historic vote to partition Palestine arrived on November 29, 1997, the UN ignored it and it went unnoticed. However, two days later it showed its bias by holding the International Day of Solidarity with the Palestinian People. Solidarity Day is held each year at the UN and includes

> a "solemn meeting" of the Committee on the Exercise of the Inalienable Rights of the Palestinian People, a series of films, and a cultural exhibit called "At Home in Palestine."[239]

Apart from the "Palestinian refugee" issue (mentioned briefly on pages 190–191), the number of "Palestinian Arabs" in "Palestine" has also been systematically exaggerated. The UN body charged with helping Arab refugees, whose staff is mainly Arab, has been cooperating with the PLO in the matter.

UNIFIL (United Nations Interim Force in Lebanon) troops are purported to be in Lebanon to keep the peace, but in actual fact they give succor to the enemies of Israel. In the days when Yasser Arafat had his multi-thousand terrorist army in Lebanon, the UNIFIL gave the PLO free passage through to Israel's northern border to conduct terrorist operations against Israel.[240] Some UNIFIL units even signed non-aggression pacts with the PLO.[241] Today the UN allows Hizb'allah terrorists to shoot Katyusha rockets and mortars at Israeli troops from just outside UN compounds, or from within the actual enclave itself. This provides the terrorists with a refuge as they know Israel cannot fire upon the compounds. In a single two-week period

> Israel's military produced a list of 31 incidents in which Hizb'allah fired at Israeli targets from UN enclaves, using the camps of the peace-keeping forces as a safe haven."[242]

And an investigation revealed that

> UNIFIL buildings have been used to shelter Hizb'allah fighters and their families.[243]

And UNIFIL's "peace keeping" activities are costing taxpayers many millions of dollars every year.

The European Union

Several countries of the EU have more than once offered their services as mediators between the PLO and Israel. But these were not genuine offers of mediation; they were declarations of support for Arafat's demands. The EU wants to safeguard its multi-billion dollar investment in the PLO, and in EU eyes Israel must not be allowed to thwart the economic benefits of a union between Europe and the Arab world. France, Britain and Germany are all trying to supplant U.S. influence in Syria, Lebanon, Iraq and Iran by being more pro-Arab than the Americans. Thus Israel does not and cannot ever expect to receive fair press or treatment from the EU.

In 1998, the European Commission President called on European governments to "get tough with Israel,"[244] and the EU has stuck its nose into every place where it has not been welcome.

In May 1998, the EU called for a boycott of any produce originating in eastern Jerusalem, *Judea*, *Samaria*, Gaza and the Golan Heights. Israel's prime minister Bibi Netanyahu said the boycott would

> put an end to any attempt of the European Union to have any kind of facilitating role in Middle East peacemaking efforts.[245]

He said the boycott makes it clear that the EU was a "'one-sided player' rather than an impartial mediator."[246]

The Oslo accords forbid PLO activity in Jerusalem, but the EU foreign ministers decided that the EU leadership must visit Orient House—the unofficial PLO headquarters in Jerusalem—while on official trips to Israel.[247] Israel has filed complaints with the EU time and again about its official visits to Orient House, but it persistently refuses to change its arrogant attitude. In a March 1999, formal reply to yet another Israeli demand that foreign ministers stop visiting Orient House as it contravenes the Oslo Accords and the Wye Agreement, German Ambassador Theodor Wallau wrote on behalf of the EU:

> We have no intention of changing our custom regarding meetings in Jerusalem.[248]

This is the EU's way of informing Israel that it recognizes Jerusalem as the capital of the PLO state-to-be, and Israel had better get used to the idea.

In March 1999, EU foreign ministers meeting in Berlin approved the text of a declaration stating that the European Union "backs the Palestinian's unqualified right to self-determination."[249] According to the document,

> Israel would have no power to veto a Palestinian declaration of statehood.[250]

Reacting to the EU declaration, former Prime Minister Netanyahu vocalized his opposition to an establishment of a Palestinian state by saying:

> ...a Palestinian state would be able to "establish a large army, support itself without limit, frame treaties with regimes seeking the destruction of Israel and serve as a base for enhanced terror against Israel and thus endanger its existence."[251]

Netanyahu also said:

> ...it was regretful that Europe, where a third of the Jewish people perished, would see fit to attempt to impose a solution that endangers the state of Israel and its interests.[252]

International law gives Israel full right to occupy the land captured in wars of self-defence. For several years following the Six Day War, Israel offered to trade captured land for peace with its Arab neighbors. All offers were bluntly rejected. The Arab answer to Israeli peace overtures was the same as Gamal Abdel Nasser's famous Three Noes of the Khartoum summit in August 1967: "No recognition of Israel, no peace, no discussions."[253] So, in the 1970s Israel finally began building cities and towns on the land. But now the pro-Arab EU slams Israel for having moved onto the land and issued a statement saying, "Settlements contravene international law."[254] Apparently, international law is drawn up daily to suit particular parties quoting it against Israel. The UN's 22-member Arab group of nations even said that any 1998 Israeli celebrations in Jerusalem to mark the state's 50th anniversary "will violate international law."[255]

Some people find it rather amusing to hear the EU and the media pushing their anti-Israel biases by continually referring to Arab "villages" on the one hand, but Israeli "settlements" on the other. Apparently, there is a world of difference between an Arab "village" and an Israeli "settlement," even between Israeli "settlements" that are substantially older than some Arab "villages." However, while the EU and the media use the word "settlement" in a derogatory way, it is also the word Joshua used when he brought the Israelites across the Jordan in order to "settle" the land. Therefore "settlement" is not a dirty word, but rather a divine decree to "settle" permanently on their 100,000-year-long God-given inheritance.

The EU's Middle East policy is bankrolled by the never-have-enoughs of European business, and thus the EU states fall over one another in their greedy scramble to line their coffers with Arab and Iranian money. The West armed Iraq and made billions from the business; then it spent billions to blow Iraq apart because it seriously threatened the profits of Western oil companies, lucrative contracts for Western business in the Gulf states, and its huge arms exports to these states and Egypt. Of course, neither U.S. presidents nor the leaders of the EU nations regarded these arms exports as a threat to the stability of the Middle East or a probable catalyst for future wars. Business is business. In his Ph.D. thesis, Henry Kissinger laid out the need for

> ...developing ongoing small wars around the planet to maintain the economic alignment of the superpowers.[256]

After Iraq had been battered into submission and the Gulf War came to an end, EU businesses were once again beating a path to Saddam Hussein's door in their never ending quest for financial profit.

France[257] was first to elbow its way back into Baghdad in search of a commercial toehold, long before the UN eased Iraqi oil restrictions. Germany[258] was soon back on the trail of hot profits, while UNSCOM was spending millions hunting the German chemicals[259] and technology that had been sold to Iraq earlier. Germany knew that Iraq was hoping to "export" some of its "technology" to Israel by air via missiles, but business is business and twinges of conscience are quickly forgotten.

Germany also sells Iran many of the resources that the U.S. seek to embargo, as well as providing massive credits to pay for them. The trade enriches German businesses, which make even bigger profits due to the absence of U.S. competition for the Iranian market.

> German financing allows the Iranians to divert foreign currency to the purchase of advanced weapons and technology, including nuclear components, material and training from Russia and China, and missile technology from North Korea.[260]

Twenty-seven Spanish companies[261] were latecomers that joined the armada of European businessmen winging their way into Iraq with the gleam of petrodollars in their eyes. The Spaniards held a trade exhibition in Baghdad, and one water-pump manufacturer foresaw the possibility of $200 million in sales for his firm.[262] The Middle East—the most volatile region on earth—is a commercial carnival for EU businessmen and their blinkered governments.

In 1996, France sent "humanitarian aid" to Lebanon through the Iranian-funded and Syrian-backed Hizb'allah terror organization. France knows full well that Hizb'allah is merely an arm of the Syrian regime. And it would well remember that when Syria wanted

American and French peacekeepers out of Lebanon in 1983, Hizb'allah suicide bombers were used to kill 241 Americans and 58 Frenchmen sleeping in their barracks.[263] The French enrichment of Hizb'allah's coffers not only made the terror group richer, allowing it to fight against Israel with greater force, but it also bolstered Hizb'allah's standing and prestige in the eyes of the world.

It was not a sudden concern for the welfare of the Lebanese that animated French generosity, but a desire to clearly let the Arabs and Iranians know whose side France was on. This is the same France that slapped an immoral arms embargo on Israel on the eve of the 1967 Six Day War, when the besieged state was almost entirely dependent upon it for weaponry. In effect, France appointed itself God over the fate of a people awaiting mass-invasion by five Arab armies.

In the summer of 1973, France joined Egypt's initiative to force a settlement on Israel via the UN Security Council.[264] The Egyptian proposal did not succeed, but the manoeuvre was preparing the ground for the Yom Kippur War that followed some weeks later. Today, France has joined the Arab world in its endeavor to force yet another settlement upon Israel.

In 1996, French Defence Minister Charles Millon announced that relations between France and Israel would be lowered "if the peace process were stopped."[265] He did not threaten to cool ties with the PLO, Syria or Lebanon if the "peace" talks stopped—only Israel. Thus France places the onus squarely upon Israel for achieving Middle East "peace."

France "is seen as the most pro-Palestinian force in Europe,"[266] and French President Jacques Chirac received rousing applause from the Palestinians, when he told the PLO legislature in Ramallah that Jerusalem must be a part of any deal with the Israelis.[267] And, just as war followed the French-backed Egyptian manoeuvre in 1973, so war will also follow the latest crude meddling by France.

Britain, that paragon of propriety, has a rich history of arrogant, crude and patronizing diplomacy toward Israel. Like France, it places sole responsibility for Middle East "peace" upon the shoulders of Israel. In December 1997, senior British officials set Europe on another collision course with Israel when they said:

> London will exert intense pressure on Israel to be more forthcoming in the peace process after Britain assumes the presidency of the European Union on January 1.[268]

And in a March 1998 magazine article, Britain's overtly pro-Arab Foreign Secretary Robin Cook accused Israel of endangering the "peace" process. Cook renewed calls "for increased pressure on the Jewish state."[269]

In May 1998, the *Times* of London reported that British Prime Minister Tony Blair "was shocked at the conditions he saw in Palestinian refugee camps"[270] during his visit earlier in April. As a consequence of Blair's visit, Britain would increase its annual contribution to UNRWA (United Nations Relief and Works Agency) by one-third, bringing it to £8 million. The *Times* article reports that UNRWA is

> the largest of the UN agencies set up to deal with the 750,000 Palestinians made homeless by the creation of Israel.[271]

And according to Blair, there is "a political case for doing more for the refugees."[272]

The *Times* article is a perfect example of the British media's disinformation. The creation of Israel did not make 750,000 Palestinians homeless. When Israel was reborn there was no such thing as a "Palestinian Arab." The "Palestinian Arab" myth only came into being 25 years after the creation of Israel.[273]

The "refugees" fled when seven Arab armies attacked Israel in 1948 in the first Arab attempt to destroy the Jewish state. The Arabs themselves are the cause of the Arab refugee problem, not Israel. And, in her internationally best-selling book, *From Time Immemorial: The Origins of The Arab-Jewish Conflict Over Palestine*, Joan Peters proves from Britain's own records that the maximum number possible for refugees that fled after Israel was attacked in 1948 was 343,000,[274] a figure less than half of that claimed by the *Times*. The number of "Palestinian" refugees is calculated by the number of UN ration books circulating among the "refugees."[275]

A United States investigation into the refugee problem in 1960 found that even five years earlier some "refugees" were known to be holding as many as 500 ration books.[276] How many ration books must some be holding today, 45 years later? The UN "Palestinian refugee" count is ludicrous to the extreme and bears no relation to reality.

Tony Blair says there is "a political case for doing more for the refugees," but the refugees are themselves a political weapon.

The refugee weapon is continually used against Israel with devastating effect. Blair says he "was shocked at the conditions he saw in Palestinian refugee camps." Of course he was shocked. He was meant to be. The Arab world has purposely kept the refugees in disgusting conditions for over 50 years. Some refugee camps have been denied even the most basic amenities, such as electricity and sewerage systems, so that those forced to remain in the camps "might never forget they are refugees."[277]

The reader might stop here for a moment and ponder why a newly-reborn state of Israel, with a total Jewish population of around 650,000,[278] could absorb between 820,000 and 850,000 Jewish refugees[279] driven from Arab lands, while the vast Arab world—possessing 10 percent of our planet's land surface and countless billions of petrodollars—could not absorb 343,000 Arab refugees all sharing the same tongue and culture? The Arab refugees were not and are not absorbed because Arab leaders will never let them be all the while Israel exists. And the UN cooperates with the Arabs by consistently blocking Israel from providing its Arab refugees with new homes of their own outside of the camps.[280] The refugees will continue living in miserable, shameful conditions because both the Arab world and the UN have thus decreed it to be so. However, cosmically-ignorant leaders like Britain's Tony Blair will continue to lay the blame for the refugees' appalling conditions upon Israel.

High level British contempt for Israel showed up in the devastating July 1994 bombing of the Israeli Embassy in London. A 22 kilogram car bomb that injured 13 people and almost destroyed the Embassy was one of the worst terrorist bombings London had ever seen. Later that same night a second bomb injured six people at the London offices of Britain's main Jewish charities and pro-Israel institutions. However, on November 2, 1997 the London *MAIL* reported that an advance warning of the attacks had been sent to the British intelligence service MI5.[281] According to the *MAIL* MI5 had not bothered to inform either the police or the Israeli government.[282] The officer who received the report failed to act upon it and passed it to another officer who simply buried it in a filing cupboard.[283] Neither of the officers were disciplined by MI5 management after the hidden report came to light.[284] Two Palestinians were later convicted of carrying out the attacks.[285]

The Role of the U.S.

The United States has been the umbrella under which Egypt, Jordan and the PLO have "negotiated" their "peace" agreements with Israel. No Arab nation or entity wishes to conduct face-to-face negotiations with Israel without the powerful U.S. "mediator" being involved. This is only partly due to the Arab hatred of Israelis (the late King Hussein of Jordan used to wave and smile at Israelis from his sailboat as he sailed past them in the Mediterranean). It is mainly due to the established fact that more concessions can be extracted from Israel if America play-acts the part of being an "honest broker" in the "negotiations."

Thus far, with "peace" agreements signed with two Arab nations and one terrorist organization, the Arabs have received the following: tens of thousands of square kilometers of land; the oilfields developed by Israel in the Sinai desert (which met most of Israel's oil requirements); millions of cubic meters of precious drinking water annually (which Israel cannot spare); and billions of dollars in cash from Israel—and even more from the U.S. Israel, on the other hand, has received three sets of papers—each with the words "Peace Agreement" written on them.

Egyptian peace bars an Israeli presence from attendance at international scientific and academic events held in Egypt. Jordan expels journalists, theatre directors and such from its unions— with an inevitable loss of jobs—if they visit Israel. And the PLO peace brought a 900 percent increase in terror attacks against Israelis.

Through America's "honest brokerage," Israel purchased, at an extremely high cost, two semi-ceasefires from Egypt and Jordan ("semi-ceasefires" because both Egyptian and Jordanian soldiers have since gunned down unarmed Israeli tourists including women and children), and an escalation in terror attacks against Israelis from the PLO. And each of Israel's "peace" partners consider Israel to be their number one enemy today. A great achievement indeed!

8

Friend, or Foe?

Most people, unaware of the true facts, consider America to be Israel's greatest friend, ally and patron. This is an illusion, a myth that the left-wing and its media yes-men like to propagate at home and abroad. It is a myth that needs to be shattered. The American public is kind, warm, generous and hospitable, but its leaders and State Department wise men have never been a true friend to Israel.

Beginning with Franklin D. Roosevelt, the first American president who had to form an opinion on "Zionism," each president (with the exception of Ronald Reagan) followed much the same path of pro-Arab policies.

Chaim Weizmann, who later became Israel's first president, met with Franklin Roosevelt on a number of occasions. After his 1941 meeting with King Ibn Saud, the feudalistic ruler of Saudi Arabia, Roosevelt said:

> I have learned more about the problems of Palestine from his majesty Ibn Saud in five minutes than in 15 years of meetings with Dr. Weizman.[1]

During World War II, Roosevelt

> vehemently opposed bombing the Nazi extermination camps, using every means at his disposal to prevent such attacks. He did this despite the hard evidence—which left no room for any doubt—that every day in the camps, from late 1942 until 1944—every single day—the Nazis were exterminating some 5,000 to 10,000 Jews.[2]

Harry Truman's friendship toward Israel is well known. He represented the first country to recognize the State of Israel, in stark opposition to his State Department's wishes and recommendations. However, the real facts concerning Truman's policies toward Israel are not so well known. His administration did everything it could to prevent the declaration of the State of Israel on May 14, 1948, and even examined the possibility of changing the UN resolution and canceling the articles that dealt with the establishment of a Jewish state in a corner of Palestine.[3] Following the formal declaration of the state (when Israel was facing a major military threat from seven fully trained, fully equipped Arab armies), Truman imposed a total arms embargo against Israel.[4]

President Eisenhower succeeded Truman, and he exerted un-relenting pressure upon Israel to cede part of its minuscule amount of land area to make contiguous territory between Egypt and Jordan.[5] Had Israel given in to U.S. pressure, it would have been cut in half and been made ripe for annihilation by the next Arab invasion. Like Truman, Eisenhower refused to receive Israeli prime ministers at the White House, but received Arab leaders with full pomp on the White House lawn.[6]

After Egypt had blocked the Straits of Tiran against Israeli shipping and sparked the Suez Campaign in 1956, Eisenhower joined up with the Soviet Union to force Israel to withdraw from Sinai and the Gaza Strip. In 1957, against the possibility of another Egyptian blockade of the Tiran Straits, Eisenhower committed America to guaranteeing Israel free passage through the Straits of Tiran. But he continued the arms embargo imposed by Truman.[7]

John F. Kennedy followed the pattern of not receiving Israeli prime ministers at the White House and exerted massive pressure to force Israel to accept international monitoring of its nuclear plant at Dimona.[8] So great was the pressure at that time that some cite it as the reason for David Ben-Gurion's retirement.[9]

Lyndon B. Johnson entered the Oval Office following Kennedy's assassination. He was the first president to receive an Israeli prime minister (Levi Eshkol) at the White House.[10] However, on May 23, 1967 Egypt blockaded the Straits of Tiran again. Israel appealed to Johnson to uphold the American commitment made by Eisenhower and open the Straits of Tiran to Israeli shipping. Johnson said he "could not find" the 1957 document recording the pledge to aid Israel if Egypt were to close the Tiran Straits.[11]

The deceitful, blatant violation of America's commitment sent a signal to the Arabs that Israel was completely isolated in the international arena, and this paved the way for the Six Day War which broke out a matter of days later. Israel was surrounded on all sides by five powerful Arab armies poised for attack. Certain to be defeated if it waited for the Arabs to pounce, Israel was forced to strike first. Its pre-emptive strike was so quick and powerful that it completely decimated all five armies, along with each of their respective air and sea powers in less than a week.

On top of its shameful avoidance of the commitment that America had willingly taken upon itself, the Johnson administration supported Britain's submission of a resolution to the UN Security Council in an attempt to push Israel back to the borders it held prior to the war.[12]

One of the worst presidents—from Israel's point of view—was Richard Nixon. This was apparently due to the presence of Henry Kissinger throughout Nixon's entire period in office. Kissinger's career "always took precedence over the good of his own people,"[13] and

> he was only too eager to demonstrate his determination to implement...anti-Israel American policy.[14]

In 1970, during the War of Attrition, Israel agreed to a Kissinger-negotiated ceasefire on the U.S.-endorsed condition that Egyptian SAM (Surface-to-Air Missile) missiles would not be moved forward to the Suez Canal. Soon after the ceasefire was signed, the SAMs were moved forward without any U.S. reaction or protest.[15] Those missiles took the lives of many Israeli pilots in the 1973 Yom Kippur War.

Kissinger took the Arab position and his pro-Arab rhetoric helped pave the way for the devastating 1973 Yom Kippur War. When the war finally broke out in October of that year,

> the Nixon administration—through Kissinger—did everything it could to delay aid to Israel, in order to weaken it as much as possible and enable the United States to exert as much pressure as it could.[16]

Following Nixon's resignation due to Watergate, Gerald Ford became president. The Ford administration coordinated with Egypt and forced Israel to concede territory without Egypt having to make a single concession. In 1975 Israel gave up the strategic Mitla and Gidi Passes and the Abu Rudeis oil fields in Sinai in return for U.S. signed undertakings to supply F16 fighter planes exclusively to Israel, not to negotiate with the PLO without Israel's consent and not to provide Saudi Arabia with AWAC spy planes.[17] As a further inducement to relinquish the Abu Rudeis oilfields to Egypt, Ford wrote a letter to then Prime Minister Rabin, dated September 1, 1975, promising that any peace agreement with Syria must be predicated on Israel remaining on the Golan Heights.[18]

When negotiations with Syria began in the 1990s, the Ford letter was not cited in U.S. policy, and Rabin was encouraged to cede the entire Golan to Syria.

Jimmy Carter, a devout Southern Baptist, became president in 1976. He was, without doubt, the most anti-Israel president to hold office since Israel became a state. He applied "inexorable pressure" upon Israel's Menachem Begin to give up all of the Sinai, including the Rafah Salient and all of its settlements.[19] In 1978, Carter reneged on the U.S. commitments signed with Israel in 1975.[20] Carter also insisted that Israel recognize "the legitimate rights of the Palestinian people,"[21] a statement that became Yitzhak Rabin's justification for the Oslo process.

Carter's successor was Ronald Reagan, the only president with positive feelings for Israel and an understanding of the real issue. In 1979 Reagan said:

> The real issue in the Middle East had to do with the Arab refusal to recognize that Israel has a right to exist as a nation. To give up the buffer zones Israel took in the Six Day War, would be to put a cannon on her front walk aimed at her front door by those who have said she must be destroyed.[22]

However, due to the long-held pro-Arab policies the Reagan administration also adopted the Arab position, and worked hard to stop the PLO's capitulation and removal from Beirut[23] where Israel had bottled it. Reagan also broke the 1975 U.S. undertaking not to sell Saudi Arabia AWAC spy planes and provided them with the sophisticated airborne spy equipment.[24] Toward the end of Reagan's term his Secretary of State George Schultz announced the opening of dialogue between America and the PLO—another breach of the 1975 undertakings and a policy opposed by the Senate.[25]

The Reagan administration deplored Israel's 1981 bombing of Iraq's Osiraq nuclear reactor. During the 1991 Gulf War, however, U.S. Defense Secretary Richard Cheyney said, regarding the Israeli action: "I thank God every day for Israel's courageous actions."[26]

George Bush followed Reagan into the White House, and his administration was repeatedly described as the most unfriendly

U.S. administration in Israel's history.[27] It passed beyond being "unfriendly"—it was nothing short of "hostile"[28]—and often "assaulted"[29] Israel. Bush did not "wish Israel well"[30] and both he and his Secretary of State James A. Baker III showed their hostility toward Israel at critical moments.[31] A June 1992 Editorial in the *Jerusalem Post* said:

> Many feel that no administration has been as unfriendly to Israel as the current one. This may have as much to do with the crudeness of the pronouncements made by President George Bush and Secretary of State James Baker as with their policies themselves.[32]

"Crudeness" is hardly the word to describe some of the Bush and Baker "pronouncements." Possible the coarsest came from Secretary of State Baker, a supposed born-again, Spirit-filled "Christian" when he said, "F--k the Jews, they won't vote for us anyway."[33] Bush was also the first American president who "did not hesitate to openly interfere in Israeli elections."[34]

William Jefferson (Bill) Clinton has proven himself to be a greater liar than Richard Nixon. Clinton acted in a completely unreliable fashion, but managed to effuse conviction and credibility nonetheless. His adulterous relationship with Monica Lewinsky and his claim—"I did not have sexual relations with that woman"—can be justly compared with his dealings with Israel.

On the surface, Clinton showed remarkable depths of affection for Israel. However, everything he did in relation to Israel was aimed at getting the Jews to give up large parts of their meagre portion of land. He actively worked to redivide their God-given inheritance with the Arabs, who between them, possess 690 times more land than Israel—10 percent of the world's land area—more land than any ethnic body on this planet. He stressed faith in Yasser Arafat's commitment to "peace" when almost every other utterance from Arafat mentions the Arab goal of destroying the Jewish state and occupying every last inch of its land.

The U.S. State Department has also issued numerous statements either indicating or stating outright that Arafat has complied with the Oslo agreements while Israel has not. Many of the statements contain nothing less than bald-faced lies, but truth and international law today is what Washington wants it to be. The State Department's ability to disregard facts and lie when this suits its agenda is not only deplorable, but also contemptible. "Facts" are suited to the policy, not policy to the facts.

Court Jews have made things even more difficult for Israel and are liberally used by the Clinton administration. Court Jews are assimilated Jews who have gained power in the courts of the Gentiles. Several have been sent to apply pressure to the Netanyahu government; these include Special Peace Envoy Dennis Ross, Secretary of State Madeleine Albright, Assistant Secretary of State for Middle Eastern Affairs Martin Indyk and former secretary of state Henry Kissinger. The latter has met with top Israeli leaders behind closed doors for years—forcefully giving them his "advice." In July 1996, shortly after the election of Bibi Netanyahu and just prior to his maiden trip to the U.S. as Israel's prime minister, Kissinger arrived in Israel and met in Jerusalem with Netanyahu for two hours. Kissinger was reported as saying afterwards:

> Furthering the Middle East peace process is necessary for Israel and Binyamin Netanyahu will soon realize this.[35]

According to those who were present,

> Netanyahu emerged from the meeting white and pale, refusing to repeat what Kissinger had said to him.[36]

What better way to apply pressure to Israel than by using court Jews? These bend over backwards to retain or increase their individual and corporate political clout, readily adopting the Arab position in order to show their Gentile bosses they do not show favor to their Jewish brethren.

Congress unsupportive of Clinton's M.E. policies

All of Oslo's basic assumptions have failed the test of time, but the Clinton administration could not bring itself to acknowledge its failure. And for months Oslo was bogged in the mire of Arafat's non-compliance, but Clinton received Arafat at the White House several times while snubbing Bibi Netanyahu in another snide form of pressure.

Pressure was continually applied to Netanyahu without any corresponding pressure upon Arafat. Oslo was doomed even before it began, but Netanyahu was an effective scapegoat for its failure. Netanyahu managed to resist most American pressure designed to force him to accept American dictates in the "peace" process.

The U.S. State Department is a very real and dangerous enemy of Israel. Not the American people, not the U.S. Congress, but the State Department working through succeeding administrations. The U.S. State Department has done more harm to Israel with its lies, pressure and policies of deceit than the Arab armies have been able to do using conventional weapons of war against the Jewish state. Congress openly opposed the Clinton administration in its treatment of Israel and has, also, shown firm support for the Jewish state.

Twenty U.S. Congressmen sent a letter of support to Prime Minister Netanyahu on the eve of his talks with U.S. Secretary of State Madeleine Albright in December 1997. The signatories said they wanted to convey their

> support for your government and its efforts to resist pressures to cede ever larger parts of Judea, Samaria and Gaza to the Palestinian Authority.
>
> We believe that such pressures from the international community are misguided, dangerous, and harm the national security interests of both Israel and the United States.
>
> In addition, we would like you to know that while it may appear that there are many in the Clinton administration and elsewhere clamoring for an Israeli withdrawal from such strategic assets as the Jordan River Valley, the mountains overlooking this piece of territory, and other parts of Israel, the US Congress is firmly on your side.[37]

Eighty-one out of 100 U.S. Senators signed a letter to President Clinton in April 1998 urging him not to use public pressure against Israel.[38] The letter stated *inter alia* that public pressure

> would be particularly unfair and counterproductive since Israel has kept the promises it made at Oslo.[39]

Two hundred and twenty members of the U.S. House of Representatives sent a letter to Clinton in May 1998 also urging him "to avoid public pressure on Israel."[40] The letter said *inter alia*:

> Our most loyal democratic allies in the region should not be punished with threats and ultimatums, but given our fullest confidence as they attempt to balance their needs of peace and security.[41]

The letter also said that the Palestinians

haven't done any of the things they are supposed to have done, and yet the Clinton administration continues to be pro-Arafat, continues to prop up the Palestinian position and has now moved in a public way, to deliver an ultimatum, "decide by next week or else."[42]

U.S. Secretary of State Albright voiced, albeit rather unwittingly, both the Administration's reason for pressuring Israel so unrelentlessly and also the Administration's prime concern:

…when the peace process is stalled, our influence in the region is affected.[43]

Peace, obviously, is not the American objective in the Middle East or anywhere else for that matter. The prime thrust of U.S. foreign policy makers is—in probable order of importance—American influence, American power, and large financial profits from American big business. The U.S. only intervenes where the pickings are the richest.

Changing Fortunes

Even when Israel was an important, strategic U.S. ally against the Soviet influence in the Middle East, it was often betrayed by U.S. administrations. Therefore, being betrayed into the hands of the Arab world today should not really elicit much excitement in Israeli circles. Yesterday, Israel was an important ally. Today, Israel is hampering American interests in the Middle East and is, therefore, expendable. The U.S. "honest broker" plan is to rearrange the entire Middle East according to its interests. It will also change loyalties according to the changes in strategic and economic interests.

The collapse of the Soviet Union and the emergence of America as world arbiter coincided with the political resurgence of the oil-rich and militant Muslim world. The new situation profoundly affected the behavior and thinking of American policy makers. Israel was no longer the strategically important U.S. oasis of influence in the former Soviet-dominated Middle East. The Arab nations had lost their Soviet patron, and America was bent on filling that void—at Israel's expense if necessary.

The political and economic clout of around five million Israelis pale against that of over 200 million Arabs. U.S. policies changed toward Israel, and have continued to bob and weave ever since. At the close of 1997, a senior diplomat at the Israeli Embassy in

Washington expressed concern at the continuing shifts in American policy:

> Senior Arab elements feel these days that they are about to receive something very big as a result of a U.S. policy change, and they are, therefore, sure that if they exert pressure and wait, they will get more.[44]

Waiting is all the Arab leaders need to do. American big business expects to make an estimated $200 billion from the Arab world when "peace" is achieved in the Middle East. Handing the Arab world a truncated Israel that cannot effectively defend itself could mark the end of the Jewish state. Washington will not lose any sleep if Israel is annihilated by the Arabs—five million Israelis stand in the way of $200 billion, and that calculates at $40,000 per head. And business is business.

Bill Clinton is frequently photographed holding or waving a Bible. The Bible-waving "Christian" president, however, wore his "Christian" heart on his sleeve, when he was caught with his pants down in several adulterous relationships and, also, the ensuing lies he told before the Grand Jury regarding them.

The Clinton administration pursued a vigorous and aggressive pro-Muslim foreign policy to the detriment of both Christians and Jews. And as the Islamic fasting month of Ramadan drew to a close in January 2000, Clinton declared that Ramadan was a "gift from Islam to the world."[45] He added, "We pray that the new moon will bring a new era of peace...."[46]

Blinded by the glare of U.S. influence, power and petrodollars, the American State Department is fully prepared to give a weakened Israel into the hands of the Arab and Muslim worlds. It does not see nor care that Israel has one of the greatest concentrations of high IQs in the world. Israel is discovering medicines and medical procedures that are benefitting the whole world. It has produced agricultural benefits like drip irrigation that literally change the face of the world. And its high-tech computer software industry is unmatched by any nation. To hand Israel over to destruction will cost the Americans much more than $200 billion.

Jews make up less than half of one percent of world population yet they have taken nearly 30 percent of all Nobel prizes. Jews have excelled in Medicine, the Sciences and the Arts. They have given to this world out of all proportion to their number. One-third of all world Jewry was liquidated by the Nazis during the Holocaust. Just what did the Nazis steal from this world besides the six million Jewish souls and their gold and works of art? Perhaps they stole the cure for cancer and a thousand other cures besides. They stole the lives of one-third of all living Jews, therefore they stole the discoveries, work and humanitarian services that would have gained 10 percent of the Nobel prizes since that time. What will America steal from the world by handing another five million Jews over to the Arabs for annihilation?

The U.S. is more powerful than any power since classical antiquity.[47] It can decide what the "international community" decrees, choose its allies and enemies, and even create or destroy states at will. As the world's only superpower, the U.S. cannot be neutral because it always has a hidden agenda. American intervention in any situation or conflict is ultimately an intervention on one side or the other. Thus America, as an "honest broker" between Israel and the Arab world, is a joke. The Arabs have the political and economic clout of a 200 million plus populace living on 10 percent of the world's land area that contains two-thirds of the world's known oil reserves. Israel was once important to U.S. policy, but that policy has changed. Like a soiled diaper, Israel has been bought, used, changed, and thrown out.

New World Chaos

America's foreign policy aims to establish a New World Order with the U.S. at the head. Any nation opposing American global domination is a rebel—a rogue state to be disciplined by sanctions or military action until it toes the U.S. line.

In June 1997, U.S. Secretary of State Madeleine Albright outlined a global order under U.S. global leadership to an audience of Harvard alumni.[48] Albright told her applauding, patriotic listeners:

> No nation in the world need be left out of the system we are constructing.[49]

America's New World Order directs the Israeli-PLO "peace" process. The latest agreement in the Oslo process was worked out at the Wye River Plantation which is a facility owned by the Council on Foreign Relations (CFR). The membership of the CFR is a who's-who of every New World Order leader in the world. The

Wye River Plantation is the designated meeting place for finding a political solution to the Middle East's problems. Its think-tank committee is patterned after the Helsinki Convention which was instrumental in the breakup of the former Soviet Union.[50]

The New World Order is a humanistic attempt by *"fools"* to usher in a utopian global peace and will ultimately lead to the greatest deception of all time—the Antichrist. The New World Order will eliminate the sovereignty and powers of nations to form a one-world-government, and global policies will be instituted at will. It will monitor the world's population by electronic surveillance methods and completely destroy freedom and privacy.

Every person's movements will be monitored as will their every sale or purchase—no one will buy or sell without the NWO's authority or knowledge. The cashless society that is currently being forced—forced, not instituted—upon the world is simply a powerful method of surveillance.

Many readers will sing the praises of a cashless society and some will even repeat the NWO's propaganda that cash and checks are labor-intensive and costly to handle. If this were true, why does an electronic bank transaction cost up to five times that of a guaranteed check from the same bank? A "labor-intensive, costly" check sent by mail in the U.S. or Europe takes between three and five days for delivery. A simple electronic interbank transaction often takes a minimum of seven days and sometimes up to ten days, if banks do not have direct contact. Cash and checks are costly and labor-intensive to process? Who is kidding whom?

The New World Order, alias the One World Government, is too far advanced to be stopped. As the year 2000 is often mentioned by NWO leaders we can reasonably expect a dramatic acceleration of its activities in this, the 21st century.

U.S. Double Standards, Hypocrisy and Betrayal

American foreign politics stink. Many people are sure to respond to that by countering that America is generous to the extreme in giving aid worth many billions of dollars to any number of nations each year. When a crocodile appears to smile at a man it is not being cordial, it is contemplating how to catch and eat him. Thus, it is with America and its foreign aid, too. Washington appears to smile and holds out fistfuls of dollars in aid, but it has carefully weighed how much profit its money will bring and is about to swallow the recipient whole, if it goes for the bait.

Israel has been a faithful and important "ally" of the U.S. America guaranteed Israel a qualitative edge in military equipment, as it is surrounded by hostile Arab nations in a state of war with Israel and who have already initiated three major wars against the Jewish state. U.S. foreign policy, however, concerns itself with what it calls an "arms balance" in the region, so while it sells arms to Israel it sells a greater amount to the Arab states. There is no logic to selling greater amounts of weapons to the Arabs, because there are more Arabs than Jews. There is no logic to selling less arms to one's ally than to the ally's enemies. The only logic is keeping the balances right—bank balances, that is.

If Israel is, as the U.S. says, a faithful ally, why then have the Americans been passing classified information regarding this ally's military dispositions and defenses to Arab nations for years?[51]

In 1983, Israel and America signed an Executive Agreement on sharing intelligence between the U.S. and Israel. In 1986, Jonathan Pollard, a civilian intelligence analyst for the U.S. Navy, was sentenced to life imprisonment for passing U.S. intelligence information to Israel. In the course of his duties, Pollard had come face to face with the fact that America was violating the Agreement by withholding vital information. Being Jewish, Pollard felt he had a moral obligation to Israel and passed the information on. Casper Weinberger, a self-hating court Jew, fought hard to put Pollard away "so he will never see the light of day."[52] Of a consequence Pollard received an unprecedented life sentence.

In May 1997, it was revealed by the *Washington Post* that the National Security Agency (NSA) had intercepted a conversation between Israeli intelligence agents.[53] The breach of their security caused consternation in the Israeli Intelligence Services. They had to face the harsh fact that the United States was spying on Israel— one of its finest allies—had broken its code and was eavesdropping on its agents' telephone conversations. The NSA was spying on Israel in the full meaning of the word. Pollard only passed on intelligence information vital to Israel, a U.S. ally, which America was obligated to share, but had withheld. If Pollard had spied for Russia he might have received two to five years in prison, but for making it known that America was holding out on Israel he got life without parole. This was disproportional punishment for the crime he committed.

Former Israeli Prime Minister Bibi Netanyahu accuses President Clinton of "reneging on an unambiguous promise"[54] to free Pollard in return for Israel's participation in Washington-sponsored peace talks at the CFR's Wye River Plantation in Maryland, in October 1998. When Clinton asked Netanyahu at the White House in September 1998 to attend an intensive session of intensive negotiations in Maryland, Netanyahu said that he would need Pollard's freedom as something to take back to the Israelis.[55] Clinton unequivocally agreed to the condition.[56] Later, when it came time for Israel to collect, Clinton reneged on his promise.

Israel is not the only ally that the U.S. has betrayed. America did not become the pre-eminent world power by playing according to the rules. If the U.S. stood to gain by stabbing its "friends" in the back, it unhesitatingly stabbed. And there are a large number of nations bearing scars from American-inflicted back wounds today. In 1998, it was revealed by a former U.S. Ambassador to Britain that America had even passed British intelligence information to the IRA![57] As a consequence

London stopped passing sensitive intelligence to the White House.[58]

America is way out in front of civilized Western nations with its astronomical crime and murder rates, burgeoning drug problems and a pornographic industry larger than its huge movie and music industries combined. U.S. school authorities confiscate knives and handguns from pupils at school entrances and hand out condoms in order that the pupils may enjoy "safe sex." And Secretary of State Albright envisions a new world order of nations made in the image of the United States? God help us!

Even though the U.S. is unable to police its own backyard, it is a self-appointed world policeman. The Clinton Administration's ambition is "to control the international economy and international politics."[59] At the time of writing the U.S. is still involved with its years-long bombing of Iraq, and has just completed the destruction of Yugoslavia. In addition to its active military involvement in a number of nations the U.S. is also maintaining sanctions against a number of others: Iran, Libya, India, Pakistan, North Korea and Russia, to name just a few.

The Two Faces of the U.S.

The sanctions against Iran are supposedly because that nation sponsors terrorism. Iran does indeed sponsor terrorism, but Syria, with whom the U.S. is courting and cultivating relations, is equally as great a sponsor of terrorism as Iran.

Syrian terrorism lashes out 360 degrees from Damascus and not only against neighboring Turkey, Jordan and Israel, but much further afield. Hizb'allah, Hamas, Islamic Jihad and the Popular Front for the Liberation of Palestine (General Command) are just some of the terrorist organizations based in and operating out of Damascus. The U.S. State Department is well aware of Syria's involvement in the 1992 bombing of the Israeli Embassy in Buenos Aires[60] and also the 1994 bombing of the Buenos Aires Jewish Community Center that killed 86 people "which it "tried unsuccessfully to foist on Iran."[61] America also knows that Syria oversees the actions of Hizb'allah against Israel in Syrian-controlled Lebanon. After all, that was why it sent Secretary of State Warren Christopher shuttling between Damascus and Jerusalem and not between Beirut and Jerusalem to bring 1996's Operation Grapes of Wrath in Lebanon to an end.

The U.S. State Department has been engaged in an effort to wipe Damascus clean of the taint of terrorism, and the lengths to which it is willing to go simply boggles the mind. America blamed two Libyan intelligence agents for the terrorist bombing of Pan-Am flight 103 over Lockerbie, Scotland, in 1988 which took the lives of 270 people. At American insistence, Libya became the target of UN sanctions that remained in place until April 1999, and were only partially lifted when Libya finally gave in to the pressure and handed over the two "suspected" agents for trial in Holland. However, Libya is blameless in the matter of Pan-Am flight 103. The U.S. has known this from the beginning, but it imposed UN sanctions upon a whole nation on trumped up charges, nevertheless.

Israeli intelligence had known for years that Ahmed Jibril's Damascus based Popular Front for the Liberation of Palestine (General Command) was responsible for the bomb on board Pan-Am flight 103. The CIA also knew this, and therefore knew that Syria was deeply implicated in the bombing. But it was only in April 1996 that hard evidence of the above was provided through the whole story coming to light. The full story of Pan-Am flight

103 first appeared in the German magazine *Focus* which conducted an interview with a CIA department head. A few weeks later a summary of the interview was published in the June 1996 Digest of the *Jerusalem Institute of Western Defence*, and an edited version of this was published in the *Jerusalem Post* in July of the same year. The full interview with questions and answers is much too long to reproduce here. The following is the full portion concerning the bombing that appeared in the *Jerusalem Post* on July 22, 1996:

> Until recently, President Assad could peddle drugs, provide a haven for terrorists operating against Turkey, Israel and Jordan, keep Secretary of State Christopher twiddling his thumbs for hours and still be courted by the US? Why?
>
> One compelling reason might well be the story behind the downing of Pan-Am Flight 103 over Lockerbie, Scotland in 1989.
>
> Israeli intelligence had long known that Syria's pet terrorist chief, Ahmed Jibril, was involved in that incident. So has the CIA. But the details only came to light earlier this year when a CIA department head who had worked in Mideast antiterrorism gave an interview to the German magazine *Focus*.
>
> A CIA agent code named V-man infiltrated a Palestinian organization and met Ahmed Jibril, head of the PFLP-General Command, in Teheran in 1989. Jibril told V-man privately that he had been responsible for the Lockerbie bombing.
>
> Later the CIA discovered that the bomb that blew up Flight 103 had been made in a PFLP camp in Lebanon's Beka'a valley. Syria's national airline had transported it from Damascus to Berlin, where a Jibril terrorist cell awaited it. The bomb was smuggled aboard Flight 103 by an American PanAm employee, a drug addict paid in cash and Lebanese drugs.
>
> Why Flight 103? The PFLP chose it because it was flying US secret service and drug enforcement personnel home for Christmas.
>
> The incriminating evidence was there. But the US wanted Syria's participation in the peace process, thus no real pressure was ever exerted on Assad.
>
> Then Iraq invaded Kuwait, and as the CIA department head told *Focus*, "We needed Syria as a partner in the great

anti-Iraq coalition. We forced Assad to take part in the Gulf War." The CIA head didn't elaborate further.

Asked why, some months later, Washington suddenly blamed Libya for the Lockerbie bombing, the answer was, "That's realpolitik. How could we unmask our partners during such a difficult period and present them as responsible for one of the worst terrorist outrages of all time? We had to protect Syria and simultaneously blame someone for 270 deaths. So we picked Libya, with which our relations have always been strained..."

Added the CIA department head: "It is doubtful whether my government will ever be able to backtrack from the Libyan version. Too much has happened since 1991. The fronts have clearly been established. The UN embargo [on Libya] has caused serious damage. And Syria is on the brink of peace with Israel.

I don't deny that the price of this peace is [the truth about] Lockerbie."[62]

At the time of writing, the two Libyans agents are awaiting trial for a crime they had no part in. Only time will provide the answer as to whether they will be thrown completely to the lions and found guilty in order to save Washington's ugly face.

In June 1996, a horrendous truck-bomb exploded outside the U.S. Air Force complex in Dhahran, Saudi Arabia, killing 26 Americans and injuring hundreds. Blame for the bombing was laid upon Iranian-backed fanatical anti-American Saudi Muslims. In July 1996, however, *Agence France Presse* reported that

> the perpetrators of the bombing of US military quarters in Dhahran ... were trained near Lattaqia in Syria.[63]

And according to the London *Sunday Telegraph* of January 19, 1997, both

> the Saudi and U.S. investigations revealed that Syrian intelligence officers were the key movers in the Dhahran bombing of American military quarters last year. The bomb was prepared in Lebanon's Beka'a valley (which is under Syrian control) for several weeks and a lorry transported it to Dhahran via Syria and Jordan.[64]

Further, Saudi Arabia eventually concluded that

Iran was not involved in the bombing of the American troops in Dhahran.[65]

Which leaves us with fanatical Saudi Muslims and Syria, and

One of the main Saudi suspects sought refuge in Syria after the explosion. When the Saudis asked Syria to extradite him, he was murdered by Syrian intelligence agents.[66]

It is very obvious that Syrian terrorism is a fundamental threat facing not only Mideast states, but also the entire free world. But the U.S. whitewashes the pariah state, institutes sanctions against a nation of 5.5 million people to cover for Syria's involvement in the bombing of Pan-Am flight 103, and on the eve of his meeting with Assad in 1994, President Clinton said he was

fascinated to be meeting with this somewhat notorious character.[67]

And Martin Indyk, one of Washington's "Court Jews," said that "Syria should not be treated as the rogue state."[68] The pandering to Syria by the U.S. because of the Middle East "peace" process, shows the total moral bankruptcy of the whole American-driven process. For Iran, America wants foreign action. For Syria, it wants aid because Damascus plays too important a role in U.S. foreign policy objectives.

Europe: America's next conquest?

America also has plans to dominate Europe. It seized upon the crisis brought about by the civil war in the Balkans to establish its foothold, and consolidated its interests through the Kosovo crisis. The U.S. leadership has a lot to learn. It earned billions from its arm sales to Iraq, but has spent far more in its efforts to destroy the weapons it sold, and, also, to contain Iraq and prevent Saddam Hussein from threatening his neighbors. America has yet to learn that all the financial and physical aid it has poured, and will yet pour, into the Arab and Muslim worlds, has not bought one friend who will not side with a fellow Muslim country in any serious crisis. In fact, America is already more hated today by the Islamic and Arab worlds than before it opened its coffers and began appeasing them.

Yugoslavia was created by the Treaty of Versailles at the end of the First World War. It was an amalgam of six republics and initially

comprised Slovenia, Croatia and Serbia, but Bosnia and Herze-
govina, Macedonia and Montenegro were later brought in. In 1990-
91 Croatia attempted to secede from Yugoslavia, and this was the
spark that ignited the Balkans. Yugoslavia possessed a Constitution,
and it was a violation of that legal Constitution for any republic to
secede from Yugoslavia.

The Croats cooperated with the Nazis in the Second World
War and the fascist Ustashe government murdered 750,000 Serbs,
60,000 Jews and 40,000 Romani gypsies. Germany rewarded its
friend by being the first country to recognize Croatia. Yugoslavia,
however, did not want one of its republics to secede and sent in the
Yugoslav National Army to suppress the secession attempt. But
America, using NATO as a pretense, put pressure on Yugoslavia
by its military involvement—on the ground as well as in the air[69]—
on the side of the Croats, led by the late pro-Nazi Franjo Tudjman,
and forced Yugoslavia to back off. The secession of Croatia not
only forced thousands of Serbs to live unwillingly under Croatian
rule, but also fired the Bosnian president's imagination to secede
and start a fundamentally Islamic state which also locked Eastern
Orthodox Christian Serbs under Islamic rule. The Croats and
Bosnian Muslims were pro-Nazi while the Serbs fought for the
allies and were kind to the Jews whom the Nazis were exterminating.

It was a spectacle at once pathetic and horrifying: Hundreds
of thousands—perhaps a half million or more—terrified
civilians driven from a land their people had lived in for
centuries. Those not fortunate enough to flee fell prey to the
depredations of merciless paramilitary death squads, who
committed hideous acts of plunder, rape, and mass murder.
Thousands of civilians perished, and the human tidal wave
generated by this triumph of 'ethnic cleansing' was described
by some observers as the largest human population dis-
placement Europe had seen since World War II.

Are these snapshots of Kosovo, April 1999? No – these
are scenes from Krajina, August 1995. The victims were not
ethnic Albanians driven from Kosovo by the security forces
of Serbian dictator Slobodan Milosevic, but rather ethnic Serbs
driven from Croatia by troops under the command of Croatian
dictator Franjo Tudjman.

...Croatian assembly deputy Mate Mestrovic explained

that the Clinton Administration "gave us the green light to do whatever had to be done."[70]

Tudjman became president of Croatia after its secession from Yugoslavia. Due to his World War II pro-Nazi, anti-Jewish activities, he was consistently refused any invitation to visit Israel with other heads of state right up until the time of his death in 1999.

Throughout the upheaval in the Balkans, the Serbs have been branded as the "bad guys" by Western leaders and their kowtowing media. Cynical media manipulation has placed the greater part of the western world on the side of all those opposing the Serbs. The Western media has done to the Serbs what Walter Duranty, the first _New York Times_ Pulitzer Prize winner, did to the Russians:

> One of the most distinguished journalists of his time, Duranty almost single-handedly changed Western opinion on the Soviet Union with his reports from the USSR in the 1930s. His stories were monstrous lies and deceptive half-truths, whose full extent was discovered only with the fall of the Soviet empire.[71]

The Serbs have been demonized—graphically depicted as nothing less than jungle animals. Supposed Serbian atrocities termed "ethnic cleansing" were, more often than not, grossly exaggerated by the media or complete fabrications. These lies were given continuous worldwide media coverage while real Croatian and Muslim atrocities did not merit even a mention, especially by the American media. Thousands upon thousands of Serbs were killed, sometimes hideously, by the Croats and Bosnian Muslims without any mention of it in the U.S. media. The Serbs were blamed for "ethnic cleansing," but the facts are that in 1995 America helped drive 300,000 Serbs from their homes in the Krajina region of Croatia where they had lived as a people for 600 years. There is ample documentation available if anyone really wants to know the truth.

America, the UN and NATO (the UN and NATO are virtual U.S. puppet organizations) have taken a violently anti-Serbian stand and interfered militarily in a civil war in a sovereign state. That NATO is a U.S. puppet organization is borne out by Stratfor's _Global Intelligence Update_ of December 24. 1999, when it says NATO is primarily a political system

> for allowing the United States to have an instrument for influencing and controlling European affairs.[72]

And another high-profile intelligence agency says:

> The United States has already proved that it is ready to start wars on the flimsiest of pretexts when this furthers its political goals.[73]

The NATO strikes set a dangerous precedent in international affairs. Israeli Foreign Minister Ariel Sharon was right to criticize NATO's airstrikes against the Serbs in April 1999 as "airstrikes against a sovereign state engaged in a civil war.[74] Noting that Arabs in Galilee were pushing for autonomy, Sharon went on to say:

> If we support force to resolve regional conflicts, we could be the next victim.[75]

NATO was formed as an alliance to defend NATO nations from attack by hostile countries. Yugoslavia is not a NATO member, and it has never attacked any NATO member country. Yugoslavia is a sovereign state involved with a civil war within that state. NATO has absolutely no right to take sides in a civil war and ferociously attack a sovereign state which has right on its side. However, Washington defines its meddling according to its ambitions.

War is a terrible thing, but it makes a lot of people wealthy— especially Western arms manufacturers and arms dealers. Conflicts, therefore, are not only welcomed, but often instigated or the flames fanned by these powerful men. And the Clinton Administration shamelessly seized every opportunity of exploiting the Balkan crisis to America's advantage.

Some might parrot Madeleine Albright's line and say that America has been defending Western values in the Balkans. This is absolute rubbish. Prior to American-led NATO intervention, deaths in the Balkans could not even be measured in the hundreds, only in the dozens:

> More people died last week in Borneo than expired this year in Kosovar bloodshed – more died in a single Russian bomb blast; in a single outburst of violence in East Timor; in a single day in Rwanda. China has been bloodier this year.[76]

Defending Western values? American values are immoral and the U.S. certainly does not get involved in anything unless it is going to benefit substantially from it. The American-led NATO bombing of Yugoslavia was nothing less than a U.S.-sponsored terror campaign of which

> The estimates of costs to rebuild the damage range up to $100 billion, but the costs in human misery are incalculable.[77]

Why this U.S. obsession with the Balkans? Why Croatia? Why Bosnia-Herzegovina? Why Kosovo? Could the knowledge of there being oil worth four trillion dollars in the Caspian region possibly hold any interest for the Western greed merchants? Or perhaps the fact that Kosovo sits atop the richest lead, silver and gold mine of Eastern Europe? Defending Western values indeed. Ponder this report from the *New York Times* a good two years before the Kosovo war became a twinkle in Madeleine Albright's eye:

> Forget mutual funds, commodity futures and corporate mergers. Forget South African Diamonds, European currencies and Thai stocks. **The most concentrated mass of untapped wealth known to exist anywhere is in the oil and gas fields beneath the Caspian (Sea) and lands around it.**... The strategic implications of this bonanza hypnotize Western security planners as completely as the finances transfix oil executives.[78]

The above is confirmed by the *International Herald Tribune* in January 1998, when it reported that Leon Fuerth, Vice President Al Gore's national security advisor, was—

> leading a U.S. effort to guide development of Caspian Sea oil and gas, **the world's largest untapped reserves**.[79]

The U.S. was nowhere to be seen when millions were being butchered in Rwanda in the worst "ethnic cleansing" since the Nazi Holocaust against the Jews. There was no profit for the U.S. in Rwanda, so it let millions of innocents die. It has not gotten involved in regional conflicts in Ethiopia, Uganda, Kenya, etc., because there is no profit for it in those areas. As was mentioned earlier, America only gets involved where the pickings are richest.

Turkey invaded Cyprus in 1974 and still occupies the northern part of the island. Why has the U.S. not intervened and defended Western values by pushing the Turks off the Cypriot's land? Because that would not be profitable for American interests. Instead, the U.S. has entered into a military alliance with Turkey.

For all its noise about containing Iran, and the strict enforcement of UN sanctions the U.S. initiated against the radical Islamic regime, Washington secretly approved Iranian arms shipments to the Croats and Bosnian Muslims fighting Serbs in Bosnia-Herzegovina in 1996 in direct contradiction of UN policy. Amid denials by both the State Department and the White House, the *Sunday Telegraph* and also the conservative *Sunday Times* carried much the same articles on April 7, 1996, saying the U.S. State Department had approved an Iranian arms pipeline to Bosnia and that President Clinton had personally approved the covert shipments.[80] And in response to American pressures in May 1996, former Iranian president Ali Akbar Hashemi-Rafsanjani warned the U.S. that he

> would reveal "secret documents" showing how the Clinton administration co-operated with Iran in delivering arms to the Bosnian Muslims.[81]

The U.S. State Department wanted a Muslim government headed by Alija Izatbegovic in Bosnia, so it simply arranged it, just like it arranged the elections in "Palestine" in January 1996. If Washington wants Izatbegovic and Arafat to become elected presidents, this happens, irrespective of what the real election results happen to be.

The only two powers that are expanding today are America and fundamental Islam. The U.S. State Department is ready to join forces with Bosnian and Kosovo Muslims against the Christian Serbs because the greed of the globalists see huge personal and institutional profits. The U.S. needs to empty its warehouses of old arms and test modern ones, and it is most beneficial to the U.S. economy when others are paying the bills. Remember Henry Kissinger's Ph.D. thesis quoted earlier? Henry said it was necessary to develop

> ongoing small wars around the planet to maintain the economic alignment of the superpowers.[82]

Most people, however, do not realize the degree of the election fraud the U.S. pulled off in Bosnia.

Mr. Izatbegovic "won" the elections with a 41,000-vote margin over his Bosnian-Serb rival Momcilo Krajisnik. Independent election monitors, however, demanded the Bosnia elections be declared null and void after returns showed seven percent more votes than voters.[83] A despatch dated September 24, 1996 from correspondents of *The Guardian* was headlined: "West covering up mass fraud in Bosnian polls."[84] But the U.S. pressured the Organization for Security and Cooperation in Europe (OSCE) "to play down the evidence of fraud."[85] Thus, Bosnian Christian Serbs were forced to live under Muslim rule.

Under the guise of NATO airstrikes against Yugoslavia in 1999, America is now carving off a piece of Serbia for the Albanian Muslims—Kosovo has been part of Serbia for 600 years.

NATO's forced "peace" talks to be held in France between ethnic Albanian Muslims (KLA – Kosovo Liberation Army) and representatives of Serbian President Slobodan Milosovic's Yugoslav government, broke down in March 1999. Milosovic's negotiators refused to sign a peace agreement giving Kosovo to the ethnic Albanians for an independent Muslim state. The ethnic Albanians— now given the poetic title of "Kosovars"—have been viciously fighting the Serbs in an attempt to force Milosovic to give them independence. Milosovic was willing to grant Kosovo autonomy, but not independence. For his refusal to grant independence to the Muslim "Kosovars," Serbia was systematically destroyed by weeks of devastating round-the-clock NATO (read U.S.) bombings involving hundreds of U.S. warplanes and cruise missiles. The U.S. followed the law of the jungle in Yugoslavia and violated all international norms.

Before readers—especially American ones—start cursing this writer and scream that the bombing of Yugoslavia was a NATO action in response to Serb atrocities against the "Kosovars," they should first take a look at some cold, hard facts.

Firstly, NATO announced early in its action that it had "over 400"[86] warplanes carrying out airstrikes against Serbian targets. Two weeks later it was announced that

the United States had sent 82 more planes to the NATO action, bringing the number of American planes involved to 480.[87]

So, out of NATO's original "over 400" planes 378 were American which left the balance of some 25 planes divided between the 18 other NATO members (not counting newly admitted members). Britain, with its Harrier jets, provided more than half of the non-U.S. planes, and this, therefore, left most members only tokenly involved with a single plane or, as in the case of Germany, two, in order to keep up appearances.

Some NATO members refused to get involved at all, while

others protested the action. Therefore, the bombing of Yugoslavia was a U.S. campaign in which it managed to coerce a few others to reluctantly join it. Britain needed little coercion as Tony Blair has proven himself to be hell-bent on regaining some of Britain's lost power in order for it to be reckoned as a force within Europe. Germany welcomed the opportunity to flex its muscles and get involved in its first military action since World War II—against the Serbs who defeated them in the Balkans during that war.

Two weeks after it received the 82 additional U.S. planes, "NATO" "requested" a further 300 planes from the U.S.[88]

Secondly, on April 6, 1999, after days of round-the-clock bombing, European evening news broadcasts carried President Slobodan Milosovic's call for "a unilateral ceasefire."[89] Early European news broadcasts the following morning reported that "Washington had rejected"[90] the call for unilateral ceasefire. NATO headquarters is in Brussels, Belgium, not Washington. Only later in the day were there news reports stating that "NATO had rejected the Yugoslav offer of a ceasefire."[91]

After yet another intensification and widening of the airstrikes against Yugoslavia on April 15th—including bombing the capital of Montenegro, an autonomous, neutral republic in Yugoslavia, and one critical of Slobodan Milosovic—President Clinton said:

> The intensive NATO air attacks will continue. **If we don't the United States' power can never be used again.**[92]

The facts again leave no room for doubt that the bombing of Yugoslavia was clearly a U.S. military action against Slobodan Milosovic using NATO as a screen. And, despite the total immorality of the action—the devastation of Yugoslavia; the bombing deaths of thousands of innocent civilians (both Serb and ethnic Albanian); the massive ethnic Albanian refugee problem from freewill flights and also from forced expulsions due to "NATO's" carpet bombings; and despite the fact that NATO said the airstrikes

> had little effect on Serbian air defense systems or Serbian attack forces,[93]

—Clinton said the U.S. must continue the monstrous war against Yugoslavia. If it did not, America might lose its ability to intimidate, bully and cower nations in the future. That was nothing short of blatant hypocrisy from a proven draft-dodger[94] and an opposer of the Vietnam War.[95]

Thirdly, on April 7, 1999, U.S. Secretary of State Madeleine Albright had to defend both herself and the NATO action on American television. She is on record as saying that the NATO action in Yugoslavia was "not my personal war."[96] Albright went on to say, "The United States is fighting for its values in the Balkans."[97] Values? U.S. foreign policy values are as immoral as president Clinton. Both the U.S. State Department and Bill Clinton are determined liars, and each seem to compete with each other in deviousness. No individual or organization can take a moral holiday and remain moral. However, the U.S. State Department and Clinton did not take moral holidays, they emigrated.

The first time the Bible mentions Babylon is in Genesis 10:10. After the Flood people tried to scale the heights of heaven by building a mighty tower. The tower's name literally means "Confusion," but it stands for the pride of man. The reason for Babylon's fall in the Bible was her bad influence. Babylon made the nations drink of the wine of her impurity—corrupted them with her evil ways—and this impurity brought down on Babylon the wrath of Almighty God. America today fits the biblical description of Babylon, and it must surely be only a matter of time before the wrath of God falls upon it.

The media demonizes the Serbs, and NATO does no less. NATO's spokesman, Jamie Shea, quoted "reliable sources" when reporting Serb "atrocities." However, after the Serbs produced several ethnic Albanians that "reliable NATO sources" had affirmed to have been tortured or executed at different intervals, even the *BBC* said the

> reliable sources" had proven to be patently unreliable and this threw doubt on all NATO statements.[98]

Anyone who knows anything about journalism knows that when a "reliable source" is quoted, it is often hearsay that a particular reporter wants readers to accept as fact. Why is it that people in general think that only an enemy resorts to outright lies, half-truths and distortions in its propaganda? The West's propaganda machine is second to none.

At the commencement of the bombing of Yugoslavia, the Serbs sent thousands upon thousands of ethnic Albanians out of Kosovo into the surrounding countries. This was not "ethnic cleansing," this was the weak party's attempt to cause immense problems and raise such an outcry that NATO, the strong party, would be forced to stop the bombings. However, this strategy did not work. On the contrary, the bombings were intensified.

Hundreds of thousands of refugees also fled the bombings in fear for their lives. They fled to neighboring states of their own free will, but the Serbs were reported to have forced them all to go which was completely untrue.

Very early in the airstrikes Yugoslavia claimed to have brought down four NATO aircraft (downing four planes out of an attack force of 400 was a modest claim). However, NATO dismissed the claim as Yugoslavian propaganda. NATO denials continued unabated for days, but Serbian television continued to show wreckage from planes Yugoslavia claimed to have shot down. NATO reports were almost mocking in saying that Yugoslavian claims of destroying NATO planes was absurd. But, some days after the airstrikes began it was reported that America was sending 12 more Stealth bombers into the conflict—

> to double its number of Stealth bombers available for the airstrikes and to replace the Stealth bomber shot down a week ago.[99]

If one of the "invisible" planes was shot down by the Serbs, how much credence can be given to NATO's repeated denials of having lost any planes? We should also take into account NATO's own admission that its strikes had done little damage to Serbian air defenses.[100] Apparently, no one responsible for the airstrikes wanted to tell the folks "back home" that some of their boys were being lost in the "low-risk" attack on Yugoslavia. Only one time during the whole *BBC News* coverage of the "NATO" action, did this writer ever hear the standard air attack report that, "All planes returned safely to base."[101]

On April 15th, "NATO" planes bombed an ethnic Albanian convoy of refugees traveling in private cars, on tractors and on foot, killing around 70 people.[102] Blame was immediately placed upon the Serbs for the tragedy, but independent Western observers quickly established beyond doubt—by serial numbers found on bomb fragments scattered "among limbs, torsos and carbonized bodies,"[103] —that the bombing was carried out by "NATO."[104] The following day "NATO" apologized for the bombing of the refugees (who were fleeing the bombings), but said the airstrikes must continue despite the terrible mistake.[105] Accounts of the convoy bombing from surviving refugees were unanimous: four Yugoslavian planes had bombed them.[106] These reports were given credence despite the fact the bombing had been conclusively proven to be the work of "NATO."

Anti-Serb "eyewitness" testimonies from ethnic Albanian Muslim refugees fleeing Kosovo should be given much the same credence as Arab Muslim testimonies of "eyewitness accounts of Israeli atrocities." One "eyewitness" account of Israeli soldiers who, according to the "witness," shot an innocent Arab to death for no reason was televised on March 13, 1992:

> I saw it with my own eyes, with my own eyes, how the three soldiers who killed him bent over on the ground and drank his blood.[107]

Muslim Albanian "eyewitness" accounts of Serbs massacring defenseless ethnic Albanian civilians and the Muslim Albanian refugee testimonies of Serb atrocities, is a rerun of Muslim Arab reports of Israeli brutalities. And just as Muslim Arabs lined up to be paid for their anti-Israel demonstrations staged for Western television networks,[108] so *BBC TV News* showed NATO officials paying ethnic Albanians for their stories.[109]

The match that really lit the "NATO" airstrikes against Slobodan Milosovic was a supposed massacre of 45 ethnic Albanian Muslims in Racak village on January 15, 1999. Of course, there were the usual plentiful supply of ethnic Albanian "eyewitnesses" to the massacre. There was, however, also a non-ethnic Albanian Muslim eyewitness to the events—a *Le Figaro* special correspondent in Kosovo, Renaud Girard. Following is the full text of a summary of the translation from the French report from Girard in Kosovo that was published in *Le Figaro* on January 20, 1999:

> The photographs taken during the clash a Racak village and those taken yesterday by our special correspondent in Kosovo, Renaud Girard, disprove the claims by OSCE and Albanian separatists that Serb forces had slaughtered 45 civilians there on Friday, January 15th. Yugoslav forensic experts, who began the autopsy of the bodies yesterday, said that no evidence was found that any of the victims had been executed. As doubts persist, the exact chronology of what happened is crucial:
>
> At dawn on January 15th, Serb police surrounded and

attacked Racak, a stronghold of the Kosovo Liberation Army (KLA). Having nothing to hide, it invited two *Associated Press* TV reporters to record the operation at 8:30 a.m. The police also warned OSCE, which sent two vehicles with US diplomatic plates to the site. The observers remained the entire day on a hill overlooking the village. At 3 p.m., a police report published by the International Press Center in Pristina announced the death in combat of 15 KLA terrorists and the seizure of a large quantity of arms. At 3:30 p.m. the Serb police left Racak followed by the *AP* TV team, taking away a heavy 12.7 mm machine-gun, two automatic rifles, two sniper rifles and 30 Chinese-made Kalashnikovs. At 4:40 p.m. our reporter drove through the village and saw three orange OSCE vehicles. The OSCE verifiers were talking to three old ethnic Albanian civilians. Returning at 6 p.m., our reporter saw the verifiers taking away four lightly wounded men and women. They told the reporter, not seeming very concerned, that they could not assess the death toll of the clash.

The bodies of 45 ethnic Albanians, wearing civilian clothes and lying side by side in a ditch, were discovered by reporters only on the following day at 9 a.m., while Racak was swarming with armed KLA members, who directed foreign observers and OSCE verifiers to the alleged massacre site as soon as they arrived. The US Ambassador, William Walker, came to Racak about noon and voiced his indignation. All Albanian witnesses gave an identical version of the clash, saying the Serb police raided the village at noon on the 15th, separating women from men and taking the men to a hilltop to execute them on the spot. However, the TV film of the *Associated Press* team, viewed by '*Le Figaro*' radically contradicts these testimonies. It shows the Serb police entering an empty village early in the morning, moving along house walls for protection. They were fired on from KLA trenches dug into an overlooking hill. The fighting intensified. The *AP* team, sheltering near a mosque, understood that the surrounded KLA guerillas were making desperate attempts to break out, about 20 of them succeeding, as the police confirmed.

What really happened? Did the KLA gather bodies of men killed in the fighting overnight between the 15th and 16th January to fabricate an image of execution in cold blood?

Reporters saw few empty cartridge shells around the ditch where the bodies were found. [110]

The above *Le Figaro* report gave rise to a great deal of speculation in France and Renaud Girard was interviewed on *Europe 1* and *France Info* radios, confirming the facts. [111] The Information Advisor to Ibrahim Rugova admitted in a statement published by the Albanian paper *Koha Ditore*, that terrorists in the village of Racak were "waging a war for bodies." [112] The presence of the KLA in Racak on the 16th is explained by the Serb forces leaving it the preceding afternoon. William Walker arrived there before an investigation was held, promptly blaming the Serbs for a "horrible massacre" [113] He was proclaimed *persona non grata* and asked to leave Yugoslavia within 48 hours. He refused. However, "NATO's" declared intention was to "destroy everything dear to Milosovic" [114] and this was largely based upon "eyewitness" accounts of a "massacre" from Serb-hating Muslims—accounts that were rebutted by a *Le Figaro* correspondent report, a film taken by *Associated Press* and the actual bodies themselves (the "witnesses" said the men had been separated from the women, taken away and executed, but the line up of bodies shown around the world on television included several female bodies).

The media loves to portray Serbs as monsters so it would only be fair to include an extract of a report by Bill Schiller on the Serb-hating Bosnian warlord, Nasir Oric, printed in Canada's *Toronto Star*:

> ...Oric is a fearsome man and proud of it. I met him in January 1994, in his home in Serb-surrounded Srebenica. On a cold and snowy night, I sat in his living room, watching a shocking video version of what might have been called "Nasir Oric's Greatest Hits." There were burning houses, dead bodies, severed heads, and people fleeing.
>
> Oric grinned throughout, admiring his handiwork. "We ambushed them," he said when a number of dead Serbs appeared on the screen. The next sequence of dead bodies had been done in by explosives: "We launched these guys to the moon," he boasted. When footage of a bullet-marked ghost town appeared without any visible bodies, Oric hastened to announce: "We killed 114 Serbs there." Later there were celebrations, with singers with wobbly voices chanting his praises. [115]

Obviously, the Serbs are not always the "bad guys" the media has intentionally made them out to be. For more years than they would care to remember, the Serbs have been attacked in turn by Croat Nazi-sympathizers, ethnic Bosnian Muslims and latterly by ethnic Albanian Muslims. In the three months following the signing of an agreement between U.S. Special Envoy Richard Holbrook and President Milosovic—the period from October 13, 1998 to January 14, 1999—there were 599 attacks on Serbs by ethnic Albanian terrorists—186 against civilians. [116]

The Serbs proved themselves to be real friends of the Jewish people during World War II. Could the reason for the intense media dislike of the Serbs be due to their sympathy for the Jews? The Serbs receive similar treatment from the media as has been dished out to Israel, and it is on the receiving end of similar Islamic rhetoric as Israel:

> Muslims everywhere are obliged to fight against the Serbs who are fighting against Muslims in the Balkans—physically, financially and verbally until all Muslim land is liberated. [117]

It is not just ethnic Albanians that make up the KLA force against the Serbs. Muslims from Saudi Arabia, Yemen, Afghanistan and Iran are known to be a part of it. And unconfirmed reports indicate that Osama bin Laden is also involved.

The Serbs are literally lumped together with Israel:

> We declare that we will not rest until Kosovo is returned to the Muslims and they achieve their independence as a Muslim nation. We declare that we will not stop the Jihad against the Serbian or Israeli occupiers no matter what the UN may say or do. [118]

It should be noticed that Muslims consider verbal attacks to be equal to physically fighting or the funding of weapons purchases. Thus, Muslim "eyewitness" accounts of Serb or Israeli "atrocities" are part and parcel of the Jihad, the Muslim "holy war."

Much false and distorted information has been served to the public on media-plated dishes regarding Kosovo. Numbers of journalists and analysts, however, have provided some facts that drive shafts of light into the deliberate grey and black reporting of the kowtowing U.S. media. The horrendous evil done to the Serbian people by the U.S. led devastation of Kosovo and Yugoslavia is being deliberately hidden from the eyes of the public. Can the reader even begin to imagine the carnage done to Serb civilians from thousands of American cluster bombs dropped from 15,000 feet? The whole truth will get out; it always does. Perhaps Clinton will yet find himself dragged before the International Criminal Tribunal that his administration established,[119] as a war criminal on charges of genocide. Phyllis Schlafly wrote in her column:

> The Clinton/NATO bombing was carried on for 78 days with total disregard for human life. **The bombs killed thousands of innocent civilians** and even destroyed hospitals and schools.[120]

According to Human Rights Watch, as at November 1999, some 164,000 Serbs had been driven out of Kosovo by ethnic Albanians, leaving more NATO troops in Kosovo than Serbs.[121] NATO has shown itself to be both uncaring and powerless to prevent ethnic Albanians from slaughtering Serbs in Kosovo,[122] and more Serb civilians have been killed since the bombing stopped than ethnic Albanians before the bombing began.[123]

Another journalist, John Laughland, of the British *Express*, wrote a lengthy article in July 1999. Following is part of the summary of that article published by the *Jerusalem Institute of Western Defence*:

> Officially there are no refugees at all in Serbia. Their existence proves that Yugoslavia has lost control of Kosovo. Though on paper NATO conceded that Kosovo is an integral part of Yugoslavia, in reality NATO and the Kosovo Liberation Army are now in charge. But for NATO, the flood of refugees destroys the fiction that the war was fought for moral principles. Time and again during the war Mr. Blair said: "This is not a war for territory but for values." Ethnic cleansing was unacceptable and had to be stopped. However, if this were the real reason for the war, NATO should now be bombing the Albanian capital, Tirana, or attacking KLA headquarters all over Kosovo. Instead, NATO is turning a blind eye to Albanian atrocities. Far from exerting pressure on the KLA, Mr. Blair was photographed recently enjoying a joke with its leader. And while the International Criminal Tribunal prosecutor, Louise Arbour, travels around Kosovo to draw attention to Serb atrocities against Albanians committed months ago, she is

ignoring atrocities now committed by Albanians under her very nose. The Western military even looks the other way when the Albanian Mafia charges Albanian refugees ransom money before allowing them to leave camps and return home.

Hundreds of Serb and gypsy refugees pour across the Serbian border every day. They told me how they were chased from homes which were then burned before their eyes; how women were raped; how neighbors were shot or had their throats slit. They complained that Albanians were killing Albanian Kosovars who had worked for the Yugoslav state as postmen or in factories. NATO troops were doing nothing to protect the refugees. One 30-year-old mother of three tried to alert a British soldier to looting and violence by Albanians. He replied: "We have no mandate to arrest people." In the French sector, uniformed KLA soldiers walk around unmolested, in contravention of the demilitarization agreement.

The gypsies' fate is particularly tragic. All over Eastern Europe they are a persecuted minority. Only in Serbia did they live free from discrimination. Albanians seem to have a particular hatred for them. I was taken to the former gypsy quarter in the town of Kosovska Mitrovica. All the houses stood empty, torched and smashed up by the Albanians. "We cannot live with the Albanians any more," cried one desperate gypsy woman waiting by the roadside with her family and a few suitcases. "They are animals."

If NATO now rejects the principles it enunciated only a few weeks ago, how credible is its justification of the war? Two elements must make us skeptical. First, there was no refugee crisis (and thus no 'ethnic cleansing') until the bombing started. There were many displaced people in Kosovo fleeing the civil war, but the mass movement into Macedonia and Albania began only after the bombing started. The more we bombed, the more fled. So many fled from the bombs, not from the Serbs. And hundreds of thousands of Albanians remained in Kosovo during the war untouched by Serbs. Second, as a KLA leader told an American journalist two years ago in Istanbul, the KLA strategy for Kosovo independence (executed from January 1998 onwards) was to attack and kill Serbs in order to provoke reprisals. These were presented to the West as racially motivated ethnic cleansing.

In reality they were a brutal reaction to a brutal terrorist insurrection – a fact systematically obscured by NATO propaganda.[124]

Laughland's article exactly bears out what this writer has presented. But what of the Serbian "genocide" reportedly carried out in Kosovo's "killing fields"? These reports came from ethnic Albanian Muslims, and the quoted numbers of ethnic Albanians "massacred" by the Serbs, according to the U.S. foreign policy wise men, began at 10,000 then quickly jumped to 11,000. Figures of 100,000[125] dead were then tossed out, and the U.S. State Department even claimed that some 500,000[126] were feared to have been massacred. This was the supposed motivation for the destruction of a nation, even though State Department spokesman, James Rubin, acknowledged that the atrocity accounts he provided to reporters came from the KLA commander Hashim Thaci, and were "not necessarily facts."[127]

Addressing NATO combat pilots at the air base in Aviano, Italy on April 8, 1999, U.S. Secretary of Defense William Cohen said:

> Milosevic and his minions are engaging in rape, pillage, and mass murder on a scale that we have not seen since the end of World War II.[128]

However, at the end of November 1999, after five months of investigation and exhumation of all the dead in Kosovo, the UN war crimes investigators had found only 2,108 bodies[129] which included lots of strange deaths that could not be blamed on anyone in particular.[130] And it was the figure of 2,108 that the chief prosecutor for the UN war crimes tribunal, Carla Del Ponte, confirmed in her report to the UN Security Council.[131] So, where are all the thousands upon thousands of massacred ethnic Albanians buried? Where are all the graves containing the bodies of the victims of the mass murder that Cohen said was on the scale of World War II—worse than the "ethnic cleansing" that took place in Rwanda by his reckoning? There was no "ethnic cleansing" or "genocide" ever carried out by the Serbs. The reports were but the result of Islam's drive to completely overthrow Christian Serbia. When will a gullible and naive West understand that lies are part and parcel of Islam's Jihad—holy war—against the West? Jihad is simply "an Islamic word which other nations use in the meaning of 'War.'"[132] And the word Jihad is defined by a Muslim authority as:

> To struggle in the cause of Allah with pen, speech or sword—
> that is Jihad.[133]

The Serb atrocity stories were nothing less than Islamic lies designed to bring more U.S. military intervention in Yugoslavia. The KLA knew the U.S. needed a very small pretext in order to break up more of Yugoslavia in favor of the Muslims, and by doing so, move closer to getting its hands on the greatest concentration of wealth in the world.

There can be no disputing of the facts this writer has presented concerning Kosovo. Forensic teams came from 15 nations: Austria, Belgium, Canada, Denmark, Finland, France, Germany, Iceland, Luxembourg, Netherlands, Spain, Sweden, Switzerland, the United Kingdom, and the United States. The teams combed Kosovo, and inspected hundreds of sites which ethnic Albanian Muslims had "testified" to being mass graves. The FBI made the biggest effort to find bodies, but they came up with fewer than 200.[134] The combined result from the 15 forensic teams was given above, but no apologies or compensation from those who destroyed Yugoslavia are forthcoming. Yugoslav president, Slobodan Milosevic, is unable to venture out of his country since he would be arrested under an "international warrant" issued against him.[135]

The drive by ethnic Albanians for an independent Muslim state in Kosovo is only one of a dozen or so Muslim conflicts attempting to establish independent Muslim states by force of arms around the world today. The number of casualties caused by Islamic violence is of no consequence to Muslims. When it was pointed out that NATO airstrikes against Yugoslavia would cause Serb retaliation, a KLA leader replied:

> We don't care. 400,000 Kosavars can be sacrificed for our independence.[136]

But how many American Christians realize today that their defense dollars are being used to attack other Christians on behalf of Islam?

The United States of America came together under the leadership of godly men—One Nation Under God. Today, it is a nation deep in sin. Be warned, America! It is but a very short distance between being under sin and being under judgment.

An additional point to ponder is this:

The average age of the world's greatest civilizations has been **200 years**.[137]

America's official birthday is July 4, the date which marks the formal adoption of the Declaration of Independence in 1776, although members of Congress did not sign the Declaration until August. Irrespective of whether America's birthday is July 4, or August 2, during the year 2000 the United States will celebrate its **234**th anniversary: *Lord, how long will the wicked, how long will the wicked triumph?* (Psalms 94:3).

This writer reiterates that the U.S. attack upon the Serbs was as immoral as its president. And like the cruel sanctions imposed against the entire people of Libya in order to protect Syria, America could not stop the bombing of Yugoslavia, because it would lose credibility and face. When Japanese people lose face they kill themselves, when Arab people lose face they kill others, but to save America's face the Clinton administration bombed an entire nation into desolation. Kosovo is a very deadly precedent—

> The most dangerous lesson of the Yugoslav war is that it can happen again anywhere and anytime. If US interests require the destruction of this or that state or the silencing of this or that political movement, the buildup and use of forces will begin. In contrast to the Cold War period, there is only one superpower now, and no importance at all is attached to the views of other parties or allies. And there are grave indications that our [Middle East] region will be the next American playground.[138]

How true the above observation is: Yesterday it was Yugoslavia, tomorrow it could be Israel.

On April 15, 1999, senior Palestinian Authority official Ahmed Abdel Rahman told reporters that

> the war in Yugoslavia is a sign of a new development in international relations, by which the international community uses force to impose international agreements.[139]

Abdel Rahman hinted

> that the international community adopt measures similar to those being employed in the Balkans to end "Israeli occupation."[140]

Before readers dismiss this Arab hope, they would do well to remember that the Bible informs us that all nations will come up against Jerusalem. Those who survive the experience will not forget the biblical truth that the Name of *the Holy One of Israel* dwells there.

American and European drives for "peace" are not drives for real peace at all. They are tyrannical pressures to force a situation where political power is increased and carefully calculated business profits are harvested. Whoever gets shoved around or destroyed during the process is of no consequence to the power monger and greed merchant elite—business is business.

Since the breakup of the Soviet empire in 1991, America has humiliated Russia time and again by treating the former world power with almost total disdain. Russia gulped and swallowed numerous diplomatic insults. But when the U.S. decided it would bomb the American-imposed "no-fly zones" in Iraq—along with its new-found British lackey without UN Security Council approval or Russian consultation—Russia was more than exasperated and began a push to regain its lost influence.

Russia vociferously opposed the Clinton/NATO bombing of Yugoslavia, and the destruction of its friend and ally was the straw that broke the Russian camel's back. Boris Yeltzin stepped down as Russian president on the eve of the year 2000, and Vladimir Putin became acting president until elections could be held in March.

Putin is a no-nonsense ex-KGB high-ranking official. Yeltzin nominated Putin as his successor before he stepped down, saying the country was in good hands. Putin gained substantial support from the Russian people by his handling of Russia's military siege of Grozny, in Chechnya, and also by ignoring Western condemnations of the war. But Putin's January 2000 reversal of Russia's vow never to be the first to use nuclear weapons[141] was a very clear message to the U.S. that the post-Cold War period has ended. Putin's announcement of the rescinding of the no-first strike vow sent shock waves around the world. It was Russia's way of telling the U.S. that it is sick and tired of being treated like a tertiary power, and that any repeat Kosovo type of action could bring nuclear warheads raining down upon American heads. It remains to be seen whether the hot heads among Clinton's foreign policy wise men will heed Russia's cold shoulder and cool off.

War has so permeated history that there is no place to assume that war cannot occur, because a country is at "peace." History is replete with examples, and it is sheer folly to rest national security on the childish premise that peace is eternal.

The historical record proves that "peace" today is no guarantee for the future. Those ages which in restrospect were the most peaceful were the ones where "peace" was sought least. Countries prepared for war are more likely to prevent war. Israel must ensure national survival by resisting U.S. pressures to unconditionally surrender to every Arab demand. Israel must guarantee the security of its people by maintaining a powerful military, and the maximum of strategic territory. To do otherwise is suicidal.

The tide of world opinion and condemnation against Israel for not giving in to PLO and other Arab demands rises daily. The U.S., the UN and the EU pressure Israel into making "peace," but it is impossible to make peace with those whose greatest desire is to destroy the one with whom they are supposedly negotiating peace.

The Jewish people have survived the tyrant, the well meaning, and, at this time of writing, the "peace" process. They have not only survived, but are home on their land. This is due to one reason only—Almighty God. The U.S. now acts as if it were God, and the UN, EU and NATO are all aspiring to that position. However, if these powers really determined Israel's destiny, the Jews would likely have been back making bricks in Egypt years ago.

The "peace process" is a farce. It is a "piece process"— Israel being broken down piece by piece. The West is driven by an insatiable appetite for wealth and political power, and Israel is altogether dispensable, because it reduces the West's financial and political profits.

The more Jewish *"fools"* focus on peace, the more it will illude them. Their only chance for true peace lies in making their own peace with God. Jewish *"fools"* omitted the name of God from Israel's Declaration of Independence that proclaimed the establishment of the Jewish state, and now they are losing their God-given inheritance to those who worship Allah.

Millions of people, including many Christians, are pinning their hopes upon "peace" in the Middle East. They should, however, realize that any "peace" brokered between Israel and the Arab world will only last as long as all other peace agreements have lasted in this region—until the next war. The last word here should come from God, and it concerns all those who pin their hopes on a soon-coming peace:

> *For when they say "Peace and safety!" then sudden destruction comes upon them, as labor pains upon a pregnant woman. And they shall not escape* (1 Thessalonians 5:3).

9

In the Footsteps
of Muhammed

Subtle changes are taking place in many avenues of today's world. Quickly becoming the new norm, these changes accelerate the slide of a previously more moral world into that of an almost totally immoral one—a world ripe for judgment by an incensed God. Abortion is now no longer the killing of an unborn child; it is the "terminating of a pregnancy." Sodomy (homosexuality), lesbianism and transvestism are no longer sexual perversions; they are "alternative life-styles." Yasser Arafat, unrepentant murderer of tens of thousands of men, women and children, is no longer the godfather of international terrorism whose name was near the top of the list of the ten most wanted men in the world; he is now the "Nobel Peace Prize laureate" and "President of Palestine." Poor Arabs, who came from various impoverished Arab states to benefit from the industrious efforts of Jews in barren pre-Israel Palestine, are no longer poor Arab immigrants; they are now "Palestinians robbed of their ancient homeland by the avarice of Jews." And Allah, the pagan idol and demonic spirit-god of Islam, has now been elevated to the role of God. Part of the shame belongs to the millions of "Christians" who find no fault with these things. They have listened, as Eve did, to Satan's *Hath God said?* (Genesis 3:1).

Unable to defeat Israel militarily, Arab aggressors now wage religious war around a "peace" table against Hellenistic Jews. The Arab objective remains the same, to annihilate the Jewish state. The faithless, secular humanist Hellenistic Jews are being defeated through their appeasement of the Arab aggressors. The Hellenist *"fools"* are handing their new-found "peace partners" the victory that escaped them for 50 years on the battlefields. It reminds this writer of a quote by Sir Winston Churchill: "An appeaser is one who feeds a crocodile hoping it will eat him last."[1]

The *"fools"* are so deep into appeasing the aggressors that every time the Arabs spit upon them they say "it's raining."[2] These *"fools"* have, in a few short months, thrown away much of Israel's divine inheritance. The inheritance, lost almost two millenniums ago through the sin of previous _"fools,"_ had been purchased back with the blood of over 22,000 Israelis shed in more than 50 years of bloody attacks. The "right of redemption" for the land, which the new _"fools"_ have squandered due to their godlessness, will cost Israel far more blood than that of 22,000 souls.

Islam is the sole reason why no "peace agreement" on earth can bring peace between Israel and the Arab and Muslim worlds. American and European greed for wealth and political power may lead Israel faster and deeper into Islam's trap, but it was Islam that baited and set the trap in the first place. If the _"fools"_ sitting in Israel's Knesset, the White House and the U.S. State Department were not spiritually bankrupt, they would know that Muslims are forbidden to make peace with their enemies. Arabia—from whence came the Arabs—is the birthplace and heartland of Islam, and it is incumbent upon the Arab nations to continue their war with Israel until Israel is destroyed. Islam only allows the creation of a false "peace" in order to lull the enemy into relaxing its guard. And such is the Middle East "peace" process.

At this very moment of writing, a news item was broadcast on _Israel Radio_ that the head of Israel's Mossad, Ephraim Halevy, has stated that Israel will never achieve normal relations with its Arab neighbors because

> Arabs look upon peace agreements as no more than cease fire agreements.[3]

It was Muhammed, the founder of Islam, who paved the way for Muslims to make temporary peace with enemies in order to attack at a later, more opportune time. Muhammed laid the foundation by making a "peace treaty" with the Kuraish tribe in Mecca in 628 A.D. Two years later, when Muhammed was considerably stronger through having gained more followers, he abrogated the treaty and attacked. Muhammed and his followers subsequently slaughtered every male among the Kuraish people.

The agreement between Muhammed and the infidels (unbelievers) of Mecca is known as the Truce of Hudaybiyyah, and is written into the Hadith (Muhammed's teachings, sayings, or acts). A world renowned professor of Islamic history says of Muhammed's Truce of Hudaybiyyah:

> This truce became a model and a precedent in Islamic law for

all agreements with infidels: never permanent, never lasting more than 10 years (with the possibility of another 10 years extension, no more). Islam is not permitted to stop its war against non-Moslems for more than this period.[4]

In his book, "The Political Language of Islam," another authority on Islam, Bernard Lewis, Professor Emeritus of Near Eastern Studies at Princeton University, confirms that Muslims can interrupt their war against non-Muslims when it is expedient to do so:

According to the law books, this state of war could be interrupted, when expedient, by an armistice or truce of limited duration. It could not be terminated by a peace, but only by final victory.[5]

Yasser Arafat, recorded several times on tape and in print, makes it perfectly clear to Muslims that the "peace" agreement the PLO has signed with Israel is, indeed, only a temporary interruption of its war against Israel. The following extracts are taken from a recorded speech given by Arafat in a South African mosque a few days after the "historic" signing of the Oslo "peace" agreement with the Jewish state:

In the name of Allah ... believe me there is a lot to be done. The Jihad will continue ... Our main battle is Jerusalem. Jerusalem ... And here we are, I can't—and I have to speak frankly, I can't do it alone without the support of the Islamic nation. I can't do it alone ... No, you have to come and fight and to start the Jihad to liberate Jerusalem ... no, it is not their capital. It is our capital. It is your capital ... This agreement—I am not considering it more than the agreement signed between our prophet Muhammed and the Kuraish tribe—a despicable truce. The same way Muhammed had accepted, it we are accepting now this peace effort ... From my heart, and I am telling you frankly from brother to brother, we are in need of you. We are in need of you as Muslims, as warriors of Jihad ... Again I have to say ... onward to victory, onward to Jerusalem![6]

Arafat's intentions are crystal clear to anyone with two ears and half a mind: Muhammed's false peace with the Kuraish people—the Truce of Hudaybiyyah—is the model for the PLO's "peace" with the Jewish people. The "despicable truce" with Israel is the coin that the PLO is forced to pay in order to bring about Israel's destruction. Listen now to a later speech by Feisal al-Husseini, Arafat's cousin and chief PLO official in Jerusalem:

> Peace for us means the destruction of Israel. We are preparing for an all-out war, a war which will last for generations. Since January 1965, when Fatah was born, we have become the most dangerous enemy that Israel has. We shall not rest until the day when we return to our home, and until we destroy Israel.[7]

It should now be quite clear to the reader that peace is not the objective of agreements signed by Arab nations or the PLO. The agreements are signed only in order to lull Israel into a reduction of its military forces and arms' industry, while at the same time buying the Arabs time to regroup and rearm. Fatah, which al-Husseini mentioned, is the PLO military faction that Arafat personally heads. Fatah has been responsible for many thousands of Jewish deaths, maimings and injuries in Israel and elsewhere. The name Fatah is derived from the reverse letters of the Arabic word _hataf_, meaning "sudden death." Fatah was formed in 1965— two years before the Six Day War—for the sole purpose of carrying out terrorist actions against Jewish targets in Israel and overseas.

Love versus Hate

The Koran is to Islam what the Bible is to Christianity. But there is a very real difference between the Koran and the Bible. The Koran is approximately the same size in volume as the New Testament, but whereas the New Testament contains 57 direct commands to "love"—"love your God, enemies, neighbor, wives, one another," etc., and 191 other indirect commands to love, the Koran contains no such commands to love, direct or indirect. Instead, it has 123 commands to fight and kill for Allah.

Will the Real God Please Stand Up!

Most people—including Christians—believe the argument that "Allah" is the Arabic word for God, because it is used in the Arabic Bible. This is patent nonsense. The personal name of the God of the Bible is Yahweh. And "Allah" is the personal name of a pagan deity who fathered three goddesses called "the daughters of Allah." The first Bible in Arabic was not published until the 9th century, some 200 years after Islam held full sway over all of Arabia and many surrounding nations. The name "Allah" had permeated the Arab mind and became its supreme god. Thus the name slipped into the Arabic translation of the Bible.

The Arabs certainly understand that Yahweh, God of Abraham, Isaac and Jacob, is not the same as Allah, the god of Islam. A Palestinian Arab—a world renowned authority on Islam—stated categorically that, "The Allah of the Koran is not the same as the God of the Bible."[8]

A recent anti-Semitic blood-libel article in the Egyptian newspaper, *Al-Shaab*, also makes a clear distinction between Islam's Allah and the God of Abraham, Isaac and Jacob when it said *inter alia*: "Jews carry out human sacrifices to please their bloodthirsty God."[9] A high school text book in Jordan contains much the same sentiments about the God of Jews and Christians:

> If you knew the attributes which they attributed to their god, those which they wanted and those which they have adorned him with, then you would certainly be astounded. Jehovah, lord of hosts, lord of Israel, commands them to smear their houses with sheep's blood in order to save their sons and let the Egyptians perish. He is a god who feels remorse for creating Adam and for setting Saul on the throne. He is bloodthirsty, fickle-minded, harsh and greedy. He is pleased with imposture and deceit. He is loquacious and passionately fond of long speeches.[10]

Without doubt the Muslim's Allah is not Yahweh, the God of the Bible. We will end this section by hearing the considered opinions of top Islamic authorities on the name and nature of Islam's Allah:

> Allah is a purely Arabic term used in reference to an Arabian deity.[11]

> "Allah" is a proper name, applicable only to their peculiar God.[12]

> The origin of this goes back to pre-Moslem times. Allah is not a common name meaning "God."[13]

> "Allah" is a pre-Islamic name ... corresponding to the Babylonian Bel.[14]

Allah was known to the pre-Islamic Arabs; he was one of the Meccan deities.[15]

Allah-worship, as well as the worship of Ba'al, were both astral religions in that they involved the worship of the sun, the moon, and the stars.[16]

In Arabia, the sun god was viewed as a female goddess and the moon as the male god. The name Allah was used as the personal name of the moon god.[17]

Allah, the moon god, was married to the sun goddess. Together they produced three goddesses who were called "the daughters of Allah." These three goddesses were called al-Lat, al-Uzza, and Manat.[18]

The desert Arab ... feared and worshiped incalculable deities in stars and moons.... Now and then he offered human sacrifice; and here and there he worshiped sacred stones. The center of this stone worship was Mecca with the Ka'aba and its sacred Black stone ... in its southeast corner, five feet from the ground, just right for kissing....

Within the Ka'aba, in pre-Moslem days, were several idols representing gods, One was called Allah ... three others were Allah's daughters—al-Uzza, al-Lat, and Manat.[19]

There should now be no shadow of doubt left in the reader's mind that the Muslim god Allah is, indeed, a pagan deity who was worshiped a thousand years before Islam. And this demonic spirit is an extremely powerful, evil and savage force in today's world.

Through the ages Christians have done Yahweh, the God of Creation, the God of Abraham, Isaac and Jacob, a terrible injustice. This injury has been done by substituting the rather nebulous "LORD" in place of His personal name. Every Hebrew name in the Bible is rich in meaning, and the pronouncing of a Hebrew name makes an emphatic statement into the spiritual realm. In our English Bibles we read that God says to Moses:

Thus you shall say to the children of Israel: "The LORD God of your fathers, the God of Abraham, the God of Isaac, and the God of Jacob, has sent me to you. This is My name forever, and this is My memorial to all generations" (Exodus 3:15).

The correct and exact translation of the Hebrew text, however, is as follows:

> *Thus you shall say to the children of Israel: "Yahweh God of your fathers, God of Abraham, God of Isaac, and God of Jacob, has sent me to you. This is My name forever, and this My memorial to all generations."*

In this passage God tells Moses that He, Yahweh, is sending Moses to the children of Israel. That Yahweh has been God's personal name from the beginning of time is clear from the Hebrew text of the creation account in the book of Genesis:

> *These are the generations of the heavens and the earth when they were created, in the day that Yahweh God made the earth and the heavens* (Genesis 2:4).

To Moses, God says that it is by His name, Yahweh, that He is to be known for all eternity, it is the memorial name by which His people shall worship Him.

The Christian church has all but buried God's personal name. Yah, a contraction of God's personal name also appears 50 times in the Hebrew text of the Bible, but rarely is it ever included in our translations. The *King James* and *New King James* versions do translate it occasionally—for example:

> *Sing to God, sing praises to His name; Extol Him who rides on the clouds, by His name YAH, and rejoice before Him* (Psalms 68:4),

but for the most part it is hidden.

In addition to the 50 times mentioned above, the contracted name, Yah, is also found numerous times in a hyphenated word that every Christian knows, and, most use—*hallelujah*. In Hebrew the word is hyphenated thus: *hallelu-Yah*. Most translations render this as: *Praise the LORD!*

The name Yahweh, however, has deep significance for the reader who has a little patience. A careful reading of the following, could unearth a golden nugget for many readers.

In Hebrew the name Yahweh has only four letters: ' (yod) ה (hay) ו (vav) ה (hay) and it looks like this (reading from right to left), יהוה. This personal name of God appears 6,356 times in the Hebrew Old Testament. Far from being a great un-discovered mystery, the meaning of the name Yahweh is relatively easy to ascertain in Hebrew.

In biblical Hebrew there is sometimes an interchange between the letters ' (yod) and ו (vav). This can be seen, for example, in Genesis 3:20 where Adam's wife is given the name (reading from right to left) חוה—*Chava*, because she was the mother of all חי—life. The added ה (hay) at the end of חוה (*Chava*) simply tells us that the object is feminine.

Looking at God's personal name in Hebrew, there is an easily recognized pattern: ה (hay) ו (vav) ה (hay)—*hoveh*, which is the Hebrew word for "the present;" ה (hay) ' (yod) ה (hay)—*hiyah*, the Hebrew word meaning "was;" and, using the interchange of letters, ' (yod) ה (hay) ' (yod) ה (hay)—*yihiyeh*, and this word is the Hebrew for "will be." So, we arrive at a very special name: "Is now, was and will be." And God confirms this in the Scriptures for us. For example—

"I am the Alpha and the Omega, the Beginning and the End," says the Lord, "who is and who was and who is to come, the Almighty" (Revelation 1:8).

Again, we have greatly dishonored Yahweh by merely referring to him as Lord, when He is the One *who is and who was and who is to come, the Almighty*.

There are many Lords. Even the main Hindu god is called "Lord" Rama. There are also many lords. In fact a whole "house of lords" help make up the British parliament!

Christian, Yahweh is no common Lord! He is *Yahweh God of gods, Yahweh God of gods...* (Joshua 22:22). Oh that we would begin to reverently use the mighty and wonderful name of Yahweh instead of trying to reduce Him to the level of man. Had this been done 1,400 years ago, the Muslim god, Allah, would never have gotten referred to as God.

A few years ago Allah was Allah. Pick up almost any newspaper or magazine, and the pertinent articles would be found to have used the name Allah. When it was necessary to mention the Islamic god in speeches given in English, by Arabs and other Muslims, Allah was the name used. Today it is not so. Pick up any newspaper or magazine now and "God" has everywhere been substituted for the name Allah. And so it is also with English speeches given by Arabs and other Muslims, in public, on television, and on radio. The substitution of "God" for Allah has been foisted upon us, and this is how deception takes root—like the godless theory of evolution before it.

Allah, as has been shown, is a pagan idol and the demonic spirit behind Islam. Nowhere is the demonic aspect of Islam demonstrated more vividly among its adherents than when young Shi'ite Muslims

> engage in self-flagellation, cutting their scalps with sharp knives and razors.[20]

In the same manner the priests of Ba'al paid homage to their pagan god thousands of years ago:

> *...they cried aloud, and cut themselves, as was their custom, with knives and lances, until the blood gushed out on them*
> (I Kings 18:28).

Most—yes, most—of the brutal conflicts taking place in the world today directly involve the followers of Muhammed, the founder of Islam. And in an interview with the *Jerusalem Post*, another candid Palestinian Arab said:

> Muslims are human beings, but Islam is a satanic religion. When a Muslim becomes faithful and religious, he becomes a killer.[21]

And this was borne out by the actions of Idi Amin of Uganda, who slaughtered 300,000 of his people, mostly Christians, after he embraced Islam.[22]

The number of Muslim initiated conflicts and their corresponding brutality, can only increase as time passes. The 21st century is, according to Islam, the century of Islam, which will usher in "the messianic age—the acceptance of Islam by all the earth's inhabitants,"[23]—by force, apparently. They claim that the 21st century is

> the century of Islam's glory and that the collapse of the Soviet Union will be followed by the collapse of the United States,[24]

Osama bin Laden, one of the world's most wanted men, called "for an intensification of the Jihad throughout the world."[25] The century of Islam's glory will bring particular sorrow to Jewish families, especially those in Israel. For Muhammed declared:

> The last hour will not come before the Muslims fight the Jews and the Muslims kill them.[26]

A fundamentalist Muslim leader reiterated this to a group of 300 students at the Islamic University of London, in March 1994. He said that the last hour would not arrive until there is

> a mass slaughter of Jews. The Jews are our enemy and, please Allah, we should finish them.[27]

Why this obsession with the destruction of the Jewish people in general and the Jewish state in particular? Because, Islam is satanic and the Jews are the chosen people of Yahweh. In the natural realm, darkness always fights to overwhelm the light. This also holds true in the spiritual realm. Islam's Koran teaches Muslims that "Jews are the enemies of Allah, Muhammed and the angels,"[28] and that Muslims are to "kill them wherever you find them. Over such men Allah gives absolute authority."[29]

Peace agreements between Arab nations and Israel are really only Islamic jokes. While the Koran remains in existence there can never be peace between the Arab and Muslim worlds and Israel. Only Yahweh can broker a peace between Israel and Islam. This peace will not be based on any "land for peace" formula, but only on their heart's acceptance of Yahweh's Son, Yeshua (Jesus), who shall be called _Wonderful Counselor, Mighty God, Everlasting Father, **Prince of Peace**_ (Isaiah 9:6).

This writer does not recommend reading the Koran, but some knowledge of its content should be understood. The Koran insistently urges Muslims to violence against all non-Muslims, wherever they might be. Some understanding of the Koran's content will, therefore, be an aid to understanding why peace continues to elude not only Israel, but also the entire non-Islamic world. Following is a brief outline of Islam's most holy and revered book. The edition used is that of N.J. Dawood, _The Koran_: Fifth revised edition translated with notes (London: Penguin, 1990).

"Koran" means "Recital" and Muslims are to "recite," not read, the Koran. In the following treatise of the Koran, bracketed references such as (S. 6:70) denotes the Sura (Chapter) and verse. Where "etc." is included as in (S. 2:273 etc.), it means there is more than one verse, often many verses, stating the same or approximately the same thing.

Every Sura, with the exception of the ninth, begins: _"In the Name of Allah, the Compassionate, the Merciful."_ Readers should take note of the number of verses given over to fighting and killing for Allah, the severing of limbs, the cursing and the fate of those who refuse to accept Islam. There are also numerous verses in the Koran where Allah tells how he "drowned" people as a form of punishment, and says in Sura 36:41, "I drown them if I will." Only an overly fertile imagination could describe Islam's Allah as "compassionate" or "merciful."

It was mentioned earlier that the Koran is approximately the same size as the New Testament. The sections on "Paradise" and "Hell" below are compilations of quotations of what is actually written in the Koran and distributed throughout its pages. The graphic descriptions of punishment literally puts "the fear of Hell" into its readers, and detailing the "delights" of paradise is certainly sufficient to stimulate rich and poor Muslim males to readily give their lives "in the cause" of Allah.   An Arab Sheik, himself raised as a fundamental Muslim, confirmed in a letter to this writer that the Ghulmans, the "young, immortal, virgin boys" in "Paradise," are provided for sexual purposes. Also, a prominent Egyptian sheik described in a sermon how "devout Muslims entering paradise would enjoy sex with young boys."[30]

The word "Islam" means "absolute submission to the will of Allah." Allah is the pre-Islamic moon god who was worshipped by the pagans of Arabia, and Allah's ancient symbol was the crescent moon which now graces mosques and the flags of Islamic countries.

The English edition of the Koran used here is the fifth revised edition, which means to say that it has been corrected five times and thus should be literally perfect. The last of the five revisions replaced the name "Allah" with "God." As a biblical Christian, I consider this to be blasphemy, and it greatly offends me. Allah is a demonic spirit, not God. This writer has, therefore, in all quotations from the Koran replaced "God" with "Allah," the personal name of the god of Islam.

In Muhammed's day the Koran included what are known today as the "Satanic Verses," and these received worldwide attention in 1989 when a Muslim by the name of Salman Rushdie wrote a book with the same title. Readers will see that the Allah of the Koran revealed fresh verses to Muhammed that "abrogated" existing verses and "replaced" them with "better" ones. This is what happened with the Satanic Verses—they were "abrogated" and were no longer part of the Koran after Muhammed's death.

The Satanic verses permitted the worship of three goddesses—al-Lat, al-Uzza and Manat—who were the daughters of Allah. They were the result of a marriage union between the moon god and the sun goddess. And, it should be noted that two of the three daughters bear names which are, in fact, the feminine forms of Allah. It should also be noted that al-Lat, al-Uzza and Manat are mentioned by name in the Koran (S. 53:13 etc.) today, but footnotes refer to them as, "Names of Arabian idols, claimed by the pagans of Mecca to be daughters of Allah."

Allah, being the Babylonian moon god, is also an idol. And the Koran explicitly states in Sura 12:39: "We will serve _no other idols besides Allah._" Emphasis mine.

There are 123 verses concerning fighting and killing for the cause of Allah. Muslims are encouraged to be wholly occupied (S. 2:273 etc.) with fighting for Allah's cause. Allah will give "a far richer recompense to those who fight for him" (S. 4:96 etc.). Regarding infidels (unbelievers), they are the Muslim's "inveterate enemies" (S. 4:101 etc.). Muslims are to "arrest them, besiege them, and lie in ambush everywhere" (S. 9:5) for them. They are to "seize them and put them to death wherever you find them, kill them wherever you find them, seek out the enemies of Islam relentlessly" (S. 4:90 etc.). "Fight them until Islam reigns supreme" (S. 2:193 etc.). "Cut off their heads, and cut off the tips of their fingers" (S. 8:12 etc.).

If a Muslim does not go to war, Allah will kill him (S. 9:39). He is to be told "the heat of war is fierce, but more fierce is the heat of Hell-fire" (S. 9:81).

A Muslim must "fight for the cause of Allah with the devotion due to him" (S. 22:78 etc.).

Muslims must make war on the infidels (unbelievers) who live around them (S. 9:123 etc.).

Muslims are to be "ruthless to unbelievers" (S. 48:29 etc.).

A Muslim should "enjoy the good things" he has gained by fighting (S. 8:69).

A Muslim can kill any person he wishes if it be a "just cause" (S. 6:152 etc.).

Allah "loves those who fight for his cause" (S. 61:3).

Anyone who fights against Allah or renounces Islam in favor of another religion shall be "put to death or crucified or have their hands and feet cut off on alternative sides" (S. 5:34).

The "Truce of Hudaybiyyah" is an Islamic military tactic whereby a peace agreement is made with the enemy in order to destroy him at a later date. On page 7 of the Koran it is called: *Treaty* of Hudaybiyyah, on page 8: *Truce* of Hudaybiyyah, and on page 362 *Peace* of Hudaybiyyah.

The *Treaty/Truce/Peace* allows Muslim forces to build up strength, while the "enemy" reduces its strength due to having a "signed peace agreement." The "Peace of Hudaybiyyah" was first used by Muhammed in the year 628 and has been periodically used by Muslims throughout the succeeding centuries. Several times Yasser Arafat has confirmed that the PLO-Israel "peace agreement" is nothing more than the "Peace of Hudaybiyyah."

The only true believer is one who adheres to "Islam—the True Faith, and fights for Allah" (S. 8:74).

Muslims must "pronounce the name of Allah" over animals as they are "slaughtered" (S. 22:33). (Only Muslim slaughtermen can ritually kill meat in countries that produce meat for export to Muslim markets. Countries such as New Zealand, for example, were forced to realign its slaughter houses in order for the slaughter-men to face Mecca. Thus the spiritual declaration of the name of Allah resounds throughout the earth 24 hours each day and night, tens of millions of times every year).

Allah plots and is "the supreme Plotter" (S. 3:54 etc.). Allah schemes, and is "most profound in his machinations" (S. 8:30).

A Muslim must "give in the cause of Allah," and if he does not give, Allah will kill him (S. 47:38).

Only Muslims will be saved—all others will be tormented in Hell (S. 3:86 etc.). Allah himself "perfected Islam" (S. 5:3 etc.).

A Muslim man is allowed several wives, numerous concubines (sex partners) and unlimited slave girls (S. 2:224 etc.) with which he is allowed, and encouraged, to have sex (S. 23:5 etc.)

> ("if a Muslim man purchases a slave girl, the purchase contract includes his right to have sex with her"[31]).

Slave girls are given by Allah "as booty" (S. 33:50).

There are four types of people depicted in the Koran: "believers, Jews, Christians and Pagans." The latter three are all unbelievers. Both Jews and Christians are "hypocrites" (S. 4:146), but Jews are also "deceivers."

Jews and Christians are cursed (20 times) by Allah, and "shall be rewarded with disgrace in this world" (S. 3:58 etc.). They have "incurred Allah's most inexorable wrath," and are to be "sternly punished in this world." Only the few that embrace the "True Faith" (Islam) will escape Hell fire, the rest are evildoers and "ignominy" shall attend them wherever they go (S. 3:110-112 etc.).

Muslims must fight against Jews and Christians until they "embrace the true Faith," or "until they pay tribute" (S. 9:29 etc.). (To pay tribute means to accept _dhimmi_ status and live as second class citizens, ruled by Muslims and paying a poll tax to their Muslim masters).

Jews and Christians "may be compared to Satan" (S. 59:11 etc.).

Jews and Christians are "perverse" and "imitate the idolaters of old" (S. 9:30).

Allah has no son (nine verses): it is "a monstrous blasphemy"— "a lie of the Christians who are cursed—no one is more wicked than the one who invents a falsehood about Allah" (S. 18:1 etc.). "A monstrous falsehood, at which the very heavens might crack, the earth break asunder, and the mountains crumble to dust" (S. 19: 88).

Christians are cursed because they claim that they are "children of Allah" and "loved by Allah" (S. 5:13 etc.).

Christians are cursed because "they claim that Jesus the Messiah is Allah" (S. 5:17 etc.).

Christians are cursed because they claim Allah is a Trinity and has "partners in His kingdom." For this they are to be "sternly punished" (S. 5:73 etc.).

The Koran specifically states in three verses that the Jews were cursed by Allah and were "changed into apes and swine, and those that serve the devil" (S. 5:59 etc.). (Here is the reason for media reports of Muslims celebrating the killing and injuring of "sons of monkeys and pigs" after terrorist attacks in Israel).

Jews have never been "wronged" by Muslims, only by other Jews (S. 16:19).

Jews "vie with one another in sin and wickedness." "Evil is what they do" (S. 5:62 etc.).

Jews are not only "cursed by Allah" (S. 5:64 etc.), but also "by David and Jesus" (S. 5:80).

Jews are the enemies of Allah, Muhammed and the angels (S. 4:101 etc.). Muslims are to "kill them wherever you find them" (S. 4:91 etc.).

Jews are the "most implacable enemies" of the Muslims (S. 5:82 etc.). The "nearest in affection" to them are "the Christians."

It is a "wicked lie" (S. 2:140 etc.) to say that Abraham, Isaac and Jacob were Jews—they were Muslims, as were all the biblical prophets, together with Jesus, the disciples and apostles (S. 2:132 etc.). Abraham's father was an "enemy of Allah," and Abraham "disowned" him (S. 9:114 etc.).

Only the "Glorious Koran" is "shorn of falsehood" (S. 18:1 etc.) and contains "the Truth" (S. 2:175 etc.). The Old and New Testaments were "corrupted, perverted and tampered" with by the Jews and the Christians, and both the Jews and the Christians are deceived by the lies of their religions (S. 3:24 etc.). Much of the Bible is just the imaginations of Jews and Christians.

The Koran is "free from any flaw" (S. 39:28 etc.).

Allah "abrogates" and "changes" verses of the Koran in order to "replace it with a better one" (S. 2:106 etc.). Verses were "abrogated" to accommodate Muhammed's personal sexual desires. (E.g., Muhammed required a new verse in order to get his adopted son, Zayd, to divorce his wife so that he could marry her himself.) Thus, what was formerly forbidden became for Muhammed, "Allah's will" which "must needs be done." There is also added personal protection for Muhammed in the next verse which says: "No blame shall be attached to the Prophet for doing what is sanctioned for him by Allah."

Muslims must always face the Ka'aba in Mecca that was built by Abraham and Ishmael (S. 2:27 etc.). (Muslims used to face Jerusalem, but that command was "abrogated" because the Jews refused to follow Muhammed—footnote to p. 24).

Muhammed addresses critics of the Koran 11 times, mainly "the Israelites" (S. 27:79). He says that he himself did not "invent" what the Koran contains, that it is not "a medley of dreams," and that he is not "an impostor" simply because Allah "changes one verse for another." Neither is he "possessed," or "bewitched." (Muhammed was believed to have been epileptic. He would roll on the ground, convulse and foam at the mouth before giving "revelations." (In Luke 9:42, the Bible firmly indicates that epilepsy is demonic).

For those that refuse to recognize the Koran as divine, Allah will "obliterate their faces" (S. 4:47 etc.) and "curse" them. They will be burnt in the Fire until their "skins are consumed," and when their skins are consumed Allah will give them "other skins" to be burnt off "so they might truly taste the scourge" (S. 4:56 etc.).

Those that do not believe Islam will be victorious in this world, and the world to come, should "tie a rope to the ceiling of his house and hang himself" (S. 22:15).

The Koran was revealed in the month of Ramadan (S. 2:184 etc.). In actuality it took Muhammed years to write it as it was "revealed gradually" (S. 2:175 etc.). At least half the Koran's bulk is made up of endless repetitions).

Muhammed says that if the Koran was not of divine origin, "they [unbelievers] could have surely found in it many contradictions." (Readers will be able to judge for themselves if the Koran has "contradictions," and if it is "without flaw.")

A day is a space of "a thousand years" (S. 32:5).

A day is a space of "fifty thousand years" (S. 70:3).

The Koran "fully explains" the Bible (S. 10:38 etc.). (Not one single passage of the Koran dealing with the Bible is factually correct—see last grouping of quotations for a few examples).

The Koran states: Muhammed was "immortal" (S. 21:34).

Jesus was sent by Allah to herald the coming of Muhammed (S. 61:6).

Jesus, according to the Koran, was: the "Messiah" (S. 3:45); the "Word" (S. 3:24); the "Unlettered Prophet" who believes in "Allah and His Word" (S. 7:157 etc.); "No more than an apostle" (S. 5:75).

Shortly after Mary gave birth to Him, Jesus spoke and said "I am the servant of Allah. He has given me the Book and ordained me a prophet" (S. 19:30).

Jesus "preached to men" while in His "cradle" (S. 5:110 etc.).

Jesus was not killed or crucified (S. 4:157 etc.).

Men are "superior" to women (S. 4:34 etc.). (Women are regarded to be so inferior to men—intellectually and religiously—that female births are not recorded in Islam.[32] Women, according to Muhammed, are only "toys.")[33]

Wives are a Muslim man's "fields." He is to "go into them" and cause them to produce (S. 2:224 etc.). In his book, "Women in Islam," Rafiqul Haqq summarized the significance of the marriage contract according to three schools of Islam:

> The followers of Imam Malik declared that "the marriage contract is a contract of ownership of benefit of the sexual organ of the woman and the rest of her body."

> The followers of Imam Shafii said: "The most accepted view is that what has been contracted upon is the woman, that is, the benefit derived from her sexual organ."

> The followers of Imam Abu Hanifa said: "The right of sexual pleasure belongs to the man, not the woman; by that it is meant that the man has the right to force the woman to gratify himself sexually.[34]

If a Muslim "suspects disobedience" he is to "admonish" his wives, send them to bed "and beat them" (S. 4:34).

"Paradise" (128 verses): There are four gardens of Eden: "gardens of delight watered by running streams—as vast as heaven and earth"—in which Muslim men "will be busy with their joys—dwelling forever in towering mansions, with gushing fountains, rivers of fresh milk, clarified honey and delectable wine." There are "streams of sparkling waters, high-bosomed maidens, bashful, dark eyed virgins—*houris* of exceptional beauty—chaste as the sheltered eggs of ostriches. Dark-eyed virgins—*houris*, chaste as hidden pearls whom neither man nor Jinnee [spirits] will have touched before." These "loving companions" are "a reward for their deeds."

Homosexuals, too, will have "boys of their own, immortal youths, as fair as virgin pearls, boys graced with eternal youth, who to the beholder's eyes will seem like sprinkled pearls."

Muslim men—"blissful their reward"—will be "decked with bracelets of gold and pearls and arrayed in garments of fine green silk and rich, fine brocade." They shall be "wed to dark-eyed *houris*—to spouses of perfect chastity, and recline in shady groves on green silk cushions arranged in order, fine carpets richly spread, soft, jewel encrusted raised couches while waters roll at their feet." They shall "eat the finest of fine foods on golden dishes, drink honey nectar out of golden cups," and have their "every desire satisfied"—all that their "souls desire," and all that their "eyes rejoice in." "They shall be given a pure wine to drink, securely sealed, whose very dregs are musk (for this let all men emulously strive)." Note: Musk is a very powerful scent that a musk deer releases to attract females.

"Hell" (81 verses): All unbelievers (S. 6:70 etc.) will eat nothing except "decaying filth—choking food." Their drink shall be "festering blood" and "scalding water which will simmer in your belly and tear bowels: yet you shall drink it as the thirsty camel drinks." They are to be "branded on the nose, dragged by the hair of their scalp with faces downward" and thrown into a "blazing fire which can be heard raging, roaring and seething from a great distance—throwing up sparks as huge towers, as bright as yellow camels. Their heads will roll about in the Fire" that is "bursting with rage. They will be speechless with despair," and when they "want to come out of the fire they will be driven back." They will be "chained together by the neck with heavy chains and shackles—iron fetters, each 70 cubits long [24 feet—7 meters]. A harrowing scourge—sheets of fire and molten brass—will assail them from above and beneath." Angels will "carry off their souls, striking their faces and their backs."

Koranic facts that contradict historical and biblical facts:

King Saul had his men drink water from a pool to select a small army of men (S. 2:249). The Bible informs us that it was Gideon (Judges 7:4-6).

The wife of Amram (Exodus 6:20) gave birth to Aaron, Moses, Miriam and Mary the mother of Jesus (S. 3:36 etc.). Historical and biblical fact is that about 1,500 years separate Miriam from Mary.

Zacharias was "bereft of speech for three days and three nights" (S. 19:11 etc.). The Bible tells us that he was mute from the time of Gabriel's visit (Luke 1:20) until the circumcision of John (Luke 1:64), a period of approximately 10 months.

Mary was raised by Zacharias (S. 3:37 etc.), and Jesus was born before John (S. 3:37-40 etc.).

Mary went to "a solitary place to the east" (S. 19:14) and gave birth alone, "by the trunk of a palm-tree" (S. 19:22). She then "carried the child and came to her people" (S. 19:28). In gospel narratives the Bible tells us that Mary gave birth in

Bethlehem, in a stable, in the presence and with the help of her husband, Joseph. Shepherds saw the child in the manger and Wise Men from the East gave gifts of gold, frankincense and myrrh.

The "first temple for mankind—a blessed sight, a beacon for the nations—was built in Mecca" (S. 3:96 etc.). The Koran frequently refers to "mosques" as the place of Muslim worship (S. 7:31 etc.), thus the "temple" here is not to be understood as a "mosque." The "temple" at Mecca was built in the 7th century A.D. Historical fact is that Solomon's temple was completed around 959 B.C., and the second temple around 515 B.C.

Moses had the Egyptian magicians cast down their "rods and ropes" first, before he cast down his staff which turned into a snake and ate up all the sorcerers' snakes (S. 7:118 etc.). The Bible tells us that Aaron threw his rod down, then the Egyptian magicians, and Aaron's rod swallowed the Egyptian rods (Exodus 7:10-12). The Koran says that in the face of such a sign the magicians prostrated themselves before Moses and became Muslims. Pharaoh then had the magicians' "hands and feet cut off on alternate sides" before "crucifying" them on "the trunks of palm-trees" (S. 7:124 etc.).

Pharaoh became a Muslim by embracing Islam "as he was drowning" in the Red Sea (S. 10:91 etc.).

As Noah entered the Ark his son refused to embark. He sought "refuge in a mountain" from the flood, and was drowned (S. 11:42). The Bible tells us that Noah and all of his sons entered the Ark and were saved (Genesis 7:7).

Abraham was thrown into a furnace by Nimrod (S. 21:65). Historical fact: Nimrod lived some 350 years before Abraham.

Haman was a contemporary of Pharaoh and built the Tower of Babel (S. 28:38 etc.). In actuality the Tower of Babel was built around 2,247 B.C., Pharaoh lived around 1,500 B.C., and Haman ("the enemy of the Jews"—Esther 3:10) around 500 B.C.

Space does not allow more of these "revelations" given by Allah to Muhammed, but readers should by now have gotten a small glimpse into the Koran, and that of an Arab preoccupation with sex.

The very reading of the Koran inspires Muslims of all ages to kill Jews and Christians, most especially Jews. Early one Sunday morning in late 1998, a 15-year-old Arab girl plunged a knife into the back of an Israeli 17-year-old high school girl, as she stood talking with some friends. It took the combined strength of an Israeli soldier and another man to overpower the Arab girl. She admitted to having "decided to attack Jews after reading from the Koran on Saturday night."[35]

It is this writer's prayer that readers will now have a greater understanding of the content of the Koran and, consequently, a better understanding of the battle that lies before Israel and all Christendom.

If Islam could destroy the sovereign State of Israel, biblical Christians would be its next target. It behooves all twice-born Christians to oppose Islam with all of their strength. Muslims are imprisoned in a most terrible darkness, and this darkness can only be pierced by the light of the Risen Christ.

Deceived or Deceiver?

Aril Edvardsen, a prominent Norwegian Christian tele-evangelist who lives much of the time in Florida, U.S.A., has been making an evangelistic thrust into the Arab world. In late 1997, Edvardsen made a statement to the Norwegian media that

> The Koran's Allah created Adam. He was the God of Abraham, and he was the God of David.[36]

Edvardsen was really saying that the Allah of the Koran is the God of Bible. He was apparently trying to protect himself from a possible Christian backlash by not saying it outright. However, Edvardsen must surely be aware that the Koran[37] he cites—written centuries after the advent of Christ who is called the _Son of God_ 49 times in the New Testament—expressly says **nine times** that "Allah has no son."[38] How then, can Allah be the same God as that of the Bible? Edvardsen must also be aware that the Koran clearly forbids even saying "Allah begot a son," and to do so is "a monstrous blasphemy."[39] Again, how can this Allah be the true God when the Bible clearly states:

> _Whoever confesses that Jesus is the Son of God, God abides in him, and he in God_ (1 John 4:15).

The very heart of the good news of salvation is stated in John 3:16:

*For **God** so loved the world that He gave **His only begotten Son**, that whoever believes in Him should not perish but have everlasting life.*

If Allah is the Creator of Adam and the God of Abraham and David, as Edvardsen asserts, then according to that He must be the God of the Bible. But the Koran's Allah is adamant that he has no son. Therefore, if Allah is God, then the Bible must be a lie from beginning to end, and all Christians remain dead in their sins without hope of salvation. What nonsense indeed!

Edvardsen surely knows also that the Koran explicitly states one of the major Muslim tenets: "We will serve **no other idols besides Allah**."[40]

For Edvardsen to have made his comment about the Koran's Allah, he must have read the Koran. Only a complete fool would comment on it without having read it through. So, having read the Koran, Edvardsen must be aware that in the Koran Christians are repeatedly cursed by Allah. This is also in total contradiction to the teachings of the Bible. The God of the Bible only curses those that despise the Jewish people (Genesis 12:3). God is love, and He loves with an everlasting love:

In this the love of God was manifested toward us, that God has sent His only begotten Son into the world, that we might live through Him. In this is love, not that we loved God, but that He loved us and sent His Son to be the propitiation for our sins (1 John 4:9-10).

Edvardsen is, therefore, either naive and totally deceived, or he himself is purposely trying to deceive others for his own ends. Perhaps he hopes to curry favor with Yasser Arafat and the Arab Muslims in order to become the first Christian ever to hold an evangelistic crusade in the Arafat-ruled territories.

But how can Edvardsen get his name into Christian history books through preaching an Allah who has no son and, consequently, no plan of salvation? The heart of the gospel—John 3:16—is missing.

Edvardsen must also know the Koran states that Jesus never died, and that He was not Allah's son despite the New Testament's 49 assertions that He is the *Son of God*. Edvardsen surely knows, too, that the Koran rules out both the atonement and the forgiveness of sin, and makes both the Old and New Testaments to be a hodgepodge of lies and deception.

Edvardsen's "love affair" with Arab Muslims apparently caused him to make a complete U-turn from his former biblical stand concerning Israel. Since beginning his "love affair" with the Muslims, Edvardsen has frequently criticized Israel, and even called former Prime Minister Netanyahu "a liar" on Norwegian television while Netanyahu was still Israel's premier.

On the eve of his departure for Gaza where he hoped to receive permission from Yasser Arafat to hold a "Crusade," Edvardsen harshly criticized this writer and his books in the Norwegian media. Edvardsen said that he only needed to read a few pages of this writer's books to know they were biblically unsound. He also had the temerity to say,

> It was not scriptural to say that God would bless those who bless Israel—God rebuked Israel, and we can do no less.

Just who does Edvardsen think he is—God? And regarding the Promised Land, Edvardsen said: "The promise is to Abram's seed. Jews have to share with Arabs." This is almost too inane to comment upon. Edvardsen knows better than most Christians that all the promises, including that of the Land, were to be through Isaac. In fact, Abraham's seed is only recognized through Isaac:

> **_In Isaac your seed shall be called._** _That is, those who are the children of the flesh, these are not the children of God; but_ **_the children of the promise are counted as the seed_**
>
> (Romans 9:7, 8).

And in Psalms 105:8-11, it is written that God

> _remembers His covenant forever, the word which He commanded, for a thousand generations, the covenant which He made with_ **Abraham,** _and His oath to_ **Isaac,** _and confirmed it to_ **Jacob** _for a statute, to_ **Israel** _as an everlasting covenant, saying,_ **_"To you I will give the land of Canaan_** _as the allotment of your inheritance."_

There is no provision for Ishmael and the Arabs to inherit the Promised Land in that passage of Scripture, or in any other passage of the Bible.

Edvardsen's good friend, Yasser Arafat, has been claiming descent from the Canaanites in an effort to tie the Palestinians to the Land before the Israelite conquest 3,500 years ago. Arafat even encouraged Palestinian Arabs to celebrate festivals to "ancient fertility-deities, Ba'al and Ashtaroth."[41] That should have caused Edvardsen to stop and think before he aired his views about Jews having to share the Promised Land with Arabs because the promise was to Abram's seed. Edvardsen's silly statement is not only contrary to all Scripture, but Arafat's claimed descent from the Canaanites even places him outside of Abram's seed. Arafat apparently suffers from schizophrenia. One day he is a Canaanite and the next an Arab. Five years ago he was claiming descent from the Philistines, but he apparently found out that the Philistines were a non-Semitic people and lost interest in that track.

Edvardsen's politically-motivated statements have shocked thousands of Norwegians, causing many to withdraw their spiritual and financial support from his ministry.

An important Old Testament tenet is that God blesses those who bless His people Israel. Edvardsen said this writer's books were unscriptual because they hold to that tenet. It beggars the imagination to think what Edvardsen might say to the media regarding God's promise to Abraham and his seed in Genesis 12:3:

> *I will bless those who bless you, and I will curse him who despises you.*

Coming just prior to his arrival in Gaza, some of Edvardsen's statements would certainly appear to have been no more than political propaganda messages for the benefit of Arafat. If Edvardsen has thrown his Christian ethics to the winds in pursuit of fame and fortune, he would not be the first "Christian" to have done so.

Perhaps Edvardsen should be reminded of the fact that Balaam was willing to curse Israel for profit (Jude 1:11), and he perished. However, God first restrained Balaam's madness through the use of a dumb donkey (2 Peter 2:16).

Islamic Terrorism

Terrorism forms a sizeable part of Islamic activity. Islam officially condemns terrorism, but it draws a clear distinction between terrorism and that of fighting "alien domination."[42] This, of course, provides Islamic legality for the numerous brutal conflicts around the globe where Muslims are fighting for a number of independent Islamic states.

Islam is on the march as it was in Muhammed's day. Throughout the Western world, mosques are springing up like mushrooms in a farmer's field. In 1970, the once Christian populated Bethlehem area where Jesus was born had only five mosques. By the end of 1997, it sported 72, and on Fridays, the whole area in front of the Church of the Nativity in Manger Square is packed with Muslim worshippers, because there is no longer room for them all to pray in the Mosque of Omar.[43]

In the U.K. almost 1,000 churches have been turned into mosques, and Muslims in Britain planned to build 100 new mosques by the turn of the millennium—a quarter of them for London.[44]

In typical Western naivete, Western leaders have opened up their country's doors to a Muslim immigration that could eventually destroy Western culture. In some countries, like Saudi Arabia, no religion apart from Islam is tolerated, not even in private homes. It is illegal to be overheard praying to Jesus or to display any Christian symbol. Even foreign Christians visiting the country are not allowed to gather and worship.

> Since 1992, more than 360 cases have been documented in which Christian expatriates were arrested for taking part in private worship.[45]

Saudi Arabia is a country without one single church building, and US$10,000 is paid by the Saudi government to anyone who unearths a house church.[46]

Egyptians Christians must have personally-signed permission from the president of Egypt in order to build a new church.[47] Under Islam, churches that have been destroyed for any reason cannot ever be rebuilt, and permission to remodel a church is unobtainable. Ignoring all this, the West has opened its arms to Muslims, and Islam is spreading in the Western world today almost as rapidly as the plague in medieval times.

Islam is the biggest evil facing the Western world, but a greater threat than Islam is the Western world's own humanism, the millions upon millions of _"fools"_ who say in their hearts, _There is no God._

At the October 1999 synod of Europe's Catholic bishops, Archbishop Giuseppe Bernadini of Smyrna quoted an important Muslim figure speaking at an Islamic-Christian meeting. Addressing the "Christians" in his audience, the Muslim leader said:

> Thanks to your democratic laws, we shall invade you; and thanks to our religious laws, we shall dominate you.[48]

Another Muslim leader said, at the same meeting: "You have nothing to teach us, and we have nothing to learn."[49]

Time and time again Muslim leaders have told us of their arrogant intentions, but Western leaders do not want to believe them, so they simply ignore the rapidly developing threat. Millions of Muhammed's followers are all-too-easily invading Europe and America through immigration. And a time bomb is ticking its way toward a massive Islamic explosion in the West.

Muslim suicide bombers who blew dozens of Israelis to pieces in Tel Aviv, Ashkelon, Afula, Hadera, Beit Lid and Jerusalem, and maimed or wounded several hundred more, would use a mini atomic bomb if one were available to them. And, it is only a matter of time before such devices do become available to them.

Referring specifically to the suicide bombers who blew themselves up in Jerusalem's main pedestrian mall in September 1997, taking several Israeli lives, including three 14-year-old girls, Dr. Taksin Shea-Hrabni, an official in Iran's Foreign Office in Teheran, said:

> Every saint dies for the holy Allah and, therefore, is not a murderer. He dies in heaven's gates.[50]

Islam, like Judaism, regards suicide as sin. However, one of Egypt's most influential Muslim leaders, Muhammed Sayyed al-Tantawi, chief sheik of Cairo's Al-Azhar Mosque, ruled that

> a Muslim who serves as a human bomb in order to take Jewish lives along with his own—or the lives of anyone declared to be an enemy—is not a sinful suicide, but a noble *shahid* (martyr), "a holy witness" to the justice of the Arab/Muslim cause.[51]

The same Muslim cleric noted that Islam forbids the murder of children, old and helpless people. On this he ruled that

> Jews are "attackers," and therefore not entitled to exemption as "aged, child, or woman." And the *shahid* who takes such Jewish lives is considered to have acted in self-defense.[52]

Similarly, in a newspaper interview, Syrian Islamic Mufti (Judge) Kaftaro described Muslim suicide bombings as "legitimate in Islam because they are carried out in the name of Allah."[53]

All Muslim murderers of Jews are glorified as martyrs. Yihye Ayyash, an Arab terrorist who masterminded attacks against Israelis that took the lives of around 50 civilians, was killed by Israeli agents when they detonated a booby-trapped mobile telephone he was using. The PLO, instead of honoring its Oslo agreements to fight terrorism and hand over wanted terrorists to Israel, gave permission to rename a street in Gaza after Ayyash.[54]

Islam's battle against Israel will continue for as long as it takes the *Prince of Peace* (Isaiah 9:6) to win every Muslim heart. Even if Israel signed 1,001 agreements with every Arab nation and every other Muslim state, war would continue because Islam's "holy" book says Israel must be destroyed:

> In the end Israel will disappear as the Koran states. From the standpoint of the Koran, there is no place for Israel and its existence is not justifiable.[55]

But, the reader might say, Israel has a strong defense force. That is correct. Correct at the time of writing, that is. However, the Hellenistic *"fools"* currently sitting in Israel's driving seat severely cut the defense budget for the year 2000. They have also promised to cut the mandatory military service by at least half a year, and have indicated that thousands of reserve soldiers will no longer be required to attend the one month refresher course each year. On top of this, the *"fools"* are ceding almost all of Israel's militarily strategic high ground to their sworn enemies.

Israeli *"fools"* are desperately trying to coax Syria into signing a "peace" agreement. They are prepared to cede to Syria the strategic Golan Heights with the Banias Springs—the source of nearly 40 percent of Israel's drinking water—for this worthless scrap of paper. As Syrian Foreign Minister Farouk al-Shara and Israeli Prime Minister Ehud Barak sat down to talk "peace," an editorial in the government-controlled Syrian daily *Tishrin* exposed the true heart of Israel's new "peace" partner: "Israel is the enemy of Islam and of all Muslims."[56] And after they had sat down, al-Shara told a gathering of writers and journalists in Damascus that

> the Ba'ath party, to which I have the honor of being a member, understands that restoring Palestine in its entirety is a long-term strategic goal that cannot be achieved in one stage. The Ba'ath party ideology for more than 30 years now sets stages for the liberation. The first stage is the stage of restoring the occupied lands of '67.[57]

The Syrian Foreign Minister stated Syria's real intention to his audience. Syrian intent is the same as the PLO's—to use Islam's Truce of Hudaybiyyah and continue its war against Israel by stages. Israel's desire to cede the Golan Heights to Syria in exchange for a useless piece of paper will not bring peace. It will simply give Syria a more strategic position from which it will launch another military onslaught against Israel in the not-too-distant future.

Israel has fought seven wars of self-defense against attacking Muslim Arab armies. It should be remembered that the surprise attack launched against Israel in October 1973 nearly succeeded. It should also be remembered that Mahmud Ghaznavi, a Muslim king, attacked India 17 times before he finally conquered part of India. The consequences of Ghaznavi's victory over part of India, and the inevitable spread of Islam in that region, ultimately brought about the breakup of the Indian subcontinent. The Muslims broke off Pakistan and Bangladesh, and the bloody conflict over Kashmir rages today because Muslims want all of that province also.

Islam wants every inch of the territory Israel occupies. Why? One reason is because Muhammed said, "Never do two religions exist in Arabia."[58] The second reason is that Islam teaches that all lands once conquered by Muslim armies remain Islamic eternally. No true Muslim, therefore, will ever rest peacefully until Israel is destroyed. This is why South African Muslims—thousands of miles away from Israel—marched in Cape Town on May 14, 1998, protesting the establishment of Israel a half-century earlier. Several hundred placards read "Death to Israel" and "Long live Hamas," and slogans were chanted such as "One Zionist, one bullet."[59]

The vicious Islamic terrorist organization, Hamas, has been responsible for dozens of suicide bombings in Israel that have killed hundreds of Israelis and wounded hundreds more. The organization's Khaled Mashaal said in an interview with the Jordanian *Star*:

> Our path is clear: armed struggle until the occupiers [of Islamic land] have been banished. Nobody in the world can change Hamas's strategy.[60]

Sheik Ahmed Yassin, the blind founder of Hamas, told an audience of 3,500 at the Islamic University of Gaza:

> We have one enemy and we will wage war and fight him until we return to our [Islamic] land. No to a ceasefire, and we will

not concede one inch of our [Islamic] land, however high the price.[61]

And Yassin told a Swedish newspaper that "Israel must disappear."[62] He also said:

"a two-state solution"—the widely promoted view that Israel and an independent Palestinian Arab state should exist side by side—was not acceptable. Even a small Israel located in Tel Aviv was unacceptable.[63]

Another Hamas leader, Abdel-Aziz Rantisi, interviewed by two London-based dailies, Saudi-owned *al-Hayat* and the PLO's *al-Quds al-Arabi*, said:

Islam does not permit giving up one inch of Palestine and states that Palestine belongs to the Muslims, belongs to the Palestinian people, not to the Jews. Bartering land is not liberation and is not permissible in Islam.[64]

Sheik Ahmed Yassin expectantly awaits an early destruction of Israel during the 21st century, the century of Islam. In 1998 he told a news conference in Damascus:

The first quarter of the next century will witness the elimination of the Zionist entity and the establishment of the Palestinian state over the whole of Palestine. The strong will not remain strong forever and the weak will not remain weak forever. Things change.[65]

Israel's "peace" partner, the PLO, also makes clear what its own long-term goal is. A monument erected to the memory of Arabs killed during the *intifada* can be seen on Hebron Road, just south of Jerusalem. The stone monument is in the shape of the "Map of Palestine," with borders from the Jordan River to the Mediterranean Sea.[66] And the new official map of "Palestine State" issued by the Palestinian Authority includes all of Israel, complete with *Judea*, *Samaria* and Gaza.[67] In addition to all this, the PLO-appointed Mufti of Jerusalem, Ikrama Sabri, has said in his official capacity:

Despite all the conspiracies, Jerusalem and Palestine from the Jordan River to the Mediterranean Sea will remain Islamic until judgment day.[68]

Hizb'allah seems to have been fighting a guerilla war against the IDF for eons in Israel's "security zone," in southern Lebanon.

Hizb'allah means "Party of Allah" and is another fanatical Islamic group funded by Iran. Its equipment, fighting methods and successes have improved with each succeeding year, and the rate of casualties suffered by the IDF have induced prime minister Barak to declare a unilateral IDF pullout from Lebanon by July 2000. Barak's intention is to deploy the IDF inside Israel, along its border with Lebanon. The *"fools"* guiding Israel believe that an IDF pullout from Lebanon will end the high loss of life from constant Hizb'allah attacks despite army and intelligence reports to the contrary. The *"fools"* have chosen the humanist path rather than believe Western intelligence analysts, high-ranking IDF officers, or even the oft-stated intent of Hizb'allah itself.

Following Barak's announcement of a unilateral IDF withdrawal from the "security zone," Israeli army officers stated that Hizb'allah "does not recognize the border between Israel and Lebanon,"[69] and that after a unilateral IDF pullout "it will continue to launch attacks."[70]

Western intelligence sources even predict a rise in attacks against the redeployed IDF forces inside Israel, and also in terrorist attacks against Israeli civilians.[71]

Hizb'allah's deputy leader, Na'im Kassem, himself told *SKY NEWS* in July 1999 that

an Israeli withdrawal from south Lebanon would not be the end of the organization's struggle against the Jewish state.[72]

In the preceding March of 1999, the commanding officer of the IDF's Southern Command, Major-General Yom Tov Samiyeh, had said:

An IDF withdrawal from Lebanon is only part of what Hizb'-allah wants. What they are really driving for is the capture of Jerusalem.[73]

Samiyeh's professional assessment is nearer to the truth, but it is still far from the whole truth. The whole truth is contained in statements by Hizb'allah secretary-general Sheik Hassan Nasrallah. He told *Radio Teheran* that Hizb'allah's

fight against Israel will continue until the "final destruction" of the Jewish state.[74]

The whole Hizb'allah truth was nowhere put so succinctly by Nasrallah as in July 1999, when he spoke to a group of Lebanese journalists:

Even if the entire world recognizes Israel, even if they threaten to hang us, we cannot recognize this cancer, this racist and terrorist entity. Even if the Syrian Golan and southern Lebanon are returned by Israel, there will still be a great national and Islamic problem to resolve.[75]

Nasrallah accepts the Arab world's view of agreements signed with Israel—they are only binding upon the Jews. He said in January 2000:

All Palestinians must fight to liberate Palestine even if agreements are reached.[76]

In response to the question put to him in an interview with *Lebanese Television*: What will Hizb'allah do after Israel evacuates South Lebanon?, Deputy Secretary-General of Hizb'allah, Na'im Kassem said:

We are not saying what we will do because we don't want the enemy to know our methods of operations. First, let the enemy retreat. The Israelis will know about it in good time—after they have retreated.[77]

Sheik Hassan Nasrallah is even more optimistic about Israel's demise in the "century of Islam" than the leader of the Hamas terror group. Nasrallah said on February 16, 2000: "Israel will exist for only another 10 years, at the most."[78]

It is very obvious that no earthly "peace" agreement between Israel and the Arab nations is ever going to bring peace to the region—at least, for no longer than it will take for the Arabs to regroup, rearm, and strike again. It would be against everything Islam and the Koran teaches if Muslims were to let Israel continue to exist unmolested on Allah's land.

Members of the international club of *"fools"* are placing their bets on Islam becoming more moderate, but fundamental Islam is spreading like a brush fire after five years of drought. The *"fools"* are gambling that Western influence will moderate Islam, but it is inflaming its passions instead. Islam calls America the Great Satan, not the least because America's huge pornographic and film industries spew out filth that offends every one of the millions of radical Muslims.

A *fatwa* (Islamic decree) was issued against the life of Salman Rushdie for offending radical Islam. In addition to the *fatwa*, Islamic authorities also offered a reward of more than US$3 million to anyone who killed Rushdie. This has kept Rushdie in hiding for nearly a decade. In February 1998, another *fatwa* was issued, this time against all Americans:

> We with Allah's help, call on every Muslim who believes in Allah and wishes to be rewarded to comply with Allah's order to kill the Americans and plunder their money wherever and whenever they find it. [79]

Islam has fed on violence and deceit from its inception. It has spread like a cancer and has proven to be equally as deadly. Muhammed's expression of delight, *"Allahu ahkbar!"* (Allah is greater!), became the Muslims' battle cry. The sound of *"Allahu ahkbar!"* rings out as suicide bombers detonate themselves in the midst of Israeli civilians. It resonates from the lips of Arabs as they plunge knives into the backs of unsuspecting Israeli men, women and children. It echoes amid the mortar and gunfire directed at Israelis from Amal, Islamic Jihad, Hamas and Hizb'allah fighters. The cry of *"Allahu ahkbar!"* reverberates not only throughout the cities and towns of Israel, but also across the entire world. It sanctifies Islamic murder and mayhem and turns it into divine injunctions from Allah.

As these pages are penned in early 2000, the cry of *"Allahu ahkbar!"* is heard as Muslims continue to murder Christians in Sudan and raze their villages. *"Allahu ahkbar!"* is heard as Christian houses and churches are torched in Kenya, Nigeria, the Philippines and Indonesia. *"Allahu ahkbar!"* is heard as Chechens battle Russian troops in Grozny. *"Allahu ahkbar!"* is heard as Indian troops battle Muslim insurgents in Kashmir. And *"Allahu ahkbar!"* is heard as Muslims take control of huge tracts of Israel's land.

In recent years Sarajevo fell to Islam and the Muslim cry of *"Allahu ahkbar!"* In recent months Kosovo fell to Islam and the sound of *"Allahu ahkbar!"* In recent days a large part of Israel has fallen to Islam and *"Allahu ahkbar!"* What prize does tomorrow hold for Islam?

The World Trade Center was torn apart by a Muslim bomb. The Paris Metro was brought to a standstill by a Muslim bomb. The Israeli Embassy in Buenos Aires was destroyed by a Muslim bomb. The Jewish Center in Buenos Aires was destroyed by a Muslim bomb. The Israeli Embassy in London was destroyed by a

Muslim bomb. The British center for Jewish charities was also destroyed by a Muslim bomb. Apartment buildings, vegetable markets, shopping malls, pedestrian malls, buses and bus stations, passenger planes—on the ground and in the air—these all fall victim to Muslim terror. Bombs and still more bombs. Bombs, bullets and kitchen knives have become the Islamic calling card. Islamic bombs, Islamic terror. Bombs, bodies, wrecked buildings and wrecked lives. And Muhammed's cry of delight— _"Allahu ahkbar!"_

While love is the typical Christian attitude, love for the good carries with it a corresponding hatred for what is wrong. And while this writer loathes Islam, he does not hate Muslims. Jesus loves the sinner but hates the sin. He commended the church of Ephesus for hating the actions of a particular group of people:

> _But this you have in your favor, **you hate the deeds of the Nicolaitans, which I also hate**_ (Revelation 2:6).

Islam is a particularly dark and deadly religion. Jesus loves the Muslims, but He hates the deeds of Islam today as surely as He hated those of the Nicolaitans yesterday. It behooves all twice-born Christians to follow their Master in this. Fundamental Muslims are following in the footsteps of their master, Muhammed. They are keeping his commands and imitating his deeds. Muslims walk in a darkness that is impenetrable by everything except the light of Jesus. Every twice-born Christian should seek the face of Yahweh on behalf of the world's almost one billion Muslims. They should earnestly strive in prayer for Jesus to snap the chains of Islam and set the Muslim captives free.

10

The Wall

Oslo is a four-letter word for suicide. The Oslo "peace" is a "peace" that kills. The "peace" between Israel and the PLO that was birthed in Norway was *conceived in sin and brought forth in iniquity*. The Oslo Accords were the product of *"fools"* whose world views do not rise above man's horizon. Yahweh, *God of Israel*, nowhere entered the equation, and this is a recipe for disaster. If God-fearing men and women had been leading Israel, there would not have been any dark, undercover secret meetings in Oslo— meetings that were categorically denied as having taken place at the time. Half-truths and outright lies spilled from the politicians' mouths like water over a dam during a flood. The godless plan their furtive actions in the dark, because they cannot bear exposure to the light.

Leaving *the Holy One of Israel* out of the Oslo equation, however, will neither prevent Him from having His say nor stop Him from exercising His will. Cast aside and forgotten like an old rag doll, He still intends to rule over Israel—with an iron fist if necessary:

"As I live," says Yahweh God, "surely with a mighty hand, with an outstretched arm, and with fury poured out, I will rule over you" (Ezekiel 20:33).

The Bible is full of warnings to Israel and its shepherds, and these can only be ignored by Israel at its peril. The recorded catastrophes that befell Israel in the past are not just a record of events. They are warnings, pure and simple:

Now all these things happened to them as examples, and they were written for our admonition, on whom the ends of the ages have come (1 Corinthians 10:11).

There is a distinct parallel between modern Israel and Judah under King Asa. The Bible tells us that

Zerah the Ethiopian came out against [Asa] with an army of a million men and three hundred chariots (2 Chronicles 14:9).
Asa had less that half the number of soldiers and went out to battle vastly outnumbered. We are told that

*Asa cried out to Yahweh his God, and said, "Yahweh, it is
nothing for You to help, whether with many or with those who
have no power; help us, O Yahweh our God, for we rest on
You, and in Your name we go against this multitude. O Yahweh,
You are our God; do not let man prevail against You!" So
Yahweh struck the Ethiopians before Asa and Judah, and the
Ethiopians fled* (1 Chronicles 14:11-12).

Modern Israel has also been attacked by numerically superior
forces. Since the day following its declaration of the State, it has
been repeatedly attacked by Arab armies. For example, in 1973,
on Yom Kippur, the holiest day of the Jewish calendar, an Arab
force in excess of 1,200,000 troops, 4,200 tanks, more than 1,000
planes and thousands of artillery pieces[1] launched a surprise attack
against Israel. It took several days for Israel to mobilize a force of
300,000 men that included every available reserve. However, in a
matter of days Israel had all but obliterated the attacking force
together with its equipment.

A relatively small band of largely untrained Israeli fighters
battled seven fully equipped, fully trained Arab armies in 1948,
and won the war. And it won the next war against Egypt's massive
army in 1956. Israel also won the next war against five Arab armies
in 1967—and it won the next war...and the next...and the next.

God's intervention on Israel's behalf was apparent to the world
with miracles abounding in each war. Today, however, Israel takes
the posture of a defeated nation and sues for "peace" with its Arab
neighbors, because as far as they are concerned, Yahweh is out of
the equation. The *"fools"* leading Israel are deathly worried that
their run of "luck" will come to an end. The *"fools"* are giving
away large portions of the Promised Land, the Temple Mount where
the great temples once stood, and even the Old City—*the city of
the great King* (Psalms 48:2). How like King Asa these *"fools"*
have become:

*Asa brought silver and gold from the treasuries of the house
of Yahweh and of the king's house, and sent to Ben-Hadad
king of Syria, who dwelt in Damascus, saying, "Let there be
a treaty between you and me, as there was between my father
and your father. Here, I have sent you silver and gold; come,
break your treaty with Baasha king of Israel...*

(2 Chronicles 16:2, 3).

Yahweh was extremely displeased at being set aside by Asa after routing the Ethiopians for him. He was not only set aside by Asa, but Asa also disposed of Yahweh's own property out of His temple. Yahweh sent Hanani the seer to express His displeasure:

Because you have relied on the king of Syria, and have not relied on Yahweh your God, therefore the army of the king of Syria has escaped from your hand. Were the Ethiopians and the Lubim not a huge army with very many chariots and horsemen? Yet, because you relied on Yahweh, He delivered them into your hand. For the eyes of Yahweh run to and fro throughout the whole earth, to show Himself strong on behalf of those whose heart is loyal to Him. In this you have done foolishly; therefore from now on you shall have wars

(2 Chronicles 16:7-9).

Did not Yitzhak Rabin act the same as Asa king of Judah by giving away Yahweh's land to the PLO? Did not Shimon Peres do the same? Is not Ehud Barak surpassing the two former *"fools"* by ceding more land than Rabin and Peres between them? Is not Barak compounding the felony by allowing the Temple Mount to remain under Islam's authority? And is it not shameful that the Old City of Jerusalem is about to be given over to at least partial PLO control? If Asa and Judah were given over to continual wars for one act of unfaithfulness, we can be certain that Israel will also have continual wars despite all the pieces of paper signed with the words "Peace Agreement" printed on them. Only Israel will now have to fight using its own strength and from a weakened position, having given away so much of its militarily strategic territory.

Asa resented Hanani bringing Yahweh's message and acted like many other insecure rulers:

Then Asa was angry with the seer, and put him in prison, for he was enraged at him because of this. And Asa oppressed some of the people at that time (2 Chronicles 16:10).

Yitzhak Rabin's government took the same course of action as Asa did. Thousands of Israelis who actively demonstrated against Rabin's policies were oppressed. Many were beaten with clubs, women were dragged by their hair, and not a few demonstrators were dragged off to prison. When God is absent from the equation, chaos reigns. Chaos *is* the absence of God.

Despite being rebuked by Yahweh for his perfidy, Asa would not return to Him:

> *And in the thirty-ninth year of his reign, Asa became diseased in his feet, and his malady was severe; yet in his disease he did not seek Yahweh, but the physicians*
>
> (2 Chronicles 16:12).

So also with the *"fools"* of Israel. The more of the divine inheritance they gave away and the more they grovelled before the Arabs, all the more Israelis were savagely murdered in Arab terror attacks. Instead of returning to the Rock from which it was hewn, Israel determinedly followed the humanist path trod by *"fools."* Asa became severely diseased in his feet, but continued to shun his Creator in preference for man's remedies. Rabin turned his back on *the Holy One of Israel*, followed the Luciferic religion of Freemasonry, and was assassinated in a bizarre conspiracy.

Prophecy and Middle East "Peace"

Before we look at some biblical prophecies concerning the "peace process," we should first glance at some obstacles that trip students of biblical prophecy. In Christian circles, we often hear warnings about not taking Scripture out of context, etc. If those issuing the warnings would only but take a good, long look at the way the Holy Spirit-inspired writers used and applied Scripture, they would not be so dogmatic on this point. This writer wrote a fairly comprehensive chapter concerning biblical prophecy, including the subjects of "Interpretation," "Exegesis," and "Eisegesis" in the third edition of his book "When Day and Night Cease." Readers are referred to that work as we do not have the space here to delve deeply into the subject. We shall limit ourselves to two points only: Multiple fulfillments of biblical prophecy; and usage of Scripture by Spirit-possessed servants of the Most High.

There is often more than one "fulfillment" of a biblical prophecy. The Holy Spirit-inspired writers of both the Old and New Testaments give us examples of a fulfillment of prophecy and then another fulfillment of the same passage. Andrew Smith writes:

> It is important to note that in Jewish Midrashic interpretation, prophecy can be fulfilled once, and then again. It is a cycle—often repeating more than once, but pointing towards one "ultimate fulfillment."[2]

One example will be sufficient for our purposes. At the burning bush in the wilderness Yahweh called Moses to a specific task:

Come now, therefore, and I will send you to Pharaoh that you may bring My people, the children of Israel, out of Egypt (Exodus 3:10).

Yahweh then gave Moses an unambiguous message for Pharaoh, King of Egypt:

*Then you shall say to Pharaoh, "Thus says Yahweh: **Israel is My son, My firstborn**. So I say to you, **let My son go that he may serve Me**. But if you refuse to let him go, indeed I will kill your son, your firstborn"* (Exodus 4:22-23).

It should be noticed that it is Israel that is referred to as Yahweh's firstborn son. The *New King James* Bible (this writer's preference among English editions) capitalizes words wherever they refer to the Divine. We see in the above passage that "son" is with a lowercase "s" and is, therefore, referring to Israel, not to Jesus. The prophet Hosea records the fulfillment of Moses' mission when he writes down Yahweh's words to him: *When **Israel** was a child, I loved him, and **out of Egypt I called My son*** (Hosea 11:1). We see that Yahweh is still referring to Israel as His son, and "son" is again written with a lowercase "s."

Let us go now to the narrative concerning Mary and Joseph's flight to Egypt with the young child Jesus. We pick up the story in Matthew's account of the gospel, where the wise men decide to elude Herod by taking a different route back to the East:

*Now when they had departed, behold, an angel of Yahweh appeared to Joseph in a dream, saying, "Arise, take the young Child and His mother, flee to Egypt, and stay there until I bring you word; for Herod will seek the young Child to destroy Him." When he arose, he took the young Child and His mother by night and departed for Egypt, and was there until the death of Herod, that it might be fulfilled which was spoken by Yahweh through the prophet [Hosea], saying, "**Out of Egypt I called My Son**"* (Matthew 2:13-15).

In this passage we see another fulfillment of Hosea's prophecy. This time "Son" is capitalized and clearly refers to Jesus. Exactly which fulfillment is the "ultimate" fulfillment and which is the secondary fulfillment, this writer leaves for the reader to decide.

Holy Spirit-inspired writers often lifted an existing portion of Scripture from its "context" and applied it to where and what they were writing. The Apostle Paul's writings are replete with examples, but let us go to an even higher authority on the use of Scripture, Jesus Himself.

In Luke 4:18-19 we read that Jesus was handed the Hebrew[3] scroll (it was not a "book") of the prophet Isaiah, and He read from the following passage:

> _The Spirit of Yahweh GOD is upon Me, because Yahweh has anointed Me to preach good tidings to the poor; He has sent Me to heal the brokenhearted, to proclaim liberty to the captives, and the opening of the prison to those who are bound; to proclaim the acceptable year of Yahweh_ (Isaiah 61:1, 2).

There is no pause in the Hebrew text until the end of verse three, and no break in the text until the end of verse nine. Yet Jesus did not feel bound to even complete the sentence that makes up verse two! He completely ignored the second half of the sentence in Hebrew that begins with, _and...._ Jesus left us an example here that no one but a _"fool"_ would find fault with. May these few examples of Scripture usage throw some light into what might otherwise be grey areas for students of the Bible struggling with biblical prophecy.

"Peace, peace!"

Studying biblical prophecies can be likened to keeping ourselves informed on events in Israel and our world. The news media networks update their audiences on earth-shattering events, but they are really only corroborating what biblical prophecies told us thousands of years earlier.

A Christian who is an avid sports fan sat next to a 7 foot 4 inch (223.5 centimeters) basketball star on a U.S. domestic flight. The Christian asked the star, "When you are told to block a player, what do you look at? His eyes to see which way he is looking? His feet, to give you an indication as to which way he might run?" The star replied, "No, sir, I look at his belly button—until that moves, he ain't going nowhere." That is a true story. It is also true that Israel is the spiritual navel of the world, and until things move in Israel, no one is going anywhere.

We are in the end of the End Times. Events are heating up in Israel and that means things will soon heat up elsewhere. In the time frame of biblical prophecy, Israel has passed the halfway mark in the fulfilling of several prophecies dealing with a false peace. Here is the first of these prophecies:

> *Because from the least of them even to the greatest of them, everyone is given to covetousness; and from the prophet even to the priest, everyone deals falsely. They have also healed the hurt of My people slightly, saying, "Peace, peace!" When there is no peace* (Jeremiah 6:13- 14).

An identical passage of Scripture follows two chapters later:

> *...because from the least even to the greatest everyone is given to covetousness; from the prophet even to the priest everyone deals falsely. For they have healed the hurt of the daughter of My people slightly, saying, "Peace, peace!" When there is no peace* (Jeremiah 8:10, 11).

When Yahweh sees fit to tell us things twice, we can be sure that we are touching on something very important. It must be especially important when He says that the false peace spoken of above will only bring trouble:

> *We looked for peace, but no good came; and for a time of health, and there was trouble!* (Jeremiah 8:15).

And it must be really, really important and mean very big trouble for Him to repeat the ominous warning word for word later on:

> *We looked for peace, but there was no good; and for the time of healing, and there was trouble* (Jeremiah 14:19).

Now let us look at the prophecies in more detail:

> *...from the least of them even to the greatest of them, everyone is given to covetousness...*

As with all Western nations, so with Israel today. Inner greed makes Israelis in general want to shake off *the Holy One of Israel* and "be like all other nations." There has also been increasing tension and frequent outbreaks of violence between secular and religious Jews since the beginning of the "peace process." Rabin was the first to say publicly that Israel wants "to be like all other nations." He said it in Cairo when signing the first agreement with Arafat, with President Clinton looking on. Rabin knew his remarks were being televised worldwide. Other Israeli leaders have since stated the same thing. Israel wants to be like all other nations, because they pant for the material goods of the Western nations. Israelis long for

> _the fish which we ate freely in Egypt, the cucumbers, the melons, the leeks, the onions, and the garlic; but now our whole being is dried up..._ (Numbers 11:5, 6).

Since Rabin signed the Cairo agreement, MacDonalds, Burger King, Tom and Jerrys, Pizza Hut, etc., have opened franchises throughout the length and breadth of Israel. Many delicious traditional Middle Eastern food stands have been forced to close. Israeli _"fools,"_ like Esau before them, have sold their birthright for fistfuls of fast American junk food.

The prophecy continues: _and from the prophet even to the priest, everyone deals falsely._ Who are the "prophets" and who are the "priests"? The Scripture answers the question itself. They are those saying _"Peace, peace!" When there is no peace._ And who may they be? Ministers and other members of Israeli governments since 1992.

We are told that the "prophets" of the false peace, along with the "priests," all "deal falsely." Much of the deceit in which Yitzhak Rabin was involved in order to come to power in 1992 is presented in another book by this author entitled, "Philistine: The Great Deception" Readers are referred to that work, as there is far too many pages of material to include here. Documented proof of the deceit and outright lies by Rabin and others—especially Shimon Peres—following Rabin's ascension to the Israeli throne is also included there.

In chapter 6 of this present work, this writer has already shown that current Prime Minister Ehud Barak was also involved in illegal election activities, and his political party has been fined an unprecedented sum of NIS 13.8 million (US$3.4 million) for "trampling on election laws."[4] President Ezer Weizmann, another pro-"peace" activist, is also under police investigation for accepting large, illegal cash gifts from a foreign businessman who gave the money in order to get Weizmann to acquiesce to his political wishes.[5] The inner greed of the nation for base gain also extends to the "prophets" and "priests," all of whom practice fraud. Instead of leading the people of God on the true path, they use deceit and dishonesty to gain power and material goods.

The "priests" are largely members of the ultra-orthodox Shas party which formed an integral part of Rabin's and Peres's governments, and an even bigger part of Barak's. Within just a few months after becoming part of Rabin's coalition government, some members of the Shas party had already been imprisoned and others were awaiting trial for corruption, fraud, etc.

The leader of the Shas party, Arieh Deri, along with three other members went on trial in December 1993 on charges of bribe-taking, fraud, violating the public trust, and falsifying corporate documents. The defendants stood for an hour while the three judges read the 50-page indictment out loud.[6] The list of charges was so long, and the 107,500 pages[7] of evidence and 1,250 four-hour tape recordings[8] compiled by police investigators so intensive, that the defense attorney reasoned if only each page of evidence were to take 15 minutes to read properly, it would take 200 years to review the material.[9]

The trial finally ended in 1999. It became the costliest and longest running trial in Israel's history, and it should give the reader some idea of the extent of corruption among the "priests."

The same party is today politically blackmailing Barak even while a member of his coalition government. In order to ensure the Shas vote for the passing of the State Budget by the deadline of December 31, 1999, it was necessary for Barak to first authorize the treasury to pay Shas some NIS 500 million (US$122 million) for its private education program and other ministry requirements. Otherwise Shas would have withdrawn from the coalition, toppling Barak's government.

The prophecy goes on to say,

They have also healed the hurt of My people slightly, saying, "Peace, peace!" When there is no peace.

Israelis are tired of war. Almost every family in Israel has lost a loved one in the long-running Arab-Israeli conflict. Most Israelis, however, cannot see an end to the perpetual state of war with their Muslim Arab neighbors. In their hearts they are not convinced that ceding their land to the Arab aggressors will bring them peace. However, each successive "peace" government—of Rabin, Peres and Barak—has continually assailed them with baseless promises that giving in to Arab demands and ceding land to them will indeed bring "peace" to the region.

The real injury to the nation lies in the fact that Islam can never negotiate peace with Israel. This injury is dealt with as though it were only a trifling graze and not a serious threat to the life of the nation. While the majority of Israelis remain sceptical—especially in light of the fact that hundreds of Israelis have been brutally murdered by Arab terrorists since the signing of the first agreement on September 13, 1993—they are willing to gamble on the false hopes offered by the governments for the sake of future generations. The "prophets of peace" have spoken of peace when there is no peace, and, therefore, the "peace process" is only a superficial cure of the people's wounds. The "prophets of peace" have failed to see that there cannot possibly be peace with Islam, and they also fail to see that there can be no peace while they, and most of the nation, are sick at heart. The "prophets of peace" have, therefore, fulfilled to the letter the last portion of the prophecy:

> *They have also healed the hurt of My people slightly, saying, "Peace, peace!" When there is no peace.*

While Jeremiah the prophet was prophesying and being ill-treated in Jerusalem, his contemporary, Ezekiel, was in Babylonia, among the captives taken there by Nebuchadnezzar. A distance of some thousands of miles might separate the prophets, but the same message concerning the false peace is communicated to each by the Holy Spirit. Ezekiel's account gives us more details than Jeremiah's:

> *Therefore thus says Lord Yahweh: "Because you have spoken nonsense and envisioned lies, therefore I am indeed against you," says Lord Yahweh. "My hand will be against the prophets who envision futility and who divine lies; they shall not be in the assembly of My people, nor be written in the record of the house of Israel, nor shall they enter into the land of Israel. Then you shall know that I am Lord Yahweh. Because, indeed, because they have seduced My people, saying, 'Peace!' when there is no peace—and one builds a wall, and they plaster it with untempered mortar—say to those who plaster it with untempered mortar, that it will fall. There will be flooding rain, and you, O great hailstones, shall fall; and a stormy wind shall tear it down. Surely, when the wall has fallen, will it not be said to you, 'Where is the mortar with which you plastered it?'"*
>
> *Therefore thus says Lord Yahweh: "I will cause a stormy wind to break forth in My fury; and there shall be a flooding*

rain in My anger, and great hailstones in fury to consume it.
So I will break down the wall you have plastered with
untempered mortar, and bring it down to the ground, so that
its foundation will be uncovered; it will fall, and you shall be
consumed in the midst of it. Then you shall know that I am
Yahweh.

    Thus will I accomplish My wrath on the wall and on
those who have plastered it with untempered mortar; and I
will say to you, 'The wall is no more, nor those who plastered
it, that is, the prophets of Israel who prophesy concerning
Jerusalem, and who see visions of peace for her when there is
no peace,'" says Lord Yahweh (Ezekiel 13:8-16).

In this passage God repeatedly refers to Himself as _Lord_
Yahweh, not _Yahweh God_. It is a reverential expression of the divine
majesty, but the force of the term means "Sovereign" Yahweh,
pointing to His unequivocal omnipotence.

In verse 8, God tells the "prophets of peace" that He will act
against them as an adversary because of their false promises and
false visions of "peace." Their visions of "peace" when there is
no peace are nothing short of _nonsense_ and _lies._

Verse 9 conveys a decided threat and contains a basic declaration of hostility toward the "prophets of peace." In Deuteronomy,
speaking of the faithless spies and their faithless followers, we are
told that due to their faithlessness Yahweh also became their
adversary:

For indeed the hand of Yahweh was against them, to destroy
them from the midst of the camp until they were consumed
                                           (Deuteronomy 2:15).

As with the faithless spies and their followers, so also with the
faithless "prophets of peace" and their followers. Yahweh will come
against them, to destroy them until they are all consumed. (Yitzhak
Rabin, the initiator of the false "peace," has already been
consumed).

Their punishment for being _"fools,"_ and leading the people
astray with false promises and false hopes, will also consist of
being outlawed and excommunicated from the redeemed people of
God. They will first lose their influential positions and will no
longer form part of the council—the governing body—of the people.
Their deception and misguidance of the community under their

leadership will be matched by their exclusion from the number of the elect. The use of _My people_ distinguishes the true Israel from the apostates, and _the record of the house of Israel_ is the burgher-roll—the register—which will contain the names of citizens in the Kingdom of God. It is Yahweh's prerogative to maintain this register and to delete the names of those whose lives are diametrically opposed to His covenant. Thus, they are barred and unable to _enter into the land of Israel_ in the messianic redivision (outlined in Ezekiel 47:13-21). Exclusion from Israel also means exclusion from fellowship with God.

In verse 10 we read:

> _Because, indeed, because they have seduced My people, saying, "Peace!" when there is no peace...._

The repetition of _because_ heightens the emphasis and indicates that Yahweh is incensed. The "prophets of peace" have led Yahweh's people astray—the have _seduced_ them. To "seduce" means "to persuade to do something disloyal."[10] The "prophets of peace" have persuaded Israelis to hand their God-given inheritance to sworn enemies. They have also raised hopes of prosperity and peace and even encouraged apostasy among the people of God.

It is not just the "prophets of peace" who will come under Yahweh's judgment, however. Many of the people will also fall under it, because they are trusting in what the "prophets of peace" have said instead of trusting in Yahweh their God.

Verse 10 continues: _and one builds a wall_. This is no ordinary "wall." It is a series of stones placed together, without bonding, to form a weak, narrow wall. The Hebrew word _chayits_, translated "wall," is used nowhere else in the Hebrew Scriptures. One of the few places where this word is used is found in a section of the _Mishnah_, and there it gives us the real intent of the word. This particular section of the _Mishnah_ deals with the seventh year, the year when Israel's fields must lay fallow and no work of any sort is allowed in them. However, in times of exceptional need, one is allowed to pick up stones from what lie close at hand on the surface to form a dam, or a wall to prevent erosion of topsoil. The wall is to be on the field's boundary, and the stones used to construct the wall are restricted to—

> "any stone lying in the field which a man building the bank need but stretch out his hand to take."[11]

We can see from this that the "wall" in our prophecy is indeed a very weak one, extremely flimsy. It is also a boundary or partition wall. This means it separates one area from another. The word used in the critical Hebrew text for "partition" is also only found in post-biblical Hebrew and Aramaic writings. Yahweh's intent in using such language is designed to draw attention to His message.

The rickety wall represents the current "peace process." It partitions off the Palestinians from the Israelis. It was largely built by one man, and there is little reason not to believe that this man was Yitzhak Rabin. Other "prophets of peace" (and there are thousands of them in Israel today), however, daub (not "plaster") this weak wall of loose stones with *untempered mortar*—a sloppy mixture of mud or dung, chopped straw and water. When dry it is then daubed with whitewash to give the appearance of a substantial wall. The mortar figuratively depicts deceit and corruption as well as the string of concessions Israel has been forced to make in order for the wall to stand at all. The whitewash is the facade of respectability that has been given to the "peace" process.

The message from Yahweh is clear: Only fools would hastily construct such a wall in the open and then daub it with a mixture reserved for an interior wall well away from the naturally destructive elements of wind and rain.

Yahweh continues in verse 11:

> *...say to those who plaster it with untempered mortar, that it will fall. There will be flooding rain, and you, O great hailstones, shall fall; and a stormy wind shall tear it down.*

The wall will fall. Indeed, it must fall. It was never constructed to withstand the elements. Its fall shows the absurdity of the construction, and exposes it for the sham that it is. The three most destructive agents shall cooperate against the wall—wind, rain, and hailstones. And the three agents Yahweh is going to bring against the wall to overthrow it are all extremes of nature—*flooding rain* (that overwhelms), great *hailstones* (of crystal), and *stormy wind* (hurricane)—these are His own instruments of war (See Exodus 9:18; Joshua 10:11; Job 38:22; Psalms 18:12-14; Isaiah 28:2; 30:30; Revelation 16:21):

> *...have you seen the treasury of hail, which I have reserved for the time of trouble, for the day of battle and war?*
>
> (Job 38:22, 23).

Yahweh mocks the builders in verse 12 with a virtual "Where is it now?":

Surely, when the wall has fallen, will it not be said to you, "Where is the mortar with which you plastered it?"

In verse 13 we get a small glimpse of how upset Yahweh really is with this wall:

I will cause a stormy wind to break forth in My **fury**; and there shall be a flooding rain in My **anger**, and great hailstones in **fury** to consume it.

Does this much wrath stem from His people being led astray with false promises and false hopes? No, there is more to it than that. We saw in chapter 1—"The Promise"— that Yahweh gave Israel the unalienable right of possession of the Promised Land, but the Land itself remained His. An Israelite could sell or rent his allotment of the divine inheritance, but that piece of land was to be returned to him or his family in the year of Jubilee (Leviticus 25:10). It was forbidden to sell the Land permanently because it all personally belonged to Yahweh:

The land shall not be sold permanently, for **the land is Mine**; for you are strangers and sojourners with Me

(Leviticus 25:23).

However, the "prophets of peace" have now given away Yahweh's land to those whom He calls _My evil neighbors_ (Jeremiah 12:14)— the enemies of Israel.

Israel is, for all intents and purposes, a tenant on Yahweh's land. Yahweh is, therefore, the Landlord who collected "rent" from Israel in the form of a 10 percent tithe. Now, let us suppose that a person rents a large piece of property from some other person for a set amount of money. Let us suppose, also, that when the landlord— the owner of the rented property—came to collect the amount due him the tenant told him that he was not going to pay because he had divided the property up and given it to some neighbors— neighbors whom the landlord disliked. Would the landlord simply shrug his shoulders and say that he understood, that it was perfectly all right with him? Or would he get extremely angry and tell the tenant that he had no right to give away his property? Would he not categorically demand the property back again and use every means to ensure that it was restored to him?

Yahweh is going to want His land back. The Bible makes it perfectly clear that He does get it all back, all of it. The Bible also indicates that He is going to use considerable force, and it tells us approximately when this will happen:

> *For behold, in those days and at that time, when I bring back the captives of Judah and Jerusalem, I will also gather all nations, and bring them down to the Valley of Jehoshaphat; and I will enter into judgment with them there on account of My people, My heritage Israel, whom they have scattered among the nations; **they have also divided up My land***
>
> (Joel 3:1-2).

The times in which we are living now are the days in which the captives are returning. The Jews are returning to the Land by the hundreds of thousands—from the four corners of the earth. This regathering will no doubt continue for some years, but we are in the time frame which Yahweh speaks of. It could happen in ten or twenty years, or it could happen in the next few years, months, or even weeks.

Yahweh has a twofold controversy with the nations: First, they took part in the scattering and persecution of the Jews following the Roman destruction of Jerusalem. A renowned conservative Old Testament Bible Commentary confirms this in its exegesis of the verses quoted:

> Joel is speaking not of events belonging to his own time, or to the most recent past, but of that dispersion of the whole of the ancient covenant nation among the heathen, which was only completely effected on the conquest of Palestine and destruction of Jerusalem by the Romans, and which continues to this day.[12]

For almost 2,000 years the Jews were persecuted by the nations. Latterly, the nations have had a hand in dividing up Yahweh's land. The Promised Land would never have been cut up and huge portions handed over to the Arab nations in any "peace process" if the nations—especially America and the EU—had not pressured Rabin, Peres, Netanyahu and Barak to cede the Land.

The destruction of the wall is almost certainly linked to Yahweh's judgment of the nations in the *Valley of Jehoshaphat* — today called the Valley of Kidron—due to the "wall" being linked to the division of His land. The *all nations* in the Valley could refer to every nation who has had a finger in the "peace" pie, or it might refer to a multinational force like the UN or NATO.

Yahweh, however, is going to spend His wrath on the wall and on all those who had a part in its construction, those who have "visions of peace." The wall is not simply going to collapse due to bad weather. Verse 14 tells us that it is going to be broken down and its foundations laid bare by the full force of Yahweh's power:

> *So I will break down the wall you have plastered with untempered mortar, and bring it down to the ground, so that its foundation will be uncovered; it will fall, and you shall be consumed in the midst of it. Then you shall know that I am Yahweh.*

The wall is broken down with terrible power, and all the "prophets of peace" are buried in its ruins. It is as if the flimsy partition wall were holding up an entire structure, and when the wall comes down, it brings the whole house down upon the inhabitants.

Verse 15 says:

> *Thus will I accomplish My wrath on the wall and on those who have plastered it*

The Hebrew word, *kalah*, translated here as "accomplish," is variously translated in other English translations as "spend" "finish," "complete," "exhaust," "consume" and "satisfy." The infinitely better translation is "consume." It shows Yahweh's impressive change from "consuming" the "prophets of peace," to the "consuming" of His wrath. He says: *I will say to you, "The wall is no more, nor those who plastered it...."* His wrath has been consumed—He is angry no longer.

A great many words spoken by the Israeli left-wing "prophets of peace" has been with regard to Jerusalem. "We will never divide Jerusalem," the *"fools"* have said. "It is the eternal capital of the Jewish people," they maintained. But they also said: "We will never recognize the PLO," and did. They said, too, "We will not cede any land to the PLO without first letting the public decide in a referendum." But they went ahead, ceded land, and forgot about the referendum. They said, "We will never release any Arab prisoner with blood on his hands, Jewish blood or Arab blood." But they have released many Arab prisoners with blood on their hands, both Jewish and Arab blood. They said, "We will never come down from the Golan Heights; it is essential to the security of Israel." Yitzhak Rabin's government was willing to come down from the Golan, and Ehud Barak is crawling on his knees begging Syria to take it off Israel's hands. So how much credibility can be placed in their promises never to divide Jerusalem—especially when Barak's Minister for Jerusalem, Chaim Ramon, has stated in a radio interview that all Arab neighborhoods surrounding Jerusalem will be ceded to the PLO? And credibility is further questioned when the PLO has already built its Parliament Building with government permission in a Jewish controlled neighborhood only one kilometer (less than 1,100 yards) from the Temple Mount. The building extends over Jerusalem city's municipal boundary line. The "prophets of peace" will never divide Jerusalem? Come now, who is kidding whom?

Everything that can be done in the flesh is being done, but there can never be any real peace until Jesus, the *Prince of Peace* (Isaiah 9:6), rules from Jerusalem. All else is delusion. If only the "prophets of peace" and their followers would take note of 1 Thessalonians 5:3:

> *For when they say, "Peace and safety!" then sudden destruction comes upon them, as labor pains upon a pregnant woman. And they shall not escape.*

The last part of Ezekiel's prophecy that we have been considering zeros in on Jerusalem. It is Jerusalem that is the real focus of the "prophets of peace." It is the capital's survival or fate that is the burning issue:

> *"...the prophets of Israel who prophesy concerning **Jerusalem**, and who see **visions of peace for her** when there is no peace," says Lord Yahweh.*

As in the prophecy, so also in reality. Modern Israel's "prophets of peace" declare that all will be well with Jerusalem. They have built up false hopes and false dreams in the people. Jerusalem is the greatest prize the PLO seeks. It is the prime target on which it has set its sights. However, Jerusalem is Yahweh's own city. It is *the city of the great King* (Psalms 48:2). It is the *city of our God* (Psalms 48:8); *the throne of Yahweh* (Jeremiah 3:17); the *city of Yahweh of hosts* (Psalms 48:8); the *city of God* (Psalms 46:4); and the *mountain of Yahweh of hosts* (Zechariah 8:3). Jerusalem shall be called: *"Sought Out"* (Isaiah 62:12); *Yahweh Is There* (Ezekiel 48:35); and *A City not forsaken* (Isaiah 62:12).

The modern "prophets of peace" may well have *forsaken* the city for the sake of "peace," but Yahweh is not about to follow suit. Neither will He relinquish control of His city to a terrorist organization headed by the prince of murderers.

Jerusalem is *the throne of Yahweh* (Jeremiah 3:17). The PLO is an Arab Muslim terror group committed to the total destruction of the Jewish state. The god of the Muslims is Allah— a powerful satanic spirit—the most evil and brutal force in the world today. Satan and Yahweh have nothing in common. Satan's ambition, however, is to dethrone Yahweh in Jerusalem. Of course, he will not succeed, but try telling him that. A massive confrontation between Islam, Western *"fools,"* the people of God and *the Holy One of Israel* is about to take place over Jerusalem.

The prophet Zechariah informs us that Yahweh is the central part of this particular equation:

> *The burden of the word of Yahweh concerning Israel. Thus says Yahweh, who stretches out the heavens, lays the foundation of the earth, and forms the spirit of man within him: "Behold, I will make Jerusalem a cup of drunkenness to all the surrounding peoples, when they lay siege against Judah and Jerusalem. And it shall happen in that day that I will make Jerusalem a very heavy stone for all peoples; all who would heave it away will surely be cut in pieces, though all nations of the earth are gathered against it"* (Zechariah 12:1-3).

But it will not be easy for Israel. Remember, the "wall" must first fall and consume the "prophets of peace":

> *For I will gather all the nations to battle against Jerusalem; the city shall be taken, the houses rifled, and the women ravished. Half of the city shall go into captivity, but the remnant of the people shall not be cut off from the city*
> (Zechariah 14:2).

After the "wall" has collapsed and all the "prophets of peace" have been consumed—along with all those who trusted more in the false promises of the "prophets" than they did in Yahweh—then *Yahweh of hosts, the Mighty One of Israel* (Isaiah 1:24) goes out to fight for the true Israel, to deliver them:

> *Then Yahweh will go forth and fight against those nations, as He fights in the day of battle* (Zechariah 14:3).

We are left only with the question of when all this will take place. What will bring about the collapse of the "wall" and the consuming of the "prophets of peace"?

We saw in the proceeding chapter from two world-renowned experts on Islam that Muslims are not permitted to stop their war against non-Muslims for more than 10 years (with the possibility of another 10 years extension). Yasser Arafat has stated several times that the PLO "peace" agreement with Israel is nothing more than Muhammed's Truce of Hudaybiyyah. The Truce is, according to the Islamic experts, an armistice or truce of limited duration that cannot be terminated by a peace, but only by final victory. Therefore, the Muslim truce is probably the key to the timing of the great war that will take place.

Yitzhak Rabin and Yasser Arafat signed the first "Oslo" agreement on September 13, 1993. This date must have set the clock of the 10 year truce (with a possibility of another 10 years, no more) ticking. If we pass September 13, 2003 without the conflict erupting, then we should expect it anytime before September 13, 2013. This is the limit Muhammed set for any Muslim "peace." Of course, the Truce does not guarantee a Muslim victory. There could be several skirmishes of limited duration. But it would make far more sense if all the Muslim Arab nations, along with other Muslim nations such as Iran and Pakistan, united their armies against Israel. It is also well within the bounds of feasibility that the Arab nations might enlist the aid of the radically anti-Semitic UN or even NATO to force Israel to acquiesce to "legitimate Palestinian rights."

Only One knows the answers, and He is not telling. We do, however, know of the promised salvation for the redeemed of Israel. For this, every twice-born Christian and every true Jew should be extremely grateful to the one true God, who loves them with an everlasting love.

II

Steel Helmets
and Gas Masks

The warning signs of an impending nuclear, chemical and biological holocaust have appeared on the horizon, and our lives are in danger of being snuffed out in an inferno of cosmic proportions. The coming conflagration could be ignited at the whim of any one of many people who believe they control the destiny of nations, and whose hatred of Israel burns within them. We may shut our eyes to such facts, but this will not do away with them.

A question many have asked regarding the "peace" process is this: Is modern Israel being given over into the hands of its enemies as a form of punitive punishment, as ancient Israel was delivered into the hands of its enemies for unfaithfulness? Doubtless the answer is affirmative. The great majority of Israelis are apostate today. Many would like every vestige of religion eradicated from the land. We can, however, rejoice that there still remains a remnant of God-fearing Jews who await the redemption of their people.

Revelation 14:6 speaks of an *eternal gospel*, meaning that it is permanently valid. It is directed to *those who dwell on the earth— to every nation, tribe, tongue and people*, which includes the Jews.

There is no way for Jews to find salvation except through Jesus, despite what some prominent Christian ministries are saying today. The leader of a large multimillion-dollar Christian ministry operating from Jerusalem has said that God has an alternative plan of salvation for the Jewish people. This is heresy. Jesus Himself said to the Jews:

> *I am the way, the truth, and the life.* **No one comes to the Father except through Me** (John 14:6).

"No one" most certainly includes Jews. And in Acts 4:8-12 Peter was preaching Jesus to the high priest and other rulers of the Jews in the Sanhedrin. Peter ended his discourse with:

> *Nor is there salvation in any other, for* **there is no other name under heaven given among men by which we must be saved** (Acts 4:12).

Unfortunately, however, according to biblical prophecy, it seems the Jewish people will only look to Jesus when their nation is about to be defeated in a war. It was also that way in yesteryear: *When He slew them, then they sought Him...* (Psalms 78:34). But do not most of us require being brought low before we will reach out in our desperation to the Fount of life?

One of the great promises of the Bible is that Yahweh will make a new covenant with the whole house of Israel:

> *Behold, the days are coming, says Yahweh, when I will make a new covenant with the house of Israel and with the house of Judah—not according to the covenant that I made with their fathers in the day that I took them by the hand to lead them out of the land of Egypt, My covenant which they broke, though I was a husband to them, says Yahweh. But this is the covenant that I will make with the house of Israel after those days, says Yahweh: I will put My law in their minds, and write it on their hearts; and I will be their God, and they shall be My people. No more shall every man teach his neighbor, and every man his brother, saying, "Know Yahweh," for they all shall know Me, from the least of them to the greatest of them, says Yahweh. For I will forgive their iniquity, and their sin I will remember no more* (Jeremiah 31:31-34).

The new covenant will not be written on tablets of stone like the first covenant at Sinai. It will not be laid before the people to accept or reject. The new covenant will be placed within their being, written upon the hearts of the people. It will become a life principle, and thus the people will truly be Yahweh's own.

The above prophecy has as yet found only partial fulfillment. Many thousands of Jews—in Israel and outside of Israel—now have a personal relationship with Yeshua (Jesus), but hundreds of thousands is a far cry from the whole house of Israel. At some point in time—in the not too distant future—every living Jew will have a personal relationship with Yeshua, the only begotten Son of Yahweh, the King of the universe. A long valley of tears, however, lies between then and now.

In Revelation 4:1 we read about *things which **must** take place."* The word *must* is important—Yahweh is sovereign and in complete control. The last days, no less than the first, are in His hands. The Book of Revelation is about the end of time and the overthrow of evil. We read of horrific catastrophes and dreadful bloodshed. But all these things *must take place*. They cannot be prevented from happening. If this were possible prophecy would no longer be prophecy, and the entire 22 chapters of Revelation is considered to be a single prophecy:

> *Blessed is he who reads and those who hear the words of this* **prophecy**, *and keep those things which are written in it; for the time is near* (Revelation 1:3).

> *Behold, I am coming quickly! Blessed is he who keeps the words of the* **prophecy** *of this book* (Revelation 22:7).

> *And he said to me, "Do not seal the words of the* **prophecy** *of this book, for the time is at hand"* (Revelation 22:10).

> *For I testify to everyone who hears the words of the* **prophecy** *of this book: If anyone adds to these things, God will add to him the plagues that are written in this book; and if anyone takes away from the words of the book of this* **prophecy**, *God shall take away his part from the Book of Life, from the holy city, and from the things which are written in this book*
> (Revelation 22:18-19).

When people set themselves against Yahweh's purposes, they become the prey of demonic forces. These forces have greater freedom when people turn away from Yahweh. However, Yahweh is not defeated, stopped or even slowed—He continues to work out His purposes even through demonic forces. But, people must accept the consequences of their choices, and Israelis must also accept the consequences of theirs.

The first recorded word Jesus preached was *"Repent"* (Matthew 4:17). At that time Jesus was ministering exclusively *to the lost sheep of the house of Israel* (Matthew 10:6; 15:24), and thus He was directly addressing the house of Israel. But Israel did not repent. Nearly 2,000 years later Israel has not repented still. However, Israel will repent, otherwise Israel cannot be saved. And Yahweh says all of Israel will know Him, *from the least of them to the greatest of them* (Jeremiah 31:34).

Today, Arab nations, together with radically Muslim Iran, are arming for war against Israel at an unprecedented rate. Since the signing of the Oslo "peace" agreement, Arab nations have become by far the world's largest arms purchasers. A UN report that did not include Israel's downgraded military spending divulges:

> The region in the last few years was particularly exceptional in being the highest spender in the world on military purposes.[1]

Iran, Iraq, Libya, and latterly Egypt are also aggressively pursuing the production of nuclear weapons. Several of the Arab nations are producing huge stockpiles of chemical and biological agents in order to possess the "poor man's" nuclear bomb—non-nuclear—but a dreadful weapon of mass destruction nevertheless. All of this will be aimed at Israeli population centers.

Let us not to be hoodwinked by the number of "peace agreements" signed between Arab nations and Israel. We have already quoted a senior Israeli politician—himself a super*fool*—as having said:

> the number of agreements signed in the Middle East are as the number of the agreements annulled.[2]

The current leader of Israel's Likud party and member of the government opposition has said of the Arab nations:

> While their words may have changed, their intentions remain the same; while their tactics may have changed, their strategy remains.[3]

Israel has again forsaken Yahweh, *the Holy One of Israel*. The Jewish people have endured terrible sufferings throughout their thousands of years of history. They suffered because they repeatedly forsook their God. Their spiritual obtuseness apparently prevents them from comprehending a simple fact: When a nation forsakes its God, its God forsakes the nation.

In the concluding paragraph of chapter 6 it was written:

> ...it is this writer's firm conviction that God has fully determined to strip off the militarily strategic sections of Israel's inheritance and give it over to its enemies.

The giving over of strategic positions to the enemies of Israel is an open invitation for those enemies to mount a devastating attack against Israel. Some might contend that Yahweh would never purposely initiate a massive attack against His covenant people that would result in the loss of thousands of Israeli lives. Such sympathies are misplaced. A reading of the Old Testament will soon confirm that Yahweh has initiated dozens of such attacks against His people, often with calamitous results.

The Book of Revelation clearly shows divine involvement in war, civil war, famine and death. The opening of the seals in Revelation chapter 6 are but a series of pictures that repeat themselves in history. They show us that militarism and lust for conquest are among the forces set loose by the hand of Christ to prepare the way for His second coming. We should, therefore, expect wars, civil wars, famines and death prior to the coming of our Lord and Savior, Jesus Christ. In Revelation 15:8-16:1 a voice originating from the temple instructs the angels to release the bowls of God's wrath upon the earth. This tells us that it is Yahweh Himself that releases the final plagues upon man.

For twice-born Christians, all words from God are sweet to our tastes (Psalms 119:103), but there are a number of passages in the Bible that tell of stern denunciations by a righteous God and foretell dreadful woes upon the godless. When digested, such passages cause bitterness in our stomachs (Revelation 10:10), but if we are true to our God, we will not hold back from declaring such words.

Peace tends to elude those who pursue it as a primary objective. This is a fact to which Israel should have paid attention. Until the *Prince of Peace* (Isaiah 9:6) comes to rule and reign from Jerusalem, there will never be more peace in the Middle East than what there is now. This is as good as it gets. The dream of permanent peace is not really a dream, it is an hallucination. The only thing permanent in the region is instability and conflict.

The Middle East came perilously close to the brink of disaster in February 1991. The United States, under President George Bush, led a coalition of military forces against Iraq in January 1991, in what is now known as the Persian Gulf War.

Iraqi military forces had attacked and overrun its neighbor, Kuwait, in a matter of hours in August the previous year. The U.S. had a defense agreement with Kuwait, but it did nothing to stop Saddam Hussein's drive through Kuwait. American intelligence even admitted that it knew Saddam was going to attack Kuwait. So much for U.S. defense pacts! However, when Iraqi armor began to move towards Saudi Arabia, Bush leaped into action. Could this motivation to act have been entirely due to U.S. dependence upon oil from Saudi Arabia? Or could George Bush's personal stake of several million dollars in that Saudi oil have energized him? The reader can make the necessary calculations.

Israel was not involved in the coalition against Iraq. Nevertheless, Iraq launched 39 missiles at Israeli population centers and 31 missiles hit their targets. Israel did not retaliate against Iraq, but continued to absorb missiles that damaged or destroyed some 5,000 Israeli homes and kept Israelis shut up in sealed rooms wearing gas masks. The world was amazed at Israel's restraint, and the U.S. kept praising Israel publicly for showing such restraint. It was typical White House hypocrisy that has unfortunately become the hallmark of U.S. foreign policy.

The Americans had the Israelis by the political and military jugular throughout the entire crisis—they had withheld the International Friend or Foe (IFF) codes from Israel so that Israel could not retaliate.[4] The IFF codes are used by allied pilots to determine friendly aircraft. Without the codes Israeli warplanes could have downed allied aircraft, and allied warplanes could have downed Israeli aircraft. However, the last missile to hit Israel was not a Scud, but a Hijarah with a concrete and metal warhead.[5] The warhead remained intact, and Israeli military intelligence determined that it was a primitive biological warhead. The warhead was quickly taken out to sea and dumped.

That Hijarah missile was the straw that broke the proverbial camel's back and ended all Israeli "restraint." Israeli Defense Minister Moshe Arens called President Bush and told him that he had just three hours before Israeli warplanes would be arriving over Iraq. One hour following Arens' call the Gulf War was over. It was a fact that

> Israel was on the verge of retaliating against Iraq when Mr. Bush ended the war.[6]

Millions have expressed surprise at the abrupt ending of the war and have wondered why Bush so suddenly stopped it without achieving the full objective. Iraq's final missile brought an end to Israeli "restraint," but had it exploded it might well have brought an Israeli nuclear response that would have set the whole region on fire.

American castration of Israel during the Gulf War forced it to absorb 31 missile hits on its population centers. This has subsequently altered the Middle East military balance dramatically. Spurred by Saddam Hussein's success in grinding Israel to a halt during the 1991 war, the entire Middle East today is bristling with missiles and far more sophisticated biological and chemical warheads than what was attached to the Hijarah missile.

The most significant development in the Middle East of late has been the obtaining of ground-to-ground missiles by Arab countries, including their ability to produce the missiles themselves. For the first time since the founding of the Jewish state in 1948, Arab countries have the ability to hit any part of Israel. One small spark is all that is necessary to ignite the flame that could scorch much of our planet and its inhabitants.

The game being played in the Middle East might change as the players change, and there is a large scale reshuffling taking place today. The somebodies of today will become the political nobodies of tomorrow.

U.S. President Clinton is only months away from leaving the Oval Office, and the next president is as yet unknown, as is the successor's foreign policy.

Ehud Barak's coalition government has tottered more than once since it was formed less than one year ago, and it is questionable whether it will fulfill a four-year term. Another right-wing prime minister of Bibi Netanyahu's ilk, or Arik Sharon's, would really set the cat loose among the pigeons.

King Hussein, with whom Israel signed an agreement, lost his battle with cancer early in 1999 after ruling Jordan for 46 years. His son, Abd'allah, was hastily brought in and is still an unknown quantity. It is an accepted fact that Israel made "peace" with King Hussein, not with Jordan.

Yasser Arafat has turned 70, speaks at the podium with trembling lips and hands, and often forgets why he is in the meeting in the first place.[7] If someone like the PLO's Farouk Kaddoumi succeeds Arafat, a mushroom-shaped cloud could soon hang over the Middle East.

Seventy-eight year-old King Fahd of Saudi Arabia was two times admitted to hospital in Riyadh in less than 12 months. His brother, Abd'allah, also aged 78, is slated to ascend the throne after Fahd.[8]

Syrian President Hafez al-Assad, the 71-year-old "healthiest sick man of the Middle East,"[9] is hurriedly grooming his son Bashar to replace him after 27 years at the dictatorship's helm. One of al-

Assad's ailments is reported to be dementia.[10] Apparently, Assad is only 'in his mind' for a limited number of hours each day, and 'out of his mind' for the rest of it.[11] Assad is also suffering from diabetes as well as cancer in his urinary tract, and is "living on borrowed time."[12]

Elias Hrawi, the puppet president of Lebanon, is 73 and "fairly worn out."[13] He is fully expected to step down at the end of his current term.

King Hassan II of Morocco is another 70-year-old, and has a "pernicious disease that's been eating away at him for years."[14]

Egypt's 71-year-old Hosni Mubarak has "quietly dropped his daily squash game and cut his work hours to the minimum."[15] Mubarak has consistently refused to appoint a deputy, and the neo-Nasserite current foreign minister, Amr Moussa, is campaigning to be Mubarak's successor.[16]

With so many of the current players in the Middle East game about to change, the rules and strategy might also be about to undergo revision. Some younger, hotter Muslim blood could advance the date of the looming conflict.

The absence of strategic territory from which Israel could successfully defend itself against an inevitable Arab attack will force it to break open its arsenal of nuclear and chemical missiles and use them. Therefore, the "peace" process could very well be the spark that ignites a nuclear, chemical and biological holocaust. The trouble with the vision the *"fools"* have of a new Middle East, where peace will reign supreme, is that they assume the region is living in the 21st century. In fact, it has not yet emerged from the Middle Ages. The *"fools"* that have scoffed at the importance of territory and strategic depth in the missile age betray childish irresponsibility.

If Israel comes under a missile attack similar to what it was forced to endure from Iraq, it would be pushed into using a nuclear response. A retaliatory nuclear strike by Israel, however, would, in turn, bring hundreds of missiles raining down upon Israel from surrounding Arab and Muslim nations.

Speaking specifically of the missile capabilities of four nations—Egypt, Syria, Iran and Saudi Arabia—a 1996 *Jerusalem Post* editorial stated:

> The Islamic countries possess 3,000 missiles, virtually all of which can reach Israel. Both Egypt and Syria have vast quanti-

ties of chemical weapons, while Libya has built a monstrous underground plant for the production of such weapons.[17]

The above was an assessment in 1996. In 1995, arms sales to the Middle East totalled US$12.8 billion and comprised 42 percent of worldwide arms sales.[18] In 1997, Arab countries alone spent US$35.7 billion on weapons,[19] and this jumped to US$38.7 billion in 1998.[20] Figures for 1999 are not available at this time of writing. However, in recent years, five Middle Eastern states alone, all hostile to Israel—Saudi Arabia, Egypt, Kuwait, Iran and United Arab Emirates—have taken delivery of arms valued at US$101.5 billion![21]

The scale of the military buildup by the Arab nations can perhaps be better understood in terms of the percentage of the Gross Domestic Product (GDP). Current average percentage of GDP spent on arms—including the U.S. and Russia—is 2.4 percent.[22] The poorer Arab nations spend an average of 8.8 percent of their GDP while oil-rich states average 11.4 percent,[23] nearly five times the average of other nations.

No one knows exactly what warheads the Arab and Muslim nations will use to arm their missiles. What is known, however, are some of the horrendous biological agents that are available to them.

The most feared biological agent is **anthrax**. Ground contaminated by anthrax can remain lethal for half a century or more. Anthrax is a bacteria, and when exploded in a missile, a cloud of anthrax spores is released on the population under attack. Casualties from even an airplane flying upwind of a city releasing an anthrax cloud, could reach three million dead[24]:

> Between one and six days after inhalation, the spores cause a gradual onset of symptoms such as fatigue, fever, discomfort in the chest, and possibly a dry cough. The victim's condition can improve for a few hours or days, but then follows sudden difficulty in breathing, profuse sweating, cyanosis (bluish skin caused by lack of oxygen), shock and death within 24 to 36 hours.[25]

Botulin is another germ-warfare weapon. Botulism toxin is one of the most toxic substances known, and in biological warfare it would be dispersed as a toxic cloud. It acts by inhibiting nerve impulses and produces progressive paralysis leading to death.[26]

Bubonic plague is another potential weapon in the Muslim arsenal. The bubonic plague killed vast numbers of people in the 14th century and was known as the Black Death.[27]

Q fever is another germ-warfare weapon that would be dispersed into the air above the targeted population. Q fever symptoms appear about 10 to 20 days after inhalation and include fever, chills, headache, fatigue and muscle aches. In most cases it is not fatal.[28]

VX Nerve Gas is toxic both by breathing and absorption through the skin. Exposure to a single drop of this oily liquid on a person's finger would produce death in a few moments.[29] The nervous system is affected as is respiration and vision. Muscle control is lost, convulsions occur, and death comes when major organs fail.

Sarin Gas is lethal when inhaled. Symptoms begin to appear within minutes and include pupil constriction, headache, nausea, vomiting, coughing, excessive perspiration and muscle constriction.[30] Death occurs within 36 to 48 hours.

Cyanide Gas is toxic through both inhalation and the skin. Victims experience an immediate sensation of unusual warmth followed by headache, nausea, vomiting, and asphyxial convulsions leading to death from respiratory arrest[31] in 24 to 36 hours.

Other chemical nerve agents in addition to the above are in full production in Arab countries, and substantial arsenals of these nerve agents are being built up.

Despite the odd skirmish or two between Israel and minor Arab entities such as the PLO and Hizb'allah, the region has been relatively quiet since 1973. Israel's string of stunning victories against vastly numerically superior Arab armies earned the grudging respect of the Arab world. When Israel entered what are now called the "occupied territories" in 1967, the situation was idyllic. The local Arabs received the IDF "like kings."[32] When the IDF entered Lebanon in 1982 to eradicate the PLO terrorist network operating there, the Lebanese Arabs greeted the Israeli tanks with flowers and "threw sweets (candies) at our soldiers—what joy."[33]

But things have changed. Crawling to the Arabs with concession after concession in the "peace" process has shown Israel's weakness to the Arabs, and their respect born of fear has melted away and has now been replaced by contempt. Since the "peace" process began in 1993, the Arabs have only held respect for former Prime Minister Bibi Netanyahu. Netanyahu incurred the wrath of the Clinton Administration for not being a perceived "weakling" like Rabin and Peres, and now Barak.

Gideon Ezra, deputy head of Israel's General Security Services (GSS), worked with Arabs for many years. In 1996 Ezra said:

> After many years working with them, one sees the soul of the Arabs.[34]

Ezra went on to say:

> The Arabs appreciate strength and they fear Netanyahu's rule, and that's good. Fear brings respect. The moment they see weakness, they stop appreciating you....[35]

For Israel, there is no respect today in the eyes of the Arab world, only contempt. Egypt and Jordan have gotten all they demanded from Israel, and the PLO and Syria are about to follow suit. Israel is perceived to be weak and contemptible, because it does not even know how to bargain in a Middle Eastern manner. The Arabs make a demand, refuse to budge, and Israel capitulates every time—except when Netanyahu was Israel's premier. The Arab opening position in negotiations is also its final position, hence they always get what they demand.

The Arab objective is to obliterate the Jewish state from the Middle East. The Arab world once thought it would be impossible to defeat Israel militarily. After the "peace" process has reduced Israel to a truncated dwarf, the Arab world feels its dream is close to reality. The Muslim dream is that the Jewish state will disappear:

> Our vision for the Middle East is that it will be a center for Islam, tranquillity and peaceful life for all, from which it will spread to the whole world sooner or later.[36]

The good news is that Islam's bid for "tranquillity" and "a peaceful life for all" in the Middle East is still in the future. The bad news is that it gets closer each day.

Players in the Mid-East War Games

Israel has the lead role among all the players, external and internal, and will take the center stage during the full dress rehearsal for Armageddon. While Israel has never actually admitted to possessing nuclear weapons, this has been an accepted fact for many years.

The real significance of Israel's perceived nuclear arsenal is diplomatic and psychological. They are tools that appear to increase the stakes without increasing the risks. Nuclear weapons tend to decrease the willingness of antagonists to threaten the very existence of a nuclear state. However, in 1986, Mordechai Vanunu, a former technician at Israel's nuclear reactor in Dimona—for a "gratuity" of £60,000—gave photographs from inside the plant to Britain's _Sunday Times_. Based on Vanunu's information, nuclear experts said that "Israel has the world's sixth-largest arsenal of nuclear weapons."[37] Vanunu is today serving his 13th year in solitary confinement of an 18-year sentence for treason.

As far back as 1987, Leonard Spector, of the Carnegie Endowment, said that Israel

...had enough nuclear weaponry to level every urban center in the Middle East with a population of more than 100,000.[38]

Spector also said:

Israel, incidentally, also has a chemical weapons stockpile, one far larger than that of Iraq, according to a knowledgeable authority, as well as the potential for far more efficient means of delivery.[39]

Britain's prestigious military magazine, _Jane's Intelligence Review_, has stated that

Israel's military is the third strongest in the world, and that its air force is 7 to 8 times stronger than the combined might of the air forces of all the Arab nations.[40]

And on July 2, 1998, Israel announced that it was ordering

...three West German submarines capable of missile launching. The apparent purpose: to create a missile launch capability more secure than land based systems.[41]

In addition to its unknown number of missiles, nuclear and chemical weapons, Israel also has the first anti-missile missile system which was put into operation in mid-March 2000. The Arrow anti-missile missile's sophisticated radar system is designed to first detect hostile missiles and then despatch its own missiles to intercept and destroy them.

Obviously, Israel, with or without the strategic depth of territory to defend itself, is not going to be a pushover for any combination of Muslim aggressors wishing to eradicate it from the face of the Middle East. But Israel cannot afford to make even one mistake. Its first mistake could well be its last.

A late-breaking report of a sophisticated Russian missile system able to overcome Israel's Arrow system is contained in Addenda, 2.

External players

The United States is the most powerful of all the external players "meddling" in the Middle East. It has portrayed itself as an "honest broker" in the Middle East War Games, but we have already seen in chapter 7 that it is anything but an honest broker. It has pushed, cajoled and even threatened Israeli prime ministers in order to have its own plans for the Middle East adopted.

It was reported on Israel news at the beginning of March 2000 that "President Clinton 'wants' an Israeli-Syrian agreement by May."[42] Clinton jerks the strings and Barak dances. Clinton pushed and bullied Rabin. Rabin bowed to Clinton, but paid with his life. Clinton backed Peres, but Peres was rejected by the Israeli people. Netanyahu refused to dance, so Clinton bullied him, threatened him, and finally had him brought down and replaced by Barak. Clinton has gotten a good run out of Barak thus far—he has given more of the Promised Land away than all of his predecessors combined.

The U.S. is by far the biggest supplier of arms to the Middle East in the world. In a single 1996 sale, Egypt, Saudi Arabia, Kuwait and United Arab Emirates received arms worth billions of dollars from the U.S., including the following:

101 F16 jets, five executive jets, three observer planes, one communications plane, 14,000 bombs, five frigates, 28 Apache helicopters, 1,000 "Hellfire" missiles for Apache helicopters, 31 M1 tanks, 8,500 anti-tank "Tow" missiles, 1,200 tank fire control systems, 400 armored carriers, 350 terrain vehicles, and missile launchers.[43]

From 1994 to 1998 the U.S. sold $53.88 billion of arms.[44] Israel received only a tiny percentage of that amount. Its enemies, however, were armed to the hilt.

In March 1999, U.S. Defense Secretary, William Cohen, agreed to another Egyptian request to buy:

> $3.2 billion worth of sophisticated weaponry—24 state-of-the-art F16 fighter aircraft, 200 M1 tanks and a Pac-3 Patriot anti-missile missile battery.[45]

Earlier, he had

> offered medium-range air-to-air missiles to Saudi Arabia and Bahrain, and discussed selling warplanes and missiles to the United Arab Emirates.[46]

In March 2000, it was reported that:

> The U.S. will supply the United Arab Emirates with eighty "Block-60" advanced F-16s built by American manufacturer Lockheed Martin in a $6.4 billion deal already approved by Congress. The F-16s are to be equipped with better radar and weapons systems than those sold in recent years to Israel, threatening to further undermine the U.S. commitment to help maintain Israel's qualitative edge against any array of potential foes.
>
> The deal was signed in the UAE capital of Abu Dhabi, after being delayed several times due to U.S. objections to the advanced systems requested by the Arab purchaser. Last year, the Emirates threatened to pull out of contract negotiations if the jets were not equipped with technology considered too advanced by the Pentagon. The U.S. finally relented out of fears of losing out to a European conglomerate on the lucrative deal, and even approved including radar systems more powerful and precise than those used by the U.S. Air Force. The deal includes $1.3 billion worth of missiles and weapons for the fighter jets.[47]

This writer has maintained from the very beginning that it is all simply a matter of money. Some members of U.S. governments would sell their grandmother's teeth to a cannibal if they felt it would advance American power and wealth.

Wars are necessary to keep the U.S. economy buoyant, and U.S. weapons manufacturers and arms dealers in business. The U.S. government sells vast quantities of sophisticated arms to states hostile to Israel, and pushes Israel into giving up its strategic territory. This writer wonders if anyone in the White House or U.S. State Department will lose any sleep if all the weapons they sold were to be used against Israel in a single week. It would, after all, be extremely good for the American economy. It could even create more jobs for Americans.

Russia has begun to roll the dice again in a resurrection of past Cold War games. It is tired of being humiliated and treated like a third-world country by the U.S. Russian consensus was that it was betrayed by the U.S. bombing of Iraq, which was a tactic to delay the Clinton impeachment vote. The Duma (Russian Parliament) condemned "the barbaric bombing of the republic of Iraq,"[48] and said that it was "an act of international terrorism."[49] The resolution passed 394-2.[50]

The Post-Cold War world quietly slipped away in 1998, but the straw that really broke the camel's back and ended the Russian flirtation with the West was the bombing of Kosovo. Russia saw this as American aggression against one of its allies. Consequently, Russia has flung aside all attempt at democracy and is now militantly rebuilding its old empire.

Boris Yeltsin bowed out as the Russian leader on the eve of the year 2000 and endorsed his prime minister, Vladimir Putin, who became acting president. Putin is of the old KGB guard and devoutly nationalistic. Putin has thumbed his nose at the West, ignoring its criticism of the war waged in Chechnya by Russian forces. This has won Putin a lot of points with the Russian people and should be taken as a warning sign by the West. Putin's popularity showed in the presidential elections held in March 2000. He romped home by a huge margin and became Russia's elected president.

The rebuilding of a powerful Russian federation will take some time to accomplish—possibly a decade. According to one whose business it is to forecast these things, it would take an entire generation.[51] Irrespective of how long it takes for Russia to reassert itself, it will be worrisome for both the U.S. and Israel.

Russia's rebuilding should be a cause of concern in the U.S. because Russia is now determined to put an end to America's dominance in the world. Vladimir Putin is well aware that Russia is too weak at this point to threaten the interests of the U.S., but Putin is good at rolling the dice. He has made overtures to China to create a strategic partnership—primarily an anti-American alliance—and China has responded to this very favorably. A summit between Putin and President Jiang Zemin of China has been scheduled. Closely guarded items on the agenda for discussion between the leaders are Russian oil and advanced weapons systems for China, as well as nuclear fuel for a Chinese reactor.[52] From this Russia will receive some much needed hard currency together with economic activity for its energy and arms industries, giving them both a boost.

Alone, Russia and China are too weak to challenge present American power. However, a strategic partnership with coordinated strategy can create simultaneous problems in different parts of the world, increasing pressure on U.S. military capabilities which are already stretched thin.

The drive by Russia to reassert itself, and regain its former global power status lost through an attempt at Westernization, will also have negative repercussions for Israel. Russia has already begun to reactivate old Cold War relationships with countries hostile to Israel, such as Syria and Iraq. In early February 2000, Vladimir Zhirinovsky, head of Russia's ultra-nationalist Liberal Democratic Party, announced that an agreement had been reached with Iraqi President Saddam Hussein on the stationing of Russian warships at Iraqi naval bases.[53]

Russian arms sales are far below those of the U.S., but even in its weakened state, it still holds the number two slot for global arms sales.[54] Besides arming Syria, Egypt and virulently anti-Israel Iran (and soon probably Iraq), Russia is, according to U.S. intelligence reports, playing a key role in Iran's drive to develop two medium-range ballistic missile systems.[55] In addition to helping Iran with its medium-range missile program, Russia is also helping Iran with the Shihab-4, a long-range missile that is

> entirely a product of Russian missile technology and can carry biological, chemical or nuclear warheads.[56]

To make matter worse for Israel, Russia is also actively transferring nuclear technologies to Iran.[57] It is reported that

> at least nine companies are said to be actively involved in helping Iran develop nuclear weapons and ballistic missiles.[58]

Russia is also pressing ahead with the building of three nuclear reactors in Iran despite strong American and Israeli opposition. Russia says the reactors "will only be used for civilian purposes."[59] Israel heard the same line from Iraqi President Saddam Hussein, before it bombed the Osiraq reactor in June 1981.

China, Russia's new strategic partner, holds the number six position in the world arms sales race.[60] China is also indiscriminately arming nations hostile to Israel such as Iran, Iraq, Syria, Egypt, Pakistan and other Muslim states ready to buy its arms.[61] Chinese experts are also said to be working with Libyan technicians to help create missiles for Colonel Muammar Gaddafi.[62] And China, as well as Russia, is playing a key role in building Iran's medium-range missile systems.[63] China is, according to intelligence analysts,

> changing the military balance between the West and the Muslim world to the West's disadvantage.[64]

None of the above bodes well for Israel in the long haul.

Another factor that must be entered into the Middle East equation is that of so-called Russian "Loose Nukes." Russia has some 22,000 nuclear weapons.[65] Of this number between 10,000 and 15,000 are in storage and guarded not by elite forces, but by regular troops.[66] The trustworthiness of many of these regular troops is questionable, and numbers of the "nukes" are being sold for quick money to un-stable regimes and, supposedly, even to terror groups. (Osama bin-Laden, America's public enemy number one, is recently re-ported to have acquired nuclear weapons from former Soviet republics, but these reports remain unconfirmed at the time of this writing).

Reports that missing Russian nuclear warheads have turned up in Iran have been confirmed. Three nuclear warheads "dis-appeared" from the former Soviet republic of Kazakhstan in May 1992.[67] Two of the missing warheads "reappeared" in Iran and are under the control of the Iranian Nuclear Energy Commission.[68]

A "suitcase bomb" is a small, portable nuclear bomb capable of horrendous destruction. One of this writer's reliable intelligence sources says that as many as 250 suitcase bombs are missing from Russian arsenals, and that a number of these are now in the Middle East. Four of these suitcase bombs are already known to be in the hands of one of Israel's "peace" partners (we will come to that in due time).

Pakistan is a lesser, but nevertheless, very dangerous external player in the Middle East War Games. Pakistan has developed the nuclear bomb and is currently aiding the Iranian quest for nuclear pro-duction. But the real issue is this: Is this a Pakistani bomb or an Islamic bomb? (This, too, will be addressed more fully).

Internal players

Egypt is Israel's most powerful local antagonist by far in the Middle East War Games. After Egypt's defeat in the devastating October 1973 war that Egyptian President Anwar Sadat initiated against Israel, Sadat began a quest for "peace." While addressing the People's Assembly on November 9, 1977, Sadat declared that he was

> "ready to go to the Israeli parliament itself and discuss with them."[69]

It was a stunning declaration. Sadat's foreign minister promptly resigned.[70] A number of other senior Egyptian officials did likewise.[71] On November 16, 1977, Sadat flew to Damascus in an attempt to win Hafez al-Assad's backing. All he got was an unpleasant four-hour meeting, after which

> Assad instructed Syrian newspapers to announce a day of national mourning.[72]

On November 19, 1977, Sadat flew to Israel and received a rousing welcome. Israelis had waited 30 years for this. Sadat addressed the Israeli Knesset and declared: "No more war!"

A formal peace agreement was eventually signed by Anwar Sadat and Israeli Prime Minister Menachem Begin on March 26, 1979. Two days later, leaders of the entire Arab world assembled themselves in Baghdad and severed all political and economic ties with Egypt.[73] Large-scale economic aid that had been promised by Saudi Arabia and Kuwait was also canceled. And on October 19, 1981, Anwar Sadat was cut down in a hail of bullets during a parade on the anniversary of the October 1973 war. There were "few signs of mourning."[74] Sadat died for being a traitor to Islam, and to the Arab cause.

Anwar Sadat had appointed Hosni Mubarak as his deputy. Mubarak assumed the presidency after Sadat's murder, continues in that post today, but consistently refuses to appoint anyone to the position of his deputy. While many Israeli politicians say Mubarak has maintained a "cold peace" with Israel during the 19 years of his presidency, in reality it has been a "cold war."

Mubarak has "frozen" all cultural ties between Egypt and Israel until such time as there will be a full peace established throughout the region.[75] Mubarak has done about everything within his power to prevent Israel's participation in any event held anywhere in the Middle East. He has also attempted to torpedo cooperation between Israel and Turkey, and embarked on a campaign of criticism of Jordan and other Arab states attempting to develop economic links with Israel.

In March 2000, Hizb'allah fighters fired missiles from inside populated Lebanese villages against IDF outposts in Israel's southern security zone, killing several Israeli soldiers. The government of Israel led by Ehud Barak had pledged to withdraw all Israeli forces out of Lebanon by July 2000, but Hizb'allah continued to launch its sneak attacks. Israel finally issued stern warnings that strong retaliatory attacks would be taken against Lebanese infrastructure if the Hizb'allah attacks continued. Hosni Mubarak, however, having full knowledge of Israel's timetable and commitment to withdraw its forces, flew to Lebanon, to uphold

the "right" of the Lebanese Hizb'allah to continue attacks against Israeli troops stationed in Lebanon.[76]

Even Yitzhak Rabin spoke of an "ill wind blowing from the Egyptian Foreign Ministry."[77] And, it is perfectly clear that Mubarak did not go to Lebanon lightly. In going to Lebanon, he became the first Egyptian head of state to ever visit that country.[78] Going to Lebanon and standing with Hizb'allah was Mubarak's way of sending Israel a veiled message: You Jewish pigs, I hate you. I will stand by the side of anyone who kills you. Mubarak virtually said as much when he "vowed to support any Arab state in a war against Israel."[79] (Mubarak was not the only Arab "peace partner" to stand alongside Hizb'allah in its attacks against Israel. Foreign ministers from 20 Arab countries moved their semi-annual meeting from Cairo to Beirut in order to show their solidarity with Hizb'allah.[80] Jordan's King Abd'allah cancelled a visit to Israel as did Jordan's Prince Hassan,[81] and Saudi Crown Prince Abd'allah visited Beirut and had unprecedented praise for the Iranian-backed militia.[82])

Anwar Sadat came to Israel in late 1977, and Israeli Prime Minister Menachem Begin visited him in Cairo. Since Sadat's assassination, it has been a one-way road to Egypt for talks with Mubarak. Menachem Begin took his hat in his hand and went to Cairo to talk with Mubarak. So did his successor, Yitzhak Shamir; as did Shimon Peres, Yitzhak Rabin, Bibi Netanyahu, and now Ehud Barak.

The path to Mubarak's front door has been trodden by every Israeli Prime Minister of the past two decades, but Mubarak refuses to make a formal visit to Israel: "the time was still not right for him to make a return visit to Israel."[83] Mubarak has a standard line that he rolls out whenever necessary: "Now, with the present situation, it is difficult."[84]

President Clinton twisted Mubarak's arm and practically forced him to come to Jerusalem for Rabin's funeral. He came, but stayed for the absolute minimum amount of time and departed silently and quickly. It is extremely doubtful if he will ever set foot on Israeli soil again.

Egypt is preparing for war, and Israel is the perceived enemy. Egyptians "identify no significant potential enemies other than Israel."[85] Egypt has been preparing for war with Israel almost since the U.S. opened its arsenals to it following Sadat's murder. America has allowed Egypt, (as it has allowed the United Arab Emirates), to obtain weaponry superior to what Israel has been able to procure. An Israeli intelligence report of April 23, 1998, warned that

> recent Egyptian purchases of advanced Western weaponry had greatly altered the balance of power in the Middle East by drastically reducing the qualitative advantage enjoyed by Israeli forces. ... Egypt is building up a force of advanced warships armed with Harpoon missiles, manufacturing its own version of the U.S.-designed Abrams tank, and also equipping its fighter jets with U.S.-made AMRAAM air-to-air missiles, which even Israel has yet to acquire.[86]

The Egyptian arms buying spree has been virtually continuous for almost 20 years. In March 1999, the U.S.

> offered to sell Egypt "$3.2 billion worth of sophisticated weaponry, including 24 state-of-the-art F16 fighter aircraft, and 200 M1-A1 tanks."[87]

The U.S. sales to the Arab world goes on and on and on. Is it any wonder that the American economy is booming today?

Besides all the advanced and sophisticated weaponry being stacked in the Egyptian arsenals along with weapons from Russia, China and other sources, Egypt is pursuing a low-level nuclear program to complement its chemical weapons program. Another Argentinian-built "peaceful" reactor began operating in late 1997, bringing to three the number of reactors imported from Argentina.[88] All reactors in the Middle East—including those in Israel, Iraq, Iran and Libya—are for "peaceful" purposes despite the nuclear weapons programs carried out by all these countries.

Egypt was the first Arab country to use chemical weapons when its aircraft dropped mustard gas bombs on Yemini civilians near the Saudi border in 1963.[89] Egypt delivered its first chemical weapons to Syria in 1972 as part of the preparation for the October 1973 war against Israel.[90] Egypt is believed to be producing "highly lethal VX nerve gas" at a supposedly conventional chemicals factory near Cairo,[91] and it is also believed that Egypt has "thousands of tons" of chemical weapons.[92]

All recent Egyptian army maneuvers are programmed "to send the army into the Sinai peninsula to fight the Israelis."[93] And Egypt has also

> built tunnels under the Red Sea which can easily transport huge amounts of weaponry and people across the sea within a matter of minutes.[94]

With the aid of the U.S., Egypt has revolutionized its military forces and transformed them into the equivalent of modern Western forces. This bodes ill for Israel. Even the Egyptian navy is "larger, better equipped and more modern than the Israeli navy."[95]

The feeling in the Arab world in general, and Egypt in particular, is that Israel is a divided country and will soon be defeated by military force. This feeling is fostered by the backing of Western nations for Arab positions while blatant Arab provocations of Israel are condoned. The popular Egyptian magazine, *Ruz al-Yusuf*, dedicated almost the whole of the January 23, 1995 issue for "the future war with Israel."[96] Amin al-Huweidi, former Egyptian Minister of War and head of General Intelligence, declared:

> The war is inevitable. The war is coming, though not immediately.[97]

Syrian President Hafez al-Assad came to power in a 1970 coup. Together with Anwar Sadat of Egypt, al-Assad planned and executed the massive surprise attack against Israel in 1973 that almost saw the defeat of the Jewish state. Prior to the coup in which he seized control of Syria, al-Assad was the chief of the Syrian air force. In the June 1967 war Syria lost the Golan Heights to Israel. Al-Assad feels responsible for that loss and plans to take the Golan back no matter what cost is involved. Under his dictatorship, Syria has been heavily arming for war against Israel, and Israeli Major-General (Res.) Yossi Peled says:

If Assad makes war and loses 100,000 people, he won't face a revolution. Instead, they will turn him into a hero

If Assad finds he doesn't have an answer to our air force, he will use Scuds. If he has to, he will dare to.[98]

More than once Israeli troops have felt the inevitable war was about to begin. As *Time* magazine reports:

It was late one night this fall, and the soldiers were sleeping. Suddenly alarms began to sound across their bases on the Golan Heights. By the hundreds, members of the Israeli Defense Forces spilled out of their barracks, speeding towards their assigned tanks. Engines roared to life, maps were unfurled, and within minutes two full tank brigades were rolling out. The armored leviathans rumbled to the Syrian front and onto ramps built long ago as battle stations, many of which were overgrown with weeds from disuse. Once there, the troops parked and waited, peering anxiously into the night for the Syrian attackers.

This time they didn't come. Nor did the Syrian army appear during a repeat exercise weeks later. But the full-dress rehearsals on the Golan, unprecedented in recent years, show just how nervous Israeli commanders have become about the possibility of a genuine Syrian assault.[99]

That was in late 1996. In August 1997, Syria deployed hundreds "of upgraded T-55 tanks from Ukraine near the Golan"[100] in a provocative and dangerous act. In the same month Israel filed a complaint with the United Nations against Syria for digging military fortifications along the border of the Golan Heights.[101] The following month Israeli military sources reported that

the Syrian army has set up an illegal bunker system, about 5-kilometers (3-miles) inside the demilitarized zone, under UN control.[102]

The Syrians had built an entire fortification system under the watchful eye of the UN, without it doing anything to prevent it. Israeli complaints have availed nothing. The United Nations is not only virulently anti-Israel, but also profoundly pro-Arab.

The heightened tension on the Syrian front over the past few years has caused Israel to increase its overall standing army by some 30 percent[103]—also to stockpile millions of dollars worth of ammunition on the front.[104] Israel's former Deputy Chief of Staff, Major-General Matan Vilna'i, said the IDF's response to the Syrian situation had been twofold:

> First, it has determined targets to attack within Syria should war erupt. Second, the IDF has increased the level of its standing army while providing soldiers with more advanced equipment.[105]

Russia is forging ahead with its arms trading with Syria. Russia is even prepared to cancel some of the $12 billion debt Syria owes it to facilitate further purchases of Russian arms. Syria is purchasing advanced Russian T-80 tanks and SA-10 anti-aircraft missiles.[106] According to an *Ha'aretz* report, about 100 Russian military advisors are currently in Syria, and more than 70 Syrian officers are training in Russia.[107]

Israel is concerned that should it finally sign a "peace" agreement with Syria, it would have to face the probability that Damascus would be allowed to purchase U.S. arms as a "reward."[108]

Syria's missile stock is increasing alarmingly. A former Israeli Defense Minister, Ariel Sharon, said back in May 1996 that "Syria today has 1,000 ground missiles."[109] In 1997, a senior Syrian political figure was quoted in a London-based Arabic newspaper as saying:

> Syria was capable of causing "a great deal of damage to Israel," using its 600-kilometer range missiles and other weapons.[110]

In August 1999, it was reported that Syria was developing a long-range surface-to-surface missile capable of striking targets as far away as Ankara, in Turkey. The new missiles were being developed with the assistance of Iran. Fired from mobile launchers, of which Syria has 60, "these missiles will be able to strike any point inside Israel."[111]

It is Syria's stock of chemical weapons that causes the most worry for Israel's top military brass. Dr. Danny Shoham, a leading Israeli expert on chemical and bacteriological warfare and former senior army intelligence analyst, said in 1996:

> Syria has an arsenal of deadly nerve gases and, reportedly, anthrax, a lethal bacterium.
>
> The Syrians had the chemical agents installed in thousands of aerial bombs and between 100-200 warheads for Scud B and the more advanced Scud C ground-to-ground missiles.

The main components of Syria's chemical arsenal are the nerve agents, "Sarin" and more recently VX which is more virulent and can penetrate through the skin and not only the respiratory system, and also persists longer because of its less volatile nature. [112]

Syria has been assisted by Russian chemical experts including General Anatoly Kuntevich, a senior military chemical expert who was awarded the Lenin Prize by then-Soviet leader Mikhail Gorbachev for his secret development of a new binary chemical warfare agent. [113] Russian materials currently being shipped to Syria are intended for

> the production of the Soviet/Russian version of the VX nerve agent—code-named Substance 33 or V-gas. [114]

A report in *Jane's Defence Weekly* in late June 1998 confirmed that Syria was producing the deadly VX nerve agent. [115]

The German magazine *Stern* broke the news in 1996 of a gigantic chemical weapons plant in Aleppo in northern Syria. [116] Evidence of the awesome dimensions of the plant, said to be the largest in the world (rivaling that of Libya), [117] has been provided by American spy satellites. It has been built underground, and the CIA believes the tunnels in which it is largely hidden are indestructible by conventional weapons. [118] Syria will be a formidable foe with all its forces unleashed against Israel.

The PLO might appear to be a ragtag entity, but even today they have the capacity to inflict heavy casualties upon Israel in any outbreak of war. With a known 80,000 men under arms back in 1996, [119] whom Yasser Arafat openly refers to as "our soldiers," [120] and almost one million "Israeli" Arabs who would form a fifth-column within Israel, the PLO is already a military threat to Israel.

Miniature submarines are nothing new, not to the Middle East and not to the PLO:

> The PLO has at least two Italian-made mini-subs it got from Libya. These subs were made by the top Italian mini-sub firm, Cosmos. The PLO boats were based at a training facility on Kamaran Island, off Yemen and instructors in commando operations came from East Germany. [121]

Arafat and cadres are already preparing for war with Israel. *Time* magazine provides a few details:

Palestinian security officials had a plan…they took an inventory of all the tractors and bulldozers in the West bank. Then they devised a system for appropriating the machinery to dig ditches and build other obstacles to slow an Israeli advance. But how to test the scheme? In mid-January [1998] an opportunity was literally heaven-sent. When a rare blizzard blanketed the West Bank with snow, Palestinian authorities quickly seized the earthmovers under the pretence of clearing the roads. In fact, the action was a drill for war.[122]

According to Israeli intelligence, the PLO has

developed a formal war room that is mobile and headed by Brigadier-General Haj Ismail, overall military commander of the West Bank.[123]

Arutz 7, an Israeli radio station, reported in March 1998 that

the large-scale Palestinian attempts to bring in more and more weapons, together with the building of many underground bunkers and concrete-enforced shooting points at the entrances to PA cities, are but a few of the indications that the Palestinians are industriously preparing for a war with Israel.[124]

Israeli Major-General (Res.) Oren Shahor, the recently retired government coordinator for the territories, said:

Arafat said some time ago that the Palestinians would be willing to take tens of thousands of casualties to achieve their goals, and he asked how many casualties Israel was prepared to suffer.[125]

A 1998 report in *Yediot Aharonot* quotes Shlomo Filber, Deputy Director of the Council of Jewish Communities in Judea, Samaria and Gaza (YESHA), saying the PLO is spying on Jewish settlements.[126] Fibler says the PLO are photographing Jewish settlements and compiling files on the different communities, and that there are some 143 "thick folders" in Orient House, the PLO's Jerusalem headquarters.[127] The PLO intelligence documentation on Jewish settlements includes

photographs taken from inside and outside the communities, development plans, security arrangements, and more, with the help of the American Consulate in Jerusalem, and Peace Now.[128]

Israel is treating the PLO threat seriously and has staged a series of exercises aimed at retaking the areas handed over to the PLO. _Israel Radio_ reported that the IDF is preparing for the possibility of an all out war with the PLO.[129] _Reuters_ reports that a senior PLO official said

> Israeli forces had trained with helicopters, tanks and troops near 21 Jewish locations around Jenin in Judea-Samaria.[130]

There is more to the PLO threat than pure arrogance. For years it has been smuggling in weapons of every conceivable type. PLO officials admit they are smuggling in large, forbidden weapons including, mortars, anti-tank missiles and long-range Katyusha rockets.[131] Israeli officials, on the other hand, know that the PLO is bringing in a large variety of weapons including Sagger anti-aircraft missiles.[132] A smuggling ring which brought in Iranian arms across the Dead Sea from Jordan eluded the Israeli army and police for more than a year.[133] But that particular ring was finally broken in August 1996, and six motorized rafts piled high with weapons destined for the PLO were seized.[134] Senior police investigator, Chief Superintendent Rahamim Tuval, said after the bust:

> Who knows what else they, or others, managed to smuggle into the country.[135]

The PLO has several channels for bringing arms into the areas handed over to it by Israeli governments. One way is through tunnels under the border between Egypt and Gaza, near Rafiah. Israel has discovered many tunnels and has blown them up. A top Israeli military source says:

> They have been smuggling all sorts of weapons through the tunnels. They would be smuggling tanks, too, if they could fit them through the tunnels.[136]

A convenient channel used by the PLO to smuggle arms is through the "diplomatic immunity" afforded to Arafat's henchmen, who have been accorded VIP status. Their vehicles are exempt from Israeli searches and, thus, they return to Gaza loaded with arms and small missiles. A _Jerusalem Post_ Editorial states:

> It is no secret that the PLO leader's minions who are granted VIP status abuse the privilege, smuggling weapons and explosives with impunity into the West Bank and Gaza.
>
> An intelligence source told us that whenever Arafat travels, his vehicle is always loaded down with weaponry, its

chassis hanging low on the road. Netanyahu's security people, as well as the IDF, constantly warn that this method of transporting weapons and explosives is common in the Palestinian Authority.[137]

A senior Israeli Defense Force intelligence officer told the Knesset Foreign Affairs and Defense Committee in August 1998 that

PLO chairman Yasser Arafat has used his personal helicopter to smuggle wanted terrorists and illegal weapons.[138]

Things appear to get worse as we go along: It was reported in *Al Qabas*, a joint Arab-Russian newspaper, that in 1993

two Ukrainian nuclear warheads were sold to the "Palestinian resistance movement" for US$30 million.[139]

The newspaper also said:

five former Soviet missile officers left Ukraine for southern Lebanon where they are drilling with Palestinian groups.[140]

The newspaper did acknowledge that the Palestinians had no way of launching the warheads at the time of purchase.

Something even more disturbing than the above was a January 1998 headline in a respected Dutch newspaper saying: "Yasser Arafat in possession of atom bomb."[141] The front page lead article identifies its source as U.S. Congressman Curt Weldon, a Republican and chairman of the subcommission "Military Investigation and Military Developments" of the National Security Council of the American Congress.[142] The article—accompanied by a photograph of Weldon—states that Congressman Weldon had obtained a secret June 1996 Palestinian report titled: "The Plan For The Liberation Of Palestine From Zionism."[143] The secret report was passed to Weldon via a "Russian friend" and documents not only that the PLO has at its disposal three atomic bombs, a number of bacteriological and biological weapons and some civil aeroplanes, but also gives the details of how the PLO plans to use the atom bombs against Israel "at a suitable moment," via the use of "kamikaze-pilots."[144]

Weldon spoke to the newspaper's reporter by telephone and said:

You should not at all know the content of this report, because it is still secret."[145]

Congressman Weldon confirmed to the reporter that he had notified the National Security Council of the American Congress of the report in a meeting held behind closed doors.[146]

There is no apparent reason why credence should not be placed in these reports of PLO possession of nuclear weapons. They do, however, pluck the PLO out from its perceived image of being a stereotype Arab terror organization and place it squarely in the camp of Israel's most potentially dangerous enemies.

Iran was not a founding member of the exclusive Muslim club of potentially dangerous threats to Israel's existence. Iran is not an Arab nation. Iran is ancient Persia. It has its own language and culture, and the only thing it has in common with Arab nations is Islam. Since its acceptance into the hate Israel club after the overthrow of the Shah in 1979, it has progressively worked its way up to a senior position.

Since the Islamic revolution in which the Shah was overthrown, Iran has never attempted to keep its hatred of Israel a secret. A succession of fanatical Iranian Muslim leaders have all declared identical policies toward Israel. Iran's position with regard to Israel is twofold:

There would be no recognition of—and no negotiations with—Israel.[147]

There can be no solution to the Middle East conflict without the dissolution of the state of Israel and the declaration of a Palestinian state.[148]

In an effort to help achieve the dissolution of the Jewish state, Iran funds, backs, trains and equips several fanatical Muslim militias to carry out attacks against the IDF and Israeli civilians. Besides the Hizb'allah militia that has caused Israel so many casualties in Lebanon, Iran also funds the Islamic Jihad and Hamas terror organizations that have been responsible for hundreds of Israeli civilian deaths and thousands of injuries. Yasser Arafat revealed to the Lebanese newspaper, *Al-Shara'a*, in September 1999, that Iran had recently given Islamic Jihad and Hamas a further US$35 million for fighting Israel.[149]

Iran pursues an aggressive missile development program with the aid of not only Russia and China, but also Pakistan.[150] Successful Iranian tests of its Shihab-3 missile have been monitored by U.S.

intelligence agencies using surveillance satellites.[151] The missile has a range of around 1,300 kilometers (800 miles) and is capable of carrying a warhead weighing a metric ton (2,200 pounds).[152] The missile's range places all of Israel within its target range.[153]

The Washington Times reported that the Iranians are also trying to produce the Soviet ballistic missile SS-4,[154] and the Russians are helping Iran to leap the

> technical hurdles to develop a missile that can leave and re-enter the atmosphere.[155]

> Western analysts said the missile is meant to attack Israeli population centers from Iranian batteries 1,700 kilometers [1,050 miles] away.[156]

Iran is also building a vast arsenal of chemical and biological weapons. In August 1996, *Jane's Defence Weekly* reported that Syria and Iran have the largest stockpiles of these deadly substances in the Third World.[157] Sanctions are in place against Teheran, but

> German, French and Italian industrialists, faced with millions of restless unemployed, are supplying Teheran with vast a-mounts of raw materials and the tools to create chemical and biological weapons.[158]

In addition to its missile program, a *Jerusalem Post* Editorial states that "Iran possesses sophisticated submarines purchased from Russia."[159] The Editorial also says of Iran:

> It has acquired missile launchers and Silkworm missiles capable of delivering nuclear warheads from China. With German help it has rebuilt the Boshar nuclear center, and it is developing the region's largest nuclear network in 10 different locations.[160]

Iran's vigorous pursuit of nuclear weapons has rivaled its missile development program. Nuclear weapons in the hands of a fanatical Muslim government like Iran is a cause of concern to many:

> Iran's attempts to buy nuclear know-how from China, North Korea and former Soviet republics have triggered alarms among intelligence services around the world.[161]

Among Teheran's ruling elite the Iranian nuclear program is known as "The Great Secret Project."[162] Technical assistance has again come from Russia, China and Pakistan.[163] Besides the nuclear warheads that Iran is known to have obtained from Kazakhstan[164] (a secret deal was signed with Kazakhstan in 1992 to purchase four nuclear warheads,[165] a deal that was supposedly foiled by CIA agents. However, if two of those warheads are known to have turned up in Iran, it is likely that all four were "delivered"), Iran has now been, or will soon be, able to produce its own nuclear weapons. In November 1997, *Jane's Intelligence Review* reported that Iran was "just four months away from complete nuclear capability."[166] In April 1998, two U.S. congressmen, Jim Saxton and Bill McCollum, told the *Jerusalem Post* that

> Iran had indeed obtained nuclear weapons and "a ballistic missile command and control system to launch them.[167]

And in January 2000, the CIA published a report that "Iran has enough nuclear materials to build a bomb."[168]

The reports are conflicting: Iran has nuclear weapons; Iran is near to producing nuclear weapons; Iran has the materials to produce nuclear weapons. Perhaps we should reverse these reports and arrive at a point nearer the truth: Iran has the materials, and is very near or has already managed to produce its own nuclear weapons. Whatever stage Iran has arrived at in its quest for nuclear weapons, it spells serious trouble for Israel. A senior Israeli official said in 1997:

> Iran should know—and will know—that on the day it fires all it has at us, even if it all hits, Israel will still have the ability to wipe Iran off the face of the earth—quickly, forcefully and in the most inelegant manner.[169]

Such bravado, however, is rather childish. If Iran has, indeed, the nuclear weapons it is reputed to have, along with the capability to hit any part of Israel with them, and if it hits Israel with all it has, what would be left of Israel would hardly be worth defending.

Iraq is another implacable enemy of Israel. According to the *Sunday Times*, Iraq is now rebuilding its missile factories destroyed in the Gulf War.[170] The report also says that Iraqi sites capable of producing weapons of mass destruction have renewed activity ever since UN weapons inspectors were expelled in late 1998.[171] According to a 1998 U.S. Defense Department document:

> Iraq, second only to Israel, has secretly developed and

assembled the most advanced weapons of mass destruction and long-range missile systems in the Middle East.[172]

Rafiz al-Samurai, a former head of Iraqi intelligence who defected to the West, admitted on British TV that

Saddam Hussein has operational Al-Hussein missiles capable of delivering biological and chemical warheads on targets in Israel, as well as warheads with anthrax, VX gas, Sarin gas and Tabun gas.[173]

After the Persian Gulf War the Iraqi government admitted that it had 3.5 tons of VX nerve gas, of which a single droplet can be lethal within minutes.[174] Part of this stockpile was destroyed, but around 3,800 kilograms was never found by the UN Special Commission (UNSCOM).[175] UN inspectors believe that

as much as 200 tons of VX were produced, in theory enough to kill every human being on earth.[176]

U.S. Defense Secretary William Cohen confirmed in November 1997, that Saddam Hussein may have produced enough of the deadly chemical VX to kill everyone on earth.[177] In December 1997, Cohen announced that 1.5 million troops would receive a series of six inoculation shots against anthrax at a cost of $120 million[178] because

U.S. officials estimate that Iraqi dictator Saddam Hussein has enough anthrax to fill six warheads.[179]

According to Scott Ritter, the UN weapons inspector who resigned in August 1998 to protest what he called the failure of the UN and America to enforce international resolutions on Saddam Hussein, Iraq was also hiding three virtually complete nuclear bombs.[180] The bombs at that time were "technologically complete" and lacked only the fissionable materials to make them operational.[181] *Ha'aretz* reported on September 9, 1998, that although the UN inspectors knew the whereabouts of the three bombs and the way they were being hidden, no order was ever given to the team to conduct a surprise inspection of the site.[182]

Following the Gulf War, Saddam Hussein's hit list must now include the U.S. as well as Israel. The U.S. must be acutely aware of this for it to order the inoculation of 1.5 million of its troops. Thus, it is worth recalling the words of the late Uriel Dann, professor of history at Tel Aviv University, who in June 1991 warned,

Saddam Hussein does not forget and forgive... The day will come when he will hit... He may, by the grace of God, miscalculate, as he has miscalculated in the past. But even so the innocent will pay by the millions. This must never be put out of mind: Saddam Hussein, from now on, lives for revenge.[183]

U.S. Secretary of State, Madeleine Albright, said in relation to Saddam Hussein in February 1998, "We still want to give diplomacy a chance."[184] Diplomacy did not stop Saddam Hussein from brutalizing Kuwait in 1990. Missile strikes did not stop him in 1991. A massive aerial bombardment did not stop him, neither did a brief ground assault. The Gulf War did not convince Saddam Hussein to give up his vast arsenal of terrifying biological and chemical weapons. Nine years of sanctions has not convinced him, neither has two years of daily U.S. and U.K. bombings.

Give diplomacy a chance? To do what? Talk Saddam out of his firm belief that he is the neo-Nebuchadnezzar destined to lead Iraq into the greatness that once belonged to ancient Babylon? Does Albright seriously hope to talk him out of his dreams and into relinquishing his arsenal of weapons of mass destruction? Convincing him to take up knitting would be simple in comparison. A *Boston Globe* article by Jeff Jacoby provides us with the last word on Saddam Hussein:

> Saddam cannot make it more plain. Nothing will induce him to halt his stockpiling of biological and chemical agents—VX gas, anthrax, botulinum toxin, possibly even smallpox virus. Nothing will induce him to permit unfettered inspections. The issue the world confronts is not if Saddam has such weapons, or where: It is when he intends to use them.[185]

Libya is another Arab nation ruled by an unstable dictator. Muammar Gaddafi was only a 27-year-old lieutenant when he seized power in 1969.[186] Gadaffi has much the same mentality as Saddam Hussein of Iraq. And just as the concentrated bombing of Iraq and years of UN sanctions have not loosed Saddam from his throne, neither have the U.S. bombing of Libya in 1986 and years of U.S.-imposed sanctions chastened Gadaffi. In both cases, it simply shows the futility of attempts at assassination through air power; these two megalomaniacs "win" just by surviving.

As Saddam is obsessed with the development of weapons of mass destruction, so, too, is Gadaffi. In addition to the existing

Libyan chemical weapons projects at Sabha and at Rabta,[187] American spy satellites have shown that the Libyan leader is building what is believed to be the largest underground chemical weapons plant in the world.[188]

Egypt's President Hosni Mubarak has vehemently denied the existence of the enormous Libyan underground death plant in Tarhuna, southeast of Tripoli[189] despite irrefutable satellite evidence, and the American threat to bomb it.[190] Egypt, however, has reason to deny the existence of the vast Libyan plant because it is co-operating with Libya in the developing of chemical and biological warheads.[191]

The Americans threatened to bomb the plant, but continued surveillance by spy satellites have apparently shown that to be unfeasible. A *Reuters* report makes this clear:

> Libya is building a facility described as the "world's largest underground chemical weapons plant" and the Central Intelligence Agency cannot stop it, a report in *Time* magazine said yesterday. The plant is being built in the side of a mountain near the town of Tarhuna and only a direct nuclear hit on top of the mountain could destroy it, *Time* said, quoting CIA sources. *Time* reported the plant could be operational by 2000. "You can never stop anything like this," a U.S. intelligence source said. "You only slow it down and buy time."[192]

According to a Pentagon study released in late November 1997, Libya is among those "'aggressively seeking' nuclear, biological and chemical weapons"[193] and was one of "'the most pressing threats' to Middle East stability."[194]

Libya is also constantly attempting "to purchase, develop, or produce under license long-range ballistic missiles."[195] Subsequent reports indicate that Libya is currently "developing ballistic missiles and non-conventional warheads."[196]

Few are under any illusions why these horrific weapons are being made. Jane Harman, a U.S. Congresswoman who serves on the House National Security and Intelligence Committees, said:

> Libya and others today have in their possession, or are developing, the means to suddenly annihilate large portions of Israel's population with biological, chemical, or nuclear weapons.[197]

Libya has been placed in the same camp as radically Islamic

Iran. Both nations are a very real threat to the world at large. As White House aide, Daniel Tarullo, said:

> There is an almost universal view that Iran and Libya present enormous problems to the world community....[198]

The next Arab-Israeli war does not yet have a name, but it will be very nasty, pointless and probably quite soon. The word most frequently used in the Arab press in connection with the "peace process," is "withdrawal," not "peace." The Arab interest lies in getting Israel to withdraw from all Arab lands won in wars of self-defense; they are not concerned with peace with Israel. With the acquisition of modern weaponry and Israel reduced to a truncated state due to the "peace" process, the Muslim world hopes to strike the final blow to the Jewish state.

While Israeli, U.S. and European *"fools"* fantasize about a "New Middle East," the Arabs and other Muslims see nothing wrong in the Old Middle East—a region without a Jewish state. The thousands of missiles in the arsenals of the Arab world, together with its emerging nuclear threat and unknown number of tons of the deadliest substances known to mankind, are expressly for the purpose of liquidating the Jewish state and re-establishing the Old Middle East.

A U.S. House of Representatives Task Force On Terrorism and Unconventional Warfare report states:

> Numerous sources in the region report that the supreme leaders—both civilians and military—in most Arab states, as well as Iran and Pakistan, are convinced that the present vulnerability of Israel is so great that there is a unique opportunity to, at the very least, begin the process leading to the destruction of Israel. These circumstances are considered to be a historic window of opportunity the Muslim world should not miss. Therefore, these Muslim leaders have finalized numerous strategies and tactical alliances heretofore non-existent in the region.[199]

It is obvious from the hundreds of intelligence reports included in this book that the Muslim Arab world, along with Muslim Iran and Pakistan, are gathering their forces for a final confrontation with Israel. Between them, they possess sufficient terrible weapons to destroy all life on planet earth several times over.

Throughout this book the writer has argued that Yahweh, *the*

Mighty One of Israel, is about to judge Israel for spurning Him for the umteenth time, and that day draws ever closer.

The 50 plus years of modern Israel's existence has been accompanied by exceptional blessings from God, but Israel has neither valued them nor the Giver of them. The gods of modern Israel are materialism, the Israel Defense Forces and the Israeli Air Force. Yahweh has stripped Israel of most of its strategic defensive territory through its own godless leaders who have sought "peace" instead of Him. When the coordinated Muslim avalanche hits Israel the "Wall"[200] will fall, and the "prophets of peace" will be consumed. In their time of trouble, the "prophets of peace" will no doubt say to the One on whom they have turned their back: "Arise and save us" (Jeremiah 2:27). And He will likely say:

> *But where are your gods that you have made for yourselves? Let them arise, if they can save you in the time of your trouble; for according to the number of your cities are your gods...*
>
> (Jeremiah 2:28).

The "Wall" must fall and the "prophets of peace" must be consumed and also many from among the nations, but the remnant that makes up the true house of Israel will be preserved:

> *I want to remind you, though you once knew this, that the Lord, having saved the people out of the land of Egypt, afterward destroyed those who did not believe* (Jude 1:5).

What held good in ancient times also holds good in modern times. Yahweh has saved His people from extinction from gas chambers, from war and from assimilation. He has re-established His people on their ancient land, and is bringing them back from the literal four corners of the world. The great majority of Jews, however, have no appreciation of these blessings. They want to be like "all other nations." The Jewish nation today is ripe for Yahweh's judgment, but the God-fearing remnant will be saved.

If the Muslims could destroy all Jews today, Yahweh could not fulfill His promises that His Son would reign as King of the Jews on David's throne in Jerusalem at His second coming. If Islam could destroy all Jews and uproot them from the Land, Yahweh would be found to be both a liar and a loser, and Satan a winner. Yahweh's integrity and eternal purposes are inextricably linked to the survival of both the Jews and Israel. Therefore, both will survive.

El Niño

Yahweh is sending punitive judgments upon the nations today. All over the world nations are experiencing devastating catastrophes of flooding, earthquakes, famines, disease, tornados, hurricanes, hailstones, snow, etc. The nations do not repent, instead they "curse God" exactly as the Bible (Revelation 16:9, 11) describes it in the last days.

There is something very significant about the weather 'phenomenon' that is blamed for all these catastrophes befalling the nations today. Christians know that their God is the one that controls the weather and all other things besides, but the world's *"fools"* blame it upon something they call *"El Niño."* El Niño means, in Spanish, "the child," but it is more specifically used to denote "the Christ child." It is Yahweh's way of informing us that the second coming of Jesus is imminent.

The Book of Revelation shows us some of the dreadful catastrophes that will befall the nations before Jesus Christ takes up His rule. The Book of Revelation is literally the judgment of the nations—they are made to

> *drink of the wine of the wrath of God, which is poured out full strength into the cup of His indignation* (Revelation 14:10).

In the opening paragraph of the first chapter of this book it is written:

> …the One who predicts history with such accuracy must also control it. And the One who predicts natural events such as earthquakes with frightening accuracy must, also, control nature. Therefore, Bible believing people can take comfort in knowing that the future is a lot less out of control than is generally thought and, consequently, a lot less terrifying.

Our confidence must only be in an active, living God, whose love and whose wrath are both clearly revealed in the events of human history—a God who has played the decisive part in that history when he sent Jesus Christ among us. Only if we hold this faith can we have any real hope in this present world. It is the only faith that will dare to hold its own in our technological and nuclear age. We must, therefore, put to good use the little time left to us. Only today is ours; yesterday cannot be recalled and tomorrow cannot be assured: *Today if you will hear His voice, do not harden your heart* (Hebrews 3:15).

The living, loving, active God made provision to take away sins at Calvary's cross, but nowhere has He said He will provide a more convenient tomorrow for our procrastinations. Say "Yes," to Jesus today. All of us are in His hands. Ultimate reality is not dependent upon present appearances. Real power belongs with the risen Christ, not with the world's politicians.

If Yahweh did not spare His own Son (Romans 8:32) and spares not His own chosen people, the nations have no prospect at all of immunity from catastrophe. Revelation 14:7 says, *"Fear God,"* and, let us face facts, godless people have much to be afraid of.

Judgment is part of the redemptive way Yahweh deals with His people and with the world. Judgments are loosed against all mankind, including believers. Yahweh is in control of the whole process and is concerned for His people. Unless Yahweh's judgments hit the earth, people do not learn righteousness:

*With my soul I have desired You in the night, yes, by my spirit within me I will seek You early; for **when Your judgments are in the earth, the inhabitants of the world will learn righteousness*** (Isaiah 26:9).

Yahweh's people have nothing to fear from His judgment of the godless. They need never be dismayed. They will be preserved no matter what the tribulation.

Our world is a greedy, materialistic, brutal and merciless world, and those without a living relationship with Jesus have very good reason to fear indeed:

For judgment is without mercy to the one who has shown no mercy. Mercy triumphs over judgment (James 2:13).

All truly twice-born Christians, however, will join together in singing the song of Moses with those who overcame

by the blood of the Lamb and by the word of their testimony, and they did not love their lives to the death.... They sing the song of Moses, the servant of God, and the song of the Lamb, saying: "Great and marvelous are Your works, Lord God Almighty! Just and true are Your ways, O King of the saints!"
(Revelation 12:11; 15:3).

All the ways of Yahweh are indeed *just and true.* Nevertheless, let us bow our heads and humbly petition Him that, in His judgments, He will remember mercy. *Amen.*

"... if the watchman sees the sword coming and does not blow the trumpet, and the people are not warned, and the sword comes and takes any person from among them, he is taken away in his iniquity; but his blood I will require at the watchman's hand"
(Ezekiel 33:6).

For Your Information

Ramon Bennett, the author of this book, also writes for the *Ministry & Prayer Update*, the periodic newsletter of the *Arm of Salvation Ministries*. The *Update* keeps readers informed on current events in Israel and, also, on the ministry and movements of Ramon and his wife, Zipporah. A minimum annual donation of $15.00 is requested to offset production and postage costs, and this can be sent to *Shekinah Books Ltd.* at the address below.

Readers in Australia, New Zealand and the United Kingdom can subscribe to the *Update* in their respective currencies, and they should contact the appropriate persons listed on page 2 at the front of this book. The *Update* is also produced in German and Norwegian and readers interested in subscribing to either of these language editions should contact *Shekinah Books Ltd.* at the address below.

Arm *of Salvation*, of which Ramon Bennett is the Executive Director, is an indigenous Israeli ministry dependent upon gifts and proceeds from its books and tapes to sustain work in and for Israel and the Jewish people. These are critical times for Israel so readers' support is warmly appreciated. All donations sent to *Shekinah Books Ltd.* at the address below will be forwarded in full to Mr. Bennett, together with any letter or note attached.

Further copies of *The Wall* are available by mail from *Shekinah Books Ltd.* and can be obtained by sending $14.95 plus $3.50 ($6.00 Airmail) shipping and handling to the address below.

Books by Ramon Bennett are often not available in bookstores. We therefore encourage readers to purchase 10 or more of Ramon's books at a 40% discount for gifts, to sell to friends or to members of prayer and church groups. Add together the requested prices (given on this and following pages) for each book in an order of 10 or more to a single address, deduct 40% and then add 12% for shipping and handling (18% outside of the U.S. and Canada). Mail your check or *International M.O.* in *U.S. funds drawn on a U.S. bank* to:

SHEKINAH BOOKS LTD.
P.O. Box 846, Keno, Oregon 97627, U.S.A.
Tel: (541) 882-9777   Fax: (541) 850-4395
Email: Shekinah@kfalls.net

Addendum I

RAVIV DEFENSE IS THE TRUTH
by Barry Chamish

Since the Avishai Raviv trial is being held behind closed doors, or putting it in more accurate terms, since the Israeli public is being denied the right to know what is going on at Raviv's trial, I will do my best to follow the proceedings via the flimsy summations released to the public weekly.

After the first two hearings, which began on Feb. 22, it is clear that the prosecutor Moshe Shiloh, as I previously predicted, is running the government's cover-up. Raviv's lawyer Eyal Shomroni-Cohen complained bitterly that the state prosecutor is not releasing most of the documents requested for Raviv's defense.

No surprise so far...but look at what Shomroni-Cohen is requesting! I quote from the weekly newspaper *Makor Rishon*:

> Attorney for Shabak agent Avishai Raviv, Eyal Shomroni-Cohen has demanded a copy of the State Pathologist's Report on the death of Yitzhak Rabin. He also demanded copies of the other medical reports. He announced, "Until I see these reports, until I examine the actual murder, I won't sleep at night and will disbelieve the murder." The prosecutor has charged Raviv with not preventing Rabin's murder and Shomroni-Cohen observed that his client cannot defend himself unless the murder itself is examined. Although he has not claimed there was a conspiracy, Shomroni-Cohen stressed that, "A major question is raised within the documents." He added that the documents he is demanding challenge the accepted version of the Rabin murder. He pointed out that Rabin's daughter, the Knesset member Dahlia Rabin-Pelosoff stated that there is a clear contradiction between the State Pathologist's Report and those of Ichilov hospital. He accused the state prosecutor of denying him the documents based on the protection of personal privacy. He noted that the right to defend oneself in a court of law takes precedence over personal privacy.

Well, well, well, well, well. Look who has discovered the Rabin assassination conspiracy thesis! And give Raviv's attorney credit for defending his client properly. If given access to the very same documents I have published in the Hebrew and Russian versions of my book "Who Murdered Yitzhak Rabin," Shomroni-Cohen will prove his client is innocent of not preventing Rabin's murder because Amir didn't commit the murder. If he wants copies of said documents, all he has to do is call me. We wish him good luck. and some of us are going to press and press and press for this trial to be opened to the public and media.

The court may be hiding the Raviv trial, the media may be covering it up, but the people want to know the truth already. Raviv's trial may be hidden but the issue of how Rabin really died will not go away until the facts are known. I leave you with two brief items recently relayed to me:

1. Edgar Bronfman is paying millions to send American Jewish college students to Israel for free under a program called Operation Birthright. He is selling the plan as a charitable gift to the Jewish people but many of the first 6000 who arrived in Israel are reporting that they were subjected to a sophisticated propaganda exercise designed to instill a love of the Israeli left and the unpopular "peace" process. Students complained that their requests to visit Judea and Samaria were turned down. One tour guide told me that the vast majority of the guides hired by Bronfman were from the far left and touted the "Peace Now" line to their trapped students. Bronfman is a leading member of the Council On Foreign Relations. He and two other CFR members, Lawrence Tisch and Henry Kissinger provided the initial funding for Ehud Barak's political career in 1995.

2. While it is known that Yitzhak Rabin's deal with Hizb'allah after Operation Accountability included the right to kill IDF soldiers, it was widely reported that shelling Israeli towns or dropping Katyushas on them was forbidden by the pact. That is not precisely the case. Hizb'allah agreed not to bomb almost all towns including Metulla, Nahariya, Rosh Hanikra, kibbutzim such as Dan and Daphne, etc. which support the Labor Party and whose residents are mostly Ashkenazi. However when Katyushas had to be launched, they were restricted to the mostly Moroccan, right wing city of Kiryat Shmoneh. Hizb'allah has stuck to the deal and only Kiryat Shmoneh has borne the brunt of the rockets for nearly the past decade.

Addendum 2

RUBIN WASN'T SHOT
by Barry Chamish

Dr. David Chen is currently the most successful Rabin assassination researcher at work. Using his insider contacts and impressive initiative, he has uncovered stunning new evidence proving the conspiracy to murder Rabin. He has requested that the new evidence be gathered in one explosive package and then presented to the justice system.

My response to his strategy was, "What justice system?" Dr. Chen has faith where mine has disappeared. Last week he faxed me a document of such import that I could wait no longer to release it. I called Dr. Chen and expressed the view that events are out of control in Israel and every weapon must be released in a last ditch effort to save our nation. The report he sent me had the potential to short-circuit the government. He reluctantly accepted my logic.

I have in my possession the clinical report on Yoram Rubin, Rabin's personal bodyguard and as my latest evidence proves, the prime suspect as his murderer. Recall that on the night of Rabin's assassination, Rubin was reported badly wounded in the arm trying to save Rabin. The new Prime Minister, Shimon Peres, immediately appointed the courageous Rubin as his personal bodyguard.

Recall that Rubin testified under oath that a bullet entered his arm, "like an electrical charge," at the elbow and traversed the forearm until exiting at the armpit. The bullet was never found. Recall that the Shamgar Commission, and the judges at Yigal Amir's trial concluded that Rubin was wounded by a bullet which entered the arm at the elbow and exited at the armpit. These rulings were central to the government cover-up of the murder, since they served the dual purpose of proving that a *Shabak* (General Security Services) officer did risk his life trying to save Rabin and of deflecting suspicion of murder from Rubin.

THESE CONCLUSIONS WERE FALSE. THE PUBLIC WAS LIED TO.

* * *

Surgery Dept. Elias Sorosky Medical Center
SUMMARY OF PATIENT

Name: Yoram Rubin
ID No.: 5959979
Address: Morgenthau 31, Jerusalem
Admittance level: Emergency

Admission Date: 4.11.95
Date of Birth: 1965
Telephone: 02 863489
Release Date: 10/11/95

Patient, aged 30, was transferred from Surgery G for continuation of treatment. He was previously transferred in emergency condition from ER.

Wound description: Gunshot wound to forearm from under the elbow, leaving two wounds in the upper forearm under the armpit, causing a slight swelling and sensitivity in upper forearm. Patient reported inability to straighten arm beyond 110 degrees because of the pain. Bruise in distensible region.[†]

Treatment: The wounds was cleaned with a toxoid in ER. Afterward, in our department, Polydine was applied locally along with antibiotics. The swelling was quickly reduced. The wounds in the arm were clean. The patient was released in good health with no fever.[††]

Signed by Dr. Laslo Kalmanovitch

* * *

So why did our government tell us Rabin's bodyguard was seriously wounded and why did he remain in hospital for 6 days? And why did our government's commission of inquiry rule that Rubin was actually wounded by a bullet IN his arm?

Further; Shamgar accepted that Rubin was shot while lying atop Rabin, by Amir who was shooting above him. No one shooting from above could have caused the horizontal friction wound described in this report. The only way Amir physically could have caused the wound is if he stood in front of Rubin and asked him to hold his arm out for him.

[†]   (Note: To imagine the wound, point your finger from under the elbow continuing at an angle toward the top the the underarm. There the fold in the skin will be hit twice by the passing of a bullet. Yes, passing of a bullet, because no bullet enters the flesh. This is a friction wound. Now imagine Rubin shooting a gun from under his elbow to under his armpit via the underside of the forearm and you'll see what happened. BC)

[††]   (Note: Rubin's "wounds" were washed and Polydine (an iodine-based cleanser) applied. The swelling disappeared and Rubin was released. That's it. Rubin's boo-boo was treated with soap and iodine and he was home free. BC)

Addendum 3

THE OTHER RABIN MURDER BOOK:
A Review Of Natan Gefen's "The Fatal Sting"
by Barry Chamish

My expose of the true Rabin assassination, "Who Murdered Yitzhak Rabin" received a great deal of attention because it was the first and because it was published in four languages. The release of a second book on the conspiracy, "The Fatal Sting" by Natan Gefen was greeted with less fanfare, partly because that's what happens when you're number two, and in greater part, because so far, the book is only available in Hebrew.

Those who read Hebrew often ask if there is a rivalry between me and Gefen. The answer is no; we are on the same team. And I'm not being overly magnanimous when I conclude that his book is as valuable as mine for those seeking the truth of what really happened to Rabin. In fact, Gefen adds several documents missing from my work that round out the study of the assassination. Allow me to point out his most striking revelations.

Amir Did Not Confess At The Beginning

A month after the murder, on December 3, 1995, a court hearing was held to consider Israel Police's request for an extension of its investigation of the murder. Before the hearing began, Amir shouted at the reporters present, demanding to know why they were not investigating the murder of the security officer Yoav Kuriel. Most of Israel saw his outburst on television and heard the following interchange between him and Judge Dan Arbel, who ordered Amir to desist from speaking to the media.

From *Ma'ariv* 4/11/95:

> One Of The Reporters - Would you do it again?
> Amir - Yes. After you understand why, you'll see the system is rotten. Everything is set up. What you're seeing is a facade. I didn't think they'd start killing people. Since Oslo B...
> Judge Arbel - Don't talk about Oslo B. You're not the Foreign Minister.
> Amir - They're killing people. Don't you understand that? It's all a lie.
> Judge Arbel - What's a lie?
> Amir - That I killed Rabin. I never even tried to kill him.

I included that remarkable exchange in my book but had no idea that Amir's denial appeared in the court records. Gefen managed to track down the protocols of this hearing and he reprints them in full in "The Fatal Sting." After the reporters are removed from the court and the session continues in camera, Amir tells Judge Arbel, "About the request for an extension, what you've seen now has all been a facade. I request to be allowed to explain the background to my actions. They're killing people. If you listen to the truth, the whole country will be up in arms."

Amazing it is that one month after the murder Amir was still trying to tell an Israeli court the truth and the judge turned down his request to speak. The justice system was rigged against Amir from the beginning and Gefen proves it. After this incident, Amir was taken away for over a month and a half and when he returned from _Shabak_ prison to face the investigators of the Shamgar Commission and the judges at his own trial, he had changed. Now he was an ever-smiling buffoon who confessed every time a witness testified in his favor. If only Judge Arbel had let him speak the truth.

The Bullets

On page nine of his book, Gefen makes an astute observation about Hagai Amir and Dror Edni. Both were tried and given long prison sentences for supplying the ammunition to the murderer. Most of the case against them was based on the following events.

On the night of the murder, the police searched the Amir home in Herzlia and came up nearly empty-handed. Two days later, the _Shabak_ (General Security Services, Israel's FBI), researched the home and came away with two pistols and a huge armory of bullets. Gefen observes that if Hagai Amir and Dror Edni were really involved in the assassination, they would never have left such an armory in the Amir house.

Now we jump to page 30 and Gefen reports on the bullet that supposedly shot Rabin's personal bodyguard, and my prime candidate as his murderer, Yoram Rubin. The actual bullet was never found and Rubin was not actually shot. But traces of the bullet which passed through his jacket were found by Israel Crime Lab technician, Chief Lieutenant Baruch Gladstein and he discovered brass, a metal that was not found in the bullets which wounded Rabin.

Gefen makes three points which I missed in my book. First, the prosecution explained away the different bullet by claiming that Amir loaded two types of bullets into his clip. Gefen puts the argument to rest by referring to the police ballistics report. No bullet with the chemical composition of that which pierced Rubin's suit was found in Amir's clip or in the armory allegedly kept by his brother Hagai and his "accomplice" Edni.

Next, Gefen notes that hollowpoint bullets are rarely used in Israeli murders and it would have been mad for a political assassin to use them since they are much less effective at penetrating a bulletproof vest, which Rabin should have been but wasn't wearing. How would Amir have known Rabin wouldn't be wearing one? However, hollowpoints shatter upon impact and cannot be traced back to a specific weapon.

Finally, a major revelation, nowhere in the court or police records are Amir's gun, clip or extant bullets tested for fingerprints. There is no fingerprint evidence that Amir ever held the murder weapon or loaded its clip. Gefen insists this could not have been an oversight and implies that the fingerprint evidence was deliberately withheld.

Tampering With The Film

Many people have found ways to prove that the "amateur" film of the murder, wrongly attributed to a *Shabak* flunky named Ronnie Kempler, was obviously tampered with. The shooter in the still-frame from the film has a different haircut and face than Amir, is wearing a long-sleeved shirt, when Amir wore a short-sleeved shirt and is shooting with his left hand, while Amir shot from the right. It can't be Amir and I have concluded that someone else was superimposed into the frame to bring Amir closer to the point blank range the police found Rabin was shot at. Central to the case against Amir is the frame which supposedly captures the flash of the gun as he shoots. Bernard Shechter, head of the Police Forensics Laboratory at the time of the assassination, told me that he had never seen a flash appear like that in any other shooting he had examined and suspected that it was drawn in. Arther Vered, a computer expert pulled the flash frame from the Kempler film and placed it atop the flash still which was first published by *Yediot Ahronot*. They are not the same. Still, there are lingering suspicions that the gunflash was real.

Not any more. Gefen consulted a physicist who explained

most rationally, that the light generated by the flash of an ignited bullet cartridge is as brilliant as lightning. If the flash was real, it would have lit up Rabin's back, which it clearly does not. "The Fatal Sting" proves the photo of Amir shooting Rabin has been altered drastically.

Understanding Dr. Barabash

One of the biggest headaches I have when lecturing is explaining away the TV interview given by Ichilov Hospital director, Dr. Gabi Barabash on the evening of the assassination. While, the official version of Rabin's murder has him shot twice in the back, both Gefen and I agree that all the evidence proves that Rabin was shot three times, the final fatal shot coming from the front and ultimately shattering his spine, a wound the government claims never occurred.

I present two televised interviews from Ichilov to my audiences. First, I show Health Minister Ephraim Sneh announcing that Rabin was shot three times; in the chest, stomach and spinal cord. Then comes Barabash who confirms the chest to spine wound but claims Rabin was only shot twice.

"The Fatal Sting" more than suggests he was lying. Two hours later, Dr. Barabash was interviewed on Channel Two and he is much less certain about the number of shots. Gefen provides the text of this startling interview and keeps the original tape in his archive.

> Channel Two Reporter - How many bullets are we talking about?
> Dr. Barabash - Pardon me?
> Channel Two Reporter - How many bullets are we talking about?
> Dr. Barabash - I think two, no three, I think two. One of them injured the area around the heart and wounded the spinal cord, cutting it off.

Barabash can't get the story straight. He mixes up the cover-up with the truth.

When Was Rabin Shot?

"The Fatal Sting" includes a shocking document I had never seen before and frankly, I just can't digest it. I had concluded based on court testimony and hospital records that Rabin was shot at 9:40, placed in his limousine a few minutes later and arrived at the hospital at 9:52. Since the ride should have taken only a minute, I concluded that Rabin's driver, Menachem Damti, got unexplainably lost for eight minutes.

Two months ago, one of Rabin's surgeons, Dr. Kluger told _Ha'aretz_ that, in fact, Rabin was twelve minutes late. How could I have been off by four minutes?

(I digress. A close associate of his informed me last week that Dr. Kluger has been afflicted by a mysterious malady and looks, "like a living corpse." He is the second doctor to be so mysteriously stricken recently. Last September, the head of Rabin's surgical team, Dr. Mordechai Gutman suffered neurological pain that left him unable to function for six weeks. The cause of the pain was never identified but my informant told me, "He got the hint.")

To confuse the issue more, Gefen presents the hospital conclusion based on blood coagulation that Rabin was shot 4-5 minutes before he arrived at Ichilov. This would mean, according to my published calculations, that Rabin was shot some three minutes after he entered his car. If Kluger is right, then Rabin was shot, some seven minutes into his final journey. This is just too much of a discrepancy and it must be explained.

Gefen does so in such a drastic fashion that, until I figure out what it means, I must remain speechless. Reprinted in "The Fatal Sting" are Amir's arrest records. According to them, he was arrested by the police at 9:30 PM, or a full ten minutes before, officially, Rabin was shot by him.

I tried and tried to work it out, until finally I phoned Nathan Gefen and asked him, "Is this arrest report mistaken? Didn't people check their watches to see when Rabin was shot? Why is it accepted that Rabin was shot at 9:40 if Amir was already in custody by then?"

He replied, "This is the first police report and it's the most authentic. After that, the arrest time was readjusted five minutes at a time to suit the cases of Shamgar and Amir's prosecutors."

In "The Fatal Sting," Gefen quotes a police expert who explains that the time of arrest in such a form is the most vital information of all and it is rarely, if ever, so wrong. Gefen concludes, "If Amir had chosen to pursue his innocence, he has the best alibi of all. He was already under arrest when Rabin was shot."

There is much more in this book, but the arrest records shook me up the most. Gefen dares where I merely hinted: he names Shimon Peres as the organizer of the murder and he has strong arguments to back his accusation up. Today, I have even stronger ones than Gefen. However, the real strength of "The Final Sting" lies in the documentation, which when combined with the ample documents of my book, proves beyond any doubt that Yigal Amir could not possibly have murdered Rabin.

Now there are two books that reach the same conclusion. A third is on the way. It is called "Lies: The Israeli Secret Service And The Rabin Assassination" by David Morrison. It will be published by Gefen Books of Jerusalem (no relation to Nathan Gefen). Write isragefen@netmedia.net.il for information.

Last October, Rabin's son Yuval went on television and demanded a reinvestigation of his father's murder because, "If not, there are going to be a lot more books likes Chamish's soon." His prediction is, thankfully, coming true.

* * *

"The Fatal Sting" is sold through the Steimatzky chain in Israel or can be ordered by phone from Ram Marketing. Call (972) (0)3 6775630 or 03 5745367. Natan Gefen can be reached at gfn@inter.net.il.

My book "Who Murdered Yitzhak Rabin" is distributed in English in America by Brookline Books, call 1 800 666 BOOK and is available again over Amazon.

Please visit www.webseers.com/rabin

Addendum 4

Russia to sell multi-warhead missiles that can beat Israel's new anti-missile system

SPECIAL TO WORLD TRIBUNE.COM
Thursday, March 23, 2000

MOSCOW – The designer of advanced multi-warhead missiles capable of overcoming Israel's new anti-missile system said Russia would sell them to its clients in the Middle East, a newspaper here reported.

The new weapon is the Iskander-E, with a range of 280 kilometers. Defense industry sources said the missile can deliver multiple warheads of 480 kilograms each to their targets.

Each warhead, they said, consists of 54 separate bomblets. The sources said the missile is suitable for both point and targets and can overcome any anti-ballistic missile system.

Nikolay Gushchin, chief of the Kolomna Mashinostroyeniye design office, said the Iskander-E is different from all of its predecessors. "Technical designs have been incorporated in Iskander-E which also enable the missile to overcome easily an ABM system of an enemy," he said.

U.S. officials have expressed concern that Russia might export the missiles, whether formally or through smugglers.

In Washington, CIA director George Tenet told the Senate Foreign Relations Committee on Tuesday that Moscow continues to be a major arms proliferator to Iran and the Middle East. He said that the new missiles being developed make it easier to deliver biological and chemical weapons.

"We are concerned that countries are acquiring advanced technologies to design, test, and produce highly effective munitions and sophisticated delivery systems," Tenet said.

Gushchin, designer of the Iskander-E, said Russia would seek to sell the missile to such countries as Algeria, Jordan, Kuwait, Syria and the United Arab Emirates. But he said the most significant market is East Asia, including Singapore, Vietnam, Malaysia, and South Korea.

Russia has sold older generation preceding weapons systems to Syria and Yemen. Industry sources said the Iskander is an improvement of the Tochka tactical missile system.

"In my view, there is a very special place in the world arms market for such weapons complexes as Iskander-E," Gushchin told the Russian newspaper _Krasnaya Zvezda_. "The point is that even a small number of such installations will radically change the layout of power in regional conflicts. Imagine, even an enemy having a superiority in military forces and weapons by a factor of 10 will not dare to start aggression, similar to the aggression of the members of NATO against Yugoslavia, if his cities, air bases, and troops are in the sights of missiles which, in the next 10 - 15 years, an enemy will not be able to destroy in battle positions and will not be able to intercept in flight."

Last week, senior Israeli defense officials acknowledged that Russia has multi-warhead missiles but said they are not being offered to Middle East clients. The officials said the Arrow anti-missile system, developed by the United States and Israel, has not been designed to counter multi-warhead missiles.

The Iskander-E does not depend on satellites and can be directed by a man on the ground, the sources said. The missile has an optical seeker that can operate in all weather.

"All of the existing active electronic warfare equipment is powerless against such a homing head," Gushchin said. "There is not a single tactical system in the world other than Iskander-E that can carry out such tasks."

The above report, which is reprinted in full, came to hand just as this book was going to print. The news of such a missile system will obviously be a further source of grave concern to the heads of the Israel Defense Forces. Russian clients in the Middle East will be clamoring to obtain the weapon, and Israel will soon be encircled by hundreds of these lethal projectiles. Adding them to the thousands of existing missiles that are also capable of carrying chemical and biological nerve agents as well as nuclear warheads, the Battle of Armageddon might be a lot closer than we care to imagine.

Chapter I

1 Abraham Rabinovich: "Why should Jews emigrate to Israel?," *Jerusalem Post*, June 28, 1996.

2 Benjamin Netanyahu, *A Place Among The Nations: Israel and the World* (New York: Bantam, 1993), p. 41.

3 *The World Almanac and Book of Facts*, (New York: Pharos Books, 1993), p. 766.

4 John F. Walvoord, *Armageddon, Oil, and the Middle East Crisis* (Grand Rapids: Zondervan, 1990), p. 55.

5 This phrase appears 31 times in the Old Testament, 25 of them in the book of the prophet Isaiah.

6 *Jane's Intelligence Review*—world renowned for its accuracy. Cited in *Petah Tikvah,* Vol. 15, No. 3, July 1997, p. 50.

7 President Clinton, quoted in: "An Open Letter to President Clinton," *Jerusalem Post*, Nov. 13, 1998.

8 *NIV Study Bible*, (Grand Rapids: Zondervan, 1985), notes on Genesis 15:17, p. 29.

9 *The Oxford English Dictionary* (Second Edition), (New York: Oxford University Press, 1989).

10 "Anglican Archbishop Critical of Israel's Jerusalem Policy," *ICEJ News Service*, Feb. 1, 1999.

11 "US Churchmen Want Aid To Israel Stopped," *ICEJ News Service*, Jan. 29, 1999.

Chapter 2

1 Achmed Tibi, quoted in: "Settlers must be disarmed," *Jerusalem Post*, July 12, 1996.

2 Ya'acov Tsur, quoted in: "The Halhoul Revelation," *Jerusalem Post*, Sept. 17, 1995.

3 Yisrael Harel: "Netanyahu's ticket to insincerity," *Jerusalem Post*, Nov. 29, 1996.

4 Shimon Peres, quoted in: "Editorial," *Jerusalem Post*, May 29, 1996.

Chapter 3

1 A popular misbelief is that there were only five attacking nations. For confirmation and details of the seven attacking armies see, for example, Howard M. Sacher, *A History of Israel: From the Rise of Zionism to Our Time,* (New York: Alfred A. Knopf, 1991), p. 315; Ramon Bennett, *When Day and Night Cease,* 3rd Edition (Jerusalem: Arm of Salvation, 1996), p. 171, 210; William L. Hull, *The Fall and Rise of Israel: The Story of the Jewish People During the time of their Dispersal and Regathering* (Grand Rapids: Zondervan, 1954), p. 328; etc.

2 Ian V.Hogg, *Israeli War Machine: The Men; The Machines; The Tactics*, (London: Hamlyn, 1983), p. 20.

3 Bennett, *When Day and Night Cease,* p. 171.

4 Hogg, *Israeli War Machine*, p. 20.

5 Sacher, *A History of Israel*, p. 633.

6 *Ibid.*, pp. 633, 634.

7   *Ibid.*, p. 640.

8   For further details see: Bennett, *When Day and Night Cease,* pp. 173-175.

9   Sacher, *A History of Israel,* p. 759.

10   *Ibid.*, p. 781.

11   Sacher, *A History of Israel,* p. 779.

12   Hogg, *Israeli War Machine,* p. 6.

13   *Jane's Intelligence Review*—world renowned for its accuracy. Cited in *Petah Tikvah,* Vol. 15, No. 3, July 1997, p. 50.

14   Jim Ledeman, *Battle Lines: The American Media and the Intifada*, New York: Henry Holt, 1992, p. 319.

15   Asher Wallfish: "Palestinian leaders: Baker promised us a state," *Jerusalem Post*, Feb. 7, 1993.

16   Shmuel Katz: "Golan: more than geography," *Jerusalem Post*, March 5, 1993.

17   *The Jerusalem Institute For Western Defense: Periodic New Digest from the Arab World and Iran*, Digest 6, June 1994, p. 3.

18   "Synopsis," *Naviv*, Jan. 1996, p. 11.

19   Sarah Honig: "Likud urges no-confidence," *Jerusalem Post*, Jan. 12, 1993.

20   P. David Hornik: "Looking in, looking out," *Jerusalem Post*, Aug. 16, 1996.

21   *Ibid.*

22   *Ibid.*

23   *Ibid.*

24   Yitzhak Rabin's speech to Jewish leaders in New York on September 28, 1995 after the Oslo 2 signing ceremony. Quoted in: "They don't 'criticize' as much as hurl epithets," *Jerusalem Post*, Dec. 8, 1995.

25   *Ibid.*

26   *Ibid.*

27   Shimon Peres speaking to faculty and students at the University of Pensylvania in October 1994. Quoted in: "The roots under the topsoil," *Jerusalem Post*, May 29, 1996.

28   Liat Collins: "His Own Man," *Jerusalem Post*, Jan. 3, 1997.

29   *Ibid.*

30   Esther Wachsman: "About Rearranging Priorities," *Jerusalem Post*, June 7, 1996.

31   *Ibid.*

32   Ruth Matar quoting Naomi Chazan's own words in a fax to Chazan on Feb. 10, 1998.

33   Sarah Honig: "Aloni: Machpela cave not sacred to Jews," *Jerusalem Post*, March 25, 1994.

34   Carl Schrag: "Class of '93," *Jerusalem Post*, July 2, 1993.

35   *Ibid.*

36   "Bolshevik Tactiics – A Successful Transplant To Israel," Media Release, *Women For Israel's Tomorrow*, Nov. 29, 1995.

37   *Ibid.*

38   Charley J. Levine: "When young faces off against old," *Jerusalem Post*, Nov. 5, 1993.

39   Bill Hutman: "Olmert disputes Rabin's claim that his election is bad for peace process," *Jerusalem Post*, Nov. 4, 1993.

40   "We Are Our Own Worst Enemies," Media Release, *Women For Israel's Tomorrow*, Dec. 29, 1997.

41 *Ibid.*
42 Esther Wachsman: "About Rearranging Priorities," *Jerusalem Post*, June 7, 1996.
43 Editorial: "The Polarization danger," *Jerusalem Post*, Dec. 9, 1993.
44 Quoted by Stan Goodenough in: "Bible Briefing," Supplement to the *Middle East Digest*, Dec. 1996.

Chapter 4

1 *ICEJ News Service,* Sep. 20, 1998.
2 *Encyclopaedia Britannica, 1997.*
3 *Ibid.*
4 Immanuel Jakobovits: "A nation unlike any other," *Jerusalem Post*, May 15, 1994.
5 See p. 47.
6 Spoken to world renowned *Dry Bones* cartoonist Ya'akov Kirschen by a supporter of the peace process. Printed in *Middle East Intelligence Digest*, Oct. 1994, p. 2.
7 Ari Stav: "Peres: Without a secure border, the State faces annihilation in war," *Nativ* Feb. 1996, p. 9.

Chapter 5

1 Ari Stav: "Peres: Without a secure border, the State faces annihilation in war," *Nativ* Feb. 1996, p. 9.
2 Moshe Kohn: "What 'Peace Process'?," *Jerusalem Post*, Dec. 24, 1993.
3 Yedidya Atlas: "Rabin's unwanted child," *Jerusalem Post*, Nov. 1, 1993.
4 *Ibid.*
5 Asher Wallfish and David Rudge: "Rabin: Golan settlers can 'spin like propellers,'" *Jerusalem Post*, June 8, 1993.
6 Moshe Kohn: "'Rabin *was* us...'", *Jerusalem Post*, Oct. 25, 1996.
7 *Ibid.*
8 *Ibid.*
9 *Ibid.*
10 Greer Fay Cashman: "Clinton ran out of gas, so Christopher jogged solo in Jerusalem," *Jerusalem Post*, April 11, 1994.
11 Marilyn Henry: "Tearful Clinton bids farewell to 'friend' Rabin," *Jerusalem Post*, Nov. 5, 1995.
12 David Graniewitz: "Private grief, public stance," *Jerusalem Post*, June 5, 1996.
13 *Ibid.*
14 David Bar-Illan: "'Der Spiegel' divides our nation," *Jerusalem Post*, Dec. 1, 1995.
15 Paul Wasserman: "Poor Taste," Letters to the Editor, *Jerusalem Post*, May 8, 1997.
16 Liat Collins: "Who really killed Yitzhak Rabin?," *Jerusalem Post*, Nov. 24, 1995.
17 *AP:* "Leah Rabin: Bodyguards told me gun was a toy pistol," *Jerusalem Post*, Nov. 7, 1995.
18 *Ibid.*

19   Raine Marcus: "Amir subdued in realistic courtroom reenactment," _Jerusalem Post_, Jan. 30, 1996.

20   Security man interviewed by _Israel Radio_, Nov. 5, 1995—the morning following the assassination.

21   Raine Marcus (Herb Keinon contributed): "Eyal leader held as suspected Amir conspirator," _Jerusalem Post_, Nov. 9, 1995.

22   Uri Dan and Dennis Eisenberg: "Truth, and nothing but," _Jerusalem Post_, Feb. 29, 1996.

23   Batsheva Tsur: "Avishai Raviv: from childhood trickster to GSS mole," _Jerusalem Post_, Nov. 20, 1995.

24   Steve Rodan: "Was Raviv under orders or out of line?," _Jerusalem Post_, Dec. 1, 1995.

25   Uri Dan and Dennis Eisenberg: "Truth, and nothing but," _Jerusalem Post_, Feb. 29, 1996.

26   Uri Dan and Dennis Eisenberg: "Schoolgirls speak up," _Jerusalem Post_, Feb. 1, 1996.

27   Raine Marcus: "Defense witness Ojalbo: Raviv told Amir Rabin must die," _Jerusalem Post_, March 11, 1996.

28   Uri Dan and Dennis Eisenberg: "Bring Raviv to Trial," _Jerusalem Post_, June 18, 1998.

29   Uri Dan and Dennis Eisenberg: "Lies in high places." _Jerusalem Post_, Dec. 14, 1995.

30   Steve Rodan: "Was Raviv under orders or out of line?," _Jerusalem Post_, Dec. 1, 1995.

31   Raine Marcus: "Yigal Amir's lawyers looking for Avishai Raviv," _Jerusalem Post_, June 19, 1996.

32   Alon Pinkas: "'Eyal leader Raviv was GSS agent.' Arrested due to failure to warn GSS of Amir," _Jerusalem Post_, Nov. 19, 1995.

33   Steve Rodan: "Was Raviv under orders or out of line?," _Jerusalem Post_, Dec. 1, 1995.

34   Uri Dan and Dennis Eisenberg: "Lies in high places." _Jerusalem Post_, Dec. 14, 1995.

35   Raine Marcus: "Yigal Amir's lawyers looking for Avishai Raviv," _Jerusalem Post_, June 19, 1996.

36   Batsheva Tsur: "Rabbi Elon: Raviv had support from authorities," _Jerusalem Post_, Nov. 28, 1995.

37   Steve Rodan: "Was Raviv under orders or out of line?," _Jerusalem Post_, Dec. 1, 1995.

38   Uri Dan and Dennis Eisenberg: "Schoolgirls speak up," _Jerusalem Post_, Feb. 1, 1996.

39   Alon Pinkas: "'Eyal leader Raviv was GSS agent.' Arrested due to failure to warn GSS of Amir," _Jerusalem Post_, Nov. 19, 1995.

40   Uri Dan and Dennis Eisenberg: "Schoolgirls speak up," _Jerusalem Post_, Feb. 1, 1996.

41   _Ibid._

42   Uri Dan and Dennis Eisenberg: "Lies in high places." _Jerusalem Post_, Dec. 14, 1995.

43   _Ibid._

44 Uri Dan and Dennis Eisenberg: "Truth, and nothing but," *Jerusalem Post*, Feb. 29, 1996.
45 Steve Rodan: "Was Raviv under orders or out of line?," *Jerusalem Post*, Dec. 1, 1995.
46 *Ibid.*
47 Michal Yudelman: "Winners, losers, and sounds of silence," *Jerusalem Post*, Nov. 24, 1995.
48 Uri Dan and Dennis Eisenberg: "The sting that backfired," *Jerusalem Post*, Nov. 30, 1995.
49 *Ibid.*
50 Liat Collins: "Who really killed Yitzhak Rabin?," *Jerusalem Post*, Nov. 24, 1995.
51 Aaron Lerner: ""Discrediting campaign," *Jerusalem Post*, Jan. 2, 1996.
52 Steve Rodan in "Ben-Yair, Beinish hold their tongues on Raviv case," *Jerusalem Post,* Dec. 1, 1995.
53 *Ibid.*
54 Steve Rodan: "Raviv knew Amir was assassin," *Jerusalem Post*, Dec. 1, 1995.
55 *Ibid.*
56 Uri Dan and Dennis Eisenberg: "Smoke Screen," *Jerusalem Post*, Dec. 22, 1995.
57 Steve Rodan: "Raviv knew Amir was assassin," *Jerusalem Post*, Dec. 1, 1995.
58 *Ibid.*
59 *Ibid.*
60 Uri Dan and Dennis Eisenberg: "The Sting that backfired" *Jerusalem Post*, Nov. 30, 1995.
61 Steve Rodan: "Was Raviv under orders or out of line?" *Jerusalem Post*, Dec. 1, 1995.
62 "'Rabin assassination plot' reporter kept off the air," *ICEJ News Service*, Oct. 29, 1997.
63 *Ibid.*
64 Raine Marcus: "Amir Defense argues for Manslaughter," *Jerusalem Post*, Mar. 18, 1996.
65 *Ibid.*
66 *Ibid.*
67 *Ibid.*
68 Raine Marcus and *Itim*: "Amir brothers remanded: Police suspect they belong to Kahane Hai," *Jerusalem Post*, Nov. 7, 1995.
69 Raine Marcus, Sarah Honig and Alon Pinkas: "Rabin assassinated. Pronounced dead at 11:15 p.m. after being shot," *Jerusalem Post*, Nov. 5, 1995.
70 *AP:* "Leah Rabin: Bodyguards told me gun was toy pistol," *Jerusalem Post*, Nov. 7, 1995.
71 *Ibid.*
72 Liat Collins: "Shahal rejects conspiracy theory," *Jerusalem Post*, Dec. 14, 1995.
73 Raine Marcus: "Amir subdued in realistic courtroom reenactment," *Jerusalem Post*, Jan. 30, 1996.
74 *Itim:* "Ichilov Director: Delay in getting Rabin to hospital probably not significant," *Jerusalem Post*, Dec. 1, 1995.
75 *Ibid.*

76 Dalia Rabin-Perlosoff in: "Rabin family airs doubts over his death 4 years ago," _ICEJ News Service_, Nov. 5, 1999.
77 Raine Marcus: "Amir Defense argues for Manslaughter," _Jerusalem Post_, Mar. 18, 1996.
78 Liat Collins: "Who really killed Yitzhak Rabin?" _Jerusalem Post_, Nov. 24, 1995.
79 _Ibid._
80 _Ibid._
81 Barry Chamish writing in: "Gillon Protest?" fax, Feb. 21, 1998.
82 _Ibid._
83 Uri Dan and Dennis Eisenberg: "Schoolgirls speak up," _Jerusalem Post_, Feb. 1, 1996.
84 Steve Rodan: "Ben-Yair, Beinish hold their tongues on Raviv case," _Jerusalem Post,_ Dec. 1, 1995.
85 "Rabin assassination anniversary tensions," _ICEJ News Service_, Nov. 5, 1997.
86 "Something fishy in 'Pig's Head' plot," _ICEJ News Service_, Dec. 30, 1997.
87 _Ibid._
88 _Ibid._
89 _Ibid._
90 Barry Chamash, quoted in: _Ibid._
91 _Ibid._
92 Emanuel Wilson, quoted in: _Ibid._
93 Aaron Peretz: "District Court judge denies bail for accused pig's head plotter," _Ha'aretz_, March 6, 1998.
94 _Ibid._

Chapter 6

1 _Israel's population also includes over 800,000 Muslims and some 250,000 Christians._
2 Sarah Honig: "Labor angry at hiring of security chief," _Jerusalem Post_, Dec. 19, 1997.
3 _Ibid._
4 Liat Collins: ""The tumultuous Knesset that was," _Jerusalem Post_, May 31, 1996.
5 _Ibid._
6 David Makovsky: "Eye on the government," _Jerusalem Post_, Dec. 20, 1996.
7 Editorial: "Inauspicious beginning," _Jerusalem Post_, Feb. 16, 1996.
8 Michal Yudelman and Sarah Honig: ""Stop attacking media, Netanyahu urges," _Jerusalem Post_, June 4, 1996.
9 _Ibid._
10 _Ibid._
11 _Ibid._
12 _Ibid._
13 Zvi Harel: "Former aide to premier sues most of media, _Ha'aretz,_ Feb. 13, 1998.
14 _Ibid._
15 Sarah Honig: "Should the PM watch his back?," _Jerusalem Post_, Oct. 10, 1997.

16 Allison Kaplan Sommer (Liat Collins contributed): "Prime minister slams article on Sara as 'evil,'" *Jerusalem Post*, Dec. 12, 1997.
17 *Ibid.*
18 Geoffrey Hansen: "Israel TV staff punished for 'false' report," *The Times* U.K.), May 28, 1998.
19 "Netanyahu deplores attempts to smear him,'" *ICEJ News Service*, Aug. 18, 1998.
20 Michal Yudelman: "Journalists accused of offering bribes for 'dirt' on Netanyahus," *Jerusalem Post*, Nov. 15, 1996.
21 *Ibid.*
22 Sarah Honig: "Should the PM watch his back?," *Jerusalem Post*, Oct. 10, 1997.
23 Ari Shavit: "Why we hate him: the real reason," *Ha'aretz*, Dec. 26, 1997.
24 Sarah Honig: "Should the PM watch his back?," *Jerusalem Post*, Oct. 10, 1997.
25 *Ibid.*
26 *Israel Radio*, Feb. 9, 1998.
27 "Rapprochment sought after Weizman shoots from the lip," *ICEJ News Service*, July 1, 1998.
28 Dan Nimrod: "Judging a Widow in Her Moment of Grief and Beyond," *Dawn Publishing*, June 19, 1996.
29 Editorial: "Netanyahu's challenge," *Jerusalem Post*, June 2, 1996.
30 Michal Yudelman: "Labor starts finger-pointing," *Jerusalem Post*, May 31, 1996.
31 *Panim Hadashot*, Nov. 10, 1995.
32 Leah Rabin, quoted in: "Rabin family airs doubts over his death 4 years ago," *ICEJ News Service*, Nov. 5, 1999.
33 Kevin Abrams writing in an Internet posting: "Greatness Still Awaits You Leah Rabin," July 3, 1996.
34 Sarah Honig: "TV election ad campaign ends," *Jerusalem Post*, May 28, 1996.
35 Moshe Sharett's Personal Diary, 1957. Vol. 8, p. 2301.
36 Sarah Honig: "TV election ad campaign ends," *Jerusalem Post*, May 28, 1996.
37 Yosef Goell: "A Likud government faces potential pitfalls beyond the peace process," *Jerusalem Post*, May 31, 1996.
38 Pinkas Sherut, p. 417. Quoted in "Peres: 'Without a secure border, the state faces annihilation in war," *Naviv*, Feb. 1996, p. 12.
39 *Yediot Aharonot*, Jan. 2, 1990. Quoted in *Ibid.*
40 Ari Stav: "Peres: 'Without a secure border, the state faces annihilation in war," *Naviv*, Feb. 1996, p. 13.
41 Moshe Kohn: "When shame is absent," *Jerusalem Post*, May 17, 1996.
42 Moshe Kohn: "Of shameless 'candor'," *Jerusalem Post*, March 15, 1996.
43 "Peres, The Fox Inside The Chicken Coop," Media Release, *Women For Israel's Tomorrow*, April 13, 1997.
44 Editorial: *Jerusalem Post*, May 13, 1997.
45 Sarah Honig: "Warding off the evil eye," *Jerusalem Post*, May 16, 1997.
46 Ari Stav: "Peres: 'Without a secure border, the state faces annihilation in war," *Naviv*, Feb. 1996, p. 12.

47   *Ibid.*

48   *Yediot Aharonot*, May 3, 1996. Quoted in: "Election Quotes to Note," *Middle East Intelligence Digest*, June 1996, p. 2.

49   Yosef Goell: "The proof of the pudding," *Jerusalem Post*, May 31, 1996.

50   Amotz Asa El: "Death of a statesman," *Jerusalem Post*, May 16, 1997.

51   Ari Stav: "Peres: 'Without a secure border, the state faces annihilation in war," *Naviv*, Feb. 1996, p. 4.

52   Shimon Peres, quoted in: *Ibid.*, p. 13.

53   Martin Sherman: "Peres's perfidy," *Jerusalem Post*, May 28, 1997.

54   Quoted in: "Peres: 'Without a secure border, the state faces annihilation in war," *Naviv*, Feb. 1996, p. 5.

55   Quoted in: *Ibid.*, p. 13.

56   Aaron Katz: "Truth and Revelation," *Jewish Press*, Aug. 9, 1996.

57   Ari Stav: "Peres: 'Without a secure border, the state faces annihilation in war," *Naviv*, Feb. 1996, p. 7.

58   *Ma'ariv*, Mar. 2, 1988.

59   Ari Stav: "Peres: 'Without a secure border, the state faces annihilation in war," *Naviv*, Feb. 1996, p. 7.

60   Quoted in: "Back Again To Rig The Elections," *Inside Israel*, March-April 1995, p. 2.

61   Quoted in: *Ibid.*

62   *Ibid.*, p. 8.

63   *Ibid.*

64   *Ibid.*

65   Sarah Honig: "If I campaign for thee, O Jerusalem," *Jerusalem Post*, Feb. 23, 1996.

66   *Ibid.*

67   *Ibid.*

68   Moshe Kohn: "When shame is absent," *Jerusalem Post*, May. 17, 1996.

69   Yossi Ben-Aharon, director-general of the Prime Minister's Office between 1986 and 1992, writing in: "A skilled manipulator," *Jerusalem Post*, May 22,1996.

70   *Ibid.*

71   Quoted in: "Back Again To Rig The Elections," *Inside Israel*, March-April 1995, p. 2.

72   Ezer Weizman, *On Eagles' Wings*, (Jerusalem: Steimatzky, 1976, p. 211.

73   Yoram Aridor: "A misplacing of confidence," *Jerusalem Post*, May 10,1994.

74   "Synopsis," *Naviv*, Jan. 1996, p. 11.

75   *Ibid.*

76   Zvi Harel: "Barak: If I were Palestinian, I'd also join terror group," *Ha'aretz*, March 6, 1998.

77   Liat Collins: "His Own Man," *Jerusalem Post*, Jan. 3, 1997.

78   Aaron Katz: "Truth and Revelation," *Jewish Press*, Aug. 9, 1996.

79   *Ibid.*

80   Yohanan Ramati: "A virus called defeatism," *Jerusalem Post*, Nov. 19, 1996.

81   "Labor plan saw Old City sovereignty relinquished," *Middle East Digest*, September/October 1996.

82   *Ibid.*

83 Allan E. Shapiro: "A government of exiles is what it looks like," *Jerusalem Post*, Dec. 20, 1996.

84 Arieh O' Sullivan (Batsheva Tsur contributed): "Netanyahu defends suspension of Shahor," *Jerusalem Post*, Nov. 4, 1996.

85 Arieh O' Sullivan, Liat Collins and Sarah Honig: "Netanyahu suspends Shahor as negotiator. Decision a scandal and embarrassment – Peres," *Jerusalem Post*, Nov. 3, 1996.

86 Michal Yudelman and Liat Collins: "Knesset turmoil follows reports Peres advised Arafat," *Jerusalem Post*, Nov. 19, 1996.

87 Eldad Beck: "Peres: When time is right I will move to save peace process," *Jerusalem Post*, Oct. 3, 1996.

88 Steve Rodan: "The boomerang effect of freezing ties," *Jerusalem Post*, Dec. 27, 1996.

89 Published in Eldad Beck's: "Peres: When time is right I will move to save peace process," *Jerusalem Post*, Oct. 3, 1996.

90 Sarah Honig: "Likud probe panel resigns," *Jerusalem Post*, Nov. 28, 1997.

91 "Netanyahu's govt. survives, budget is passed," *ICEJ News Service*, Jan. 6, 1998.

92 Lili Galili: "Foreign Minister Sharansky?," *Ha'aretz*, Feb. 13, 1998.

93 Ari Shavit: "He hates us, too," *Ha'aretz*, Dec. 26, 1997.

94 Editorial: "Clinton's intervention," *Jerusalem Post*, May 30, 1996.

95 *Ibid.*

96 Quoted in: "Three Days that Shook the World," *Middle East Intelligence Digest*, June 1996, p. 4.

97 AndreaLevin: "Media votes 'No' to Israeli democracy," *Jerusalem Post*, June 21, 1996.

98 "Clinton's Campaign King to Help Israel's Opposition," *ICEJ News Service*, Dec. 2, 1998.

99 *Ibid.*

100 "Election 99 Developments," *ICEJ News Service*, Jan. 18, 1999.

101 Michal Yudelman: "Ben-Eliezer: Weak Arab vote caused Labor's loss," *Jerusalem Post*, June 2, 1996.

102 Evelyn Gordon: "Court refuses to overturn election results," *Jerusalem Post*, July 5, 1996.

103 Evelyn Gordon: "Central elections panel: Labor's fraud charges almost entirely baseless," *Jerusalem Post*, July 4, 1996.

104 Ari Shavit: "He hates us, too," *Ha'aretz*, Dec. 26, 1997.

105 Editorial: "Foot-in-mouth disease," *Jerusalem Post*, Oct. 24, 1997.

106 *Ibid.*

107 "Living by the sword," *Middle East Digest*, October 1997.

108 *Israel Radio*, April 18, 1999.

109 Steve Liebowitz: "Binyamin Netanyahu is not John Jay Sullivan," *Jerusalem Post*, July 9, 1996.

110 *Ibid.*

111 Steve Liebowitz: "They've got his number(s)," *Jerusalem Post*, Aug. 11, 1996.

112 *Ibid.*

113 *Ibid.*

114 Steve Liebowitz: "Binyamin Netanyahu is not John Jay Sullivan," _Jerusalem Post_, July 9, 1996.

115 Steve Liebowitz: "They've got his number(s)," _Jerusalem Post_, Aug. 11, 1996.

116 Eli Groner: "Pressing the Issue," _In Jerusalem_, Dec. 20, 1996.

117 _Ibid._

118 _Ibid._

119 _Ibid._

120 _Ibid._

121 _Ibid._

122 _Ibid._

123 _Ibid._

124 _Ibid._

125 _Ibid._

126 Ari Shavit: "All on his own," _Ha'aretz_, Dec. 26, 1997.

127 Steve Rodan: "Arabs are cutting off relations with Israel," _Jerusalem Post_, Oct. 18, 1996.

128 Uri Dan and Dennis Eisenberg: "Our local quislings," _Jerusalem Post_, Aug. 29, 1996.

129 Sarah Honig: "Uzi Landau slams Ben-Eliezer's 'false peace' plan," _Jerusalem Post_, Jan. 13, 1996.

130 _Ha'aretz_, Dec. 21, 1998.

131 "Beilin lobbying for independent Palestine in 2000," _ICEJ News Service_, Jan. 22, 1999.

132 David Makovsky: "The candidate now becomes the leader," _Jerusalem Post_, June 7, 1996.

133 "Laughing the world to scorn," _Middle East Digest_, November/December 1997.

134 "US-Israel tensions simmer," _ICEJ News Service_, Dec. 11, 1998.

135 _Ibid._

136 Colonel David Hackworth in a January 1998 interview on the Baltimore-based Zoe Show.

137 _Ibid._

138 "America's Jews and Israel's leader," _U.S. News & World Report_, Nov. 17, 1997.

139 Jay Bushinsky: "TV: European heads attack PM in letter, _Jerusalem Post_, Nov. 11, 1997.

140 _Ibid._

141 Israeli official interviewed by _The Jerusalem Post_ and quoted in: "Chiraq rejects Israel's offer to leave Lebanon," _ICEJ News Service_, Sept. 6, 1998.

142 "Europe to boycott Jewish goods," _ICEJ News Service_, Aug. 6, 1998.

143 Geoffrey Hansen: "Arab boycott," _The Times_ (U.K), Aug. 8, 1998.

144 "Laughing the world to scorn," _Middle East Digest_, November/December 1997.

145 _Ibid._

146 "British FM warns: Israel too must comply with UN resolutions," _ICEJ News Service_, Feb. 11, 1998.

147 e.g. _Middle East Diary 1917-1956_ by Colonel Richard Meinertzhagen, Chief of British Intelligence in the Middle East at that time.

148   Editorial: "The Mellor Affair," *Jerusalem Post*, Sept. 27, 1992.
149   Uri Dan and Dennis Eisenberg: "With Prejudice: 'But there's a time to serve and a time to sin,'" *Jerusalem Post*, April 9, 1993.
150   Kenneth Y. Tsui: "It Wasn't the Sex Scandal," *Wall Street Journal*, Sept. 24, 1996.
151   Uzi Benziman: "The death of Sami Karameh," *Ha'aretz*, March. 20, 1998.
152   Uri Dan and Dennis Eisenberg: "The British tradition," *Jerusalem Post*, March 19, 1998.
153   Liat Collins: "Rabin sets out vision of final settlement," *Jerusalem Post*, Oct. 6, 1995.
154   *Ibid.*
155   *Ibid.*
156   *Ibid.*
157   *Ibid.*
158   *Ibid.*
159   Ahmed Tibi, *Ha'aretz*, Nov. 5, 1996.
160   "PA support for Saddam continues," *ICEJ News Service*, Feb. 16, 1998.
161   *The Jerusalem Institute for Western Defence*, Vol. 9, Digest 9, Sept. 1997, p. 10.
162   David Rudge: "Israeli Arab loyalties," *Jerusalem Post*, Dec. 29, 1992.
163   Dan Izenberg: "Harish orders probe of Mahameed," *Jerusalem Post*, Dec. 29, 1992.
164   Ari Shavit: "All on his own," *Ha'aretz*, Dec. 26, 1997.
165   Ari Shavit: "Why we hate him: the real reason," *Ha'aretz*, Dec. 26, 1997.
166   *Ibid.*
167   *Ibid.*
168   *Ibid.*
169   Lili Galili: "Just say 'Bibi' before bedtime," *Ha'aretz*, March 3, 1998.
170   Ari Shavit: "Netanyahu's secret," *Ha'aretz*, March. 4, 1999.
171   Patrick Goodenough: "Election feature: US consultants 'trivialize' campaign," *ICEJ News Service*, May 14, 1999.
172   "Is the US again interfering in an Israeli election?" *ICEJ News Service*, March 7, 1999.
173   "Leftist professor would be happy if Sharon died," *ICEJ News Service*, May 14, 1999.
174   Alon Pinkas: "New Chief of Staff faces greatest challenges ever," *Jerusalem Post*, Oct. 7, 1994.
175   Editorial: "PA minimum, Israeli maximum," *Jerusalem Post*, Feb. 12, 1995.
176   Alon Pinkas: "New Chief of Staff faces greatest challenges ever," *Jerusalem Post*, Oct. 7, 1994.
177   Alon Pinkas: "Shahak to be appointed next Chief of General Staff," *Jerusalem Post*, Oct. 7, 1994.
178   Amnon Lipkin-Shahak speaking on *Israel Radio*, Jan. 4, 1999.
179   Sarah Honig: "Netanyahu, PM to discuss transfer of power," *Jerusalem Post*, June 4, 1996.
180   "Mordechai Sacked, Shoots to Top of Centrist List," *ICEJ News Service*, Jan. 25, 1999.
181   Liat Collins: "Knesset briefs," *Jerusalem Post*, Jan 4, 1996.

182 Sarah Honig: "Netanyahu, PM to discuss transfer of power," _Jerusalem Post_, June 4, 1996.

183 _Ibid._

184 Yitzhak Mordechai in: "Mordechai drops out, endorses Barak," _ICEJ News Service_, May 16, 1999.

185 _Israel Radio_, March 7, 2000.

186 "Mordechai accused of sexual harrassment," _ICEJ News Service_, March 8, 2000.

187 _Israel Radio_, March 10, 2000.

188 "Netanyahu's mentor to challenge him for top Likud post," _ICEJ News Service_, Jan. 11, 1999.

189 "Begin declares his candidacy," _ICEJ News Service_, Dec. 28, 1998.

190 Benny Begin speaking with _Israel Radio_, May 19, 1999.

191 Julie Stahl, CNS Jerusalem Bureau Chief in: "Israel marks Rabin's death: Netanyahu detained by police," _ICEJ News Service_, Oct. 22, 1999.

192 _Israel Radio_, Feb. 16, 1999.

193 "Lord Levy caught in NPO scandal," _ICEJ News Service_, Feb. 25, 2000.

194 _Israel Radio_, Feb. 16, 1999.

195 _Ibid._

196 _Israel Radio_, Jan. 3, 2000.

197 _Israel Radio_, Jan. 4, 2000.

198 "Israel releases last batch of Palestinian terrorists," _ICEJ News Service_, Dec. 29, 1999.

199 _Ibid._

200 _Israel Radio_, Jan. 11, 2000.

201 "Levy: Syria intransigent; safe passage route set to open,"" _ICEJ News Service_, Sept. 27, 1999.

202 "Tamir advising PA on absorbing refugees," _ICEJ News Service_, Sept. 22, 1999.

203 _Israel Radio_, Jan. 14, 2000.

204 See p. 113.

205 "Students uncover Temple Mount artifacts discarded by WAQF," _ICEJ News Service_, Dec. 29, 1999.

206 _Ibid._

207 "Safe passage differences unresolved," _ICEJ News Service_, Oct. 4, 1999.

208 "Safe passage" only in name," _ICEJ News Service_, Nov. 1, 1999.

209 _Israel Radio_, Feb. 24, 2000.

210 "Hamas terror cell crushed just in time," _ICEJ News Service_, March 3, 2000.

211 _Ibid._

212 Yitzhak Rabin, quoted in: "Rabin's giving away of the Golan," _Jerusalem Post_, Dec. 3, 1993.

213 Lt.-Gen. Ehud Barak, quoted in: "In their own words," _Middle East Intelligence Digest_, Oct. 1994, p. 5.

Chapter 7

1 _Websters New Universal Unabridged Dictionary_ (Second Edition), (New York: Simon & Schuster, 1986).

2 _Ibid._

3 _Ibid._

4   *Ibid.*
5   See pp. 42, 43.
6   *Ibid.*
7   Ramon Bennett, *Philistine: The Great Deception* (Keno, OR: Shekinah, 1997), pp. 138,139.
8   *The World Almanac and Book of Facts 1997* (Mahwah, NJ: K-III Reference Corp.), pp. 785,788.
9   *Ibid.*, pp. 785,788.
10 King Hussein in an interview with *Al-Nahar Al-Arabi*, Dec. 26, 1981.
11 King Hussein in an interview with *Al-Anba*, Oct. 30, 1984.
12 Former Crown Prince Hussein addressing the Jordanian National Assembly and reported in: *Al-Destour*, Feb. 5, 1970.
13 Yasser Arafat reported in: *New Republic*, July 1974.
14 Abu Iyad interviewed in: *Al-Majallah*, Nov. 8, 1988.
15 For serious documentation see Bennett, *Philistine: The Great Deception*, pp. 105-162.
16 *Pravda*, Sept. 2, 1964.
17 See pp. 13-17.
18 See p. 32.
19 *Ibid.*
20 See p. 141.
21 The proverb quoted by Basam Abu Sharif, PLO spokesman and Arafat's Aide, *Kuwait News Agency,* May 1986.
22 Source: *Realities, A Journal of Timely Analysis,* reprinted in *Dispatch From Jerusalem,* Jan.-Feb. 1994, p. 2.
23 *Ibid.*
24 Paul Josef Goebbels quoted in: Benjamin Netanyahu, *A Place Among The Nations: Israel And The World* (New York: Bantam, 1993), footnote p. 27.
25 "Arafat demands Israel sanctions," *Reuters*, Aug. 14, 1998.
26 *Ibid.*
27 *Ibid.*
28 Self-Portrait of a Hero: The Letters of Jonatan Netanyahu. Jonatan (Yoni) Netanyahu, the older brother of Israeli former prime minister, Bibi Netanyahu, was the only commando killed when, on July 4, 1976, an Israeli rescue team saved more than 100 hostages in a raid on Uganda's Entebbe airport. Yoni led the raid after Arab terrorists hijacked an Air France airliner and directed it to the Idi Amin-led African nation.
      Shortly after Yoni was killed in the Entebbe raid a collection of his letters to family and friends was compiled and published in a book entitled "Self-Portrait of a Hero: The Letters of Jonatan Netanyahu."
29 John Laffin, *The PLO Connections* (London: Transworld, 1982), p. 18.
30 *Ibid.*
31 "More rot at Oslo's core," *Middle East Digest,* Dec. 1996.
32 Quoted from a communique to the author from then *Dagen* journalist, Lars-Toralf Storstrand, Sept. 22, 1998.
33 "The Norway Connection II," *Middle East Digest,* Sept./Oct. 1996.
34 "More rot at Oslo's core," *Middle East Digest,* Dec. 1966.
35 *AP:* "Norwegian peacemaker gets UN post," *Jerusalem Post,* May 26, 1994.

36 Editorial: "The UN antisemitism resolution," _Jerusalem Post,_ March 13, 1994.

37 _Israel Radio,_ Aug. 20, 1994.

38 _Jerusalem Post,_ July 9, 1982. Cited in: Dr. Irving Moskowitz, _Should America Guarantee Israel's Safety?,_ (New York: Americans For A Safe Israel, 1993), p. 24.

39 Greer Fay Cashman: "Jordanian envoy goes public – thanks to his Norwegian host," _Jerusalem Post,_ Jan. 20, 1995.

40 David Makovsky: "Norway agrees to extend TIPH mandate," _Jerusalem Post,_ Aug. 13, 1996.

41 _AP:_ "Terje Larsen named to Norwegian cabinet," _Jerusalem Post,_ Oct. 27, 1996.

42 "More rot at Oslo's core," _Middle East Digest,_ Dec. 1996.

43 _Ibid._

44 Stan Goodenough: "No honest broker," _Jerusalem Post,_ May 8, 1996.

45 _AP:_ "Terje Larsen named to Norwegian cabinet," _Jerusalem Post,_ Oct. 27, 1996.

46 "More rot at Oslo's core," _Middle East Digest,_ Dec. 1966.

47 _Ibid._

48 _Ibid._

49 _AP:_ "Terje Larsen resigns after month in Norwegian government," _Jerusalem Post,_ Nov. 28, 1996.

50 News agencies: "Arafat opens European trip," _Jerusalem Post,_ Oct. 29, 1996.

51 _Ibid._

52 _Ibid._

53 Quoted from a communique to the author from then _Dagen_ journalist, Lars-Toralf Storstrand, Sept. 22, 1998.

54 _AP:_ "Peres, Arafat: Progress in Oslo talks," _Jerusalem Post,_ Jan. 23, 1994.

55 Michael Parks writing for _Los Angeles Times:_ "Israelis, Palestinians posed as professors in secret Oslo talks," _Jerusalem Post,_ Sept. 15, 1993.

56 David Makovsky: "When enemies made peace – a night to remember," _Jerusalem Post,_ Aug. 19, 1994.

57 _Reuter:_ "Holst widow to work for UNRWA," _Jerusalem Post,_ June 19, 1994.

58 "The Norway Connection II," _Middle East Digest,_ Sept./Oct. 1996.

59 Quoted from the book "As I See It, Part Two by a former secretary-general of Norway's Labor Party, Haakon Lie, and quoted in: "Norway's foreign minister Bjorn Tore Godal demanded Israel's annihilation in '71," _Dagen,_ May 3, 1996.

60 Steve Rodan: "Norwegian leaders supported termination of Jewish state," _Jerusalem Post,_ May 5, 1996.

61 _Ibid._

62 _AP:_ "Norwegian peacemaker gets UN post," _Jerusalem Post,_ May 26, 1994.

63 "The Norway Connection II," _Middle East Digest,_ Sept./Oct. 1996.

64 "More rot at Oslo's core," _Middle East Digest,_ Dec. 1996.

65 Ben Lynfield: "Morocco hits back at Amnesty," _Jerusalem Post,_ Feb. 28, 1990.

66 Boutros-Ghali quoted in "An ill wind blowing," _Middle East Intelligence Digest,_ March/April 1995, p. 8.

67 _Ibid._

68   Stan Goodenough: "No honest broker," Jerusalem *Post,* May 8, 1996.
69   Shimon Peres quoted by: *The Jerusalem Institute For Western Defense: Periodic New Digest from the Arab World and Iran,* Digest 6, Dec. 1994, p.1.
70   "Dark Night of the Soul," *Time,* Sept. 14, 1998.
71   *Ibid.*
72   *Ibid.*
73   *Ibid.*
74   This figure given in: "Covenant deadline unmet," *Jerusalem Post,* Oct. 27, 1996. Actual number of PLO Police could exceed 80,000.
75   Arafat quoted in: "A counterproductive letter, *Jerusalem Post,* Dec. 6, 1996.
76   Feisal al-Husseini, member of the PLO negotiating team, Nov. 1994, quoted in: "Terrorism and the PLO: September 13 plus seven months," *Bulletin of the Jerusalem Institute for Western Defence,* Bulletin 2, June 1994, p. 11.
77   "Arafat calls for jihad, makes bid for Christian support," *ICEJ News Service,* Aug. 6, 1999.
78   "Graft in his government weakens Arafat's grip," *Business Week,* Aug. 25, 1997, p. 61.
79   *Ibid.*
80   *Radio Monte Carlo,* June 30, 1999. Reported in *Jerusalem Institute of Western Defence,* Digest 8, Aug. 1998, p. 3.
81   "Corruption in the PLO's financial empire," *Middle East Digest,* June, 1998.
82   *Ibid.*
83   *Ibid.*
84   *Ibid.*
85   *Ibid.*
86   Tom Gross: "Hackers uncover secret billions of Arafat's PLO," *Electronic Telegraph,* Dec. 5, 1999.
87   Former Prime Minister Netanyahu in a speech to foreign diplomats in Jerusalem on May 22, 1998. He quoted a figure of 4.1 billion shekels given to the PLO from 1995 - 1997 by Israel and said the figure for 1998 was not yet available.
88   *Ha'aretz,* Oct. 8, 1999.
89   Editorial: "Puzzling negotiating tactics," *Jerusalem Post,* May 2, 1993.
90   Former Prime Minister Netanyahu in a speech to foreign diplomats in Jerusalem on May 22, 1998. He quoted a figure of 4.1 billion shekels given to the PLO from 1995 - 1997 by Israel and said the figure for 1998 was not yet available.
91   Former Prime Minister Netanyahu in a speech to foreign diplomats in Jerusalem on May 22, 1998. He quoted a figure of 110,000 Palestinian workers per day.
92   Editorial: "Covenant deadline unmet," *Jerusalem Post,* Oct. 27, 1996.
93   *Ibid.*
94   Shmuel Katz: "Less cozy, more clear," *Jerusalem Post,* June 21, 1996.
95   Emil L. Fackenheim: "The right to be here," *Jerusalem Post,* Jan. 3, 1996.
96   "PNC votes to amend Palestinian covenant," *Jerusalem Post,* April 25, 1996.
97   *Ibid.*
98   *Jerusalem Post,* April 25, 1996.
99   *Jerusalem Post,* April 26, 1996.
100 *Ibid.*
101 Editorial: "Covenant deadline unmet," *Jerusalem Post,* Oct. 27, 1996.
102 *Jerusalem Post,* April 26, 1996.
103 Sarah Honig: "Netanyahu cautious over covenant changes," *Jerusalem Post,* April 26, 1996.

104 "The PNC Covenant Sham," *Jewish Press,* May 3, 1996.
105 *Ibid.*
106 *Ibid.*
107 *Ibid.*
108 *Ibid.*
109 Editorial: "Footnote to the covenant," *Jerusalem Post,* May 8, 1996.
110 *Ibid.*
111 *Ibid.*
112 Shmuel Katz: "Mischief by other means," *Jerusalem Post,* May 28, 1996.
113 *Washington Post* Correspondent: "Christopher: Covenant has been changed," *Jerusalem Post,* May 27, 1996.
114 *Ibid.*
115 Editorial: "The Covenant deadline," *Jerusalem Post,* May 6, 1996.
116 *Ibid.*
117 Editorial: "Covenant deadline unmet," *Jerusalem Post,* Oct. 27, 1996.
118 *Israel Radio,* June 24, 1996.
119 Moshe Zak: "Cairo: Land for threats," *Jerusalem Post,* June 26, 1996.
120 *Reuter:* "Israeli press barred from Gaddafi news conference, *Jerusalem Post,* June 24, 1996.
121 Evelyn Gordon: "Gov't.: PA Charter must be amended," *Jerusalem Post,* Jan. 27, 1997.
122 Moshe Zak: "It takes two to reconcile," *Jerusalem Post,* June 24, 1996.
123 *Syrian News Agency,* Feb. 1, 1998. Reported in *Jerusalem Institute of Western Defence,* Digest 3, March 1998.
124 *Jerusalem Post* Staff and news agencies: ""Netanyahu: I'm disappointed with Arafat letter," *Jerusalem Post,* July 25, 1996.
125 "Israel annoyed about Clinton's itinerary," *ICEJ News Service,* Dec. 7, 1998.
126 *Jerusalem Post* quoted in *Ibid.*
127 David Makovsky: "Clinton raises Palestinian expectations," *Jerusalem Post,* Dec. 15, 1998.
128 *CNN*'s Jean Meserve quoting Hilary Rodham Clinton, March 11, 1999.
129 "THERE IS NO PEACE... the Show of Hands Was Totally Bogus," *Los Angeles Times Syndicate.* Reprinted in *Christians For Israel Today,* First Quarter 1999, p. 4.
130 *Ibid.*
131 "Israeli Suspension of Withdrawals Remains in Effect," *ICEJ News Service,* Dec. 7, 1998.
132 *Ma'ariv,* Dec. 6, 1998.
133 David Makovsky: "Netanyahu wants deeds, not words," *Jerusalem Post,* Dec. 15, 1998.
134 Yossi Beilin: "A lot of needless fuss," *Jerusalem Post,* Oct. 30, 1996.
135 Emil L. Fackenheim: "The right to be here," *Jerusalem Post,* Jan. 3, 1996.
136 Yasser Arafat speaking on *Jordan Television,* Sept. 13, 1995.
137 Jibril Rajoub quoted in an Israel Government Press Office release, June 3, 1998.
138 *Ibid.*
139 Yasser Arafat quoted in *Ha'aretz,* and reprinted in *Arm of Salvation* Newsletter, Sept. 1998.

140 *Ibid.*

141 *Ha'aretz,* Aug. 16, 1998.

142 Israel Government Press Office, Sept. 13, 1998.

143 P. David Hornik: "A selective myopia," *Jerusalem Post,* Jan. 14, 1997.

144 Patrick Goodenough: "Palestinian security forces," *Jerusalem Post,* June 9, 1997.

145 Steve Rodan: "Palestinian have 80,000 fighters defense sources say," *Jerusalem Post,* Sept. 27, 1996.

146 Editorial: "Siamese twins: Arafat and Saddam," *Jerusalem Post,* Nov. 19, 1998.

147 "PLO prepares youth for conflict," *ICEJ News Service,* Sept. 7, 1998.

148 *Ibid.*

149 *Ibid.*

150 *Ibid.*

151 Editorial: "Siamese twins: Arafat and Saddam," *Jerusalem Post,* Nov. 19, 1998.

152 Muhammed Sabih interviewed on *Orbit Television,* Oct. 24. 1998 and published in *Jerusalem Institute For Western Defence,* Digest 12, 1998, p. 5.

153 "GSS: Many PA security officials are wanted terrorists," *ICEJ News Service,* June 7, 1999.

154 *Ibid.*

155 Editorial: "Two wrongs," *Jerusalem Post,* Feb. 10, 1997.

156 "PA-Hamas clashes in Gaza following death sentence," *ICEJ News Service,* March 12, 1999.

157 *Ibid.*

158 "Rajoub Denies PA Freed Suspects in Killings of Americans," *ICEJ News Service,* Jan. 29, 1999.

159 *Ibid.*

160 *Ibid.*

161 *Ibid.*

162 *Ibid.*

163 *Ibid.*

164 *Ibid.*

165 *Ibid.*

166 "Terror victim's mother recalls Clinton's promise – and waits," *ICEJ News Service,* June 18, 1999.

167 *Ibid.*

168 *Ibid.*

169 "Reduction of Jail Terms Causes Row," *ICEJ News Service,* Feb. 5, 1999.

170 *Ibid.*

171 *Ibid.*

172 *Ibid.*

173 "Israeli Suspension of Withdrawals Remains in Effect," *ICEJ News Service,* Dec. 7, 1998.

174 Jeremy Holt: "War of Words on Mideast Peace Pact," *International Herald Tribune,* Nov. 17, 1998.

175 "Hillary's Palestine: Blunder or test balloon," *ICEJ News Service,* May 8, 1998.

176 *Al Hayat Al-Jadida,* July 2, 1998.

177   *Ibid.* Nov. 7, 1998.
178   Moshe Zak: "Soil from which it springs," *Jerusalem Post,* Jan. 10, 1997.
179   P. David Hornik: "A selective myopia," *Jerusalem Post,* Jan. 14, 1997.
180   *Ibid.*
181   Moshe Zak: "Soil from which it springs," *Jerusalem Post,* Jan. 10, 1997.
182   For documented examples see Bennett, *Philistine: The Great Deception,* pp. 30, 31.
183   Suleiman Al-Khash writing in *Al-Thaura,* the Ba'ath party newspaper, May 3, 1968.
184   Editorial: "The authority transfer," *Jerusalem Post,* Aug. 26, 1994.
185   "US Congress to stop funding PA TV and Radio," *ICEJ News Service,* Aug. 31, 1998.
186   David Bar-Illan, Aug. 9, 1998.
187   The Fatah Constitution is at: http://www.fateh.org/e_public/constitution.htm.
188   Yasser Arafat quoted in "Arafat demands Israel sanctions," *Reuters* report in *New Zealand Herald,* Aug. 14, 1998.
189   Michael East: "War of Words on Mideast Peace Pact," *International Herald Tribune,* Nov. 17, 1998.
190   Dan Izenberg: "Unwanted neighbors," *Jerusalem Post,* Dec. 5, 1997.
191   *Israel Radio,* May 8, 1997.
192   "News in brief," *Jerusalem Post,* May 15, 1997.
193   "Arab Lawmaker Encourages the Murder of Land-Dealers," *ICEJ News Service,* June 24, 1998.
194   David Harris: "JNF: Arab real estate purchases prove land-reform plan is bad," *Jerusalem Post,* May 22, 1997.
195   *Ibid.*
196   *Ibid.*
197   "New PA Law Outlaws Israeli Ownership of Land in 'Palestine'," *ICEJ News Service,* Dec. 7, 1998.
198   *Ibid.*
199   *Ibid.*
200   *Ibid.*
201   Yasser Arafat quoted in: "Beyond Hebron ... the future is now," *Jerusalem Post,* Dec. 13, 1996.
202   Yasser Arafat addressed in an advertisement inserted by R. Joseph Gripkey for "Medlabs – Palestine" (a division of "Children International"), *Jerusalem Post,* May 31, 1996.
203   David Makovsky: "PM: Goal of peace is to separate Israelis, Palestinians," *Jerusalem Post,* Jan. 24, 1995.
204   *Ibid.*
205   *Ibid.*
206   "Peace and 'Separation'," *Jerusalem Institute of Western Defence,* Bulletin 3, Sept. 1997.
207   Liat Collins: ""Mission of goodwill - or mission impossible?," *Jerusalem Post,* Aug. 15, 1997.
208   *Ibid.*
209   "Peace and 'Separation'," *Jerusalem Institute of Western Defence,* Bulletin 3, Sept. 1997.
210   *Ma'ariv,* Aug. 11, 1997.

211 Liat Collins: "Mission of goodwill - or mission impossible?," *Jerusalem Post*, Aug. 15, 1997.
212 *Ibid.*
213 *AP:* "Israeli Arab delegation arrives in Syria," *Jerusalem Post*, Aug. 10, 1997.
214 "Population Up, Immigration Down," *ICEJ News Service*, Jan. 4, 1999.
215 "Peace and 'Separation'," *Jerusalem Institute of Western Defence*, Bulletin 3, Sept. 1997.
216 i.e. "Israeli Arab arrested for Megiddo murders," *ICEJ News Service*, Nov. 16, 1999.
217 i.e. "Israeli Arabs implicated in Tiberias, Haifa car bombs," *ICEJ News Service*, Sept. 8, 1999.
218 i.e. "Two explosions rock northern Israel," *ICEJ News Service*, Sept. 5, 1999.
219 "Arab candidate for prime minister," *ICEJ News*, March 26, 1999.
220 David Makovsky: "The criminal drive," *Jerusalem Post*, Aug. 7, 1998.
221 David Makovsky: "The road to terrorism," *Jerusalem Post*, Aug. 24, 1998.
222 David Makovsky: "The criminal drive," *Jerusalem Post*, Aug. 7, 1998.
223 *Ibid.*
224 *Ibid.*
225 Documented examples are given in Chapter 9 - "The Media," Ramon Bennett, *Philistine: The Great Deception.*
226 *Ibid.*
227 *Ibid.*
228 Peter Jennings quoted by Kevin E. Abrams, Israel's Representative for Holocaust Truth, Aug. 5, 1996.
229 Frank Sesno speaking on *CNN Live*, Jan. 12, 1999.
230 Drudge Report, Feb. 21, 1998.
231 ABC's Tel Aviv Bureau Chief Bill Seamans quoted in Jim Lederman, *Battle Lines: The American Media and the Intifada* (New York: Henry Holt, 1992), p. 138.
232 David Bar-Illan, *Eye on the Media* (Jerusalem: *The Jerusalem Post*, 1993), p. 102.
233 Committee on Accuracy on Middle East Reporting in America.
234 "Guest Report: CAMERA Charges Reckless Anti-Israel Bias at CNN," *ICEJ News Service*, Feb. 18, 1998.
235 *Ibid.*
236 *AP:* "7 Gunmen try to kill Mubarak," *Nashville Banner*, June 26, 1995.
237 See: Gary H. Kah, *En Route to Global Occupation* (Lafayette, LA: Huntington House, 1992).
238 "The Myth of UN Fairness to Israel," *Dispatch From Jerusalem*, 3rd Quarter, 1991.
239 Marilyn Henry: "UN ignores partition vote jubilee," *Jerusalem Post*, Nov. 28, 1997.
240 Documented examples are given in Chapter 8 - "The United Nations," Ramon Bennett, *Philistine: The Great Deception.*
241 *Ibid.*
242 Editorial: "The UN and its allies," *Jerusalem Post*, May 10, 1996.
243 *Ibid.*
244 *Associated Press*, Feb. 24, 1998.

245 "Netanyahu slams European boycott move," _ICEJ News Service_, May 20, 1998.

246 _Ibid._

247 David Makovsky: "Levy wants to explain to EU why Israel won't allow Orient House visits," _Jerusalem Post_, Aug. 19, 1996.

248 Steve Rodan: "EU questions Israel's right to Jerusalem," _Jerusalem Post_, March 11, 1999.

249 "EU recognizes Palestinians' right to a state," _ICEJ News Service_, March 26, 1999.

250 _Ibid._

251 _Ibid._

252 _Ibid._

253 Gamal Abdel Nasser quoted by Moshe Sharon: "Mideast security after Saddam," _Jerusalem Post_, Nov. 23, 1990.

254 _Reuter:_ "EU heads slam settlements," _Jerusalem Post_, Dec. 15, 1996.

255 "UN Arab group calls for boycott of Jerusalem's 50th anniversary events," _ICEJ News Service_, March 6, 1998.

256 Dr. Len Horowitz in a published interview with _Common Ground Magazine_, May, 1999.

257 Editorial: "Reconstructing mass destruction," _Jerusalem Post_, June 20, 1996.

258 _Ibid._

259 _Ibid._

260 Gerald M. Steinberg: "Cynical use of emotion," _Jerusalem Post_, July 29, 1996.

261 Editorial: "Reconstructing mass destruction," _Jerusalem Post_, June 20, 1996.

262 _Ibid._

263 Editorial: "Lebanon's French connection," _Jerusalem Post_, May 5, 1996.

264 Moshe Zak: "Crisis over, now for the next," _Jerusalem Post_, Oct. 25, 1996.

265 Sam Orbaum: "Only France," _Jerusalem Post_, July 15, 1996.

266 David Makovsky: "Behind Chirac's foreign policy activism," _Jerusalem Post_, Oct. 25, 1996.

267 _Ibid._

268 Douglas Davis: ""UK plans to pressure Israel when it assumes EU presidency," _Jerusalem Post_, Dec. 19, 1997.

269 "England has a plan, the US 'doesn't'," _ICEJ News Service_, March 6, 1998.

270 "Blair increases aid for Palestinians," _The Times_ (U.K.), May 28, 1998.

271 _Ibid._

272 _Ibid._

273 Documentation is given in Chapter 7 - "Palestine," Ramon Bennett, _Philistine: The Great Deception._

274 Joan Peters, _From Time Immemorial: The Origins of The Arab-Jewish Conflict Over Palestine_ (London: Michael Joseph, 1984), p. 262.

275 Documentation is given in Chapter 7 - "Palestinian Refugees," Ramon Bennett, _Philistine: The Great Deception._

276 _Ibid._

277 _Ibid._

278 _Ibid._

279 _Ibid._

280 _Ibid._

281 "MI5 failed to warn Israel of planned bombing," *ICEJ News Service*, Nov. 3, 1997.
282 *Ibid.*
283 *Ibid.*
284 *Ibid.*
285 *Ibid.*

Chapter 8

1 "The Myth of America," *Christians For Israel Today*, First Quarter 1999, p. 16.
2 *Ibid.*
3 *Ibid.*
4 *Ibid.*
5 *Ibid.*
6 *Ibid.*
7 *Ibid.*
8 *Ibid.*
9 *Ibid.*
10 *Ibid.*
11 *Ibid.*
12 *Ibid.*
13 *Ibid.*
14 *Ibid.*
15 "Our Greatest Danger–Signed Undertakings of the United States," *The Research Center for International Relations*, published in *Jerusalem Post*, June 26, 1996.
16 "The Myth of America," *Christians For Israel Today*, First Quarter 1999, p. 17.
17 "Our Greatest Danger–Signed Undertakings of the United States," *The Research Center for International Relations*, published in *Jerusalem Post*, June 26, 1996.
18 "The dangers facing Israel," *Jerusalem Institute of Western Defence*, Bulletin 4, Dec. 1998.
19 "The Myth of America," *Christians For Israel Today*, First Quarter 1999, p. 17.
20 "Our Greatest Danger–Signed Undertakings of the United States," *The Research Center for International Relations*, published in *Jerusalem Post*, June 26, 1996.
21 "The Myth of America," *Christians For Israel Today*, First Quarter 1999, p. 17.
22 Ronald Reagan quoted in "Recognizing the Israeli Asset," *Washington Post*, Aug. 15, 1979.
23 "The Myth of America," *Christians For Israel Today*, First Quarter 1999, p. 16.
24 "Our Greatest Danger–Signed Undertakings of the United States," *The Research Center for International Relations*, published in *Jerusalem Post*, June 26, 1996.
25 *Ibid.*
26 *Ibid.*

27   Editorial: "Subtle meddling," _Jerusalem Post_, June 19, 1992.

28   Douglas Bloomfield: "Bush's second front," _Jerusalem Post_, March 6, 1991.

29   _Ibid._

30   _Ibid._

31   Dore Gold: "US and Israel enter new era," _Jerusalem Post_, Feb. 28, 1992.

32   Editorial: "Subtle meddling," _Jerusalem Post_, June 19, 1992.

33   Some Israeli newspapers published Baker's gutter remark as: "The Jews can go to hell." The correct quotation is found with Mark Aarons & John Loftus, _The Secret War Against the Jews_, (New York: St. Martins Press, 1994) p. vii.

34   "The Myth of America," _Christians For Israel Today_, First Quarter 1999, p. 17.

35   Yochi Dreazen: ""Kissinger: PM will learn peace is in Israel's interest," _Jerusalem Post_, July 8, 1996.

36   Barry Smith: "Kissinger's plan for Israel in NWO," _Omega Times_, Dec. 1998, p. 9.

37   "US Congressmen voice support for Netanyahu," _ICEJ News Service_, Dec. 18, 1997.

38   "81 Senators urge Clinton not to pressure Israel," _ICEJ News Service_, April 6, 1998.

39   _Ibid._

40   "Congressmen get annoyed with Clinton," _ICEJ News Service_, May 8, 1998.

41   _Ibid._

42   _Ibid._

43   Moshe Zak, OP-ED: "We're waiting for Albright's public apology," _Jerusalem Post_, Dec. 5, 1997.

44   "US threatens to support PLO state," _ICEJ News Service_, Dec. 8, 1997.

45   "Clinton to the rescue of Israel-Syria talks, again," _ICEJ News Service_, Jan. 7, 2000.

46   _Ibid._

47   "The American Century in Europe," _Jerusalem Institute of Western Defence_, Bulletin 3, Sept. 1996.

48   "Albright sees new world order," _LA Times-Washington Post Service_, June 6, 1997.

49   _Ibid._

50   "'Wye' no real peace?, _Christians For Israel Today_, Fall 1998, p. 1.

51   _Jerusalem Institute of Western Defence_, Digest 2, Feb. 1995, p. 2.

52   Editorial: "Pollard pardon due," _Jerusalem Post_, Dec. 28, 1992.

53   Jonatan Black: "Israeli spy story has a few bugs," _New York Daily News_, May 12, 1997.

54   "Clinton reneged on promise to free Israeli spy," _ICEJ News Service_, June 25, 1999.

55   _Ibid._

56   _Ibid._

57   "America 'leaked British secrets to IRA'," _Sunday Telegraph_, Jan. 18, 1998.

58   _Ibid._

59   Ashraf Al-'Ajrami: "A Victory for the United States... A Defeat for the World!" _Al Ayyam_, June 10, 1999.

60   _Jerusalem Institute of Western Defence_, Digest 1, Jan. 1996.

61   _Ibid._

62   Yohanan Ramati: "All for 'realpolitik,'" *Jerusalem Post*, July 22, 1996.

63   *Jerusalem Institute of Western Defence*, Digest 8, Aug. 1996, p. 5.

64   *Ibid.*, Digest 2, Feb. 1997, pp. 7, 8.

65   *Global Intelligence Update*, Stratfor Systems, Inc., May 28, 1998.

66   *Jerusalem Institute of Western Defence*, Digest 2, Feb. 1997, p. 8.

67   *AP:* "'Moments of tension' in Clinton-Assad talks. 'US leader fascinated to meet with notorious character,'" *Jerusalem Post*, Jan. 17, 1994.

68   *Ibid.*, July 5, 1996.

69   William N. Grigg: "Why Kosovo?," *The New American*, May, 1999.

70   *Ibid.*

71   David Bar-Illan, *Eye On the Media*, p. x.

72   "Decade Forecast: Europe," *Global Intelligence Update*, Dec. 24, 1999. Stratfor, Inc. Austin, Texas.

73   "Points to note and developments to watch," *Jerusalem Institute of Western Defence*, Digest 11, Nov. 1999, p. 1.

74   *Yediot Ahronot*, April 2, 1999.

75   *Ibid.*

76   William N. Grigg quoting *Detroit News* columnist Tony Snow, March 29, 1999: "Why Kosovo?," *The New American*, May, 1999.

77   Phyllis Schlafly: "The Truth Leaks Out About Kosovo," *Phyllis Schlafly column*, Nov. 24, 1999.

78   *New York Times*, Sept. 21, 1997. Cited by Carl Limbacher and Caron Grich in: "The Caspian Connection: Pipeline Politics and the Balkan War," June 9, 1999.

79   Barton Gellman, *Washington Post Service*: "Iran Missiles Mire U.S. in A Debate on Sanctions," *International Herald Tribune*, Jan. 2, 1998.

80   Barry Smith: "Clinton faces curse of Iran in arms to Bosnia scandal," *Omega Times*, May 1996.

81   Jeremy Burns: "Time to end critical dialogue with Iran," *Wall Street Journal*, June 10, 1996.

82   See p. 188.

83   *Guardian* despatch, Sept. 24, 1996. Reported in *Jerusalem Institute of Western Defence*, Bulletin No. 4, Dec. 1996, p. 11.

84   *Ibid.*

85   *Ibid.*

86   *BBC Radio News*, March 24, 1999.

87   *Ibid.*, April 4, 1999.

88   *Ibid.* April 13, 1999.

89   *Ibid.* April 6, 1999.

90   *Ibid.* April 7, 1999.

91   *Ibid.*

92   Clinton's speech broadcast on *Ibid.* April 16, 1999.

93   *BBC Radio News*, April 9, 1999.

94   "The rise and rise of Bill Clinton," *Jerusalem Post*, July 16, 1997.

95   David J. Forman: "Can't get no satisfaction," *Jerusalem Post*, Jan. 6, 1993.

96   *Israel Radio,* April 8, 1999.

97   *Ibid.*

98   *Ibid.* April 6, 1999.

99   *Ibid.* April 3, 1999.

100 See p. 216.
101 *BBC Radio News*, April 9, 1999.
102 *Ibid.* April 16, 1999.
103 *Ibid.*
104 *Ibid.*
105 *Ibid.*
106 *Ibid.*
107 David Bar-Illan: "'Eyewitness' accounts: Yes, people do lie," *Jerusalem Post*, March 27, 1992.
108 Bar-Illan, *Eye on the Media*, p. 409.
109 *BBC TV News*, May 10, 1999.
110 *Le Figaro,* Jan. 20, 1999. Published in *Jerusalem Institute of Western Defence*, Digest 2, Feb. 1999, pp. 12, 13.
111 *Jerusalem Institute of Western Defence*, Digest 2, Feb. 1999, p. 13.
112 *Ibid.*
113 *Ibid.*
114 *Israel Radio*, April 17, 1999.
115 *Toronto Star,* July 16, 1995. Reprinted in *Jerusalem Institute of Western Defence*, Digest 9, Sept. 1996, p. 12.
116 *Jerusalem Institute of Western Defence*, Digest 2, Feb. 1999, p. 13.
117 Anjem Chouday, secretary-general of the Society of Muslim Lawyers. Quoted in Al Muhajiroun's *Press Release*, March 25, 1999.
118 *Ibid.*
119 William N. Grigg: "Why Kosovo?," *The New American*, May, 1999.
120 Phyllis Schlafly: "The Truth Leaks Out About Kosovo," *Phyllis Schlafly column*, Nov. 24, 1999.
121 *Ibid.*
122 *Ibid.*
123 *Ibid.*
124 Extracted from a summary of John Laughland's article, "Kosovo," *The Express,* July 20, 1999. Printed in *Jerusalem Institute of Western Defence*, Digest 9, Sept. 1999.
125 Phyllis Schlafly: "The Truth Leaks Out About Kosovo," *Phyllis Schlafly column*, Nov. 24, 1999.
126 *Ibid.*
127 William N. Grigg: "Why Kosovo?," *The New American*, May, 1999.
128 U.S. Secretary of Defense William Cohen quoted by William N. Grigg: "Why Kosovo?," *The New American*, May, 1999.
129 Phyllis Schlafly: "The Truth Leaks Out About Kosovo," *Phyllis Schlafly column*, Nov. 24, 1999.
130 *Ibid.*
131 *Ibid.*
132 Sheik Abdullah Ghoshah in: D.F. Green, *Arab Theologians on Jews and Israel* (Genčve: Editions de l'Avenir, 1974), p. 22.
133 *Islam at a Glance*, a brochure distributed in Birmingham, England, in July 1985.
134 "Where Are Kosovo's Killing Fields," *Global Intelligence Update*, Stratfor Systems, Inc., Oct. 18, 1999.
135 "Arafat invites Milosevic for Orthodox Christmas," *ICEJ News Service,* Dec. 3, 1999.

136 A diplomatic insider quoted by *Chicago Tribune*, April 1, 1999 and reproduced in William N. Grigg: "Why Kosovo?," *The New American*, May, 1999.

137 Fraser Tytler, *The Decline and Fall of the Athenian Republic*, circa 1810.

138 Ashraf Al-'Ajrami: "A Victory for the United States... A Defeat for the World!" *Al Ayyam*, June 10, 1999.

139 "PA official: NATO should also act to end Israeli 'occupation,'" *ICEJ News Service*, April 16, 1999.

140 *Ibid.*

141 "The Putin Doctrine: Nuclear Threats and Russia's Place in the World," *Global Intelligence Update*, Stratfor Systems, Inc., May 28, 1998.

Chapter 9

1   Quoted by Elan Hirshfeld in: "Appeasement," *Jerusalem Post*, Nov. 22, 1996.

2   Margot Dudkevitch: "Gush Katif thankful for a miracle," *Jerusalem Post*, April 2, 1997.

3   Mossad chief, Ephraim Halevy, quoted on *Israel Radio,* Jan.23, 2000.

4   Moshe Sharon, professor of Islamic history at the Jerusalem's Bar-Ilan and Hebrew Universities, writing in: "Behind the PLO boss's words," *Jerusalem Post,* May 27, 1994.

5   Bernard Lewis, *The Political Language of Islam* (Chicago: University of Chicago, 1988), p. 73.

6   Yasser Arafat addressing a closed meeting of Muslim faithful in a Johannesburg mosque, May 10, 1994.

7   Feisal al-Husseini, member of the PLO negotiating team, Nov. 1994, quoted in: "Terrorism and the PLO: September 13 plus seven months," *Jerusalem Institute for Western Defence*, Bulletin 2, June 1995, p. 11.

8   Haim Shapiro interviewing Dr. Anis Shorrosh: "Evangelist takes off his gloves to fight Islam," *Jerusalem Post*, April 21, 1993.

9   "The Talmud, the Jews and Human Sacrifice," *Al-Shaab*, Nov. 16, 1998.

10 Jordanian text book for second-year high school art students, *General History, Ancient and Medieval Civilizations*, p. 160.

11 Robert Morey, *The Islamic Invasion: Confronting the World's Fastest Growing Religion* (Eugene: Harvest House, 1992), p. 48.

12 Hastings *Encyclopedia of Religion and Ethics,* cited in: *Ibid.*

13 Morey, *The Islamic Invasion*, p. 49.

14 *Encyclopedia of Religion,* cited in: *Ibid.*, p. 48.

15 *Encyclopedia of Islam,* cited in: Morey, *The Islamic Invasion*, p. 48.

16 E.M. Wherry, *A Comprehensive Commentary on the Quran* (Osnbruck: Otto Zeller Verlag, 1973), p.36, cited in: Morey, *The Islamic Invasion*, p. 50.

17 Morey, *The Islamic Invasion*, p. 50.

18 *Ibid.*

19 Will Durant, *The Story of Civilization*, IV: p. 160-161. Cited by Dave Hunt in: *The Berean Call*, Feb. 2000.

20 David Rudge: "Hizbullah continues attacks in zone," *Jerusalem Post*, Nov. 5, 1997.

21 Haim Shapiro, in an interview with a Palestinian Arab whose identity was suppressed for safety reasons: "Palestinian Baptist slams Islam," *Jerusalem Post*, Sept. 23, 1994.

22 Abdullah Al-Araby writing in a tract:"Save America," *The Pen vs The Sword Publications*, Los Angeles, CA.

23 David Bar-Illan quoting a fundamental Muslim leader at the Islamic University of London: "ADL picks apart PBS on distorted reports on Israel," *Jerusalem Post*, Feb. 25, 1994.

24 *Ablamabad* (Pakistan), Sept. 12, 1999.

25 *Ibid*.

26 Dave Hunt quoting Muhammad in: "King of the Jews," *Berean Call*, Dec., 1999.

27 David Bar-Illan quoting a fundamentalist Muslim leader at the Islamic University of London: "ADL picks apart PBS on distorted reports on Israel," *Jerusalem Post*, Feb. 25, 1994.

28 *The Koran*, Sura 4:101: Fifth revised edition translated with notes by N.J. Dawood. Penguin Books, London, 1990.

29 *Ibid*., Sura 4:91.

30 Abraham Rabinovich: "Economic catastrophe awaits its turn," *Jerusalem Post Magazine*, June 21, 1996.

31 Dr. Saleem Almahdy: "A Look Beyond the Veil," *Voice of the Martyrs*, April 1998, p. 9.

32 "Saudi Arabia: The Country Without a Church," *Ibid*., p. 7.

33 Ahmed Zaki Tuffaha,*The Woman and Islam*, p. 180. cited in: *Ibid*., p. 8.

34 Dr. Saleem Almahdy: "A Look Beyond the Veil," *Ibid*., p. 9.

35 Margot Dudkevitch: "Arab teen stabs settler schoolgirl," *Jerusalem Post*, Dec. 14, 1998.

36 Aril Edvardsen in an interview with *Stavanga Aftenblad*, Nov. 11, 1997.

37 *The Koran*. Fifth revised edition translated with notes by N.J. Dawood.

38 Sura 18:1 for example.

39 *Ibid*.

40 Sura 12:39.

41 Editorial: *Dagen*, Sept. 4, 1996.

42 Ashraf Fouad: "Islamic conference slams Israel," *Jerusalem Post*, Dec. 12, 1997.

43 Christopher Walker: "Tensions darken festive mood in Bethlehem," *The Times* (U.K.), Dec. 22, 1997.

44 "Muslims in Britain To Build 100 New Mosques," *Euro Charisma, Charisma Magazine*, May 1997.

45 "Saudi Arabia," *Voice of the Martyrs*, 2000 Special Issue, p. 12.

46 "Saudi Arabia: The Country Without a Church," *Voice of the Martyrs*, April 1998, p. 6.

47 Dr. Saleem Almahdy: "A Look Beyond the Veil," *Voice of the Martyrs*, Feb. 1998, p. 9.

48 Archbishop Giuseppe Bernadini of Smyrna quoted in the Catholic weekly, *The Wanderer,* Nov. 1999, and reported in *Jerusalem Institute of Western Defence*, Digest 12, Dec. 1999.

49 *Ibid*.

50 Dr. Taksin Shea-Hrabni quoted in: "Fears of another attack before Albright arrives," *ICEJ News Service*, Sept. 8, 1997.

51 Moshe Kohn: "Objectivity," *Jerusalem Post International Edition*, Nov. 1, 1997.

52   *Ibid.*
53   Jay Bushinsky: "Muslim theologians defend suicide bombers," *Jerusalem Post International Edition*, Sept. 24, 1997.
54   *Israel Radio,* Dec. 16, 1996.
55   Islamic Jihad leader, Ramadan Abdalla Shalah, in an interview with *Mid-East Mirror,* Nov. 10, 1996.
56   *Tishrin*, Nov. 14, 1999.
57   Farouk al-Shara quoted in: "IDF wants Barak to get tougher in Lebanon," *ICEJ News Service*, Feb. 16, 2000.
58   Muhammad quoted by Sheik Abd Allah Al Meshad in D.F. Green, *Arab Theologians on Jews and Israel*, p. 22.
59   "Arafat to visit South Africa," *ICEJ News Service*, May 18, 1998.
60   Jay Bushinsky, Steve Rodan and Muhammad Najib quoting Khaled Mashaal in: "Hamas promises more bombings," *Jerusalem Post International Edition*, Nov. 1, 1997.
61   Hamas founder, Sheik Ahmed Yassin, in *Ibid*.
62   Sheik Ahmed Yassin: "Israel must disappear," *ICEJ News Service*, Oct. 19, 1997.
63   *Ibid.*
64   Douglas Davis quoting Abdel-Aziz Rantisi in: "Hamas activist vows to continue fight agains Israel," *Jerusalem Post*, May 25, 1997.
65   "Israel will cease to exist early next century," *ICEJ News Service*, May 27, 1998.
66   City Notes: "Monument with a Message," *In Jerusalem*, March 21, 1997.
67   "Israel swallowed whole in new map of Palestine," *ICEJ News Service*, March 27, 1997.
68   Ikrama Sabri on *Voice of Palestine Radio*, May 9, 1997.
69   "Hizb'Allah's real aim goes beyond south Lebanon," *ICEJ News Service*, March 7, 1999.
70   *Ibid.*
71   "Islamic Jihad on the rise in south Lebanon," *ICEJ News Service*, Nov. 15, 1999.
72   Na'im Kassem, Deputy Secretary-General of Hizb'allah, in an inteview with *SKY NEWS*, quoted in: "SLA – Treasonous sellouts or noble resistance fighters?" *ICEJ News Service*, Aug. 2, 1999.
73   "Hizb'Allah's real aim goes beyond south Lebanon," *ICEJ News Service*, March 7, 1999.
74   Sheik Hassan Nasrallah in an inteview with *Radio Tehran*: "Hizb'Allah: We won't let up until Israel is destroyed," *ICEJ News Service*, Oct. 24, 1997.
75   Sheik Hassan Nasrallah quoted in "Hezbollah Vows to Continue the Fight," Global Intelligence Update, *Stratfor Inc.*, July 28, 1999.
76   Sheik Hassan Nasrallah: *Israel Radio*, Jan. 22, 2000.
77   Na'im Kassem, Deputy Secretary-General of Hizb'allah, in an intergview with *Lebanese Television,* Dec. 29, 1998. Reported in *Jerusalem Institute of Western Defence*, Digest 2, Feb. 1999.
78   Sheik Hassan Nasrallah quoted on *Israel Radio*, Feb. 16, 2000.
79   Osama bin Laden: *Associated Press* report, Aug. 20, 1998.

Chapter 10

1   Bennett, _When Day and Night Cease_, p. 173.
2   Andrew Smith in: "Whose God is He Anyway??" _Omega Times_, June 1999.
3   Hebrew was the religious language of the day. Aramaic, Greek and Latin were spoken in the streets, but religious Jews considered it to be sacrilegious to discuss the things of God in anything other than the Hebrew tongue. Many of the ultra-orthodox Jews of today will still not speak Hebrew as a common language in Israel. They will only use Hebrew when in the synagogue or when speaking of things pertaining to God.
4   See p. 133.
5   _Ibid._
6   Bill Hutman: "Deri trial delayed until September 1," _Jerusalem Post_, Dec. 23, 1993.
7   Bill Hutman: "Technicality causes 2 week postponement of Deri trial," _Jerusalem Post_, Dec. 10, 1993.
8   Bill Hutman: "Deri trial delayed until September 1," _Jerusalem Post_, Dec. 23, 1993.
9   Bill Hutman: "Technicality causes 2 week postponement of Deri trial," _Jerusalem Post_, Dec. 10, 1993.
10   _Websters New Universal Unabridged Dictionary_.
11   Herbert Danby, D.D., _The Mishnah,_ (London: Oxford University Press, 1977), p. 42.
12   _Commentary on the Old Testament in Ten Volumes_ by C.F. Keil and F. Delitzsch, (Grand Rapids: William B. Eerdmans, 1986), Vol. 10, p. 221.

Chapter 11

1   Hazem Beblawi, secretary-general of the UN Economic and Social Commission for Western Asia, addressing a news conference in Beirut, Lebanon, on Dec. 22, 1999.
2   See p. 96.
3   _Itim_: "Sharon troubled by pace at which Arabs are rearming," _Jerusalem Post_, Oct. 18, 1996.
4   Jim Lederman, _Battle Lines: The American Media and the Intifada_ (New York: Henry Holt, 1992), p. 319.
5   Strategic analyst, Avigor Haselkorn, _Los Angeles Times_. Cited by: _ICEJ News Service_, Oct. 13, 1997.
6   Lee Hockstader: "Israel Signals It Would Strike Back," _International Herald Tribune_, Feb. 6, 1998.
7   "The Ailing Middle East," _The Jerusalem Report_, Aug. 31, 1998.
8   _Ibid._
9   _Ibid._
10   _Israel Radio_, March 6, 2000.
11   _Ibid._
12   Douglas Davis: "Report: Mossad has Assad urine sample," _The Jerusalem Post_, Jan. 10, 2000.
13   "The Ailing Middle East," _The Jerusalem Report_, Aug. 31, 1998.
14   _Ibid._
15   _Ibid._

16 *Ibid.*
17 Editorial: "Wanted: Realism," *Jerusalem Post*, May 31, 1996.
18 "$12.8b in M.E. Arms Sales," *Dispatch From Jerusalem*, Nov., 1996.
19 UN report presented in Beirut:"Arabs biggest spenders on arms," *ICEJ News Service*, Dec. 24, 1999.
20 *Ibid.*
21 "Arming For War," *Jerusalem Institute of Western Defence*, Bulletin No. 3, Sept. 1999.
22 *Ibid.*
23 *Ibid.*
24 Laurie Mylroie quoting official U.S. estimates: "The threat of biological terrorism," *Jerusalem Post*, April 3, 1998.
25 Judy Siegel-Itzkovich:"Preparing for the unthinkable," *Jerusalem Post*, Feb. 6, 1998.
26 *Ibid.*
27 *Ibid.*
28 *Ibid.*
29 U.S. Defense Secretary William Cohen, quoted in: "Iraq could destroy the world," *ICEJ News Service*, Nov. 27, 1997.
30 Ron Cantrell: "Shalom from Jerusalem," Feb. 16, 1998.
31 *Ibid.*
32 Dan Leon quoting deputy head of the GSS, Gideon Ezra in: "Respect born of fear," *Jerusalem Post*, Aug. 6, 1996.
33 *Ibid.*
34 *Ibid.*
35 *Ibid.*
36 Steve Rodan quoting students at Hebron's Islamic College: "'There are no innocents in the bombings,'" *Jerusalem Post*, March 8, 1996.
37 Moshe Reinfeld: "Vanunu will be allowed a daily walk and conversation," *Ha'aretz*, March 13, 1998.
38 Haim Adler: "Dropping the Big One," *The Nation*, Sept. 10, 1990.
39 *Ibid.*
40 *Jane's Intelligence Review,* reported in *Petah Tikvah*, July-Sept. 1997.
41 *Global Intelligence Update*, Stratfor Systems, Inc., July 2, 1998.
42 *Israel Radio*, March 3, 2000.
43 "News bytes," *Middle East Intelligence Digest*, May, 1996.
44 "Arming For War," *Jerusalem Institute of Western Defence*, Bulletin 3, Sept. 1999.
45 "US to sell arms worth billions to Arab states," *ICEJ News Service*, March 14, 1999.
46 *Ibid.*
47 "US sells 80 top F-16 fighters to UAE," *ICEJ News Service*, March 8, 2000.
48 *Global Intelligence Update*, Stratfor, Inc., Jan 4, 1999.
49 *Ibid.*
50 *Ibid.*
51 *STRATFOR.COM Weekly Global Intelligence Update*, March 6, 2000.
52 *Ibid.*
53 *STRATFOR.COM Weekly Global Intelligence Update*, Feb. 29, 2000.
54 "Arming For War," *Jerusalem Institute of Western Defence*, Bulletin 3, Sept. 1999.

55 *Washington Times*, June 16, 1998.
56 Steve Rodan: "Shihab-4 missile 'will have nonconventional warhead,'" *Jerusalem Post*, July 31, 1998.
57 Douglas Davis: "Iran hints it may rein in Hizb'allah," *Jerusalem Post*, Aug. 25, 1998.
58 Arieh O'Sullivan: "Mordechai tells Russian intelligence chief: 'Stop aiding Iran missile program,'" *Jerusalem Post*, July 17, 1998.
59 *Ibid.*
60 "Arming For War," *Jerusalem Institute of Western Defence*, Bulletin 3, Sept. 1999.
61 "The West's Dilemma: Democracy or a Pro-Moslem Policy," *Jerusalem Institute of Western Defence*, Bulletin 2, Sept. 1998.
62 *The Times* (U.K.), June 17, 1998.
63 *Ibid.*
64 "The West's Dilemma: Democracy or a Pro-Moslem Policy," *Jerusalem Institute of Western Defence*, Bulletin 2, Sept. 1998.
65 Joseph Cirincione, director of the Non-Proliferation Project at the Carnegie Endowment for International Peace, speaking to the San Francisco Examiner on August 30, 1998 and reported in: "US experts worried about Russian 'Loose Nukes,'" *ICEJ News Service*, Sept. 2, 1998.
66 *Ibid.*
67 Yedidya Atlas: "Islamic policy in action," *Jerusalem Post*, Feb. 16, 1993.
68 *Ibid.*
69 Howard M. Sacher, *A History Of Israel Volume II: From the Aftermath of the Yom Kippur War,* (New York: Oxford University Press, 1987), p. 49.
70 *Ibid.*
71 *Ibid.*
72 *Ibid.*, p. 50.
73 *Ibid.*, p. 75.
74 Yaakov Shimoni, *Biographical Dictionary of the Middle East,* (New York: Facts On File, 1991), p. 201.
75 *Israel Radio,* Oct. 19, 1996.
76 *STRATFOR.COM Global Intelligence Update*, Feb. 23, 2000.
77 Yitzhak Rabin, quoted by Gerald M. Steinberg: "Egypt loses statue by snubbing summit," *Jerusalem Post*, Oct. 4, 1996.
78 *Ibid.*
79 Egyptian President Hosni Mubarak, quoted in: "Gaza—soft underbelly of the Jewish state," *Middle East Intelligence Digest*, Feb. 1993, p. 4.
80 "Arab League adopts hard-line Syrian stand," *ICEJ News Service*, March 13, 2000.
81 "Mubarak changes tone ahead of Arab League summit," *ICEJ News Service*, March 10, 2000.
82 *Ibid.*
83 Douglas Jehl: "Netanyahu Due to Take One-Way Road to Egypt For Talks With Mubarak," *Internaional Herald Tribune*, March 4, 1997.
84 Egyptian President Hosni Mubarak, quoted in: *Ibid.*
85 Aaron Lerner, director of Independent Media Review & Analysis, quoted in: "The perils of 'peace,'" *ICEJ News Service*, March 17, 1999.
86 *STRATFOR.COM Global Intelligence Update*, May 7, 1998.

87   "The perils of 'peace,'" *ICEJ News Service*, March 17, 1999.
88   "Nuclear reactor for Egypt," *ICEJ News Service*, April 7, 1997.
89   Douglas Davis: "Cairo: Egypt to PM: Don't come empty-handed," *Jerusalem Post*, Dec. 19, 1997.
90   *Ibid.*
92   *Ibid.*
93   *Ibid.*
94   "Did You Know," *Omega Times*, Oct., 1996.
95   "War in Israel in 1999?," *ICEJ News Service*, July 13, 1998.
96   Professor Moshe Sharon: "Synopsis," *Nativ Journal*, June, 1995, p. II.
97   *Ibid.*
98   Maj.-Gen. (Res.) Yossi Peled quoted by Steve Rodan: "To war or not to war," *Jerusalem Post*, Nov. 1, 1996.
99   Lisa Beyer: "Preparing For War," *Time*, Dec. 9, 1996.
100 *AP:* "'Syria deploying tanks near Golan,'" *Jerusalem Post*, Aug. 30, 1997.
101 "Israel Complains to United Nations About Syria," *IINS News Service*, Aug. 4, 1997.
102 "Syrians Building Bunkers Near Israeli Border," *IINS News Service*, Sept. 4, 1997.
103 Steve Rodan: "Vilna'i: IDF prepared for Syrian attack," *Jerusalem Post*, Dec. 27, 1996.
104 Steve Rodan: "Leading strategist urges secrecy for war preparation," *Jerusalem Post*, Dec. 6, 1996.
105 Steve Rodan: "Vilna'i: IDF prepared for Syrian attack," *Jerusalem Post*, Dec. 27, 1996.
106 *Ha'aretz*, June 11, 1998.
107 *Ha'aretz*, Dec. 7, 1998.
108 "The perils of 'peace,'" *ICEJ News Service*, March 17, 1999.
109 Ariel Sharon: "The Likud's plan, simply put," *Jerusalem Post*, May 17, 1996.
110 "PLO prepares youth for conflict," *ICEJ News Service*, April 7, 1997.
111 *STRATFOR.COM Global Intelligence Update*, Aug. 11, 1999.
112 David Rudge, quoting Dr. Danny Shoham, a senior researcher a Bar-Ilan University's Begin-Sadat Center for Strategic Sudies: "Syria has arsenal of nerve gas, expert says," *Jerusalem Post*, Nov. 22, 1996.
113 Daniel Leshem: "Syria's deadly secret," *Jerusalem Post*, May 6, 1997.
114 *Ibid.*
115 June 1997 Jane's Defence report cited in: "'Syria to produce VX,'" *ICEJ News Service*, July 3, 1998.
116 *Stern* magazine quoted in: "Syria 'building poison gas factor,'" *Evening Standard* (U.K.), June 5, 1996.
117 Editorial: "Change policy on Syria," *Jerusalem Post*, June 7, 1996.
118 *Ibid.*
119 See pp. 164-165.
120 Yasser Arafat speaking to the late King Hussein of Jordan. Quoted by Jon Immanuel in: "King Hussein returns to Jericho," *Jerusalem Post*, Oct. 16, 1996.
121 Stephen Bryen, a former U.S. deputy under-secretary of defense, writing in: "Potent weapon," *Jerusalem Post*, Oct. 6, 1996.

122 Lisa Beyer: "Getting Ready For War," _Time_, Feb. 2, 1998.
123 _Ibid._
124 _Arutz 7,_ March 2, 1998.
125 Abraham Rabinovich quoting Israeli Major-General (Res.) Oren Shahor in: "An intifada with guns," _Jerusalem Post International Edition_, Sept. 27, 1997.
126 "PA spying on settlements – Report," _ICEJ News Service_, March 27, 1998.
127 _Ibid._
128 _Ibid._
129 _Israel Radio,_ Sept. 26, 1997.
130 Cited in: "IDF trains for war with PA," _ICEJ News Service_, Sept. 29, 1999.
131 Lisa Beyer: "Getting Ready For War," _Time_, Feb. 2, 1998.
132 Steve Rodan and Arieh O'Sullivan: "PA smuggling anti-tank arms," _Jerusalem Post_, April 14, 1997.
133 Bill Hutman: "Weapons smuggling ring from Jordan to PA revealed," _Jerusalem Post_, Aug. 16, 1996.
134 _Ibid._
135 _Ibid._
136 Christopher Walker: "Arabs stockpiling Gaza arms, says top Israeli source," A clipping from _The Times_ (U.K.) sent to the author, but without date indicated.
137 Editorial: "An end to self-respect," _Jerusalem Post_, March 20, 1997.
138 "'Arafat is smuggling terrorists, weapons,'" _ICEJ News Service_, Nov. 5, 1999.
139 Cited by Michael Widlanski in "Arab News Digest," _Jerusalem Post_, April 21, 1993.
140 _Ibid._
141 Van onze redactie: "'Yasser Arafat is in bezit van atoombom,'" _Christenen voor Israël acktueel_, January, 1998.
142 _Ibid._
143 _Ibid._
144 _Ibid._
145 _Ibid._
146 _Ibid._
147 Iranian president elect Mohammed Khatami in May 1997, quoted in: "Different face, same rhetoric," _Middle East Digest_, July, 1997.
148 Iranian President Mohammed Khatami, quoted on _Israel Radio,_ Dec. 31, 1999.
149 _Al-Shara'a,_ Sept. 13, 1999. Reported in _Jerusalem Institute of Western Defence_, Digest 11, Nov. 1999.
150 _STRATFOR.COM Global Intelligence Update_, Aug. 11, 1999.
151 Barton Gellman: "Iran Missiles Mire U.S. in A Debate on Sanctions," _International Herald Tribune_, Jan. 2, 1998.
152 _Ibid._
153 _Ibid._
154 Cited by Steve Rodan in: "Leading strategist urges secrecy for war preparations," _Jerusalem Post_, Dec. 6, 1996.
155 Barton Gellman: "Iran Missiles Mire U.S. in A Debate on Sanctions," _International Herald Tribune_, Jan. 2, 1998.
156 Cited by Steve Rodan in: "Leading strategist urges secrecy for war preparations," _Jerusalem Post_, Dec. 6, 1996.

157   Cited by Uri Dan and Dennis Eisenberg in: "The business of terror," *Jerusalem Post*, Aug. 15, 1996.
158   *Ibid.*
159   Editorial: "Kohl logic," *Jerusalem Post*, June 7, 1995.
160   *Ibid.*
161   "'Iran came nuke hunting in South Africa,'" *ICEJ News Service*, Aug. 20, 1997.
162   Douglas Davis: "Western worry: Iran shops for Islamic bomb," *Jerusalem Post*, Sept. 8, 1995.
163   *Ibid.*
164   See p. 299.
165   Douglas Davis: "Western worry: Iran shops for Islamic bomb," *Jerusalem Post*, Sept. 8, 1995.
166   "Iran soon to have nuclear bomb," *ICEJ News Service*, Nov. 18, 1997.
167   "Russian nuclear technology seized en route to Iran,'" *ICEJ News Service*, April 27, 1998.
168   "Iran might have nuclear capability,'" *ICEJ News Service*, Jan. 21, 2000.
169   Britain Israel Public Affairs Centre (BIPAC) report: "Senior Israeli Source," *Prophecy Update Magazine*, Vol. 1. No. 6, 1997.
170   *Sunday Times* (U.K.) report cited in: "Iraq rebuilding weapons facilities," *ICEJ News Service*, Sept. 8, 1999.
171   *Ibid.*
172   Arieh O'Sullivan: "Saddam, again, pushes the envelope," *Jerusalem Post*, Feb. 6, 1998.
173   Rafiz al-Samurai, quoted by *Jerusalem Institute of Western Defence*, Digest 8, August 1998, p. 9.
174   Arieh O'Sullivan: "Saddam, again, pushes the envelope," *Jerusalem Post*, Feb. 6, 1998.
175   *Ibid.*
176   *Ibid.*
177   U.S. Defense Secretary William Cohen, quoted in: "Iraq could destroy the world," *ICEJ News Service*, Nov. 27, 1997.
178   "US takes stock of Mideast germ warfare threat," *ICEJ News Service*, Dec. 17, 1997.
179   *Ibid.*
180   "'Iraq has three nuclear bombs,'" *Middle East Digest*, Oct., 1998, p.2.
181   *Ibid.*
182   Cited in: *Ibid.*
183   Laurie Mylroie: "The threat of biological terrorism," *Jerusalem Post*, April 3, 1998.
184   Jeff Jacoby:"We're left with one option: get rid of Saddam," *Boston Globe,* Feb. 5, 1998.
185   *Ibid.*
186   *AP:* "Gadaffi: Imperialism still rules," *Jerusalem Post*, May 29, 1996.
187   Daniel Leshem: "Two cheers for the Vatican," *Jerusalem Post*, March 18, 1997.
188   Editorial: "Change policy on Syria," *Jerusalem Post*, June 7, 1996.
189   *AP:* "US: Libya building weapons facility despite Egyptian claims," *Jerusalem Post*, May 31, 1996.

190 Editorial: "Change policy on Syria," _Jerusalem Post_, June 7, 1996.

191 Yoash Tsiddon Chatto: "We mus reshuffle priorities," _Jerusalem Post_, Jan. 3, 1997.

192 _Reuters:_ "CIA can't stop Libyan chemical weapons plant," _Jerusalem Post_, March 25, 1996.

193 Liat Collins—Hillel Kuttler adds: "Iraqi threat not over," _Jerusalem Post_, Nov. 26, 1997.

194 _Ibid._

195 Daniel Leshem: "Two cheers for the Vatican," _Jerusalem Post_, March 18, 1997.

196 Steve Rodan: "Israel buys 'world's most advanced fighter plane," _Jerusalem Post_, Nov. 7, 1997.

197 Jane Harman, writing in:"Security and support build peace," _Jerusalem Post_, March 14, 1997.

198 David Makovsky quoting White House aide, Daiel Tarullo, in:"US, Europe to clash on Iran at G-7," _Jerusalem Post_, June 24, 1996.

199 Task Force On Terrorism & Unconventional Warfare: "Approaching the New Cycle of Arab-Israeli Fighting," _U.S. House of Representatives, Washington, D.C._, Dec. 10, 1996.

200 See ch. 10.

Notes

Notes

Notes

Notes

_____ *Notes*

Notes

_____ *Notes*

Notes

_____ *Notes*